Forest Futures

T0364865

Forest Futures

Global Representations and Ground Realities in the Himalayas

ANTJE LINKENBACH

LONDON NEW YORK CALCUTTA

Seagull Books

Editorial offices

1st Floor, Angel Court, 81 St Clement's Street
Oxford OX4 1AW, UK

1 Washington Square Village, Apt 1U, New York
NY 10012, USA

26 Circus Avenue, Calcutta 700 017, India

Published in arrangement with Permanent Black, India

ISBN-10   1 9054 2 252 0
ISBN-13   9781905422524

British Library Cataloguing-in-Publication Data
A catalogue record for this book is available from the British Library

Printed and bound by Rockwel Offset in Calcutta, India

Contents

Tables, Maps, Figures, and Illustrations

ILLUSTRATIONS (between pp. 146 and 147)

Acknowledgements

T HIS BOOK PRESENTS THE RESULTS OF RESEARCH CARRIED out in Garhwal (North India) in the years 1993–6, funded by the German Research Foundation. Starting from the general problems of forest degradation and livelihood security in the Himalayan mountains, the project set out to explore the relationship of local residents with their forests as well as the history of forest protest in the region. The research put focus on the perspectives of the people concerned, on local discourses as well as on the rationale of local agency.

A large number of individuals and institutions supported my research. I thank the late Professor Dr Richard Burghart and Professor Dr Klaus-Peter Koepping, both Department of Ethnology, University of Heidelberg, for valuable discussions and critique. My thanks go to Professor Dr Veena Das, now of Johns Hopkins University, for stimulating discussions and for helping me to become affiliated with her department when she was at Delhi University. I thank Professor Dr Roger Jeffery, University of Edinburgh, who read a draft of the book and spared no effort commenting on it. I am also grateful to the Ministry of Human Resource Development, New Delhi, and the then Director for Higher Education, D.D. Gupta, who granted me permission to research in the Garhwal Himalayas.

The Branch Office of the South Asia Institute in Delhi, then represented by Dr Peter Zingel, and afterwards by Professor Dr Lothar Lutze, gave strong administrative and infrastructural support for which I am obliged. Many thanks also go to Gabar Singh Chauhan of the Branch Office who helped me with my first contacts in Garhwal. I am especially grateful to Jayendra Singh Chauhan, who worked with me during most parts of my research with great personal involvement. His personality and command of different local dialects was a great help in my gaining access to local residents and organizing research over different regions of Garhwal. I also thank his family members in Vikasnagar and Bangan for their hospitality.

I thank my friends and informants in Nakoli and in the neighbouring villages for hospitality, friendship, and valuable information. I felt, and still feel, at home in the village and in their company, as does my husband, and even more our daughter, who first came to the village when she was four years old. She learned the language; she played, talked, and lived with the people. Now seventeen, and after many revisits, she still confesses that she has 'two homes'.

My special thanks go to Ganga and Kamal Singh Panwar, to Bharti, Arti, Raju, Sulochna, Asha, Mahendra, Surendra, and Birendra. They all accepted us as members of their family. At Nakoli I further thank Pulma and Badri Singh Panwar, Tari and Bajan Singh Panwar, Shyamu Lal, Premdas Pancholi, Bindra and Soban Singh Chauhan, Sundari and Attar Singh Panwar, Dirgpal Singh Chauhan, Mal Singh Chauhan, Birendra Singh Rana, Sundar Singh Panwar, Jubliya Lal, Surmiya Lal, and many others.

In the neighbouring villages I thank especially Sundar Singh Rawat, Jot Singh Rawalta, Maipattu Lal, and Sitaram Nautiyal. From places in the Yamuna valley I thank Gulab Singh Rawat and Thakur Surat Singh Rautela. Special thanks for support, help, and hospitality to Amar Singh Kafola and his family, as well as to Rajesh K. Agarwal, his parents, and his sisters.

In Eastern Garhwal I am extremely obliged to activists of the Dashauli Gram Swarajya Mandal, Gopeshwar, who provided much help and information. They allowed me to join them during an eco-development camp and introduced me to villages and their residents. My gratitude goes to Chandi Prasad Bhatt, Shishupal Kunwar, Chakradatt Tiwari, Murari Lal, Chandra Singh Rana, to the women and men of Papriyana, Tangsa, and those I met during the camp in Lasiyari. I also thank Anand Singh Bisht from the Jakeshwar Shikshan Samsthan, Gopeshwar, and his daughter. My gratitude also to Sunderlal Bahuguna, Tehri, and Vimla Bahuguna, Silyara Ashram; they both received us with great friendliness and made every effort to convey to me their experiences and outlook.

I thank the late Govind Singh Rawat from Joshimath who helped me get a more differentiated picture of the Chipko struggle. I also thank all the villagers of Lata and Raini, especially the members of the *mahila mandal* and the family of Gaura Devi. I am most indebted to Devendra Singh Rawat and his family as well as to Dhan Singh Rana (both from Lata). With their help I obtained valuable information in a comparatively short time. With his beautiful poetry (and the pup he gave my daughter) Dhan Singh Rana made sure we will always remember the village and its people with special affection.

When I returned from my field trips to Delhi I was always warmly received by our friends. I thank Deepa and Dr Suresh Sharma, 'Bhabi', Neha, Raghav, and Aparna (Bitiya) for the hospitality and friendship I enjoyed during all the years.

Many other people took interest in my research and supported it in different ways. I want to thank Professor Dr Irmtraud Stellrecht, who gave me the opportunity to present parts of my research at international conferences in Germany and Pakistan. With Dr Monika Krengel, who has done research in Kumaon, and with Dr Claus-Peter Zoller, who has worked in Bangan (West Garhwal), I had many stimulating comparative discussions about our work and our regions. For that I thank them both.

I received continuous support from my husband, Martin Fuchs. He discussed the research project with me at every stage, and in between he took part in the field work as often as his time schedule allowed him to visit the hills. Our daughter Sandhya opened many doors (and hearts) for me, in Nakoli and in other villages in West and East Garhwal. I thank her for that—as also for her patience with a mother who, for days, disappeared to work on her book.

I thank Marga Hanser-Cole, who had to cope with the administrative work of the research project. Finishing the manuscript would not have been easy without the strong support I got from colleagues at the Zentrum Moderner Orient, Berlin. I thank especially Vincent Ovaert and Michael Schutz for preparing the maps, tables, and figures; they were later brought into camera ready files by Daniel Bruckner and Tankred Wettstein from the Institute of Ethnology, Heidelberg, whom I thank as well. Many thanks, finally to Nadja Christina Schneider who checked the translations and transcriptions.

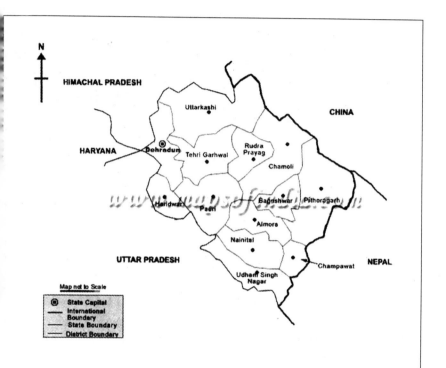

Map 1: Uttaranchal District Map

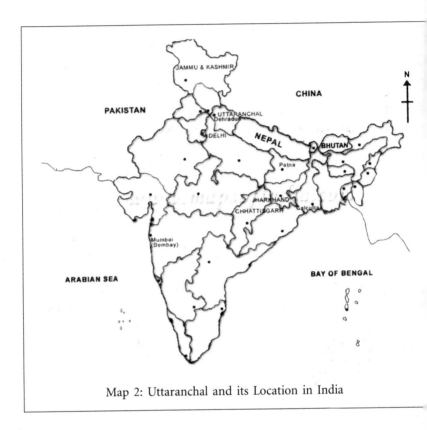

Map 2: Uttaranchal and its Location in India

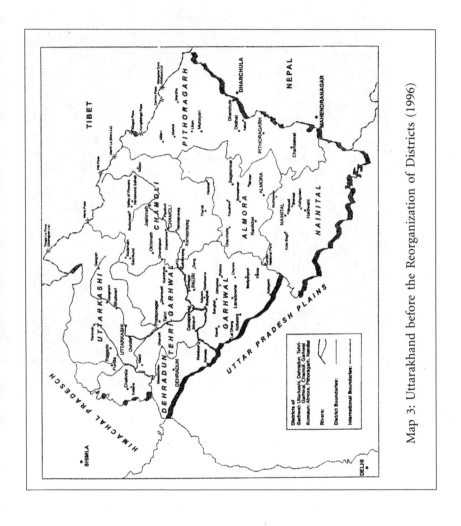

Map 3: Uttarakhand before the Reorganization of Districts (1996)

In the wealth of the woods since the world began
The trees have offered their gifts to man.— **Henry van Dyke**

Chipko had the potential of being a movement of peasants' rights over forests. The Centre, however, defused this potential by incorporating peasants' rights into environmental considerations. The message of Chipko was thus read as 'only' protection of the forests. The legitimacy accorded to peasants' rights was only an impression created by this 'prose of counter-insurgency'... it was not real.

—**Akhileshwara Pathak, 1994**

1
How to Make One's Interlocutors Present? Approaching Local Perspectives on Forest and Ecology in Garhwal

1.1 Context, Questions, and Methodology of Research

IN THE LAST THREE DECADES TWO NOTIONS HAVE GAINED prominence in public discourse: 'ecology' and 'environment'. 'Ecology', in its popularized, anthropocentric version, used by academics, activists, and politicians of every shade, and communicated in the media, refers to the responsibility of mankind for its 'environment', i.e. for nature and the globe as a common basis for survival. In this general form, ecology has developed into a socially accepted concept and moral commitment. Ecological damage and the destruction of natural resources have come under close scrutiny on a global scale and local and trans-local initiatives for the protection of the environment have appeared on the scene in different parts of the world. Particular notice is taken of the worldwide degradation of forests, and the denudation of these has become a key symbol of man's destructive capacity. In this context, a local movement—the Chipko andolan—which emerged amongst villagers in Uttarakhand in the early 1970s in opposition to the large-scale commercial felling of local forests, received international attention as a strategy of healing the environment.[1] It now serves as a prime example of a local solution to global environmental problems.

---

[1] Uttarakhand (literally meaning 'land in the north') comprises the regions of Garhwal and Kumaon and was formerly part of Uttar Pradesh (UP). Since 9

With the global emergence of the ecological debate the fame of the Chipko andolan (i.e. the 'hug the trees' movement) spread in India and abroad.[2] This andolan was represented nationally and internationally by two of its leading figures, Chandi Prasad Bhatt, and, especially, Sunderlal Bahuguna. Both received several awards for their ecological commitment and are widely accepted as spokesmen in ecological matters. Chipko developed into a popular subject in print and audio-visual media; it has been taken up as an issue in academic debates; it served and still serves political and ideological arguments. Numerous publications have dealt with, or have at least referred to, Chipko's incidents. And differing re-presentations of the Chipko andolan show that the movement became instrumental for various interest groups: it has been presented to the public as an 'ecological movement', as a 'peasant movement' with ecological impact, as a 'women's or eco-feminist movement', as a 'Gandhian movement' (forest satyagraha). In most of these publications a protective ('ecologically friendly') attitude is assumed to guide traditional relations with nature and the social practices of the people in Uttarakhand, who, accordingly, are believed to perceive environmental degradation as primarily an ecological problem.

In representations of the Chipko andolan those who actually rose against forest exploitation—the village women and men of particular regions in Garhwal and Kumaon—are almost absent or silent. The Chipko events, the targets and motives ascribed to the actors involved, and the visions which are said to have inspired them have been communicated to the public by leaders, academics, journalists. All these have spoken *for* the villagers. Even more striking, in the aftermath of the Chipko andolan a broad range of entangled discourses developed in Uttarakhand relating to forests, forest policy, and forest degradation, as well as to participatory strategies and policies of environmental protection, regional development, and natural resource management.

November 2000 the hill regions of UP constitute the Himalayan state of Uttaranchal.

[2] The Hindi word *andolan* means movement, campaign, agitation (McGregor 1993). The Sanskrit meaning is swinging, trembling, oscillation (Monier-Williams 1994).

Representatives of these discourses are the state and its administrative organs on the one hand, and institutions of civil society such as local voluntary organizations, political parties, academics, and the above mentioned Chipko leaders on the other. The voices of the local inhabitants are again marginal in this discursive field, never mind that the issues discussed are of central concern to the villagers: they affect their everyday life, and they are an essential part of visions and projects within which they imagine a future life for themselves in the hills. What is the reason for the silence of village people? Do they not get involved in discourses? Or are their contributions ignored and overlooked? For two reasons, the latter seems to be the case. First, local discourses often do not exist in an explicit language or even in written form. They are hidden in the practices of everyday life and need to be translated into the 'language of modern ideas' (Chandra 1994). To explore local discourses asks for long-term field research and it seems that most of the publications on Chipko and the question of Himalayan development are based on short field trips of several weeks which have led researchers only into the well-known centres of Chipko activities and to well-known representatives of the movement. Second, many researchers have presumed *a priori* that ecological thinking is a basic feature of hill people's (in particular women's) relation to nature. Why get involved in local discourses and practices when their structure and contents are already well known? It is against this background of ignorance as well as essentialization that I designed my research. To grasp the environmental, social, and political situation in Uttarakhand as well as local responses one cannot start from a meta-perspective or an *a priori* assumption about people, their actions, their projects. One needs to discover the different—often divergent and contested—perceptions and interpretations of a changing lifeworld, to localize and analyse different discourses as well as practices, and pay attention to the dynamics of their interaction.

Understanding the degradation of forests in the Himalayan hills primarily as an ecological problem seems to be the result of an ecological awareness which originated in the countries of the Western world and only later gained momentum in India. 'Ecology' and 'environment' have been integrated as linguistic terms into the Indian languages only recently. By an examination of Sanskrit and Hindi dictionaries Hagen Berndt (1987: 92f.) has tried to prove that the Hindi term *paryavaran* did not originally refer to the natural environment but was used in a more general sense (atmosphere, surrounding, circumstances). Only later did it become popular as a translation of the English term 'environment'. By a similar process 'ecology' has been incorporated into the Hindi language by translating it as *paristhiti vigyan*. The lack of a particular term in a language may indicate either that the 'object' is non-existent or it is interpreted differently. Although we cannot assume 'ecology' to be a concept in the traditional life and worldview of Himalayan people, certain practices or even concepts which indicate an attitude sustaining the preservation of nature may have existed. Therefore it would be interesting to investigate the way people, de facto, relate to nature, particularly to the forest, in their everyday life, as well as examine processes by which the concept of ecology has been implanted into existing perceptions and probably altered them. This question leads to others: How was the situation in the Himalayas—which *we* have termed an ecological crisis—perceived by the inhabitants of the Himalayas? What were (and are) their strategies to cope with the situation? Was Chipko the only or most adequate answer or were there other ways of coping with it? How do hill villagers imagine their future? Do they relate to, or, in which ways do they relate to, the idea or concept of development? In this context it becomes necessary to narrow down the encompassing category 'people', 'local inhabitants', 'local population' and differentiate according to region or subregion, according to gender, age, and social stratification. To sum up, I was interested in investigating how different individuals and groups in Uttarakhand represent the Chipko andolan, how they project their own future, and the role of nature (natural resources, the forest) in local discourses and practices.

To answer these questions I did intensive field work in the region of Garhwal. I deliberately took a decision not to settle in a locality such as Gopeshwar (Chamoli District) which has been overrun by short-term researchers, journalists, and eco-tourists fascinated by the Chipko events and in most cases eager to confirm their assumption that the people of Uttarakhand are outstanding for their 'ecological' consciousness. I established myself in a village at the edge of Rawain in the western part of Garhwal (District Uttarkashi) and, in the first phase of my research, concentrated on the everyday life of local inhabitants.[3] Later I also paid several longer visits to places which have become popular during the Chipko struggle and interacted with participants as well as with the leaders of the movement. During this multi-sited field work, varying research methods were employed. I am reluctant to use the term 'participatory observation' to characterize my basic field method for it suggests a concept which lays the focus on the visual, assumes an external point of view, and privileges the researcher. But learning from and with others in the course of everyday life, rituals, festivals, etc. is based on observation as well as interaction and dialogue. I want to call my research simply 'participatory field work', a term with a double meaning. It implies, seen from the researcher's perspective, approaching one's research questions by living with others, sharing *their* lifeworld (to a large, though still limited, extent) as well as sharing (fragments of) one's own life world with them. And it alludes to the interactive moment of research, i.e. that others influence and take part ('participate') in my research, that reality is negotiated during the research process. As additional research methods, narrative interviews (in different research regions) as well as a village survey (in the main research region) were carried out.

In the course of the field work and the interaction with villagers my research programme had to undergo certain modifications, and particular questions had to be added. The complexity of the issue revealed itself only in stages. The following aspects became especially significant in course of time and influenced as well as (re-)shaped the whole thrust of my research.

Regional Disparity

- Garhwal is marked by regional differences *vis-à-vis* local perceptions of the environmental and socio-economic situation in the hills as well as with respect to the strategies applied to cope with this situation.[4]

---

[3] Rawain has been an administrative unit (*pargana*) in the former kingdom of Tehri Garhwal, but the name is still important for the subregional identity of its inhabitants.

[4] The term 'hills' is often used in northern India to refer to the Himalayas.

- In the different regions of Garhwal villagers did not support the Chipko andolan with the same intensity. Between the 'core areas' in Central and East Garhwal (around Tehri, Gopeshwar, Joshimath) and the more marginal areas in West Garhwal (Rawain, Bangan) differences exist regarding the level of mobilization and active participation in the movement.

Contextualization of 'Ecology'

- Environmental degradation or the destruction of forests cannot be seen as an 'ecological' problem in the narrow sense, i.e. a problem concerning the equilibrium of external nature (flora and fauna, soil, air, and water). Humans have to be considered as part of nature as well, and any intervention in nature has consequences for humans and their living conditions. Therefore the interdependence of social beings, living and acting in a certain sociocultural lifeworld and nature as part and basis of this lifeworld, has to be taken into consideration.
- As part of a particular lifeworld, nature is always culturally constructed and villagers relate to it in their economic and cultural practices and discourses. But these relations elude any *a priori* and one-dimensional definition; they can neither be categorized as basically 'conservationist' or as 'destructive'. In any case, they have to be examined in the context of the particular social reality.
- Forests play an important part in local projects of 'development' (*vikas*). Villagers state that development is a necessary precondition for a future life in the hills, because only social and economic changes allow the village population to lead a life of human dignity and prosperity in their traditional/ancestral surroundings. But what is understood as 'development' differs widely and is subject to local and translocal discourses as well as to processes of negotiation.

Existence of a Discursive Field

- As the cradle of Chipko, Garhwal (or Uttarakhand) has emerged as a point of reference in national and international debates on ecology and development. But in the locality as well, a broad range of local discourses relating to this subject has developed. Explicit discourses exist side by side with implicit ones, hidden in the praxis of everyday life among villagers. All the discourses are interwoven with and refer to each other—by force of argument or by virtue of practices and strategies of action.

- To 'read' the explicit and implicit local discourses, and—if necessary—translate them into the language of modern ideas means breaking the silence of those who have so far been 'object and victim' (Fabian 1983, 1990) in discourses led by others, and making them co-present, at least to a certain extent.

It turned out that discourses in the Garhwal Himalayas, as they contest and reflect each other at the level of performative practice as well as in argument and policy-making, became the central focus of my study. I looked into current understandings as well as the historical dimension of the forest issue and forest struggles in the region. Adhering to a notion of anthropology as an interpretive (hermeneutical) enterprise, I was particularly interested in the way local actors—as well as trans-local ones whose ideas and practices reach back into the region—report events and (re-)construct and constitute interactions. Thus the emphasis is not just on the actors' points of view and interpretations, and on everyday practices; rather, particular focus has been placed on the historical developments and genealogy of the current state of things as they are discursively constructed. This has been done not only to understand how interpretations inform social actions and the negotiation of relationships and strategies, but also because the central event which, in many respects, became a turning point in the recent history of the region, the Chipko andolan, itself exists only in different and contesting narrative versions. It is neither an objective fact, independent of its interpretation(s), nor is there—there cannot be—an authoritative narrative version of Chipko.

Chipko has not only altered the attitude to forests and the future in Chipko's localities, but because of its trans-local impact—on international debates and national politics—it is also influential in regions which had not been, or had only marginally been, involved in the struggle. As far as targets and strategies are concerned, the movement incorporated ambivalences and tensions from its very beginning.

These tensions, and sometimes contradictions, which basically centred on the question of the primacy of ecology or strengthening local forest rights, radiated into the time after Chipko and were reflected in various local discourses and practices of hill development. The structure and organization of this book pays tribute to the key role of Chipko in these areas of debate.

The subsequent part of this section comments on the field encounter and methodological issues. Chapter 2 provides an overview of the physiographic, socio-economic, and historical conditions in Uttarakhand. Chapter 3 takes up narratives on Chipko to illustrate diverse representations of the movement and the way it becomes instrumentalized in certain discourses. Special emphasis is laid on conflicting representations in the locality itself. The chapter argues that to interpret Chipko as ecological resistance means reducing its import and failing to grasp the basic intention and motives of participants. Chapter 4 reflects on the history, meaning, and metamorphosis of the concepts of ecology and development which have become linked within the idea of 'sustainable development'. These concepts are at the core of discourses and strategies—in India in general, as well as in the Himalayan region—among state administrative bodies, social activists, and local residents. The forest, in this context, plays a special role as the symbol of nature that is violated. Chapter 5 concentrates on discourses on forest rights and forest use which took shape in the aftermath of the Chipko movement among social activists and local residents involved in the struggle. Constitutive for the discourses are particular perspectives on development or, better, development alternatives which determine the ways in which the forest is related to. This chapter opens with a short outline of forest legislation and forest policies in colonial and postcolonial India as they influence the discourses and determine, to a certain extent, the frame of action of the local population. Chapter 6 presents a case study of a village, Nakoli, in Western Garhwal. It illustrates that the forest is deeply interwoven within the local way of life. It also shows that local residents' demand for self-determination in their use of the forest are pragmatic inasmuch as they enable the use (and even the destruction) of the forest in the name of local development. With ecological considerations being part of the dominant discourse, some practices in Nakoli can be read as a form of protest against ecology's hegemonic claim.

1.2 Fieldwork and Textual Representation

1.2.1 *The Field Encounter*

Scholarly as well as popular literature on Uttarakhand and Chipko suggests that the majority of the population of the region had participated in the movement. Localities like Gopeshwar, Mandal, and Raini (East Garhwal), where the initial Chipko struggles had taken place, as well as certain places in Tehri District (e.g. Advani) have become extremely prominent. Villages in other parts of Garhwal and Kumaon are said to have fought their own battles, to have actively supported the movement. Because the 'core areas' in East Garhwal were much visited by short-term researchers and 'eco-tourists' I decided to settle in West Garhwal; and for my long-term stay I chose a village in the former pargana Rawain (today tahsil Barkot, District Uttarkashi), to which I here give the pseudonym Nakoli.

The Rawain region is well known for a historic uprising of local villagers in 1929/30, directed against the restrictive forest policy of Narendra Shah, the former Raja of Tehri Garhwal. The uprising was violently crushed by military forces at Tilari Maidan on 30 May 1930. In 1968, in the run-up to Chipko, the 'Tilari Declaration' for local forest rights was proclaimed in Barkot on the memorable day of the uprising.[5] Later, between 1970 and 1972, demonstrations on the same matter took place in some of the small towns of the region. Even though I was prepared not to presuppose anything and not seek an 'ecological' awareness at any cost, I nevertheless expected a certain degree of sensitivity to environmental issues in the village of my choice and its neighbourhood. And I expected the village men and women to relate in some very basic and essential ways to their forest, and expected this relation to form part of local discourses and practices. Very soon, I learned that the reality was rather different. Two things struck me most during my field work: first, local villagers themselves cut and denuded small patches of the local forest to

[5] In some publications the event is dated 1969.

prepare new agricultural fields for cash crops. Ideas and concepts of forest protection, as well as activities like the Chipko movement were somewhat known but treated with indifference, sometimes even hostility. Second, despite its importance for daily life as well as rituals, the forest was not generally endowed with its own subjectivity—as, for example, has been suggested in reports on tribal communities in India and other parts of the world. The forest is, rather, known as an area where supernatural powers *reside*, but it has neither supernatural quality in itself nor is it vested with supernatural powers of its own. The forest seems to be a vital and meaningful part of people's life-world, but without possessing a special immunity or being the major point of reference in representations and interpretive concepts of the local population.

The way villagers in my area of work related to their forest had obvious consequences for my research praxis. Many people in Nakoli were indifferent or reluctant to talk with me about the forest. On the one hand they could not understand why I was pursuing the issue because for them it was nothing of great importance; on the other hand they were reticent about discussing the forest because they knew that the felling of trees, which they undertook here and there, ran counter to official discourses and legislation. But whereas the people of Nakoli largely ignored the topic I wanted to focus on, they wanted to focus on other issues: on the political history of the locality and its relation to the former kingdom of Tehri Garhwal; on gods, myths, and religious practices; on their ideas and strategies for local 'development', and on the differences between their lifestyle and the way of life in 'the plains'. So, though I explored these topics, my perspective remained fixed on the forest, with the result that for some time I was uncertain and even worried about the outcome and success of my research. But because the situation in Nakoli and its surroundings seemed to be so different from the Chipko core areas, I also felt challenged and decided to make every effort to learn more about the rationales which guide local attitudes towards the forest and the everyday praxis of village men and women.

Once I stopped pursuing my own interests in a too straightforward manner and became more receptive to issues and problems that the villagers were willing to talk about, the interaction became more relaxed. In the course of time it thus turned out that I learnt of forest issues indirectly, or by indirection: the history of the locality, as narrated by the people of Nakoli, proved a clue to the relation of villagers to their forest. Moreover, the ideas and practices of forest use play an important role in local discourses on development. Finally, by not exposing myself too prominently as a researcher, I made villagers less reserved and gradually they began disclosing matters which they had formerly withheld in my presence. I gained acceptance in the village context and became more and more one of them, or at least less of an outsider.

One of the most stimulating questions relating to field work and interactions in the field has been posed by Jean-Paul Dumont: 'Who was I for them?' This question invites the anthropologist to consider the way she is seen by 'others', what is expected from her. It demands that the researcher ask how interactions and personal relations with the people researched affect them and how she even may be 'used' by particular groups or persons. But Dumont's question has a deeper level as well. It forces one to reflect on the foundations of dialogue and interaction, a problem which has been discussed with reference to two opposite models: the model of consensus (identity), and the model of difference (see Fuchs & Berg 1993).

My research in Nakoli developed as a double game of adaptation and the keeping of difference. On the one hand I had to prove that, as a woman, I was *somehow* able to manage village life. This included dressing according to the customs, doing the cooking, eating and dish-washing in the same way as other women, washing clothes in their way, behaving according to their norms and values. I was also expected to accompany women to the fields and into the jungle, and they appreciated the fact that I was able to work with them.[6] On the other hand the villagers were interested in me and my personal and

---

[6] In my area of field work no one was ready to work as a household servant, and I would have lost all credit by 'importing' somebody from the plains to work for me. I tried to live like the other villagers as far as I could, and nobody expected me to be perfect. They even liked to see me make mistakes or struggle with things which caused them no difficulties (e.g. getting the chapatis thin and round; cutting leaves with a sickle-shaped knife). I was always good as a figure of fun; the women and girls used to laugh at me especially.

cultural background because I was different and because I did not fit into their role models: I was a *videshi* (foreigner), I was educated and could move around freely,[7] I had only one child, had my separate room and kitchen in the village, etc. The younger women and girls were especially fascinated by the kind of options open to me but also by my personal belongings, which I had brought with me and which were signs of my otherness.[8] Slowly, some of the village men and women with whom I was in relatively close contact learned to utilize my otherness to carve out some liberties for themselves, whereas others tried to profit in a more informal way.

In front of my room was a small courtyard (*chauk*). This developed more and more into a public space. Often, on their way to the jungle or to the fields or to the distant market town, villagers—men and women of every age—came for a short conversation, had a cup of tea; occasionally they met acquaintances and stayed on to talk with each other. Villagers from Nakoli and neighbouring villages came daily to ask for medicines, for photographs, for some advice or help. When I visited distant villages or places by taxi, the car would invariably be crowded with villagers who took the opportunity to join us to pursue their own affairs. For those closer to me or to my research assistant, my room and kitchen became places where they could find some privacy. To have such a *private* space was especially important for young married women and girls who are usually supervised by their elders and who, normally, can only escape by going into the jungle for grass or firewood. They met in my room to gossip and laugh, to talk with each other and with me about their in-laws, about their husbands. They, as well as the older girls, asked me about marriage customs, women's education, and pre-marital relations in my country. They

---

[7] Meaning I was not subject to the control of husband or brother. As I was mostly accompanied by my research assistant, I was not without male protection. But it was essential that our relation be seen as based solely on work. Although it was accepted that we had our meals together, it was important that his room was a good distance from mine.

[8] E.g. lipstick, make-up, underwear, European clothes, camera, tape recorder. In principle, all these goods are available even to the villagers, but only 'made in India', and for most of them even these were too expensive.

enjoyed eating sweets, some women enjoyed to smoke bidis or a cigarette. In the evenings I would prepare a meal together with my research assistant. Young men who befriended him liked to come for a drink, a smoke, and to talk. They accepted my presence, not only because of my difference, but also because I was free enough to transgress local norms by joining them and having a drink with them—though this had to remain a secret. All these public and private meetings, in which I did not act as researcher but as a companion or 'partner' (Koepping 1994), proved to be a rich source of informal but extremely valuable information and became a building block in the process of my getting 'my place' in the village.[9]

It proved very important in allowing villagers to share my life in the village, and of course the other way round—the anthropologist sharing their life with them. It was of equal importance that I was able to share with them parts of my lifeworld beyond the village context.[10] They appreciated the fact that my little daughter accompanied me during most parts of the research; that my husband joined us for longer periods; and that German friends visited us in the village. They liked to see my photos and talk about my country, of how people lived and worked there. I often asked close friends from the village to accompany me on my trips to Dehra Dun, Delhi, or Eastern Garhwal. One young woman even came to Germany and lived with me and my family for three months. But the all-important condition for being accepted as somebody who 'belonged' to the village was my repeated

[9] Koepping has stressed that the authenticity of participation rests in the 'true dialogical principle of involving and confronting others as we try to understand their being different which in turn leads us to see our own difference . . .' (1994: 25). I think it is important to note that the 'others' undergo corresponding processes of understanding in the course of their interaction with the anthropologist. And it applies to both sides: true dialogue and interaction require acknowledging difference as 'value without the claim for superiority of one or the other view of reality' (1994: 25).

[10] Only with that could I really prove my willingness to 'place myself at their disposal' ('Sich zur Verfügung stellen'), which seems—according to Koepping— the only way to save oneself from degrading 'others' into mere 'objects' of research (Koepping 1987: 29).

return to Nakoli for shorter periods of research. I was taken aback and gratified at learning about things that village people had not talked before about, or had tried to hide. Even the forest issue was, on my later visits, more openly discussed.

Subsequently I came to understand one of the most basic features characterizing village life and the personality of village men and women, a feature which, in my opinion, marks a strong contrast to my own cultural context: the capacity to live with ambivalences, ambiguities, and tensions. Whereas 'we' often try to solve contradictions and make an attempt to develop a definite and unambiguous position even at the cost of open conflict and inner compulsion, in Nakoli there is a level of acceptance both of individual and social ambiguities. I argue strictly against any attempt to classify such behaviour as personal weakness or inconsistency, seeing it rather as an individually and socially inbuilt—sometimes even conscious—strategy and capacity to come to terms with oneself and with each other to cope with conflicting situations. (Maybe this capacity helped them tolerate the anthropologist!) As far as the forest was concerned, people consciously lived with ambivalence—the ambivalence caused by the official ('ecological') discourse which demands they protect their forests, and the local discourse which emphasizes the right of villagers to use their forests according to local needs—including felling the forests. They do not try to harmonize these discourses. Within families, as well as in social and religious contexts, I came across numerous examples where interaction and communication continued despite profound tensions. Setting this against my own experience, I would in such cases have expected a breakdown of communication.

When summarizing my reflections regarding my position in Nakoli and the neighbouring villages, one aspect especially seems remarkable: I was not primarily accepted as an academic researcher but as a private person who tried to learn about life in the hills by living with—and sometimes like—the local people in a village. Our communication continued not despite but because of my cultural and personal difference. In the process it led to an increasing closeness which did not mean superseding difference but overcoming distance. My interactions became more intensive and more open. Villagers arrived at the conviction that I intended no harm to the village and its inhabitants. Especially in relation to forest issues, the villagers expected me to behave in accordance with local agreement: it was understood that certain practices and opinions would not reach the public.[11]

The research situation in Nakoli differed widely from that in the Chipko core areas. In Eastern Garhwal local activists and villagers were eager to talk about forest problems, the Chipko movement, and their own efforts at forest protection and afforestation. I could focus on the forest issue without opposition. Men and women also talked openly about issues of local development and vehemently expressed their hopes and demands. As a result of their involvement in the Chipko struggle and their active participation in eco-development work, activists as well as villagers were articulate and used to appealing to a wider public in order to push their demands through. Chipko has not only succeeded in creating a public sphere but has also stimulated a particular understanding of state and civil society: the state is regarded as an institution to which people as active citizens and members of civil society can make legitimate claims and which has an obligation to care for their welfare. Social activists of the well-known NGO, the Dashauli Gram Swarajya Mandal (DGSM), as well as actively involved villagers, are used to addressing the public in order to communicate their concepts and demands for self-determined development. They approach the media direct, but interested visitors may be looked upon as a help in this as well.

People appeared to be open to discussions about forest issues, however because a number of researchers, journalists, and tourists visit the region and talk to villagers and NGO representatives in order to collect information or simply to satisfy their curiosity, I found people not only fed up with visitors but also disappointed because the increasing publicity did not necessarily translate into local benefits. After some effort, I succeeded in establishing links in certain localities

[11] A question arises: do I now violate this agreement by writing about Nakoli? A recent development in the locality made my decision easier: the practice of tree felling for cash crop production has become well known to the local administration in any case. In reaction to a recent destruction of apple orchards by the police, villagers complained at the local court. The case was pending at the time of my last visit.

and with activists, but—in comparison with Nakoli—I was less accepted as an individual or private person. Moreover, I was seen outside Nakoli as someone from the public sphere who was expected to present her research findings to the public.

1.2.2 Discourse Analysis as Mode
of Representation

The reflexive debate in anthropology has focused on the problem of 'writing' culture and on the question of how to transform ethnographic knowledge, gained in the joint and interactive process of fieldwork, into a written text without objectifying and passing over 'the other'. To solve this problem anthropologists have experimented with new forms of ethnographic writing, e.g. polyphonic or dialogic representation, and varieties of co-authorship. But is it possible to reproduce the mutuality and co-presence of anthropologists and 'others' during the field situation in a text which, in the end, is the product of a single (or perhaps two or three) author(s)? Such textual experiments only give the illusion of 'shared writing'. I think one has to concede the final *authorship* of the anthropologist even in experimental ethnography because it is she who, in the last instance, selects, arranges, and evaluates the voices of the others. This does not imply her final *authority* as well. Just as the anthropologist's is only one voice in the polyphonic encounter within the field, she herself pursues only a single and specific perspective which lies open to criticism.

In view of such critical reflections on ethnographic writing, what conclusion should I draw for the presentation of my own research findings, gained in different regions and social contexts? How to handle the different expectations that village men and women from both regions express? In search of an answer I came across a statement by Johannes Fabian in which he criticizes the denial of co-presence to the 'other' in anthropological writing: 'The absence of the *Other* from our Time has been his mode of presence in our discourse—as an object and victim' (Fabian 1983: 154). Would it be possible in an anthropological text to make others 'present' as subjects of their praxis and interpretations via *their* discourses?

I will argue below that 'discourse' must be understood as dual. First, discourses are communicative structures which may exist in an explicit form, as spoken language and/or text. Second, discourses may also be implicit, hidden in the social and cultural practices of everyday life, and only accessible through careful anthropological work and analysis. Both forms imply a certain degree of reflexivity. For Fairclough and Wodak (1997) it indicates the specificity and the strength of a discursive approach to take into account one of the over-all characteristics of contemporary social life: the 'peculiarly modern form of "reflexivity"':

contemporary life is reflexive in the sense that people radically alter their practices—the ways in which they live their lives—on the basis of knowledge and information about those practices. Technologization of discourse [conscious intervention to control and shape language practices in accordance with economic, political, and institutional objectives] is the 'top-down', institutional side of modern reflexivity, but there is also a 'bottom-up' side appertaining to the everyday practices of ordinary people. A critical awareness of discursive practices and an orientation to transforming such practices as one element in social (class, feminist, anti-racist, green, etc.) struggles—or in Giddens's terms, in the reflexive construction and reconstruction of the self—is a normal feature of contemporary social life . . . (Fairclough & Wodak 1997: 260)

The ongoing economic, political, and cultural integration of even marginal regions like Uttarakhand into the larger social context has resulted in an increase of information, knowledge, and life options at least for parts of the population. The Chipko movement has especially helped open up a public sphere where ways of life are debated, where future is imagined and projected. Reflexivity has come to exist in the 'everyday practices of ordinary people' in Uttarakhand and shows itself in explicit and implicit forms of local discourses and discursive practices even in the region's villages.

In the first instance, a discourse analytic approach has to clarify what exactly is meant by discourse, a notion or concept with a 'ubiquitous presence' (van Dijk 1977a) in the humanities and social sciences. Teun van Dijk, one of the protagonists of discourse analysis characterizes the term as 'essentially fuzzy' (1997a: 1), eluding any clear and unambiguous definition. He understands discourse (including written language) most basically as a *communicative event* characterized by three main dimensions: language use, communication of beliefs (cognition), and interaction (1977a & b). Discourse studies 'are about talk and text in context' (von Dijk 1997c: 3). But this general definition does not sufficiently explore the whole range of meanings of discourse. The term may also refer to specific types or social domains of language use, as one speaks for example of 'medical discourse', 'political discourse', 'ecological discourse'. In an even broader sense 'discourse' may refer to ideas or ideologies as in the 'discourse of liberalism'. Another complication with the notion of discourse lies in the difficulty of identifying and delimiting a particular discourse. It is not always clear where it 'begins' and where it 'ends' or whether there are one or more discourses. The analyst has to consider the unity or coherence of a discourse, the intertextual relations, intentions of speakers and writers, and the communicative context (setting, time, and place). Van Dijk distinguishes between 'simple' and 'compound' discourses, between discourses and discourse complexes (1997a: 4). For the task of discourse analysis he argues that, similar to the specialization in other disciplines, here too the analyst may lay emphasis on a particular aspect of discourse, e.g. language use (order and form, semantics, style, rhetoric, etc.), cognition (memory, knowledge, representations), action and interaction (speech acts, conversation), or social context (gender, ethnicity).

Although it seems indisputable that discourse is a complex verbal structure which can be analysed from different perspectives I would like to stress the central importance of the social, as well as the historical dimension of discourse which centrally influences and shapes its structure and meaning. Discourses are in short inextricably situated in a particular socio-historical context, they are linked with a particular social praxis, and they reflect relations of power. In this sense discourse should be seen as a *trans-individual and contextualized argumentative or narrative frame of reference relating to a specific subject or domain—which is itself constructed in the discourse in a particular way.*[12]

---

[12] That is to say, discourse and the domain shaped (or formed) by it are not fully congruent, not fully identical. It is this gap which permits (certain ways of) distanciation and reflexivity, something which is excluded in Foucault's concept of discourse and discursive formation.

I want to go a step further. Discourse has been defined as an explicit, reflexive, and meaningful complex bound to a verbal structure (talk and text). But would it be possible to apply the notion of discourse even when certain discursive practices do not build on *explicit* arguments? Would it be illuminating to analyse social practice according to a model of language which extracts implicit aspects of cognition and meaning (semantics)? I would like to postulate that people may constitute a particular discourse without verbalizing and justifying their attitudes and strategies in a 'discursive' language: meanings, beliefs, and interpretations which relate to a particular subject or domain may be interwoven in the social practice and can be context-implicit (they may also be verbalized in the language of another discourse). The anthropologist has to be sensitive to these possibilities. Therefore, she is requested on the one hand to study 'implicit' discourses by concentrating on social practices as well as everyday conversations and their propositional content in order to decipher non-verbal 'arguments'. On the other hand she has to be open to other discourses and listen carefully to arguments differently couched. In sum, the discourse analytic approach which I have in mind tries to combine two different perspectives: it aims to study *discourse in the context of social practice* as well as *social practice as a particular form of discourse*.

Certain further remarks have to be made on the theoretical and methodological status of discourses, and the aims and methods of analysis: first, the presentation and analysis of discourses seem a promising way of approaching a particular subject or domain and giving a subtle, differentiated picture of the complexity of social reality and agency in the field. As mentioned at the outset, in the Garhwal Himalayas I was confronted with a large discursive field relating to the forest and interconnected aspects of environment and development. This field included diverse discourses represented by different agents (the central and federal states, local NGOs and social activists; individuals and groups in different localities). Those interested in this subject will know that, especially in the Chipko core areas, villagers willingly comment on the forest issue—which includes official forest policy, the policies of the NGOs, and their own outlooks and strategies. They also happily discuss their own ideas of local development and the prospects of life in the hills. Outside the core area, explicit discourses on forest and environment are less frequent but attitudes to the forest can be extracted by 'reading' discourses which relate to other issues (e.g. discourses on territoriality and development), and by looking closely at everyday practices. Against the background of local research experiences in Garhwal, the discourse concept I have in mind can be outlined in a more precise way:

- Discourses express the multiplicity of voices in a certain cultural and social context and therefore indicate the fragmented character of culture and society.
- Discourses are contingent interpretations linked to a particular social practice or inherent in it. The participants of a discourse may pose validity claims of propositional truth, but for the discourse analyst there exists no theory of justification for truth claims.
- Discourses entail context-transcending elements. They are based on the creative imagination and are future oriented.
- Discourses are never self-contained, closed structures (as partly implied in Foucault's concept of discourse). They are open, and various discourses may be in interaction with each other. The modes of interaction are diverse and include mutual reference, dialogue, complementarity, conflict.
- Discourses express and address power relations. The extent to which a discourse can be asserted against other discourses, its hegemony or marginalization, depends not only on its persuasive power (rhetorics, argumentative consistency), but also on the (political, ideological) power of its representatives to push it through and translate it into a particular social practice—which then, conversely, reaffirms the definition of reality.[13]
- A particular discourse is not identical with a certain spatial or social unit (village, status group, family, institution, political party), i.e. not all people who belong to such a unit necessarily

[13] I am not satisfied with a notion of discursive formations or social systems of knowledge in the Foucauldian sense as historically *a priori* and exclusive frames, leaving no space for setting terms without options, and leaving no space for social actors to go beyond or behind (Frank 1988).

follow one discourse—even though there may be one which is dominant. Moreover, different discourses exist simultaneously, side by side. One and the same person, or one and the same text, may incorporate different discourses, which may generate inner tensions and ambivalences.

• As contingent interpretations, different discourses are in principle of the same standing. For example, an academic discourse is not *a priori* superior to a discourse of villagers. But nevertheless one has to concede that, *de facto*, academic discourses are more powerful and, often, more refined. This holds true due to the specialization of the scientists, indicated by specific knowledge, a critical mode of reconstruction and analysis, better rhetoric (argumentative style), a larger audience.

Second, we have an issue which concerns methods of discourse analysis. A discourse is not a single communicative event but an argumentative and narrative frame of reference relating to (the construction of) a particular domain. In this sense, discourses have to be re-constructed by the anthropologist and are, inasmuch, abstractions. Two strategies are possible: to take one communicative event which belongs to one genre—a narrative, an interview, a text—as representative of a whole discourse, or to base the analysis on examples of different events which may belong to different genres of language-use. I want to follow the last strategy, even though one particular communicative event may gain more prominence than others. Discourses are constituted by the three dimensions of language-use, cognition, and interaction and are linked with a socio-historical praxis (van Dijk 1997a, 1997b). Discourse studies have to integrate the analysis of each of these dimensions.[14] However I do not intend to attach equal importance to them. In my analysis I want to focus on the interactive, the social and historical, as well as the cognitive aspects of

[14] Van Dijk aims to establish discourse studies as an autonomous discipline with researchers no longer trained only in one of the mother disciplines. 'For them, writing grammars, analysing cognition, or studying interaction and societal structures will not be totally different things, but simply different aspects of one, complex scholarly enterprise, namely to describe and explain discourse' (1997a: 29).

discourses, although language use will not be ignored. Very briefly, I want to point to some of the important elements of my analytic strategy.

Language-use: The study has to include statements concerning: the type or *genre* of a communicative event (interview, narrative, song, speech, text); *performance*, i.e. visual and bodily aspects; *meaning*, such as information, topics, coherence; *style*, as context-bound variation of expression, level of discourse; *rhetoric*, such as persuasive devices, irony, metaphor.

Cognition: To analyse cognitive content requires considering individual as well as socio-cultural cognition. Important aspects are knowledge, memory, social representations, socio-cultural beliefs, ideologies.

Action and interaction in society: To study discourse as an active process includes looking for intentionality, purposes, and ways of interaction. Discourse as part of a socio-historical praxis requires concentrating on social context and power relations. One has to study participants (gender, age, class, social position, access to power), setting (locality of discourse, the grade of formality of a situation); props (personal or official markers, such as a particular way of dressing, fashioning of rooms); ways of exerting power (male, political, coercive, persuasive); and access to resources.

All these analytic aspects will not mechanically be worked off in the course of re-constructing and analysing representations of Chipko, discourses on the forest, and related issues in the Garhwal Himalayas. Rather, they function as points of reference integrated into and guiding the analysis.

2

The Region: A Geographical and Socio-historical Sketch of Uttarakhand (with Special Reference to Garhwal)

THE HIMALAYAN PART OF THE NORTH INDIAN STATE of Uttar Pradesh, was constituted as a separate state named Uttaranchal on 9 November 2000. The new state includes the districts of Uttarkashi, Dehra Dun, Tehri, Chamoli, Rudraprayag, and Pauri Garhwal (Garhwal Division), and Almora, Bageshwar, Pithoragarh, Nainital, Champawat, Udham Singh Nagar (Kumaon Division); the district of Haridwar was newly added. Haridwar and Udham Singh Nagar are located in the plains and differ from the hill districts in population and socio-economic structure. The hill-districts proper are still widely known as Uttarakhand, 'land of the north'. Because of its religious geography the region is also famous by the name of Kedarkhand, meaning holy land, or land of the gods. Four important pan-Indian Hindu pilgrimage centres—Yamnotri, Gangotri, Kedarnath, and Badrinath—are located in the upper catchment areas of the main rivers. Some episodes of the two main Indian epics, the Ramayana and especially the Mahabharat, are situated in the hills and forests of Uttarakhand, and the spiritual heritage of Hindu India is often linked with this region.

2.1 Physiographic Setting

Uttarakhand consists of four main longitudinal physiographic zones running parallel to each other: the Outer Himalaya, the Lesser (or

Lower) Himalaya, the Great Himalaya (also called Higher or Main Himalaya), and the Trans-(Tibetan or Tethys) Himalaya. The region is drained by the rivers Tons and Yamuna in the west, and in the east by the Bhagirati and Alakananda (from Deoprayag down named Ganga or Ganges) with their main tributaries Bhilangana, Pindar, and Mandakini in the central part and by the rivers Kali (Sharda) and Ramganga to the east.

The Outer Himalaya includes (from south to north) the narrow belts of Terai and Bhabar, the Siwalik Hills, and the Duns. The last are broad longitudinal valleys which separate the Siwaliks from the lesser Himalayan ranges. Most of the urban settlements of Uttarakhand are concentrated in the Outer Himalaya, like Dehra Dun, Rishikesh, Haridwar, Kotdwar, and Ramnagar. The climate is hot and moist in the Terai, Bhabar, and Dun valleys, areas which are below 600m; in the Siwalik Hills, with an elevation between 600m and 1200m, it is subtropical. The submontane forests consist mainly of *sal* (*Shorea robusta*), *khair* (*Acacia catechu*), *shisham* (*Dalbergia sissoo*), and *chir* pine (*Pinus roxburghii*).

The Lesser Himalaya rises from 1200m to 3000m. The landscape of this region is (especially in Garhwal) composed of rugged mountain ranges and ridges, separated by narrow valleys. The montane (or temperate) climate is similar to that of middle and southern Europe and very favourable for agriculture. Around 81 per cent of the total rural settlements can be found in this zone and well-known hill towns are located there, such as Mussoorie, Narendra Nagar, Landsdowne, Pauri, Srinagar, Pithoragarh, Almora, and Nainital. The forests in the lower altitudes (up to 1800m) are dominated by chir pine and *khail* (*Pinus wallichiana*), the upper parts are covered by oak forests consisting of *banj* (*Quercus leucotricophora*), *moru* (*Quercus himalayana*) and *kharsu* (*Quercus semecarpifolia*), by cedar or *devdar* forests (*Cedrus deodara*), and by fir and spruce forests of *morinda* (*Abies pindrow*) and *raî* (*Picea smithiana*). Above 1500m two other tree species are widely spread: *burans* (*Rhododendron arboreum*) and *akhrot* (walnut: *Juglans regia*). The southern slopes in the Lesser Himalaya are almost eroded, whereas on the northern slopes comparatively thick vegetation can still be found.

The Great Himalaya includes sub-alpine and alpine regions, high peaks and glaciers. The altitude varies between 3000m and 7800m. The famous peaks are (from west to east) Bandarpunch (6315m), Gangotri (6614m), Kedarnath (6940m), Chaukhamba (7138m), Badrinath (7074m), Trishul (7120m), Nanda Devi (7816m). The upper catchment areas and sources of the main rivers—Yamuna, Bhagirati, Mandakini, Alakananda, Ramganga, and Kali—are located in this area. The climate is cold and heavy snowfall occurs during the winters. In this sub-alpine region up to 3600m fir (*Abies spectabilis*), rhododendron, and birch or *bhoj-patra* (*Betula utilis*) dominates; in the alpine regions up to the snow line (between 4800m and 5200m) only scrubs and grasses grow. Alpine pastures (*bugyals*) are found up to 4000m. Important pilgrimage centres of the Hindus and Sikhs are situated in this zone: like Yamnotri, Gangotri, Gaumukh, Kedarnath, Badrinath, and Hemkund.

The Trans-Himalaya is a rain shadow zone because the monsoon does not cross the high peaks of the Great Himalayas. The climate is cold and the region is scarcely populated, mostly by Bhotiya tribes, i.e. tribes of Tibetan origin. More than 75 per cent of the area lies above 4500m and annually remains under snow for more than six months. Glacial and glacio-fluvial deposits have produced large terraces near Badrinath-Mana, Malari, Lata, and Tapovan. Tree growth is restricted to moist strips of land along the rivers and channels formed by snowmelt waters. Pine, cedar, and juniper dominate the forests.

2.2 Historical Overview

Archaeological artefacts, coins, inscriptions, and references in religious texts (Skand-Purana, Mahabharat) are the main sources for the early history of the region.[1] Historians state that the region was ruled by different 'tribal' groups such as the Khasas, Kunindas, and Kiratas, before the Katyuri dynasty established its hegemony in the fifth century. It seems that in Garhwal, because of rugged mountain tracts

---

[1] The following is based on Saklani 1987, Rawat 1989b, Joshi 1990, and Raturi 1988.

and numerous small valleys, it was difficult to exert lasting control and petty chiefs continued to rule certain pockets. The power of the Katyuris is said to have declined in the eleventh and twelfth centuries. In Garhwal their decline allowed in their place many independent chiefs, residing in small fortresses (*garhs*), each controlling a few valleys.

The dynasty of the Pamvara (Paramara, Parmar) Rajputs, who ruled Garhwal until 1949, traced its origin back to an immigrant Rajput from western India. Various chronological lists of the Parmar rulers of Garhwal exist (the lists of Hardwick, Beckett, Williams, and the Almora list, Rawat 1989b: 24–9), but, most probably, one Kanak Pal was the founder of the dynasty. The story goes that in AD 888 Kanak Pal came from western India on a pilgrimage and got married to the daughter of Son Pal, a local petty chief.[2] Kanak Pal is said to have resided at Chandpur Garh, near the temples of Adi Badri (east of Karnaprayag).

'The rise of Kumaon and Garhwal as two independent principalities marks an important era in the historical anthropology of Uttaranchal,' states M.P. Joshi (1990: 64). He refers to the sixteenth century, when Ajay Pal (*c.* 1500–47) and Rudra Chandra (*c.* 1565–97) conquered various smaller chiefdoms in Garhwal and Kumaon and gained political supremacy in their regions.[3] Historians agree that the real history of the Parmar dynasty of Garhwal started with Ajay Pal. He shifted his residence to Devalgarh near Srinagar (Alakananda valley) and installed Raj Rajeshwari as the family goddess of the Parmars. Under his successors the title of Shah was adopted.[4] The Chandras (Chands) of Kumaon, originally from Champawat (at the Nepalese

[2] According to inscriptions on the walls of a temple in Chandpur Fort, the residence of Kanak Pal, he came from Gujar Desh, which comprises today's states of Gujarat, Rajasthan, as well as parts of Maharashtra and Madya Pradesh. Many Rajput castes in Garhwal and Kumaon, who are said to have come in the time of Kanak Pal, trace their origin to Gujarat and Rajasthan (e.g. Rawat, Bartwal, Rautela, Negi, Bhandari).

[3] See Joshi (1990). Rawat (1989b) mentions Ajay Pal as the thirty-seventh in the Beckett list of rulers and the list gives the date of his death as 1389.

[4] Already Kalyan Shah, direct successor of Ajay Pal according to the Beckett list, used this title, but it became popular only with Balbhadra Shah (forty-third in the list) (Rawat 1989b). Rawat refers to a historical source which tells that

border), had shifted their capital to Almora. Relations between the Parmars of Garhwal and the Chandras (Chands) of Kumaon were characterized by political rivalry. Saklani states that the political history of the region 'appears to have been a succession of wars and counter wars' from the fifteenth to the nineteenth centuries (1987: 23). Both dynasties ruled until the end of the eighteenth century, when the Gurkhas from West Nepal started invading Kumaon (1790) and Garhwal (1791). At this time Garhwal was only forced to pay an annual tribute and accept a representative of the Kathmandu court in Srinagar, but in 1803 the Gurkhas launched an attack to conquer the region. In a battle which, according to the then *diwan* (minister) Hari Krishna Raturi, took place on 14 May 1804, the army of Pradyumna Shah was defeated; the king and most of his retainers were killed. The victorious Gurkhas, who had already occupied Kumaon, brought the whole of Garhwal under their rule and kept it for the next eleven years.

The Gurkhas were defeated by the British in 1815. Subsequently, the British incorporated Kumaon and eastern Garhwal into the Raj. The Kumaon Division, as the new administrative unit comprising Kumaon and British Garhwal was called, formed part of the North Western Provinces (after 1901 they were renamed as the United Provinces of Agra and Oudh). The other parts of Garhwal, the parganas west of the Alakananda, were restored to the son of the previous ruler. Since the former Parmar capital, Srinagar, was located within the area directly ruled by the British, the new raja, Sudarshan Shah, founded a new capital, Tehri, at the confluence of the Bhagirati and Bhilangana, after which the new kingdom was named Tehri Garhwal.[5] During

---

Raja Balbhadra was invested with the title by Aurangzeb as thanks for a favour: when Aurangzeb defeated his brother Dara Shikoh, the latter took refuge in Srinagar (Garhwal), but was betrayed and sent back to Delhi (Rawat 1989b: 39).

[5] The Tehri kingdom was one of the 'native' or 'princely' states of India, subordinate to the British government. In a *sanad* (authoritative document) of 1820, the raja was not allowed to alienate or mortgage any portion of his domain without prior permission from the British. He had to furnish hill porters and supplies to the British and guarantee trading facilities. In return he was promised protection by British troops (Saklani 1987: 42f.). After 1842 the political agency of Tehri Garhwal was given to the commissioner of Kumaon.

British rule the kingdom was one of the princely states in the Punjab States Agency and its territory corresponded to the present districts of Uttarkashi and Tehri. The princely state merged with the Indian Union in 1949. The hill region became the northern part of Uttar Pradesh and consisted of eight districts: Uttarkashi, Tehri, Chamoli, Pauri, and Dehra Dun in Garhwal; Almora, Pithoragarh, and Nainital in Kumaon. This administrative structure remained until 1996, when a reorganization of districts took place. Until the formation of Uttaranchal in the year 2000 Uttarakhand consisted of twelve districts, the new ones being Rudraprayag (formerly part of Chamoli), Bageshwar (formerly part of Almora), Champawat (carved out of Pithoragarh), and Udham Singh Nagar (carved out of Nainital).

2.3 Administrative and Demographic Structure

The new state of Uttaranchal covers an area of 53,483 km^2. Its thirteen districts are further divided into tahsils and development blocks. The total population at last count was 8,479,562. The districtwise distribution of land area and population appears in Table 1.

The figures are based on the census of 2001. Unfortunately, most of the census data concerning the different states and regions of India are not yet published. Data on natural resources is not available. Therefore the following statistical information relies on the census data collected in 1991; it refers to the period before the foundation of Uttaranchal, and before the reorganization of districts. As my research period was from 1993 to 1996, these statistics indicate the state of affairs during the research period.

Uttarakhand is a predominantly rural region, but since 1951 a certain trend towards 'urbanization' can be observed.[6] According to the census of 1991, the population of Uttarakhand (5,867 Mio.) resides

[6] In his study on urbanization in Garhwal, S. Singh (1995) emphazises the difficulty of defining and identifying an 'urban' settlement. According to the Census Commissioner of India a settlement is classified as urban if the population is more than 5000 or if it has administrative functions. But there are settlements which function as important trading and marketing points which do not fulfill these criteria (Singh 1995: 6).

Table 1

Land Area and Population in Uttaranchal
(1991 and 2001, Districtwise)

	Land area in km2 (1991)	Land area in km2 (2001)	Population 1991	Population 2001
Uttarkashi	8016	8016.0	237,000	294,179
Chamoli	9125	7613.8	441,000	369,198
Rudraprayag	included	1890.6	included	227,461
Tehri	4421	4080.0	575,245	604,608
Dehra Dun	3088	3088.0	1,014,000	1,279,083
Pauri Garhwal	5440	5399.6	664,000	696,851
Pithoragarh	8856	7100.0	557,000	462,149
Champawat	included	1781.0	included	224,461
Almora	5385	3082.8	824,000	630,446
Bageshwar	included	2302.5	included	249,453
Nainital	6794	3860.4	1.557,000	762,912
Udhamsingh N.	included	2908.4	included	1,234,548
Haridwar	./.	2360.0	./.	1,444,213
Total	51,125	53,483	5,867,245	8,479,562

Table compiled from census data, Government of India (http://www.censusindia.net)

in 16,011 rural and 74 urban settlements.[7] Table 2 shows that most of the population is concentrated in the districts of Nainital and Dehra Dun, which are both located in the lower altitudes of the Outer Himalaya; less populated are the districts of Uttarkashi and Chamoli, situated in higher altitudes.

Urbanization was part of the overall post-independence development of the Himalayan hills. The three major underlying reasons for the development efforts were, first, the Indo-Chinese conflict along the Indo-Tibetan border in 1962 and the subsequent need to make the region 'accessible' for military, administrative, and commercial purposes; second, the economic development of 'backward' areas as part of a general planning process; and third, resource development

[7] The census of 2001 mentions 84 urban settlements; of these 9 are located in Haridwar District: data on rural settlements are not yet available.

Table 2

Population, Rural and Urban Settlements in Uttarakhand
(1991, Districtwise)

	No. of rural settlements	No. of urban settlements	Population in lakh[8]
Uttarkashi	686	3	2.37
Chamoli	1681	8	4.41
Tehri	2015	4	5.75
Dehra Dun	764	16	10.14
Pauri	3551	8	6.64
Pithoragarh	2295	5	5.57
Almora	3163	5	8.24
Nainital	1856	25	15.57

Compiled from data in Aggarwal and Agrawal: 1995: 16; Pant and Pant 1995: 27f.

(raw materials, electric power) for the industrialization and the benefit of the whole country. The process of 'development' started in the
1960s and included several measures:

- *Raising people's standard of living:* Various schemes for generating
  employment in the region were implemented, encouraging
  commercial agriculture, horticulture, animal production, industrialization, and large-scale tourism.
- *Facilitating accessibility and communication by road building.* A
  long-term programme of road construction was started. The
  length of motorable (*pakka*) roads in the middle of the 1990s
  was greatest in the districts of Almora, Nainital, Dehra Dun, and
  Pauri, and least in Uttarkashi (Pant and Pant 1995: 75f. Table
  1.5). In Garhwal most of the roads follow the river valleys, often
  leading to pilgrimage centres; only about 20 per cent of the
  villages had a motorable road within 3 km distance (Singh 1995:
  95, and Table 4.4).
- *Increasing the supply of electricity by hydro-electric power projects.*
  Besides the large-scale and highly disputed Tehri Dam project

[8] One lakh is 100,000. Lakh and crore (10 million) are standard numbers in
Indian counting.

still under way, several small hydel projects had been completed
or were under construction. The projects were mainly meant to
serve the plains of Uttar Pradesh. The per capita consumption
of electricity in the hills themselves is still comparatively low
(except Dehra Dun and Nainital, see Tables 1.16 in Aggarwal &
Agrawal 1995: 31).

- *Building up urban centres for administrative and commercial
  purposes.* Building schemes for district capitals (like Gopeshwar) and other towns were implemented. The schemes included construction of office buildings and living quarters, facilities
  for trade and commerce, sewerage systems and roads.

Infrastructural development and commercialization in the hills
were accompanied by a population increase and encroachments on
forest and forest land (besides urbanization, already mentioned). For
Garhwal the population increase per district (1901 to 1951 and 1951
to 1991) is illustrated in Tables 3a and 3b. The next table (3c) shows
the population variation for all districts of Uttarakhand as well as the
population density. The figures indicate the highest increase in
population in Dehra Dun and Nainital, the two most urbanized districts. But it also increased considerably in districts like Pithoragarh,
Chamoli, and Uttarkashi, which were sparsely populated in 1901,
even though population density in these districts (located in the high
mountain parts of Uttarakhand) is still very low.[9] Nainital, with a
large part of its area located in the plains, has huge population density.

The increase in population does not simply result from acceleration
in natural growth but reflects the large degree of in-migration into
the hill regions (Dewan 1990: 42). Taragi and Kumar (1995) have analysed the role and pattern of migration in Uttarakhand. According to
their statistical data, the total in-migration into the different districts
(reported in 1981) constituted 795,774 persons, or about 16 per cent
of the total population. Of these in-migrants 34.2 per cent have migrated *within* Uttarakhand, indicating only an inter-district shift in
population. The main pulling districts were Dehra Dun and Nanital

[9] The available data on urban/rural population show a high increase in the
urban and a very low increase in the rural population.

Table 3a

Increase of Population in Garhwal
(1901–51, Districtwise)

	Population 1901	Population 1951	Population total increase (%)
Uttarkashi	69,209	106,058	53.2
Chamoli	145,670	216,972	48.9
Tehri	199,831	306,305	53.3
Pauri	283,760	422,653	48.9
Dehra Dun	177,465	361,689	103.8

Table 3b

Increase of Population in Garhwal (1951–91, Districtwise)

	Population 1951	Population 1991	Population total increase (%)
Uttarkashi	106,058	237,000	123.5
Chamoli	216,976	441,000	103.25
Tehri	306,305	575,245	87.8
Pauri	422,653	664,000	57.1
Dehra Dun	361,689	1,014,000	180.35

Compiled from District Gazetteers and Aggarwal and Agrawal 1995: 16, 18

Table 3c

Increase of Population and Population Density in
Garhwal and Kumaon (1901–91, Districtwise)

	Population 1901	Population 1991	Population total increase %	Pop density per/km² 1971	Pop density per/km² 1981	Pop density per/km² 1991
Uttarkashi	69,209	237,000	+ 243.5	18	24	30
Chamoli	145,670	441,000	+ 203.2	32	41	48
Tehri	199,831	575,245	+ 187.9	90	113	130
Pauri	283,760	664,000	+ 134.3	102	116	123
Dehra Dun	177,465	1,014,000	+ 471.8	187	247	329
Almora	323,095	824,000	+ 155.0	107	141	153
Pithoragarh	130,486	557,000	+ 327.0	43	55	63
Nainital	320,511	1,557,000	+ 386.0	3843	3769	6025

Compiled from District Gazetteers and Pant and Pant 1995 (figures for Almora and Nainital in Pant and Pant 1995, Table 2 are mixed up. They have been corrected here).

(30.99 per cent and 31.72 per cent in-migrants); comparatively high also is the figure for Uttarkashi (14.96 per cent). Of the in-migrants 65.8 per cent migrated *from outside into* the hills. This figure includes 36.5 per cent coming from the plains of Uttar Pradesh, 15 per cent from other states of India, and 14.3 per cent from outside India (mostly from Nepal). The in-migratory pattern within the hills is female-biased (due to marriages); from outside the hill region it is male-biased.

To evaluate the impact of in-flow on population growth in the hills, the in-migration rates have to be correlated with those of out-migration. The number of out-migrants (according to the data of 1981) was 8.46 per cent of the total population (409,095 in absolute numbers). From these out-migrants 66.5 per cent have moved within the hills, and only 33.5 per cent have moved to places in the plains of Uttar Pradesh.[10] A very low out-migration has been recorded for the districts of Dehra Dun and Nainital (4.9 per cent and 5.1 per cent), and those who migrate generally leave for places outside the hills. Dehra Dun and Nainital are extremely in-flow-biased districts, to which Uttarkashi may be added (5.6 per cent out-migrants, mostly moving to other areas within the hills, and 14.96 per cent in-migrants). Chamoli shows a certain balance between out- and in-migration rates (5.5 per cent vs. 6.91 per cent of total population, people migrate mostly within the hills). Tehri, Pauri, Pithoragarh, and Almora are 'losing' districts.

2.4 Socio-economic Situation

Land, forest, and water are the basic resources in Uttarakhand and the majority of the population earns a living through agriculture and animal husbandry. In comparison with regions in the plains, in the hills cultivable land is limited. Large parts of the area are covered by forests, are rocky or under permanent snow. Table 4 shows that the

[10] According to Taragi and Kumar (1995), no data are available on the number of persons moving out of Uttar Pradesh. The authors recognize this as one of the major limitations for a meaningful migration study of this area. For example, the large portion of males who have joined the military services or who have settled in urban centres like Delhi, Gurgaon, Jaipur, and Bombay could not be accounted for.

Table 4

Land Utilization Pattern in Uttarakhand, 1986–7

	('000 ha)	%
Total Reported Area	5157	100.0
Forests	3420	66.3
Area not Available for Cultivation	335	6.6
Un-Cultivated Land	657	12.7
Fallow Land	53	1.0
Net Area Sown	692	13.4

Statistical data extracted from Sharma 1996: 142, Table 2.

net area sown in Uttarakhand is only 13.4 per cent, another 13.7 per cent lies uncultivated or fallow.

The crops in Uttarakhand depend largely on rainfall, only 26 per cent of the cultivated area is irrigated. The irrigation facilities (canals, tanks, tube-wells) are unequally distributed within the region. Most of the irrigated land is concentrated in the lower hills and river val-leys. According to statistical data for 1985–6 (Rawat and Kumar 1996: 42), 82.4 per cent of the net cultivated area was irrigated in Nainital, in Dehra Dun 38.7 per cent, followed by Uttarkashi, Tehri, Pauri, and Almora (all between 15 per cent and 20 per cent). The districts with the lowest percentage of irrigation were Chamoli (11.3 per cent) and Pithoragarh (3.5 per cent).

Wheat, paddy, and millets are the principal crops, supplemented by several varieties of pulses. Whereas wheat and paddy can be grown at different altitudes, and on irrigated as well as unirrigated fields, millets are to be found in the upper regions only on rainfed land. Cash crop production gains increasing importance in the hill economy. Potatoes, peas, apples, apricots, and even citrus fruits are grown at different altitudes. The region of Dehra Dun is well known for its mangoes, and in Nainital sugarcane is grown.

Livestock plays a vital role in supplementing income from field crops. For 1986 approximately 40 lakh or 4 million farm animals are reported for Uttarakhand (Palni 1996: 349, Table 2; according to Valdiya [1996: 28], approximately 50 lakh or 5 million farm animals were counted in 1992). Palni has listed the types and numbers of livestock separately for Garhwal and Kumaon (in absolute numbers as well as in per cent of total livestock). In both regions the portion of cross-bred cattle (2.13 per cent and 1.99 per cent) and that of local cattle (45.19 per cent and 48.87 per cent) is nearly equal. In Kumaon more buffaloes are reared (25.08 per cent against 15.47 per cent in Garhwal). The number of sheep and goats is higher in Garhwal (sheep: 11.95 per cent and 6.62 per cent; goats: 23.41 per cent and 20.50 per cent). Equines play only a minor role in both regions. Palni states that the livestock population and diversity in Uttarakhand is high, whereas productivity is low. 'The feed provided to the animals in this region is neither adequate in quantity, nor balanced' (1996: 346), the author mentions. Animals get only straw, hay, green grass, and leaves from the forest, whereas nutritious and expensive foodstuffs, such as cereals and oilcakes, are out of their reach.

The industries of Uttarakhand are concentrated in the districts of Nainital and Dehra Dun (87 per cent in 1985–6), whereas for Uttarkashi and Chamoli not a single industry was reported for this period of time (Mehta 1996: 62). The classification of products for Uttarakhand indicates 39 per cent miscellaneous products, 27 per cent foods and food products, 12 per cent electrical items, 7 per cent repairing factories, 5 per cent oil products, cotton textiles, and paper products. Household manufacturing (spinning, weaving, carpet-weaving) is done in villages and provides additional income.

2.5 The State of Forests

Official data on forests in India have to be carefully evaluated. Most statistics indicate as 'forest' the areas under the control of the Forest Department (FD), even if these contain not even a single tree.[11] For more precise information on the quantity as well as quality of forests, one has to rely on satellite pictures. Between figures indicating the area under the FD and satellite data reporting area under *actual*

---

[11] In the Second Citizens' Report (Agarwal and Narain 1985) the category 'controlled by the Forest Department' is used; in the statistical database of *The Citizens' Fifth Report* (Agarwal, Narain, and Sen 1999) the category 'notified as forest' is used.

forest cover, considerable discrepancies can be observed.[12] A very
valuable compilation of statistical data on Indian forests covering the
period from 1983–5 to 1993–5 has been published by the Centre for
Science and Environment (CSE) in 1999 as a supplementary volume
to *The Citizens' Fifth Report* (Agarwal, Narain, and Sen 1999). This
volume constitutes the main source for the following remarks, com-
plemented by data on the state of forests in Uttarakhand given in
other publications.

The national forest policy of the Government of India adopted in
1952 and revised in 1988 set the entire country's forest cover at 33 per
cent as the national goal. Table 5 indicates that this goal has not been
achieved even now. The forest area of India (*notified* as forest) comes
to 23.3 per cent of the total land area, but only 19.3 per cent is under
actual forest cover. Of this, only 11.2 per cent is dense forest (with a
crown density of 40 per cent and more),[13] and 7.9 per cent is open

Table 5

Forest Area in India
(1993–5 in Relation to Total Land Area)

	million hectare	% of total land area	% of notified forest area
Total land area India	328.73	100.0	—
Forest area (notified as forest)	76.52	23.3	100.0
—reserved forest	41.65	12.6	54.4
—protected forest	22.33	6.8	29.2
—unclassified forest*	12.54	3.8	16.4
Actual forest cover	63.34	19.3	82.8
—dense forest	36.73	11.2	48.0
—open forest	26.13	7.9	34.1
—mangrove forest	0.48	0.1	0.6

*Forest Land owned by the government, but not constituted into a reserved or pro-
tected forest

Source: *The Citizens' Fifth Report*; Statistical Database, part 3: Forests

[12] Satellite data on the area under *actual* forest cover cannot differentiate between legal classifications. Therefore it includes reserved and protected forests,
civil or soyam forests, panchayat forests, private and cantonment forests.

[13] Classification according to Agarwal, Narain, and Sen (1999, supplement,
database: 11).

forest (crown density 10–40 per cent). According to the legal classification, most of the forests (83.6 per cent of the area notified as forest) are 'reserved' or 'protected'. To these forest areas local inhabitants
have no access or only limited access.

Of particular interest in the present context is the situation of forests in Uttar Pradesh. Here 17.6 per cent of the total land area was
notified as forest in 1993–5, but only 11.5 per cent was actually under
forest cover. Of the total forest area, 70.4 per cent has been classified
as reserved, and 2.9 per cent as protected forest. One has to take into
consideration that most of UP's forest (67 per cent) was concentrated
in the hill districts. Thus 67.2 per cent of the total hill area was forested, even though only 44.3 per cent was under actual forest cover
(for all data, see Agarwal, Narain, and Sen 1999, supplement, database:
70). Table 6 shows the distribution of forests in the different hill districts. The highest portion is reported for Uttarkashi; against that,
forests in Chamoli and Almora are comparatively scarce.

Table 6

Forest Area in Uttarakhand (1989, Districtwise) [14]

	Total land area (km²)	Area under Forest Department (km²)	% of total land area
Uttarakhand(total)	**51,125**	**34,359**	**67.2**
Uttarkashi	8,016	7,102	88.6
Chamoli	9,125	5,269	57.7
Tehri	4,421	3,172	71.7
Pauri	5,440	4,552	83.6*
Dehra Dun	3,088	2,192	70.9
Almora	5,385	3,303	37.2* [61,3]
Pithoragarh	8,856	3,922	72.8* [44,3]
Nainital	6,794	4,047	59.6

Compiled from Pant and Pant 1995: 312; calculation mistake for the districts of
Almora and Pithoragarh.

*Aggarwal and Agrawal (1995: 29) mention 63.26 per cent for Pauri, 54.31 per cent
for Almora, 53.39 per cent for Pithoragarh.

[14] In the literature there are slight variations in the figures on total land area
of the eight districts of Uttarakhand, while the figures on forest area, districtwise,
vary hugely. In the most spectacular cases, I will mention the deviation.

According to the revenue records of UP (cited in Nautiyal, Negi, and Nautiyal 1996: 285, source not dated), in the eight hill districts of UP 30.2 per cent (10,381 sq. km) of the forest area (under the FD) was civil and soyam, as well as panchayat forests.[15] Private and cantonment forests came to 0.6 per cent. The majority of 69.2 per cent was reserved forests.

[15] Civil or soyam forest is owned by groups of villages and utilization policies for these are decided by the villagers themselves. Panchayat forests are owned by a single village panchayat. The management of these forests is the responsibility of the district administration (Nautiyal, Negi, and Nautiyal 1996: 284). Panchayat forests do not exist in Tehri and Uttarkashi.

3

Resisting Commercial
Forest Exploitation: A Narrative
Approach to the Chipko Andolan

F ORESTS IN INDIA HAVE BEEN UNDER THREAT SINCE THE
time of ancient Indian civilization. They had to be felled to
make space for human settlements, agricultural cultivation,
and pastoral land (Gadgil and Guha 1992). But under colonial rule
forests turned into a massive commodity and 'resource', and from the
early nineteenth century timber and minor forest products were
commercially extracted on a large scale by the colonial state. The exploitation of forests and forest wealth continued in independent
India; forest degradation even increased because of the expansion of
modern infrastructure (roads, electricity) and the pressure of a
steadily growing population. Even so, forest regions continued to be
the home and life bases of many tribal and peasant communities in
various parts of India. Forests are culturally constructed and appropriated in diverse ways by local residents; they are meaningful for
economic reproduction as well as religious and social life.

Colonial and postcolonial histories tell of conflicts between the
state and the population in many regions of India over the appropriation of forests and forest wealth. In his paper at the Delhi Conference
on 'Environment and People's Subsistence' (1987a) Chandi Prasad
Bhatt, the committed Gandhian and founder of the non-governmental
organization Dashauli Gram Swarajya Mandal, Gopeshwar (Chamoli
District, Uttaranchal), who also played a leading role in the Chipko
movement, declared:

Amongst natural resources, the maximum destruction has been of forests. Nobody can deny the use of forests for the basic minimum needs of the people. But in the name of economic development, forests are being destroyed left, right and centre. . . . In a mad race to earn revenue, the government is selling away our forests to the cities and to the international markets and while doing all this, they do not take into account either the legal rights nor the natural rights of the people who live within these forests and who use these forests, thus, creating serious problems of survival for the forest people. . . . I cannot say whether the government has become conscious or not but several groups working with people have become more and more conscious, and the Chipko Movement is one such group. (Bhatt 1987a: 3)

Bhatt here draws attention to the accelerated destruction of forests by state agencies especially after independence, even as he affirms that forests have become a major concern among local inhabitants and non-governmental organizations. Chipko naturally figures here, though Bhatt does not specify that it in fact became a model for local resistance against forest destruction and restrictive official forest policy in other parts of India — for example the Appiko movement in the Western Ghats. More recently, ecologists and critics of development operating on a global scale have discovered the Indian Himalayas not only as a highly degraded forest environment but also as a stronghold of resistance against deforestation. Debates on ecology and sustainable development have repeatedly focused on the Himalayas, and Chipko is now like a showpiece of forest-related struggle, as also of the 'ecological consciousness' of a local population. Chipko has been represented thus in multiple contexts, and Ramachandra Guha notices that 'A token genuflection to Chipko has . . . become a ritual in both Indian and international debates on development alternatives' (1993: 80).

It may be rewarding to speculate on the reasons for this worldwide attention paid to the Chipko movement.[1] First, the Chipko struggle

[1] The Chipko movement was documented between 1973 and 1983 mainly in the regional press and in national weeklies. Only occasionally was it characterized as an 'ecological' movement (Berndt 1987: 76). In 1975 Anil Agarwal published an article in *New Scientist*, 'Gandhi's ghost saves the Himalayan Trees', to make

seems a convincing example of the human capacity to successfully resist. Demonstrating that even 'simple' villagers, including women, can find the courage and strength to rise against the state and economically powerful individuals and groups, Chipko's events encourage those who feel oppressed to stand up and fight against their oppressors. Second, Chipko raises a glimmer of hope in those who espy the devastation in the name of development. The movement has proved that it is possible to stop destructive practices and even exert a lasting influence on state policies and people's attitude to nature. Third, for environmental groups operating in the West, Chipko reinforces belief in their own struggle for environmental conservation and women's empowerment.

However, the interest in Chipko as a *forest* movement may also have a deeper grounding. In the early days of the international ecological debate the world's (degraded) forests had come under close scrutiny, and the violent destruction of tropical jungles (e.g. the Amazon) and the German 'Waldsterben' ('dying' of forests) had become a matter of international concern; later the Himalayas were included in this broadening picture. Forests had acquired an eminent symbolic meaning as the 'quintessence of the natural world' (Schmidt-Vogt 1994: 18); the condition of the world's forests was seen as reflecting the condition of nature as a whole and the destruction of forests became in fact a key symbol of the violence against nature. According to R.P. Harrison, the Western tradition reveals a deep empathy towards forests rooted in cultural memory:

> The global problem of deforestation provokes unlikely reactions of concern these days among city dwellers, not only because of the enormity of the scale but also because *in the depths of cultural memory forests remain the correlate of human transcendence.* We call it loss of nature, or the loss of wildlife habitat, or the loss of biodiversity, but underlying the ecological concern is perhaps a much deeper apprehension about the disappearance of boundaries, without which the human abode loses its grounding. Somewhere we still sense ... that we make ourselves at

---

the Chipko movement popular abroad. But only from the mid 1980s onwards did the popularity of Chipko really spread. The first article on Chipko, published in *Economic and Political Weekly*, was by Shobita Jain (1984).

home only in our estrangement, or in the *logos* of the finite. In the cultural memory of the West forests 'correspond' to the exteriority of the *logos*. The outlaws, the heroes, the wanderers, the lovers, the saints, the persecuted, the outcasts, the bewildered, the ecstatic—these are among those who have sought out the forest's asylum . . . . . .*Without such outside domains, there is no inside in which to dwell*. (Harrison 1992: 247, emphasis mine)

Apparently it is the basic opposition between nature and culture, wilderness and civilization, social control and freedom, inside and outside, which overdetermines the relation between human society and forests, and which accounts for the fascination with forests and the concern people evince for them. As Harrison vividly illustrats, this old and deep relation between men and forests is indicated and reflected in occidental mythology, as well as in literature and art from the ancient world to the present.[2]

The structural relation between human society and forests as its 'other', perceived from a certain interpretive gaze on cultural history and textual tradition, may also help explain the emotional commitment many people now show in their reactions towards the degradation of forests. But this dichotomy should not be understood as a general analytic concept suitable for exploring the actual relationship of members of a particular lifeworld to their forests. This relationship can only be approached by investigating their social and interpretive practices.

Therefore, the crucial question remains whether representations and constructions of Chipko, which are meant to popularize and, perhaps, instrumentalize the movement, coincide with the ways local residents and participants look at their struggle. This chapter tries to arrive at a leading narrative of Chipko, its events and episodes. It then examines local narratives on Chipko collected during field work, twenty years after the events took place.

[2] Harrison traces the relation between human societies and forests in the texts and arts of Sumer, ancient Rome and Greece, and the medieval ages. He discusses literary documents from Vico and Dante, and he refers to the Enlightenment and to Romanticism.

3.1 Public Representations of the Chipko Movement

In its public representations, the Chipko movement has been subjected to particular cognitive and political interests and been instrumentalized and glorified. The competing constructions, based on implicit social concepts of agency and gender, follow particular interpretations of the imaginary element innate in Chipko activities: each displays a certain interpretation of how Chipko actors imagine their future, how they relate to ideas of 'ecology', 'development', and the improvement of life. The constructions also assume that what· are being identified as ideals and targets by Chipko represent the view of all or most inhabitants of Garhwal and Kumaon. Regional and social differences are widely neglected.

Three of the most common modes of representing Chipko can be distinguished: it is constructed as a peasant movement, an ecological movement, an eco-feminist movement. All these interpretations refer to Chipko as an organized and widespread social uprising rooted in the Gandhian tradition. And they all emphasize its ecological concern.

The work of Ramachandra Guha (1991, 1993) stands for the first mode of representation. Guha argues that 'Chipko must be viewed as a constituent element of an overall history of *peasant protest* in Uttarakhand' (1993: 80, emphasis mine). His analysis of Chipko is instructed by the sociology of social movements, but, inspired by the Subaltern Studies project, his sociological study also has a historical foundation (1991: xii). Guha claims to take three steps in his approach to Chipko. First, he situates the contemporary Chipko movement within the history of forest conflicts and people's resistance in Uttarakhand, and explores the history of relations between state and population in British Kumaon, Tehri Garhwal, and independent India. In this context he discusses local modes of access to forest and pasture as well as state intervention and forest policy. Second, he tries to analyse earlier and present ways of life among the people of Uttarakhand to illustrate the process of commercialization and destruction of their forests. Third, he addresses issues of ideology, organizational structure, mobilization strategies, leadership, and gender roles in the context of the Chipko movement. His historical analysis is the main, and strongest, part of Guha's book, the sociological analysis being pursued mainly to underline his central argument, which places Chipko within a 'rebellious traditional culture'. For, in his representation, 'Chipko . . . can be properly viewed as a constituent element of an overall history of deprivation and protest.' Like previous forest-based movements in Uttarakhand, Chipko 'had its genesis in the perceived breach of the informal code between the ruler and the ruled known as the "moral economy" of the peasant' (Guha 1993: 100).

While subsuming Chipko within a general history of peasant movements, Guha acknowledges its ecological component. He argues that Chipko did not simply defend the values of the little communities, it also affirmed a way of life 'more harmoniously adjusted with natural processes' (Guha 1991: 196). He distinguishes between the movement's 'public' (= ecological) and 'private' (= peasant) profile. Guha opposes all attempts to label Chipko a Gandhian or a feminist movement. Although Chipko's leaders were obviously inspired by Gandhian ideology, he sees in the method to protect trees by hugging them a 'highly original response to forest felling' which should not be termed a modern satyagraha. Nor should the struggle be denoted as 'feminist', because the leading figures in the movement have always been male. During the protest campaigns men, women, and children participated equally in the local activities and, except for one case, no signs of conflict between men and women could be determined.[3]

Within their joint publications, Jayanto Bandyopadhyay and Vandana Shiva (1987a, 1987b) present Chipko as a movement in which ecological issues are centrestage. They locate Chipko in the tradition of Gandhian philosophy and emphasize that a genuine Gandhian method of resistance was applied by the Chipko actors: 'Both the earlier forest satyagrahas and the Chipko Movement, arose from conflict over forest resources and are similar as responses to forest

---

[3] How far Chipko may be called a feminist movement has been analysed by Kumud Sharma. Her conclusion: 'The Chipko movement has given women a strong forum to articulate what obviously are women's concerns. However, their participation has not helped them in their own struggle against oppression although claims have been made that it is a "feminist movement"' (Sharma n.d.: 51). For Sharma, a feminist movement must deal with women's issues and must be directed towards their emancipation.

destruction. What differentiates Chipko from the earlier struggles is its ecological basis. The new concern to save and protect forests through satyagraha did not arise from a resentment against further encroachment or people's access to forest resources but from the alarming signals of rapid ecological destabilization' (1987a: 36). To demonstrate this ecological aspect, Bandyopadhyay and Shiva quote a slogan created by 'Garhwali women': 'What do the forests bear? Soil, water, and pure air'. For these two authors the slogan embodies the 'scientific and philosophical message' of the movement and expresses opposition against concepts of development which try to achieve economic growth through the destruction of nature and the life-supporting systems of local communities. By characterizing Indian civilization as aranya sanskriti (forest culture), Bandyopadhyay and Shiva essentialize the ecological concern for forests and regard any local resistance against forest destruction as the quasi-natural reaction of a forest-loving people. Indian culture is not only identified with Sanskrit (= Hindu) culture; the protection of forests is also seen as a constitutive feature of this culture and is said to have been effective throughout its history. Such ahistorical reductionism and essentialization of culture and people seem to be even more prominent in the representations of Chipko by Sunderlal Bahuguna (e.g. Bahuguna 1987), and in the straightforwardly eco-feminist approach (Shiva 1988).

Sunderlal Bahuguna being one of the main protagonists of the movement and perhaps the sole local activist to frequently travel abroad, became famous as the spokesman and 'messenger' of Chipko. His reconstruction and representation of the events have received great global attention. Bahuguna sees Chipko as an ecological movement and emphazises that people's contemporary concern for forests originates in the teachings of classical Indian philosophy and its emphasis on reverence for nature. Trees, says Bahuguna, have always been protected by village people. He mentions an incident which was said to have happened in a Bishnoi village near Jodhpur in 1730. According to the narrative, a woman named Amrita Devi led 362 men, women, and children to protect certain khejri trees of the village from being felled by the axe-men of the Maharaja of Jodhpur. The villagers hugged the trees—as depicted on a stone carving found during the excavations of the old town of Patan in Gujarat. The axe-men did not withdraw from felling and Amrita Devi and the Bishnois, who had joined her, sacrificed their lives. Bahuguna assures us that the 'old spirit of love to nature' has always been kept alive by great Indian saints and teachers, and this tradition only received a setback under the British rulers through their commercialization of forests. But in the colonial and post-colonial revolts of forest dwellers, the 'old spirit' still seems to be alive.[4]

Vandana Shiva is the most prominent advocate of an eco-feminist interpretation of Chipko. Her work seems to me to be based on ahistorical and cultural reductionism as well as an essentialization of gender roles.[5] Shiva argues that women in general have a special relation to and a special responsibility towards nature, not only for biological reasons—as producers of life—but also by virtue of their everyday tasks, which involves doing most of the family's reproductive work. In the historical constellation of modernity, where the true principle of equal and harmonious relations between man and woman and humans and nature has been inverted, women are seen to be opposed and subordinate to men, who are conceptualized as destroyers of nature. In the current historical context, women have a special responsibility to restore nature, and Chipko, interpreted as 'explicitly an ecological *and* feminist movement' (Shiva 1988: 76), is seen as an example of women's will and power to free nature and themselves from male domination and exploitation, to bring an end to maldevelopment and the patriarchal project: 'There are in India, today, two paradigms of forestry—one life-enhancing, the other life-destroying. The life-enhancing paradigm emerges from the forest and the feminine principle; the life-destroying one from the factory and the market. . . . The first paradigm has emerged from India's ancient forest culture, in all its diversity, and has been renewed in contemporary times by the women of Garhwal through Chipko' (Shiva 1988: 76).

Besides these three prominent reconstructions of Chipko by Ramachandra Guha, Sunderlal Bahuguna, and Jayanto Bandyopadhyay and Vandana Shiva, a large number of other publications (academic, journalistic, activist) focus on the movement. Some authors

[4] Bahuguna's philosophy will be discussed in more detail in Chapter 5.
[5] Interestingly, in a recent article Bandyopadhyay heavily criticizes Shiva for her eco-feminist approach. See Bandyopadhyay (1999).

concentrate on the question of whether Chipko is a women's movement or not (Sharma n.d.; Jain 1984), others discuss critically the essentialization of women as nature (Agarwal 1991). The Gandhian
background has been stressed by Thomas Weber (1988) and Hagen
Berndt (1987).[6] Gerald D. Berreman has interpreted Chipko as an
expression of regional identity and ethnicity (1987c). Several
publications on Chipko have been written by activists—e.g. Chandi
Prasad Bhatt (1987a, 1987b, 1987c), Vimala Bahuguna (1990), Anand
S. Bisht (1993); their representations (as local 'voices') will be discussed
later; Bahuguna's construction will be considered in more detail as
well.

Public acknowledgement of the Chipko movement had reper-
cussions in its original locality which made it an issue, a matter of
controversy, among local residents of Uttarakhand. Villagers place
themselves proudly in the tradition of Chipko, communicating
Chipko messages, or explicitly take an oppositional stance, or try to
ignore it. However, all have to attend to the ideas and visions connected with Chipko.

3.2 Chipko and its Prehistory:
The Leading Narrative

Well-known and influential presentations of Chipko give a comparatively clear-cut picture of the flow of incidents and actions before
and during the movement, creating a coherent Chipko narrative.
This narrative is organized along a few central elements. First, it stresses the move from economy to ecology and brings out the ecological
content of Chipko activities and demands. Second, it elevates local
actions as well as subsequent campaigns in order to convey the idea

---

[6] Hagen Berndt (1987) has done a systematic press analysis of the Chipko
movement. He studied Indian local and national newspapers and periodicals,
the publications of NGOs involved, as well as pamphlets and leaflets covering
the period 1973–83. One of Berndt's basic sources was the weekly magazine
Dinman. Journalists who wrote in the magazine about Chipko activities were
particularly sympathetic towards the movement and towards Gandhian ideas;
for example Anupam Misra, who is active in the Gandhi Peace Foundation. Activists like Chandi Prasad Bhatt, Sunderlal Bahuguna, and the historian and
activist Shekhar Pathak were given a voice in *Dinman*.

of a closely-woven social movement which is said to have included the whole of Uttarakhand. Third, it gives the credit of mobilization mainly to outstanding Gandhian activists such as Chandi Prasad Bhatt and/or Sunderlal Bahuguna, even as their leadership role is concomitantly submerged in order to privilege and emphasize the self-organization of villagers, especially women. The narrative connects, and often reconciles, the diverse perspectives of local activists, supporters, and interpreters.

Such a reconstruction of the history of Chipko is usually based on representations of its putative 'pre-history'. Two somewhat different, even opposed, narratives of this pre-history can be distinguished: an academic version, following the argument of Ramachandra Guha, presents Chipko as the outcome of a long tradition of peasant protest. The more popular version, narrated for example by Bandyopadhyay and Shiva but also by Chipko activists, places the movement in the Gandhian tradition of village reconstruction and social work. Their representation of pre-history illustrates how the forest issue moved into the foreground and organizational networks came into being. This 'popular' pre-history is dated back to Gandhi and his programme of 'village reconstruction'. In the mid-1940s two women disciples of Gandhi settled in the Himalayas with the intention of working for the social welfare of village people. Both women were of European origin. Attracted by the ideals and ideas of Gandhi they had left their homes to join the Mahatma and the Indian freedom struggle. Mira Behn (alias Madeleine Slade) came to India in 1925, Sarala Behn (alias Catherine Mary Heilman) in 1932. Both worked for several years with Gandhi before venturing into the Himalayas. Mira Behn established herself near Rishikesh and set up Pashulok, a centre for cattle rearing. When she learned of devastating floods in the Himalayas she investigated the upper Ganga valley. Soon, she became aware of the ongoing deforestation and the substitution of broad-leaved trees by commercially valuable pine; she immediately took up this ecological issue and decided to concentrate on forest problems. She moved to Devligaon in Tehri Garhwal, roughly 40km from the capital, Tehri, and founded Gopal Ashram. Because of health problems she had to leave India in the 1950s and spent the last decades of her life in Vienna.

Sarala Behn went to Kumaon. In 1946 she founded the Kasturba Mahila Utthan Mandal at Kausani (near Almora) and established Lakshmi Ashram. She devoted herself to the improvement of the lives of hill women. Many young women were trained in her ashram as social activists. They later became involved in Vinoba Bhave's Bhoodan (land gift) movement and in the Gram Swaraj (village autonomy) movement. Sarala Behn died in 1982. She had been succeeded in 1966 by Radha Bhatt as head of Lakshmi Ashram.

The ideas and work of Mira Behn and Sarala Behn 'came together in praxis' (V. Bahuguna 1990: 113) at the Parvatiya Nav-Jivan Mandal at Silyara in Tehri Garhwal, founded by Vimala and Sunderlal Bahuguna in 1956.[7] Vimala Nautiyal had worked with Sarala Behn for several years. Sunderlal, at that time General Secretary of the Tehri branch of the Congress Party, was a young politician with a promising political career. Also strongly influenced by Gandhian ideas, he was active in the work of Harijan uplift.[8] When Vimala was to marry Sunderlal, she agreed to do so on condition that he withdraw from politics and settle with her in a village to practise social work. Sunderlal resigned, they married, and chose Silyara as the place for their ashram. Both started with educational work and opened a school for village children. They were joined by two girls who had also been trained in Kausani. To start with, the activists faced many problems. They soon realized that villagers did not send their daughters to school because—so the villagers argued—girls must care for their younger sisters and brothers; when they are older they must help their mothers in the house or cut grass or collect firewood from the jungle. Girls will never be able to get a paid job, they 'will go to another house' once they marry, so why educate them? The activists then decided to offer evening courses and tried to persuade villagers to send their daughters, arguing that education was crucial for girls as 'rearers of future citizens' (bhavi nagarik jo hai, ma ki god mein palta hai). Slowly, they gained some success. Besides providing formal education to the

[7] The following is also based on personal interviews with Vimala Bahuguna (Silyara, October 1993) and Sunderlal Bahuguna (Tehri, October 1993). See also Kishwar 1992a, 1992b.

[8] Harijan ('children of god') is the term for 'Untouchables' made popular by Gandhi.

young, they taught villagers about the need for a proper diet, offered medical help, and continued to work for the uplift of Harijans. In the early days of his involvement in social work, Sunderlal Bahuguna concentrated on the problem of local employment. He founded a cooperative to help male local residents get jobs in road building (Weber 1988: 34). He also established forest labour co-operatives and succeeded in getting small contractorships for the extraction of resin. But soon he engaged in a project which destined him to travel and become a messenger of conservation for the rest of his life. In 1960 he followed the request of the Gandhian Vinoba Bhave to take the message of *gram swaraj* to the Himalayan communities. Joined by a few others, Bahuguna crossed the hills from Himachal Pradesh to the Nepalese border. On this tour he saw deforested mountain slopes and became interested in the environmental situation of the hills.

After the Chinese–Indian border conflict in 1962, Gandhian constructive work in the Himalayan hills was continued on a bigger scale. Under the label 'defence oriented welfare projects' (Giri [1968]: 16) Gandhian organizations motivated their members to settle in all parts of the Himalayas and engage in a wide range of activities, such as community development, adult literacy, social and health education, and the provision of productive employment opportunities. The work was intended to integrate seemingly isolated border people into the Indian nation and build up their defence potential by making them 'enlightened and self-reliant' (Giri [1968]: 16). In the Central Himalayas it was the Uttarakhand Sarvodaya Mandal which supported such development work.[9]

The years 1965–71 saw an anti-liquor campaign, mainly supported by women. The campaign was launched by activists from the Silyara

[9] The Sarvodaya movement attempted social change in a non-violent way, based on Gandhi's constructive programme. Prominent members of the movement were Vinoba Bhave and J.P. Narayan. After the Indo-Chinese border war, the Border Area Coordination Committee was founded to stimulate social organizations engaged in the Himalayas. The committee, together with the Delhi School of Social Work, suggested the foundation of a national organization shouldering responsibility for work in the Himalayas. In April 1970 the Himalaya Seva Sangh came into existence, its president was J.P. Narayan. The Border Committee merged with this (Berndt 1987: 24f.).

Ashram and the first actions took place in the district of Tehri Garh-wal. Over the years, other districts of Uttarakhand (Pauri, Chamoli, and Almora) were included in the protest. Women organized demons-trations, picketed liquor shops, and were successful: the campaign ended with full prohibition in five districts in 1972.[10]

Besides the ashrams in Silyara and Kausani, a third sarvodaya cen-tre was founded in Gopeshwar (Chamoli District) in the 1960s. The Gandhian project of village reconstruction inspired many young people in the early 1950s, who joined sarvodaya work. Amongst them was Chandi Prasad Bhatt, a young man employed as a booking clerk in a transport company in Joshimath.[11] In 1953, Bhatt took leave from his job and joined the Gram Swaraj and Bhoodan movements. He became increasingly aware of economic and social problems, many of which had become extreme oppressions in many parts of the hills: insufficient agricultural production, the migration of men to the plains in search of additional monetary income (leading to the creation of a 'money order economy'), the lack of able-bodied men in villages, the disintegration of families. In 1960 Bhatt decided to quit his job and to concentrate on social work, his main aim being to create local employment. The situation in Gopeshwar was exceptional: after the Indo-Chinese conflict the border areas had been marked for development by the central and state governments. Gopeshwar was to become the headquarters of Chamoli District and the construction of roads, offices, and living quarters was booming. But local residents did not benefit from these activities. Contractors and skilled workers were brought in from outside, and only minor and temporary jobs were assigned to locals. Bhatt, together with other social workers, started to organize the local labourers and founded the Malla Nagpur Cooperation Labour Society Committee. This organization took up labour contracts for road construction and, being non-exploitative, could pay double the normal wage to labourers. Later, with the help

[10] The campaign was launched against expensive and highly intoxicating 'English wine', by which was meant rum, whisky, etc. The (illegal) distillation of local *daru*, done by the villagers themselves, continued, and continues today. 'English wine' shops have reopened in limited numbers.

[11] The following is also based on a personal interview with Chandi Prasad Bhatt (Gopeshwar, 1994). For biographical information on Bhatt, see Guha 2004, 2006.

of the Gandhian Khadi and Village Industries Commission, the co-operative also set up small-scale industries for carpentry and metal work. In 1964 the co-operative was transformed into the Dashauli Gram Swarajya Sangh (DGSS), an organization which established small forest-based industries (agricultural instruments, resin and turpentine) and took up the collection and marketing of medical herbs. The organization was renamed Dashauli Gram Swarajya Mandal (DGSM).

In the mid-1960s, therefore, both Sunderlal Bahuguna and Chandi Prasad Bhatt were involved in projects to create local employment and achieve development in the hills. In a seminar organized by Gandhian agencies for social work in the Himalayas in 1967, Bahuguna spoke up for local development schemes such as the installation of hydro-electric projects to provide electricity to villagers, and small-scale village industries—including forest-based industries. On 30 May 1968, the anniversarya of the Tilari incident (Tilari Goli Kand) of 1930, a declaration of forest rights was formulated and read out in Barkot (Rawain, Uttarkashi District) by members of the sarvodaya brotherhood. The declaration criticized the system of large-scale commercial forest exploitation and stressed the importance of forests for the hill culture and local lifestyles. It also mentioned the necessity of a harmonious relationship between forest and men, including the responsible use of forest products for sensible local life. The declaration was distributed by sarvodaya activists in towns and villages. Later, in 1972, demonstrations were organized in Barkot, Purola, Uttarkashi, and Gopeshwar to underline these demands and make them public.

The first Chipko activities took place in April–May 1973 in Mandal near Gopeshwar, as a reaction to the unequal treatment of villagers by government. Repeatedly, raw materials necessary for local industries had been denied them. When the Forest Department refused a small number of ash trees for the preparation of agricultural instruments in a village-based industry, and yet, at the same time, allotted a much larger number of those trees to Simon Company—a sports goods factory in Allahabad—DGSM activists and villagers decided to act. The idea to 'hug' (chipakna) the trees to protect them from being fell-ed was born in the course of a discussion and—according to the rele-vant publications—first voiced by Bhatt: 'Let them know that we will not allow the felling of ash trees. When they aim their axes upon them, we will embrace the trees' (Misra and Tripathi, cited in Weber 1988: 40; Misra 1978, cited in Berndt 1987: 48). This non-violent stra-tegy of resistance turned out to be a great success: the axe-men were forced to withdraw from Mandal. After this, the sports company got an allotment in the Fateh Rampur forest (80 km from Gopeshwar, 18 km below the temple of Kedarnath), but DGSM activists immediately mobilized the local villagers once more. Again, the company's axe-men were not able to fell the trees because the villagers were vigilant. Employees from the company tried hard to outwit the locals by screening a video film on the very night that the axing was to begin. Up to 31 December 1973—the expiry date of the permit to the Simon Company—villagers in the Fateh region stayed vigilant and guarded their forest. In the following months, between April and December 1974, Sunderlal Bahuguna took up the task of spreading the message of Chipko's events and set off on a 120 km *padyatra* or footmarch through the hill districts. In his mobilization work, meanwhile, Chandi Prasad Bhatt focused on Chamoli District. In the course of his work he also visited the Joshimath region, where the next well-known incident was to take place.

A forest in the upper Alakananda catchment area which belongs to Raini, a Bhotiya village situated in the Niti Ghati east of Joshimath, had been auctioned and its trees marked for felling. According to the dominant narrative, it was Chandi Prasad Bhatt who started a con-scientization campaign in the villages of the region, explaining the connections between forest degradation, landslides, and floods. In collaboration with members of the local Communist Party, he spearheaded the agitation against the felling of the Raini forest. On 15 March 1974, villagers from Raini and neighbouring places came together in a big demonstration. Notwithstanding this, the villainous contractor sent his labourers to the Raini forest. His men reached on 26 March and here the most popular story of Chipko took shape.

On that day, while Bhatt was kept busy in Gopeshwar by forest officials, men from the villages of Raini, Lata, and Malari had been ordered to leave for Joshimath, where compensation for land pre-viously appropriated by the army was to be paid them. The axe-men, meanwhile, took a small trail far from the village to approach the forest. They were spotted by a girl, who hurried to inform Gaura Devi, the head of the mahila mandal or women's organization in Raini. Gaura Devi called the womenfolk together; they marched into the forest and jointly opposed the axe-men. Gaura Devi is said to have addressed them with the following words: 'Brothers, this forest is our *maika* (mother's house). We get medical plants and vegetables from it. Do not cut the forest! If you cut the forest this hill will plunge on our village, the flood will come and the winter fields will be washed away . . .' (see the Hindi version in Berndt 1987). After negotiations between contractor, activists, and villagers over the days following, and after another big demonstration on 31 March, the trees in the Raini forest were saved. For the first time, the Raini struggle had brought ecological arguments into the limelight. Gaura Devi's words are still held up as the first proof of ecological consciousness among village women.

After the energetic efforts of the DGSM, a government committee was set up to investigate the interrelation between forests and water regulation. Following its recommendations a total ban on green felling in the catchment areas of the upper Alakananda and its tributaries for ten years was declared by the UP state government in 1977.

In the years after the Raini incident Chipko activities shifted to other places in Garhwal and thence to Kumaon; new groups joined the struggle and different methods of protest were used:

- Political parties and student organizations became active in the cities of Tehri, Uttarkashi, Dehra Dun, Almora, Nainital, and Pithoragarh. They joined demonstrations and meetings and occupied halls in which tree auctions were to take place.
- Sunderlal Bahuguna declared himself a 'messenger' of the Chipko andolan. He set off on several padyatras which took him across the Himalayas; he also undertook several fasts to enforce Chipko demands. This, together with his writings, turned him into a public figure in India and abroad; especially in the international context, the Chipko movement has been identified with him.
- Locally based sarvodaya activists (like Chandi Prasad Bhatt and Dhum Singh Negi) were operating at the village level in East Garhwal and Tehri. They tried to mobilize men and women and sought support from village councils (*gram panchayats*) and

councils of village women (*mahila mandals*). When forest lots were marked for felling, people moved to the relevant forest site to protect the trees. Some of these actions evoked a strong public response, particularily because women were in the forefront of the struggle and raised 'ecological' demands. The work of Chandi Prasad Bhatt became popular in India especially after the publication of the *First Citizens' Report* on the state of India's environment in 1981.

Almost all the publications highlight next a protest campaign which took place in 1977–8 near Advani (Hemvalghati, District Tehri Garhwal). In the Advani forest, 640 *chir* and *sal* trees had been marked for felling. The story goes that Dhum Singh Negi, who was leading the mobilization campaign, fasted for five days in the forest 'to make the people fearless' (Weber 1988: 52). Women went to the forest and tied silken threads around the trees as markers of their respect and love, as sisters typically do for their brothers at the festival of Raksha Bandhan. At a public meeting a forest officer verbally attacked the village women and shouted: 'You foolish village women! Do you know what the forests bear? Resin, timber and foreign exchange.' The village women are said to have replied in the same tenor: 'What do the forests bear? Soil, water and pure air! Soil, water and pure air are the very basis of life!' (cited in Weber 1988: 53).[12] Whether this slogan had in fact been the main slogan of the movement is not terribly relevant; more relevant is the fact that it has become the most cited and most prominent statement in publications on Chipko. It is considered 'the scientific and philosophical message of the movement' (Shiva, in association with Bandyopadhyay *et al.*, 1991: 114), a condensation of Chipko demands, an expression of the ecological character of the movement resulting from the powerful involvement of women.

Another incident has been frequently cited to underline the ecological consciousness of women: in Dungri-Paintoli (Chamoli District, in the catchment area of the Pindar river), the village panchayat had

---

[12] I found the following Hindi version: *Kya hai jangal ke upkar? Lisa, lakdi aur vyapar | Kya hai jangal ke upkar? Mitti, pani aur bayar, zinda rahne ka adhar.'* In this version, the women are not addressed as 'foolish'; and *vyapar* means simply 'trade'.

come to an agreement with the Horticulture Department to establish a potato seed farm. For this, parts of the nearby oak and rhododendron forest had to be felled; as compensation a motorable road, a health centre, electricity, and an upgradation of the primary school had been promised the villagers. But without the nearby forest the women would need seven hours to collect firewood instead of two. Therefore, despite the announced benefits for the village they decided to oppose the felling of the forest and the setting up of the seed farm. They asked Chipko activists from the DGSS for help. It is reported that because of their protest campaign, the women came into conflict with the village men who had been ready to sacrifice the forest.[13]

The Chipko andolan reached its apogee on 20 April 1981. On this day the UP government declared a total ban on the felling of green trees in all parts of Uttarakhand above an altitude of 1000m and an angle of 30 degrees and for a period of fifteen years. This moratorium (which has de facto become permanent) had been recommended in 1980 by the central government under Prime Minister Indira Gandhi. For their Chipko work, leading to this ban, Sunderlal Bahuguna and Chandi Prasad Bhatt received a number of awards.[14]

The ban brought an end to the andolan and to forest-based industries. In the aftermath of Chipko, the strategies of sarvodaya work in the hills had changed. Already, in the course of the movement, basic differences in the philosophies of Sunderlal Bahuguna and Chandi Prasad Bhatt had become clearly perceptible, and their work had started to move in divergent directions.[15] Bhatt and the DGSM activists see their main goal as securing the rights of village people to the

[13] Berndt offers another version. According to an article in the weekly *Aniket*, both men and women were prepared to oppose the setting up of the seed farm (Berndt 1987: 70).

[14] Sunderlal Bahuguna received the following awards: 1981 Padma Shree Award; 1984 National Integration Award; 1985 Men of Trees Award; 1986 Singhvi and Jamnalal Bajaj Award; 1987 Right Livelihood Award (Alternative Nobel Prize). Chandi Prasad Bhatt received two awards: 1982 Ramon Magsaysay Award for Community Leadership; 1986 Padma Shree Award. The government also distributed certificates to various villagers as appreciation of their participation in the movement.

[15] Weber 1988; Guha 1991, 1993. Guha sees three streams in the Chipko movement and differentiates between the philosophies and strategies of Bhatt,

forest, to support people's participation in afforestation and forest conservation, and to help them get their just share of forest produce. They devote most of their energy to practical work. They have initiated voluntary afforestation programmes and shifted to the even wider strategy of 'ecodevelopment'. As distinct from this, Sunderlal Bahuguna, having steadily moved in the direction of 'spiritual ecology', sees Chipko basically as a movement which does not simply aim to protect trees but one which seeks to establish a new relationship between man and nature. This is the thrust of *his* Chipko message in India and abroad. After Chipko he gained fame for his 4870 km padyatra from Kashmir to Kohima (1981–3). In the mid-1980s, he undertook a padyatra in Switzerland against acid rain. Since the late 1980s he has concentrated (and still concentrates) on the fight against the Tehri Dam. He has organized local protests, undertaken fasts, and tried to address a national and international audience with his writings, speeches, and petitions.

3.3 Local Narratives on Chipko: Conflicting Perspectives of Leaders and Participants

The contemporary landscape of thought and action in Garhwal is characterized by a variety of local discourses on forest, ecology, and development, as well as by local initiatives, projects, and strategies to translate ideas into practice. Chipko—or rather the image one has of it—is formative for most of these local discourses and practices and has gained the status of a 'key event'.[16] For me the question was: How

---

Bahuguna, and the 'marxist' Uttarakhand Sangharsh Vahini (USV), operating in Kumaon. To label the USV as 'marxist' seems questionable if one takes into account other publications as well. Hagen Berndt describes the USV as an amalgamation of young activists from different goups—namely the Uttarakhand Sarvodaya Mandal, the Parvatiya Yuva Morcha, and the Yuva Nirman Samiti. According to him the USV, founded in 1977, is committed to Gandhian principles of political work. Even though the ideology of the USV seems to be much debated, one should not overlook the militancy expressed by the name of the group, which translates roughly as Uttarakhand Militant Army.

[16] For an application of his term, see Das 1995: Das uses the term 'key event' to refer to important events of Sikh history.

is Chipko currently represented in its locality of origin? To what extent do local representations follow, or in which way do they diverge from, the popular and leading narrative? Is Chipko seen as a movement with mainly ecological objectives? The narratives on Chipko cannot be properly evaluated without mentioning the constitutive character of history and the social function of memory. For those who participated in the movement, or supported it, Chipko signifies an essential part of their personal biography, and they memorize and represent it as a crucial period in their lifetime.[17] Memory cannot simply be seen as the 'recall' of events, for it is embedded in a contemporary context of interpretation and practice which is formative for the way people remember events, represent them, or produce them.[18] The retrospective orientation often serves problem-solving in the present and that is why it is also oriented towards the future.

In the case of my field work, it was exactly twenty years after the main events that people recalled the Chipko struggle, and the context was characterized by three aspects: first, 'ecology' had been (and still is) highly valued on a global scale, and in academic and popular writings, as we have seen, Chipko is represented as the first 'ecological movement'. Second, great social and economic problems had required new ways of securing life in the hills; some groups and activists claimed to have found these new ways by following strategies of 'sustainable development'. Third, participants, supporters, and opponents of Chipko had already been pulled into discourses which, in different ways, related to the issues of forest, ecology, and development. Against this background, Chipko was retrospectively interpreted in various personal and collective accounts as a turning point which

---

[17] Kannabiran and Lalitha (1989) illustrate that women who participated in the Telangana struggle (1946–51) remember the period as an outstanding time in their lives. During the struggle they attended meetings, they were taught to read and write, and they discussed political questions. They suddenly felt catapulted into a situation 'when everything entered the realm of possibility' (1989: 185).

[18] Veena Das claims in her analysis of Sikh political discourse that '[l]anguage functions more to *produce* a particular reality than to *represent* it' (1995: 121).

altered state policies, collective strategies, and individual life histories.

After analysing the various narratives on Chipko collected from activists and villagers, I came to realize that these representations differ from the dominant narrative in various respects: (a) they give *parochial* pictures of the Chipko andolan; (b) they accentuate the *distinctiveness of targets*; and (c) they reveal a situation of *competition and rivalry* between participants in different localities, who follow divergent ideas.[19]

Parochialization

In local representations Chipko is not a coherent movement which joined people and places in Garhwal and Kumaon. Instead the focus is on singular and only partially related campaigns in particular localities at a particular time. Accordingly, a 'parochialized' picture emerges which presents not only 'one Chipko' but also many localized Chipkos with different actors. Leaders as well as participants in the different localities narrate 'their' Chipko which, at the same time, is claimed as the original and 'true' one.

Chandi Prasad Bhatt, for example, recalls Chipko incidents in Chamoli District:

> Between 1973 and 1977, the people of Gopeshwar, Mandal, Phata Rampur, Raini and Bhyundar in the Chamoli District, situated in the watershed of the Alakananda, had to protest at least half a dozen times against the forest department's working of forests. In the end, a committee of experts under Dr. Virendra Kumar . . . agreed that the issues raised by the villagers were scientifically correct and forestry based on so-called forest science was wrong. . . . This brought the Chipko Andolan to the notice of environmentalists and the government and it is today known in many parts of the world. (Bhatt 1987b: 48)

For Bhatt the ultimate success of Chipko seems to lie in the recommendations of the Kumar Committee and the ban of green felling in

[19] I refer to personal interviews and written accounts of Sunderlal and Vimala Bahuguna, Chandi Prasad Bhatt, G.S. Rawat, A.S. Bisht, villagers from Mandal, Lata, and Raini. The interviews were all conducted between 1993 and 1996.

the upper Alakananda catchment area, and not in the moratorium of 1981 which was demanded mainly by Sunderlal Bahuguna and his supporters. Bhatt calls the DGSM the 'mother organization of the Chipko andolan' and refers to Chipko campaigns in regions other than Chamoli only in passing (Bhatt 1987b, 1987c; n.d.; personal interview 1994). He sees in the current ecodevelopment work of the DGSM the continuation of the Chamoli Chipko in which he himself was involved.

Anand Singh Bisht, formerly member of the DGSM and later President of Jakeshwar Shikshan Samsthan, an NGO founded by him and based in Gopeshwar, has published a small booklet named 'Van jage vanvasi jage'.[20] Bisht tells of sarvodaya work in Chamoli District, of efforts to establish small industries and secure forest user-rights for villagers. His story of Chipko covers the Mandal and Raini incidents and, like Bhatt, he celebrates the decisions of the Kumar Committee as the movement's success.

Villagers seem to have an even more localized perception: Chipko is primarily the struggle they carried out in their particular locality. In Mandal I talked to Ganeshwari Devi, an old lady who participated in the local campaigns of 1973. She remembered the time when Chandi Prasad Bhatt, one of the neta log (leaders), mobilized villagers in Mandal and a few neighbouring villages to save their jungle. Men and women joined in the struggle, explained the old lady. The women needed especially to be guided, she added, because in those days women were shy and 'had no language' to speak in front of others. Ganeshwari says women from Mandal had been informed of Chipko events in Fateh Rampur and in Raini, but they did not take part: only the leaders went off to initiate and support campaigns.

For Bhotiya women and men from Lata and Raini, Chipko means their particular struggle to save Nilori Paing, the local forest area, from being cut by the axe-men of a contractor named Bhalla (Bhalla thekedar). Negotiations and protest campaigns continued over several weeks with the unceasing support of Govind Singh Rawat, member of the Communist Party and, in those days, Block Pramukh of Niti

[20] The grammatically correct translation would be: 'The forest and the forest-dweller should be vigilant.' But the title has an additional connotation, aimed at mobilizing the people. It is better grasped via a slightly different translation: 'Forest awake, forest dweller awake!'

Ghati. Villagers deny being mobilized by Chandi Prasad Bhatt; they give the whole credit of support to Rawat who is not considered a leader but a co-fighter—a colleague. Therefore, they claim, 'The spirit of protest was aroused in our own hearts. The forest is our basis of life and we have seen in Gairsain [south-east of Karnaprayag, near the Almora District boundary] what happens if Bhalla gets an opportunity to fell the trees. There is nothing left . . .'[21] During my stay in Lata and Raini I learned about the importance of the forest to the lives of local residents. From the forest they get not only fodder, pasture, and firewood, they also extract from it medicinal plants and roots, fruits and mushrooms. Village women have composed songs about the value of banj trees, the necessity of afforestation, and the Chipko struggle. When, during the protest campaign in 1974, the villagers moved to the forest, they went drumming, shouting slogans, and singing songs.

Chipko Song, Composed and Sung
by Women of Lata

(my translation from the Pahari, with the help of J.S. Chauhan)

Hey, didi, hey bhulli, let us all unite
    and with our own efforts let us save our jungle.
The maldars and thekedars want to make money.
Our cows and our cattle, they go to the jungle
    and with them our young people.
Hey, Rishi Maharaj, come and show yourself with your real power.
Chase far away the 600 trucks heavily loaded,
    and along with them drive back the strangers.
Hey, Lata Bhagvati, come and show yourself with your real power,
    chase far away the maldars and thekedars.
When our jungle is saved, only then will we return [to our villages].[22]

Apparently, the period of the Chipko struggle had been a 'magic time' for the Bhotiya community. The threatening behaviour of the

---

[21] Personal interview, Lata, 1995. I conducted the interviews with groups of women, or groups of women and men. For this reason, quotations are not assigned to particular persons.

[22] *Didi*: elder sister; *bhulli*: younger sister; *maldar*: rich person; *thekedar*: contractor; *Rishi Maharaj*: local form of address to a god or supreme being; *Lata Bhagvati*: goddess of Lata (Nanda Devi).

contractor and his gang and in contrast the will to save the local forest brought the villagers, men and women, close together in a joint effort. Life became out of the ordinary. Some of the women mentioned that, as girls and young women, they had loved joining the protest campaigns. They confessed that, because of their youth, they had not fully understood what was going on, but they remembered: 'We were happy in those days, when we could go to the demonstrations in Raini. We thought we'd get two hours off. We did not basically think we'd go to save the forest, or make an end to the cutting of trees. In our innocence, we thought we would get some rest [from work].' The villagers admit that, much later, they heard of the Chipko campaigns in Tehri District, but they also claim that it was *they* who started the whole struggle: 'Those people got to know from our struggle, and from this they took the courage for their own protest.'

Sunderlal Bahuguna's importance in Chipko discourses is legitimized by his authenticity as a 'local participant', and by the power of his speech—his version of Chipko has become a central constitutive element of the dominant narrative. Bahuguna (see, for example, 1987) follows a double strategy in presenting Chipko. On the one hand he constructs a narrative of repeated Chipkos, arguing that the love for trees and the desire to protect them is the expression of an ecological inclination in Hindu culture. Indian history has many instances of people resisting tree-felling and Chipko represents just one such incident in a long chain. Forerunners of Chipko, Bahuguna says, include the historical sacrifice of Amrita Devi from Khejadli near Jodhpur (1730) and the Tilari Goli Kand of 1930 which occurred in the princely state of Tehri Garhwal. On the other hand, when referring to Chipko, Bahuguna constructs a sequence of localized campaigns initiated by different activists and varying in their goals. 'Initially, *chipko* was an economic movement' (1987: 241), he argues, and the early demands reflect 'what men thought'. 'True' Chipko developed in the course of the movement, when women came to the forefront. Bahuguna lays emphasis on the Chipko campaigns in Advani and Badiyargarh (Tehri District), where the ecological message was communicated in the famous slogan 'What do the forests bear . . .', and in which he and his wife participated.[23]

[23] According to Berndt (1987: 72), who meticulously analysed the English

Vimala Bahuguna underlines the crucial importance of the Advani campaign because, so her argument goes, it was the only case of women actually hugging the trees. 'On the first of February 1978, the contractor went to the jungle with the tree fellers. . . . Before the axes could strike, the women hugged the trees and attached themselves to them. The armed force had to turn back' (V. Bahuguna 1990: 117). She points out that in Mandal the people had only planned 'to attach themselves (*chipak jayenge*) to the trees . . . the occasion for this did not arise' (V. Bahuguna 1990: 116). At variance with Bhatt and Bisht, Vimala and Sunderlal Bahuguna see the success of the Chipko andolan as being the total ban on green felling in the Himalayas for fifteen years.

Different Targets

The leading narrative constructs Chipko as an uninterrupted movement which developed in stages, with different goals having been pursued at different times. It postulates that an emphasis on ecology superseded the focus on economy. As far as the local Chipko participants are concerned, it is Sunderlal Bahuguna who shares, and is largely responsible for, this perspective. He states that the two significant targets which dominated consecutive periods of the struggle lie already at the heart of the Tilari Declaration, which he considers the 'first document of Chipko'.

The Tilari Declaration (as communicated
by Sunderlal Bahuguna)

The declaration adopted by the people on 30 May 1968 in the memory of the martyrs who laid down their lives for the protection of the forest rights on 30 May 1930.

- Forests have been the basis of our cultural and economic life from the very beginning of this civilization.
- Our main duty is to protect the forest.

---

and Hindi sources, the campaign in Badiyargarh, 30 km east of Srinagar, District Tehri Garhwal, did not find sufficient support from the villagers. The Forest Corporation had employed men from the locality as forest workers. They were afraid to lose their jobs if the protest campaign succeeded. Ramachandra Guha (1991) presents the Badiyargarh andolan as a successful campaign.

- We declare our birthright as being to fulfil our basic needs through forest products, through the forest, and to get employment from the forest.
- The harmonious relationship to the forest which is the basis of our happiness and prosperity should be permanent, for it is essential.
- The first use of forest wealth should be for the happiness and prosperity of the forest dwellers, of the people living near the forest.
- The forest products which are of daily use and which are used for village industries should be easily available for everybody.
- Forest industries based on forest products should be established near the forest.
- The present system of forest exploitation by the contractors should be replaced with forest labour co-operatives of the local people.
- In order to link love with knowledge about the forest in forest areas, botany and geology should be a part of curriculum at every stage of education in forest areas.
- On this day we pay our homage to the brave martyrs of Tilari and we remember them with great reverence.
- Their peaceful movement and brave martyrdom may inspire us and keep us alert for the protection of forest and forest rights.
- So we take a pledge to celebrate this day as 'Forest Day'.

According to Bahuguna, the fundamental inconsistency in the Tilari Declaration—the contradiction between love of the forest and the wish to get employment from it—has led to controversies and rivalries in the movement. Bahuguna knits together love, harmony, and protection as basic elements of an 'ecological' attitude towards the forest. This attitude finds its practical expression in the 'true' Chipko demands for a total ban on green felling and the closure of all forest-based industries. Against that demand, the establishment of labour cooperatives for the extraction of timber as well as the use of timber and forest products in small-scale village industries to achieve local employment is identified with an exploitative praxis, and with an attitude which gives priority to economy (in the sense of the market economy). This early 'economic' phase of Chipko—represented by Chandi Prasad Bhatt—had to give way to the 'true', i.e. ecologically inspired, Chipko, represented by Bahuguna himself.

To suggest a conflict between ecology and (market) economy seems one possible interpretation.[24] But how far do others—activists, village people—share this interpretation? Do they think there is a contradiction between protection of the forest and its use in local economies? An examination of Chipko campaigns in Chamoli District indicates that both can be seen as complementary aims. The campaigns there focused on the claim for forest rights (*van adhikar*), i.e. the *rights* of local people to control and use their jungle in ways which allow securing one's own livelihood while preserving the forest (for Kumaon, see also Berndt 1987).

In his booklet on the Chipko campaigns in Chamoli District, Anand Singh Bisht (1993) argues that people have demonstrated a desire 'to save the abundant forest wealth of the mountains from exploitation, to protect it, and to secure the hereditary rights to get daily earnings (*rozgar*) from the forest' (1993: 9). Bisht cites some of the well-known slogans, songs, and programmatic formulations which gave expression to these targets.

Chipko Slogans
(Bisht 1993: 12, translation AL)

- Protection of forests means protection of the country!
  (*Vanon ki raksha, desh ki raksha*)

- This is the call of Uttarakhand—forest rights in panchayats' hands!
  (*Uttarakhand ki yeh lalkar, panchayaton ko van adhikar*)

- Stop our exploitation by the contractor system!
  (*Thekadari loot band karo*)

- Daily earnings from forest wealth—this is a right of forest dwellers!
  (*Van sampada se rozgar, vanvasiyon ka adhikar*)

Bisht has also put down what he considers the 'five main Chipko demands' (1993: 16, my translation). The demands convey a reconciliation of protection with utilization of forests.

---

[24] Bahuguna himself offers a concept for the reconciliation of ecology and economy in the form of 'ecology as permanent economy'. Here economy means subsistence economy. See also Chapter 5.

1. The contractor system and the practice of auctioning which leads to the ruin of the forest and forest dwellers should be immediately stopped, and the utilization of forest wealth should be conducted through labour co-operatives in accordance with the guidelines of the Planning Commission.
2. Because of population growth, the rights of villages should be increased through a new forest arrangement.
3. There should be no 'export' of raw materials from the forest. Raw materials and technical assistance should be given to forest dwellers to run small forest-based industries.
4. To prevent landslides and the sinking of the water level caused by the destruction of forests, extensive afforestation plans should be made.
5. Forest dwellers must be involved in the efforts for the protection of forests and in the forest administration.

The first three points ask for a stop to exploitation by outsiders and demand a respect for the rights of forest dwellers to utilize forest wealth according to local needs. This includes the commercial use of forest products—but only to a limited and sustainable extent, and in small-scale industries. Points four and five are both concerned with forest protection, and the fifth point especially takes up an issue which became increasingly prominent in the years following: the demand for people's participation in administration and planning of forests.

One of the most famous Chipko songs, composed by the Garhwali folk poet Ghanshyam Shailani, also places emphasis on both the demand for protection and the utilization of forests (see below, Pahari version in Bisht 1993: 40–1). The song, written in a Marxist spirit, accuses those in power—the state and 'capitalists'—for the degradation of forests and their people. Shailani mentions different ways in which local residents are deprived of their rights and resources, painting a picture of the Pahari youth as a 'dish-washer'. This picture was still in people's minds during the struggle for regional autonomy (1994–7): 'We Paharis feel that we are only dish-washers, but we must learn to correct our self-image,' demanded Shamsher S. Bisht, a publisher from Almora in an interview I conducted with him in 1998.

He further emphasized the view that hill people should not see themselves as servants and subalterns, but as people who have at their disposal many resources and capabilities which they must learn to utilize in a proper and efficient way. In his poem, Shailani recommends establishing small-scale industries and using local resources for the benefit of villagers. He dreams of a future in which forest dwellers will live in fortune and prosperity, when socialism will come to the Himalayas.

Chipko Song

by Ghanshyam Shailani (my translation from the
Pahari, with the help of J.S. Chauhan)

Brothers and Sisters from the hills! Let us all gather and unite,
let us be ready to save our beloved jungle from the government's forest
    policy.
Through auctioneers and contractors all the forests have been cut
    away.
Bad times have come
    and in the hills the forest has been destroyed.
The whole benefit of the jungle has been taken away by contractors.
For years, we have cared for the forest
    and for long we have protected the jungle.
Today the rich capitalists are cutting forests and accumulating wealth,
And young people of the hills, who have real rights to the forest
    go to the plains and wash their dishes.
Today the factory for resin processing is located in Bareilly,
But the resin, the raw material, they get from here;
    and the whole profit goes to the Bareilly resin factory.
In order to earn more wealth from the *chir* pines
    deep wounds were cut in them and resulted in too many trees dying.
The government and the rich capitalists together
    are sweeping the jungle clear,
And nobody worries about planting new trees.
Instead, the Forest Department has become the destroyer of forests.
To save the jungle there are no hopes,
    to save the jungle there are no words.

Cling to the trees and don't let them be cut!
Don't let the forest's wealth be plundered!
Through the establishment of small forest-based industries
    benefit will come to the hill region,
    and through it fortune and prosperity to forest dwellers.
Everywhere in the hills socialism will come
    and from village to village the sound of the conch* will be heard.

*The conch is usually used in religious contexts.

This is not to deny that, in the course of the Chipko movement, ecological arguments have gained momentum and have substantiated the demand for forest protection. In these arguments the role of the forest as a stabilizing force within the Himalayan ecosystem has been accentuated, i.e. the protective function of forests against soil erosion and landslides, and its regulatory function for the hydrological cycle. However, this does not necessarily mean that other demands have been fully replaced, as suggested by Sunderlal Bahuguna and his followers. Chandi Prasad Bhatt has in fact laid down the demands of Chipko from his point of view, and, for the first time, a two-fold relationship of the people of Uttarakhand with their forests has explicitly been stated:

> On the one hand the forests are crucial for maintaining balance in the physical environment and on the other hand the human beings who are central to the ecological system are directly related to the forests. The various products of the forests such as firewood, timber, grass, vegetables, honey, medical herbs, fruits as well as agriculture and animal husbandry are also dependent on the forests. *For these reasons the ecological balance and the traditional human relations are so intertwined that it is difficult to perceive them separately.* In this context the Chipko movement has laid down the following six demands:

> 1. All felling of trees in the sensitive catchment area of rivers must be banned and there should be thick plantation in such areas. The trees must not be cut for the purpose of construction unless it is ascertained that this does not affect the ecosystem adversely. In such areas the forest conservation system ought to aim at protecting the forest land as well as in achieving a balance in the climatic features.

2. The contract system should be immediately stopped and rural organizations and labour co-operative societies should be established to replace it. The hill people must be actively involved. All works in the forest should be done through such organizations and societies only. The local people must also be provided with relevant training and guidelines to fulfil the objectives.

3. The daily needs of forest dwellers in the region should be duly evaluated and they should be accordingly given reasonable rights over forest resources. Forests must be surveyed properly in order to know their exact condition as well as to evaluate the rights of the natives in the proper perspective.

4. Rural industrial ventures, based on the forest resources of the region and involving the local labourers, industrial workers, and villagers, should be given all incentives. For this assistance must be provided to enable them to obtain sufficient raw material, finance, and technological knowhow.

5. The denuded hills must be made green again through afforestation drives on a war footing. Besides, the local people must be involved and should be encouraged to take up forest farming (agro-forestry). Efforts should be made to foster love and affection among the locals towards trees and plants.

6. A detailed geological, ecological, and botanical survey of the hills should be carried out before any heavy construction is begun or the Forest Department's working plan comes into operation in the region. (Bhatt n.d.: 5–6)[25]

Bhatt develops the perspective that human beings are part of the ecosystem and emphasizes the link between 'traditional human relations' and ecological balance. He also acknowledges that people's relations to the forest have changed because, in present times, they have started to recognize forests as a commercially valuable resource. The economic appropriation of forests is no longer limited to subsistence activities but necessarily includes market-oriented utilization. Chipko demands, as phrased by Bhatt, reveal a well-balanced concept

[25] The booklet was probably written in the mid 1980s: Bhatt used statistical data up to 1983. For Bhatt's concepts, see also Chapter 5.

of forest use, forest protection, and regeneration. In his concept the earlier and stronger demands for local forest rights, and for income generation from the forest and forest produce, are somewhat toned down in favour of ecological requirements. But even if this goes together with a strengthening of the influence of state, administration, and scientists, Bhatt asks for 'reasonable rights' for local residents over forest resources and an adequate participation of village people in conservation efforts. In sum, Bhatt's concept does not seem to turn away from the basic targets of early Chipko days.

When I asked villagers from Lata and Raini to explain the motives of their Chipko struggle, they put forward both ecological and economic arguments. The forest represents their 'basis of life' in a double sense. First, they *gain their livelihood* from the forest ('through the forest our stomachs are filled'—'*pet bharta hai*'). The forest provides fuel, fodder, fertilizers, vegetables, mushrooms, and fruits for six months of the year; it also provides *jadi booti* or medicinal plants, which are a main source of income for villagers.[26] Second, the forest *protects humans and human settlements from natural hazards*: with a good forest cover 'there will be no landslides; rocks and hills will not come down and destroy our agricultural fields.'

To sum up: the Chipko demands, communicated by activists and villagers in different localities, at different times and in various ways (speech, songs, text), are characterized by an ecology–economy duality. Yet for the majority of the people who participated in the Chipko andolan 'love' of the forest and a protective attitude are not necessarily in conflict with the desire to gain a livelihood and daily earnings from the forest. They perceive and approach the forest issue in its entirety and usually reject any attempt to isolate and pursue the 'economic' and 'ecological' aims as mutually exclusive or oppositional.

Competition and Rivalry

The 'many' Chipkos may be both the starting point for and the result of competition and rivalry that seems to have developed among the Chipko participants of different localities and have been sharpened

[26] Since 1981 the collection and sale of medicinal plants has been banned by the government (see Chapter 5).

by the media and responses to the movement.[27] Narrators feel inclined to present their own campaign as the 'true' Chipko and, indirectly, themselves as its 'true' and legitimate representatives. In this context the question of origin has become crucial: *Where* did Chipko really start and *who* initiated its first actions? Is there *one* place of origin? Who first articulated the idea of 'hugging' trees? Different narrators try to answer these questions in their own favour, sometimes' by accusing the others of denigrating them.

Sunderlal and Vimala Bahuguna claim that the contemporary Chipko movement originated in the Rawain area with the celebration of 'Forest Day' and the declaration of forest rights on 30 May 1969 at Tilari Maidan, and later in 1972 with the first demonstration in Purola:

> After 1947 [the year of Indian independence], 30th May began to be observed as a *shaheed divas* (martyr's day); on this day each year people would collect to hold discussions on forest problems. When, in the late sixties and early seventies, the message of gram swaraj spread in this area, and Uttarkashi was declared an independent district, a meeting on forest issues was organized at Tilari Maidan. On this occasion, a declaration on forests was prepared on behalf of the people, and thousands of people took a pledge to redeem this at the Martyr's memorial in 1969. This declaration was publicized in the villages of the area by activists of the Gram Swaraj Sangh, and became a fundamental document of the Chipko Movement. . . . The theoretical basis for the Chipko Movement was built up thus. Against this background, the practical work of the movement began. The first demonstration was on 11 December 1972 at Purola in Yamuna Ghati, the birthplace of the 1930 forest agitation. . . .
> (V. Bahuguna 1990: 115; see also S. Bahuguna 1987: 240)

Sunderlal Bahuguna has described the Tilari Declaration as 'the first document of the Chipko movement' and Tilari 'the birthplace of Chipko' because the inspiration for the movement came from here (personal interview 1993). This perspective has been sceptically questioned by Chandi Prasad Bhatt, who, alluding to Bahuguna and

---

[27] See Weber 1988: 75. He talks of 'media battles' which have developed around the figures of Bhatt and Bahuguna.

his efforts to search for historical forerunners of Chipko, remarks: 'We are people who don't read English; we are not searching in history . . .' (personal interview 1994; this and the following quotations are all translated by me). He compares 30 May with other memorable days, such as Nehru's birthday or Krishna's birthday (Janmashtami) and rejects any direct connection between this date and the Chipko movement. He says he does not recall whether he joined the May meeting in 1969 at Tilari or not ('*mujhe nahin yad ki main tha ya nahin*') and says angrily: 'You must understand, Chipko andolan did not start on the 30th of May' ('*aap samajh rahe hain . . . Chipko andolan to 30 mai ko shuru nahin hua*').

Sunderlal Bahuguna has never claimed Chipko as 'his' movement, but he positions himself as the true Chipko representative: as the only one who spreads the message of Chipko as an ecological movement; that is, a movement which, after having passed an early economic phase, finally discovered its true goals by listening to women's demands. Bahuguna admits that Chipko became controversial when he and his followers decided to raise the demand for a total ban on tree felling and brought ecology to the fore: 'Our friends from Chamoli did not agree to this new policy. They and some lefties argued that the main problem of the hills is poverty, and that there would be no other way to abolish poverty than forest based industries and tree felling' (personal interview 1993). Without mentioning names or giving further explanation, he complained that, over the years, 'some organizations tried to monopolize the movement'.

Whereas Sunderlal Bahuguna seemed to me to be comparatively cautious and restrained in his arguments—perhaps because he is aware that, internationally, he has the larger audience and publicity— Chandi Prasad Bhatt seemed more oppositional, even though he explained his point of view in an indirect way. His rhetoric indicates a double play—keeping himself in the background, yet expecting recognition for what he has done:

> You should know that we have a lot of big stones in Uttarakhand, very big stones. The people say that all these stones have been brought by Bhimsen, by the Pandavas. . . . But who really knows? . . . The same is today. The people have no idea who initiated the andolan, where the

word came from, and why. Unfortunately, newspapers say different things, sometimes they discredit the andolan. You may have heard here, and from others, that this has been a women's movement and women's names are mentioned: Syama Devi, Gaura Devi, and Indra Devi, Parvati Devi. . . . There are also the names of men. Alam Singh Bisht, Kedar Singh, Sisupal Singh Kunwar, Govind Singh Rawat, Hayat Singh, you understand, not one name—many names. And anyone who participated in the movement claimed that he had done it. . . . But when did this all begin? After 1978. After some people noticed that disturbances have started.[28] They started discrediting my name. But basically, I haven't said that there is one name or two, but dozens of names. That is, if one mentions Raini one has also to mention Gaura Devi. If one mentions Hayat Singh one must also mention Govind Singh Rawat and many others, and also our role, which we know best. Why didn't the movement start before? When we stepped in, why did it start then? But we kept ourselves as zeros.

Bhatt seems to me to feel that he and his achievements did not quite receive the deserved praise. Despite his rhetoric, the message seems unambiguous: a number of people were involved in Chipko, but people should admit that, in the end, the movement was primarily successful because of work that he and his co-activists did. In some of his articles he is less reserved and presents the DGSM as 'the mother organisation of the Chipko Andolan' (Bhatt n.d.: 7). Bhatt also claims to have written first about the andolan and publicized Gaura Devi: 'Who has told the world about Gaura Devi? Through whose writings did the world learn about Gaura Devi? ... To this place not even an ant would have come . . . this was a border area . . . Besides me, there was no second person to tell the world . . . It was I who said that we initiated the movement and that women participated in it.'

Both Bahuguna and Bhatt have become public figures and are frequently in the media. Whereas Bahuguna's audience mainly seems to be abroad, Bhatt gets his greatest response in India, and among Indian environmentalists. His work has been highly appreciated and

[28] Bhatt probably refers here to the ideological shift in Sunderlal Bahuguna after 1977, which influenced local strategies.

communicated in the Citizens' Reports of the Centre for Science and
Environment, and more recently in work by Ramachandra Guha
(2004, 2006).

Anand Singh Bisht from the Jakeshwar Shikhsan Samsthan,
Gopeshwar, suggests that it is giving of individual awards which is
responsible for disunity and rivalry between people, all of whom have
dedicated themselves to improve the lot of Uttarakhand.

When the Chipko movement started the government started presenting
awards and through it the government started putting its stamp on the
movement. After this any person who felt ambition in himself felt also
that ambition was not enough, that he also must get due importance,
that he must get a national award! I think, in this regard the biggest culprit was the government itself, in that the Chipko andolan was taken as
a national movement and the government started giving different kinds
of awards for it. Through the perspective of awards, people's enthusiasm
started increasing. I think the main reason for the unity of entire
Uttarakhand was Chipko, which brought the people together; and the
biggest culprit was the government, which worked to divide the people
and started giving awards. If awards were necessary, then these awards
should have been given in a joint form. There are differences among
peoples' perspective on the andolan. Different people participated in the
movement—village women, village men, in the various places where
Chipko began. It started in Mandal, it started in Fateh. People's minds
are now filled up with whom the government will award. I haven't been
asked up to now, but people get ambitious. (Personal interview 1995, my
translation)

Bisht recalls the time of Vinoba Bhave and Sarala Behn, when all activists who now run separate organizations—Sunderlal Bahuguna,
Chandi Prasad Bhatt and he himself—collaborated closely ('jud kar
kam karte the'). Even when Chipko began, he says, all were involved
and supported the first campaigns in Mandal and Fateh. Later, individuals became ambitious, they separated; now they do different
work and try to outdo each other.

Apart from the Chipko protagonists Bhatt and Bahuguna, and
those upheld by them (e.g. Gaura Devi), other names are seldom
mentioned and even ignored in the public discourse on Chipko. An

activist largely marginalized in the media is Govind Singh Rawat, then a communist Block Pramukh of Niti Ghati, and a resident of Joshimath. We—my research assistant Jayendra S. Chauhan and I—learned about him in our meetings with women and men in Lata and Raini. They praised him effusively as their chief adviser and supporter in the struggle to save Nilori Paing. Later we met Rawat and he recounted for us his version of the Chipko movement and its aftermath; he also gave us his views on the living conditions and development perspectives of the Bhotiyas.

In Govind Singh Rawat's narration on Chipko, three aspects dominate: the question of who created the name Chipko; a complaint about the marginalization of his own role in the Chipko struggle; the disunity of Chipko and the rivalry between activists and misuse of the name of Gaura Devi. In the dominant narrative, credit for having articulated the idea of hugging trees is given to Chandi Prasad Bhatt, a fact questioned by Govind Singh Rawat as well as by Anand Singh Bisht. I will start with the narration of Anand Singh Bisht regarding the meeting in Mandal in 1973, during which strategies for opposing the Simon Company were discussed.

Chipko Andolan began in 1973–4. On 24 April 1973 there was the first meeting in our Mandal Valley. . . . On this 24 April nobody thought Chipko would become an affair. . . . Our problem was how to drive off the people who cut the jungle, these people from the Simon Company, how to repel them. First, everybody thought of violence. We were convinced that we should try to kill workers from the Simon Company, slay them with swords, shoot them, not give them our jungle, our forest wealth. This was because the forest was absolutely necessary to our livelihood. For the people the forest was necessary to run cottage industries. Therefore everybody was sure that we would never allow outsiders to cut our trees. Formerly, we prepared the yoke for our oxen and ploughs. . . . On 24 April, when the question was raised about which method should be employed, somebody said: 'If they cut the trees we will lie beneath the trucks. We won't give our property to outsiders; we need our property for ourselves.' The whole thing was not quickly decided . . . somebody said this, another said that. Somebody said, 'We will shoot them with rifles', another said, 'We will not give them our jungle.' Different suggestions were made. Then, in this meeting, somebody

said: 'Why don't we cling to the trees [*pedon se lipat jaen*]. This would be
the idea of sarvodaya, of Gandhiji, of Vinobaji . . . and all felt that this
idea was very good. We will cling to the trees and so protect them. We will
say to the people, 'brothers, if you want to cut [the trees] you will have
to cut our body first.'. . . So this idea was born here. . . . I cannot say
from whose brain it came. . . . On 2 May there was a big and crowded
conference. On that day it was decided by all that this andolan should be
given the name Chipko Andolan. (Personal interview 1995, my
translation)

While Anand Singh Bisht emphasizes the idea of hugging the trees as
the outcome of a general discussion, Govind Singh Rawat connects
the creation of the word '*chipko*' with the Raini incidents and claims
it originated in his own inspiration. He says that in September 1973
he heard of a contractor named Bhalla who had purchased at auction
large parts of the Raini forest:

Then it came to my mind that we should fight these big contractors . . . And it came to my mind that we should launch a campaign. . . .
In the night I prepared the first pamphlet . . . I mentioned three words:
chipko–lipto–chapto. These words I used as heading. Then I asked myself
which would be the best among these words. Then I thought *chipko* a
very good word. On 15 October the pamphlet was ready and I gave it to
the press. (This and all following quotations are based on a personal
interview, 1996, my translation.)

In another statement Rawat makes his claim even more explicit: 'I
have written three words, from these I have chosen *chipko*. So it was
I who created the word. And I initiated the Chipko Andolan. I organized the people.'
    When Rawat spoke of the early times of village mobilization, he
underlined (as did Anand Singh Bisht) that in those days Gandhian
activists and communists worked jointly: 'Chandi Prasad was with
me and with his support and cooperation I did my work. In Chandi
Prasad's Chipko, in my Chipko we were equal shareholders, nobody
was a single step in front or behind. . . . I could not do my work without Chandi Prasad Bhatt and he could not do his work without me.'

Even Sunderlal Bahuguna was said to have been one of the co-operating Gandhians. Together with the others he developed a plan to start a padyatra from Arakot (West Garhwal) to Askot (East Kumaon). According to Rawat, the harmonious phase of joint effort came to an end when the media, particularly the press, showed increasing interest in the andolan. Rawat accuses the press of writing in favour of Chandi Prasad Bhatt and giving him all the credit for initiating the Chipko andolan.[29] 'For that he got the Magsaysay Award,' Rawat says with frustration, and adds: 'They have erased my name from the newspapers. Once and for all cleaned out, my name was gone. From now on Chandi Prasad Bhatt's name was in front. . . . Bhatt has become the highlight.' But in the late 1970s, Rawat continued, the picture changed again: 'After that between Bhatt and Bahuguna a competition started. Sunderlal Bahuguna is brilliant at writing. He started to write about the Chipko andolan and tried to place his name in front. Sunderlal Bahuguna wrote books, shot films . . . and Bhatt went downhill.'

Rawat listed the awards presented to Bahuguna, mentioning his journeys to foreign countries and the ensuing international publicity. 'From place to place Bahuguna's name spread', he concluded.

Govind Singh Rawat even goes so far as to accuse Bahuguna and Bhatt of having abused the confidence of village people, especially Gaura Devi. Gaura Devi seems to have gradually slipped (or rather, she was pushed) into a key role during the andolan.[30] As a village woman she perfectly represented what was popularized in the media as the central features of Chipko: an 'ecological' perspective, the self-confidence of rural woman as the true protector of nature, spontaneity, resolution, and local courage against external oppression. Gaura Devi was asked by leading activists to join them on occasions such as conferences, public meetings, the receiving of awards. Rawat suspects

[29] He accuses, especially, Anupam Misra of the Gandhi Peace Foundation. Misra was one of the first to sympathetically inform the public about Chipko. In Berndt's press analysis, Misra's publications are among the main references.

[30] When I came to Raini and Lata in 1993, Gaura Devi had already expired and I could not get her representation of events. For a hugely laudatory account of her role as catalyst, see Ramachandra Guha (2006), who compares her with Rosa Parks of the US civil rights movement.

selfish motives behind public presentations of Gaura Devi. In his opinion this was done not to emphasize the achievements of Gaura Devi and other village people but to increase the popularity of the movement as represented by those who used her. Whereas Rawat and several villagers from Lata and Raini affirmed that Gaura Devi accompanied Bhatt on many occasions, they doubt that she has accompanied Sunderlal Bahuguna. The latter is alleged by these folk to have shown a 'false Gaura' (*nakli Gaura*) to the public, that is, to have passed off a woman from the Tehri region as Gaura Devi on perhaps one or more occasions.

A certain 'instrumentalization' of Gaura Devi and inadequate acknowledgement of the contributions of villagers in the Chipko struggle were the subject of complaint, not only in my discussions with Govind Singh Rawat but also with women and men from Lata and Raini. One source of discontent was certainly the awards. People in the villages said many awards were offered to Gaura Devi and to the women from Raini, the most famous being a national award (probably the Padma Shri), and the Swedish 'Right Livelihood Award'.[31] But it was the leaders who received the awards. The national award was presented to Chandi Prasad Bhatt by Rajiv Gandhi in Delhi. Villagers criticized Bhatt for taking Gaura Devi as the sole woman from the Bhotiya region to attend the ceremony; the other women in his company are said to have been from Gopeshwar. A long and plaintive story also exists about the 'Right Livelihood Award'.

When I visited Raini in 1993 for the first time and showed interest in the local Chipko struggle, the villagers immediately asked me if I'd heard of an award worth Rs 300,000 once offered to the villagers of Raini to acknowledge their involvement in Chipko. Surprised by this question, I told the people that Sunderlal Bahuguna had received an

---

[31] The villagers of Lata complain that the name of their village has not been mentioned in the media and in publications on Chipko. Accordingly, their participation in the protest actions (and that of other neighbouring villages) has not received sufficient appreciation. During the movement Lata and Raini had a joint gram panchayat and the forest auctioned belonged to Raini; perhaps therefore Lata and the other villages were marginalized. People from Lata lay emphasis on the fact that Gaura Devi's mait (Garhwali expression for *maika*, mother's house) was in Lata.

award known under the name 'Right Livelihood Award' or 'Alternative Nobel Prize', worth that sum, on behalf of Chipko in 1987. The villagers expessed astonishment and shock at this. We were sitting at the time in the house where Gaura Devi had lived, and a young family member quickly started to search in a collection of papers. After a few minutes he took out a letter from Sunderlal Bahuguna addressed to Gaura Devi, dated 20 November 1987. In this letter Bahuguna informed the people of Raini that the Chipko movement had been nominated for the 'Right Livelihood Award', and he asked the villagers to suggest how the money should be spent. The letter concluded by requesting the villagers to suggest an answer as soon as possible. Some of the women present in the room said in those days they did not know much about awards, and, moreover, none of them was able to read or understand Bahuguna's letter properly. 'We were unknown, so we did not answer,' they said, 'and after that we never heard anything about the award—whether it had been presented or not, whether the money had been paid or not, who might have taken the money.' When I tried to read Bahuguna's letter I realized it was written in sophisticated academic language, using terms from Sanskrit and referring to the religious ideals of asceticism and devotion. For Raini's villagers, mostly illiterate or with only a basic education, it was very difficult to understand the meaning of this letter.[32]

[32] To give an idea of the language and contents of the letter, I asked an Indologist to translate its early portion:

'It is a very encouraging and reinforcing message for you, who are deeply involved in the Chipko struggle as well as for those active in similar movements, to know that the Chipko Andolan has been nominated for the 'Right Livelihood Award'. Jakob von Uexküll, who had offered this award, which in the meantime became famous as the 'Alternative Nobel Prize', justified the nomination with the following words: 'We are living in an age highly marked by global chaos and mutual distrust, which also seriously affected our strong organizations. We don't have a shortage of new philosophies, but amongst them there are only very few which seem to be useful in practice and can be applied universally in the form of projects in such a way that they can give an adequate answer to the challenges of our times. The award is meant to support such projects being a milestone on the way to a new world in which we can live a satisfactory life. In my opinion, the award is not meant to appreciate a sudden event in the history of Chipko, but it is well-deserved by people like you who have actively supported

'*Sirf nam uthaya, paisa khaya*' (Only [our] name was used, the money was swallowed), was their concluding comment. They also complained that Gaura Devi did not gain any monetary profit from her popularity. The award money was taken by the leaders, and 'the plates, the trophies, they are all kept in Gopeshwar. Gaura only got her travel expenses paid.' But even worse, Gaura Devi's popularity seems to have stirred up feelings of rivalry and envy in neighbouring villages nonetheless; she was thought by some to have received sums of money which she used only for her own profit, or only for that of Raini and her co-villagers. 'But see the condition of our village,' people from Raini argued back: 'She was given nothing.'

People from Raini as well as Govind Singh Rawat are specially disappointed at the way Gaura Devi was 'used' by 'leaders' because they describe her as an absolutely upright woman (*seedhi aurat*) who personally, and as president of the women's council, cared for the welfare of the village and felt responsible for the forest as the basis of their livelihood. When she travelled with Bhatt, said the villagers, she did not suspect she would gain advantage, she only wanted to support and strengthen the forest issue. Her handicap was her illiteracy, her lack of formal education (*bilkul anparh*). To communicate the successful struggle in Raini she, like other villagers, had to rely on leaders. None of the villagers could by themselves write articles or make speeches to take the Chipko message to the world.

We asked the villagers of Lata and Raini what, in their opinion, were the main advantages accruing from Chipko—in which way did they profit most. They thought of profit as money and answered immediately: 'Profit? We did not see any profit' (*faida—hamne kabhi nahin dekha*). They continued: 'Four years after the andolan two boxes came with old clothes, and at the same time some certificates.[33] We thought for ourselves: 'That's for us! And we did the real work!

---

the movement in their young age—the inhabitants of Uttarakhand. And it is well deserved by the noble history of renunciation (*tyag*), self-mortification (*tapasya*) and ardent devotion (*sadhna*) of women. . . .' (Translated by Nadja-Christina Schneider).

[33] In 1986 the government presented certificates to the participants of the movement.

The awards and the money are for the *samsthans* [the NGOs].' But in another sense also Bhotiya villagers saw no profit emerging from their struggle. They argued that in 1974 the men and women of Lata and Raini had joined forces and saved their jungle from an outside contractor and secured traditional rights of access; yet this perceived victory, turned out to be a dead loss. In the aftermath of Chipko, the national forest policy was adjusted to ecological requirements, and in 1980, in the Bhotiya region, the Nanda Devi National Park was established followed by the Nanda Devi Biosphere Reserve in 1988. For the local population this only led to a further curtailment of rights—the villagers perceived the environmentally sensitive government policy as a hindrance to their own development. (This aspect will be discussed in more detail in Chapter 5.)

To conclude these diverse and widely divergent representations of Chipko, I will quote the text of a song composed by Dhan Singh Rana from Lata. This song talks about the life of Gaura Devi from the perspective of a co-villager who participated in the Chipko struggle and who knew her life and personality. It communicates the self-confidence of Bhotiya women, but also the grief and disappointment which villagers feel about the fate of a woman who, in their eyes, dedicated her life and energies to save the forest, a woman who though successful in her work was not rewarded accordingly. Indirectly, the song is also an indictment of the contemporary social situation of the Bhotiyas.[34]

Gaura Devi

by Dhan Singh Rana, village Lata
(My translation from the Pahari, with the help of
J.S. Chauhan)

Today, Gaura, the people remember you,
Today again our environment is exposed to destruction.
You are benevolent, you come into our minds.
I will narrate your life, just a few things:
In 1924, in the month of Sawan
You were born in Lata village.

---

[34] I have discussed the song on Gaura Devi in more detail in Linkenbach 2001.

Since your childhood you were trouble.
Your mother was already dead; then the *mausi* came.[35]
Your *mausi* was there, but you felt as an orphan.
At twelve, still a child, you were married,
But only for a short while could you enjoy your husband's company.
You bore one child; then your husband died.
Oh, Gaura, your life was just one big trouble.
From your early days you have experienced so much grief.
Together with other children you may have been schooled.
But you were poor and barred from education.
Always, you have been poor, but never without honour and wisdom.
You cared for all the villagers both during their happiness and grief,
You never cared for yourself, only for others.
The village people paid you a lot of respect.
In 1970 there was a women's meeting and you were elected as president unanimously.
Nobody voted against you.

In the whole world people are busy cutting the jungle,
And in the hills the contractor system is a heavy burden.
In 1973 in the month of October
Bhalla Bhai came to Raini jungle.
Big tents arrived and trucks with provisions.
Hundreds of workers came and with them
    the saws and the *kulharis*.[36]
The innocent trees—the people of this whole area started to worry about them.
In those times Govind Singh was our Block leader.
When he heard the news from Gaura, he hurried to Raini.
It came to his mind to print a pamphlet.
The songs and slogans sung by the people spread fast.
Employees of the Forest Department and workers, they had already moved into the forest,
They laid ready their saws and *kulharis*.
It was Gaura who called upon the people: 'Save the forest',

[35] *Mausi*: mother's sister.
[36] *Kulhari*: axe.

Who inspired the women to come to the forest.
With their bare hands the women went to the jungle
   and explained to the *janglats* and *chiranis*.[37]
That they have sworn to allow them nothing.

Gaura realized the unity and the confidence of the women
And like the voice of the forest she spoke up:
'Do not break our affinity with the forest, rooted for generations.
Sisters, let yourselves be cut with the trees, but do not abandon them
   and leave.
Cling to the trees, hug them, but don't let them be cut.
These, the properties of the hills, don't let them steal.
Women, you who are the beloved of the forest, hug the trees!'

The *chiranis* were discouraged, and they turned back.
The people of the region assembled,
The villages one after the other donned their responsibility as
   chaukidars.[38]
Day by day people demonstrated at the edge of the forest.
All assembled and thought carefully,
They decided: The Block Pramukh should be our adviser.
From Gopeshwar they brought Bhatt as a reporter.
Bhattji took photographs, he wrote in the newspapers.
In the whole country the news from our forest spread.
As long as the jungle remains, Gaura, your memory too remains.
Lakhs have been offered to you, but you still refused.
Looking at the bribes your face turned red with anger.
Maldars and *janglats* disappeared from our region.
Women! With your bare hands you fulfilled a great mission.

Many nations have offered you awards, Gaura.
You were called to Delhi and your name made eminent
When Prime Minister Rajiv Gandhi presented you an award.
The people around you broke your trust
   and had no scruples usurping your award.
Your service has been unselfish and you were pure of heart.

[37] *Janglat*: forest worker; *chirani*: person who cuts trees.
[38] *Chaukidar*: watchman.

They have taken your award without any regret,
Without caring for you and for your respect.
In your whole life you never talked ill of others,
Your selfless actions resulted in your remaining poor.
In 1991, when you were ill, nobody looked after you.
Without money, you had no chance to heal.
Mother of the greenery, Gaura, you went to heaven.
Death called upon you and you went empty-handed.
Today your children are living poor.
You are like Bhagwati, Gaura, you have done great work.
As long as the earth exists your name will remain.

In the name of the environment people exploit the world.
Still today in your hills the forests are cut.
Take another life, Gaura, and fly into a rage,
No matter where, take another life and fly into a rage.
In this world of injustice, show us your miracle again.

3.4 Talking about Chipko: The View of Non-participants

After I became aware of the Chipko movement as a series of localized campaigns, and having listened to diverse voices in the Chipko core areas, the question that came to me was how Chipko is perceived in localities where no confrontations between villagers and contractors took place. How do people in non-Chipko areas relate to the andolan? Very briefly, I want to describe the way villagers in Nakoli and its surroundings react to the Chipko movement and its leaders.

After the Tilari Declaration, which was announced in Barkot in 1968 [1969], and initial demonstrations against the commercial exploitation of forests in 1972 in Purola, no campaigns against contractors and no tree-hugging activities were reported from this part of Rawain. Villagers did not protest even though local forests seem to have been auctioned in the 1970s.[39] B.S. Panwar from Nakoli tried to

[39] The 'Working Plan for the Yamuna Forest Divison, Tehri Circle, 1954–5 to 1968–9' (Gupta 1957), mentions four forest ranges (Purola, Rawain, Mungarsanti, Jaunpur) which are subdivided into blocks and have come under three working circles (chir working circle, devdar working circle, protection working circle).

explain why Chipko could not gain ground in the region. He argued that, in those days, people were not able to unite and join a struggle on their own steam, without leadership: 'They need somebody who guides them, and in the Yamuna valley we did not have leaders like Chandi Prasad Bhatt and Sunderlal Bahuguna.' However, there may be another reason which was probably responsible for the lack of protest. Villagers said that parts of the forests around Nakoli were felled by prominent village members who managed to get contracts for this. Under such circumstances, protest would have meant fighting a relatively powerful neighbour or even a 'brother' and bringing open conflict into the village.

Reactions to Chipko seem in fact quite myriad among villagers of the Nakoli region. When I asked men and women about the protest campaigns, the majority of respondents showed no interest in the subject. They declared they had not heard, or only vaguely heard, of Chipko. The more educated and better informed showed a critical attitude. Some devalued the Chipko andolan as 'mere propaganda' blown up in newspapers. Others appreciated the end of auctions and the ban on commercial tree-felling as well as the growing ecological awareness among uneducated hill people. But they also said ecologically sensitive politics created problems for local residents by diminishing their rights to forest access.

The blame for the difficulties on account of limited forest access is primarily laid at the door of Sunderlal Bahuguna. As common reproach, villagers argue that Bahuguna himself had been a contractor: only later did he discover his preference for ecology. J.S. Rawalta from a village in the Yamuna valley complained thus:

> There are so many restrictions on the use of forests. After 1980 the forest policy was made according to the demands of Sunderlal Bahuguna. Now the government no longer allowed felling of trees for road construction, for irrigation channels; even horse-roads and cattle-roads could not be made. All these difficulties result from Bahuguna. . . . Today he is working

---

Forests around Nakoli are included in the Mungarsanti working circle. Block names indicate that several compartments of chir and devdar forests in the vicinity of Nakoli must have been allowed to be felled. I did not have access to any later working plan.

against the felling of trees, but he was once a contractor himself. I can
show you the forest where he had his compartment.

G.S. Rawat from another village in the Yamuna valley painted a less
hostile picture of Bahuguna and his work:

> He travelled a lot in our region and now the government has taken up
> afforestations. Sunderlal works a lot and he is doing good work, but
> nobody knows where he gets all the money from. Every year he came to
> Barkot, then there was a meeting and he spoke. But for a year and a half
> he did not come. He carries a small rucksack, only walks on foot in his
> dhoti, he never takes the bus. He tells the people: do not fell trees, go and
> plant trees. He comes with cassettes, plays songs, and shows videos.

Currently, ecological considerations seem to find some resonance
among the younger generation in the Nakoli region. During one of
my revisits I learned of a young man from a nearby village who has
apparently taken the ecological teachings of Bahuguna and/or other
social activists to heart. But his commitment to tree protection had
unpleasant consequences for him as it did not remain unnoticed and
did not go unopposed by his fellow villagers (see Chapter 6).

For the majority of the inhabitants of the Nakoli region Chipko remains a distant event which does not require them to comment on it
or to take a stand in relation to it. It is past, an episode of a history that
is getting dim in people's recollections. Only indirectly are villagers
affected by Chipko events: they are under an obligation to accept the
rules and regulations passed by an ecologically sensitive forest legislation and policy, and they have to cope with the hegemonic claim of
an environmental discourse which inhibits their desired exploitation
of their forests.

3.5 After Chipko: Impact and Prospects

To understand Chipko as just one event in the long history of people's
protest against the curtailment of forest rights in Uttarakhand (or
even India) does no justice to the movement. In comparison with
other forest protests, Chipko seems to be of outstanding importance.
It took place in a period of radical socio-economic change, when, in
the name of 'development', the life and lifeworld of a hill population

was seriously affected. People saw themselves confronted with the plunder of local natural resources by 'outsiders'; with an administrative reorganization and the development of an infrastructure which brought them no profits; and with increasing inmigration. Because of their geographical location at the Chinese border, military bases were being established in the region—for example in Joshimath. The Chipko campaigns therefore have to be seen in the context of a general process of deprivation of rights and the marginalization of a local population.

The Chipko struggle is also important and significant in that, being largely dependent on the guidance and involvement of Gandhian activists, it linked economic, social, political, and ecological dimensions. Basically, Chipko fought for the rights of hill dwellers to control, manage, and use their local forests (*van adhikar*). This included the demand to utilize forests as providers of fodder, fuel, and raw materials in the traditional subsistence economy, but also as a resource to create local employment (*rozgar*) and monetary income. In the course of Chipko, activists and specific groups of participants arguably developed an explicit 'ecological' consciousness—an implicit protective attitude to nature being already part of the traditional way of life. But the way in which the relation between ecology and economy was constructed by different people and groups reflects ideological differences and resulted in varying strategies.

Chipko was also a movement which received immense resonance beyond the hill region. Chipko activities stimulated changes in forest policy at the national and state level; more environmentally-oriented legislations and strategies were implemented by politicians and the administration as a result of Chipko. The willingness of the central government as well as the state to pursue Chipko demands centring on ecology was also influenced by the international recognition gained by Chipko. The movement became a global showpiece for forest-related conflicts and the 'ecological consciousness' of a local population. The interpretation of Chipko as basically an ecological movement helped establish ecology as a guiding principle and hegemonic discourse in the region, and in India as a whole.

The impact of the Chipko campaigns, and the way they influenced personal lives as well as altered the social and economic situation in the hills, made Chipko a key event. In many parts of the hills Chipko strengthened the identification of villagers with their forests and motivated them to demand genuine rights of control. It also imparted an awareness of their role as citizens and stimulated a more general craving for self-determination and improvement. In this context it is important to say that the Chipko movement has triggered public debates on future prospects and development in the hills. These debates focus on the relation between forests and people and raise issues relating to the rights of people to make use of or exploit their local environment. In which way, and to what extent, should villagers use the natural resources at their disposal, and how should they try to overcome the obstacles posed by government agencies which currently seem to be guided by ecological claims? This question is of special importance and relates to the fact that, in the aftermath of Chipko, the apparent success of the movement revealed considerable ambivalence. Ecologically sensitive policies turned out to be hindrances in local advancement, and the rights of local residents to their forests appear to have been substantially restricted. People have started, once again, to feel alienated from their own forests.

4

Ecology and Development: Two Powerful Narratives

C HIPKO IS, AS WE HAVE SEEN, WIDELY REGARDED AS A landmark ecological movement. Yet its demands remind us that deforestation is equally an economic and social problem, for the destruction of forests poses the question of the socioeconomic and cultural survival and future of communities living in their proximity. So ecology—often narrowly understood as balance in the physical environment—has to be discussed in a much broader sense and take on a much broader meaning. It has to take into consideration the human factor, the linkages between a particular environment and human beings whose lives depend on it.

In the aftermath of Chipko, the interdependence of ecology and development—as reflected in global discourses to which Indian scholars also contributed—became equally clear. First ecology and development were brought together in the concept of 'sustainable development'; second, reflections on ecology as well as on development became moral and raised ethical questions; third, ecological consciousness and natural resource management became key issues in debates on alternative development and 'regional modernities' (Sivaramakrishnan and Agrawal 2003).

So we need to turn now to the history, meaning, and metamorphosis of the concepts of ecology and development, and see how these have become powerful global narratives which have strongly affected contemporary Indian discourses and politics.

4.1 Ecology: A Multifaceted Concept and the Search for Action Guidelines

Ecology started as a natural science in the middle of the nineteenth century.[1] Ernst Haeckel defined *Oecologie* as the science which aims to study the relations between an organism and its environment; mankind was seen as a biotic element and included in the natural world.

From its early days ecology—as discipline and concept—underwent remarkable changes. Until 1910 ecology was nearly synonymous with biology, but in the course of specialization in the natural sciences and their methodological diversification, the ecological approach was integrated into the disciplines of ethology, physiology, and genetics, as well as into the study of demography. After 1935 ecology was reconceptualized in terms of systems theory. The notion of 'ecosystem'—understood as a complex unit, composed of biotic and a-biotic elements (living organisms and their environment), and linked through the exchange of energy, materials, and information—has developed as the key concept within a new ecological approach. Ecology is now simply defined as 'the study of ecosystems' (Boughey 1971: 4) and priority is given to analysis of the 'functioning' of nature by marginalizing the study of its manifestations. The systems theoretical approach starts from the basic assumption that ecosystems are self-regulating and tend to keep an equilibrium, which however, under certain circumstances, can be disturbed. Human beings are recognized as the main factors of disturbance: as biotic element man is part of nature, but endowed with reason he also transcends and masters nature.

The perspective of *cybernetics*, the science of engineering feedback mechanisms, brought a further dimension into the concept of ecology and enlarged the idea of humanity's manipulative capacity in respect of nature. Now, systems theory 'aims at control of the second order; it strives for controlling (self-)control' (Sachs 1992: 32). The mechanisms of regulation by which a system responds to changes in its environment are now seen as open to conditioning, so that the

---

[1] For a discussion of ecology as science and concept, see Nennen 1991.

responsiveness of the system itself gets altered. 'Looking at nature in terms of self-regulating systems, therefore, implies either the intention to gauge nature's overload capacity or the aim of adjusting her feedback mechanisms through human intervention' (Sachs 1992: 32).

The new systems approach, promising a yet unknown controlling and manipulative capacity over nature, dominated ecology since the end of the 1940s. A few years later, the first environmental hazards shocked the world: smog in England (1952), radioactive fallouts in New York as the result of atomic tests in the Nevada desert (1953), oil pollution in the world's oceans. Subsequently, perspectives on nature in the industrial countries underwent a radical change. Basically, an economization of nature came about; nature was no longer a 'free' economic good but an additional cost factor, alongside soil and labour. The experience that nature 'hits back' drew attention to the social costs of industrial production (e.g. the need for elimination of dangerous wastes, preventive measures against pollution) which influence the marginal utility calculation. On the other hand a whole industry of eco-technology developed out of the necessity of environmental control and protection, so that the ecological critique of industrial production finally resulted in the establishment of new industrial sectors.

The emerging environmental problems also resulted in a moral commitment, in a feeling of responsibility among many towards nature. The 1960s and early 1970s were characterized by a rise of environmental consciousness in Europe and in the USA. In 1968 the Club of Rome was constituted, and during the following years several environmental organizations like Greenpeace and Friends of the Earth were founded. The first 'National Environmental Teach In' ('Earth Day'), held in New York in 1970, gained worldwide publicity as a milestone in the history of environmental protection. International conferences were summoned, starting with the UNESCO Conference for the Protection of Biosphere in 1968, followed by the UN Conference on the Human Environment in Stockholm in 1972. In the same year the Club of Rome published its study, *The Limits to Growth* (Meadows *et al.* 1972), and caused a great stir throughout the world.

This study was based on a method called 'system dynamics', invented by J.W. Forrester of the Massachusetts Institute of Technology (MIT), which was said to be able to analyse and predict the behaviour of complex systems. Forrester created a 'world model' characterized by 'the five basic factors that determine, and therefore, ultimately limit, growth on this planet—population, agricultural production, natural resources, industrial production, and pollution' (Meadows *et al.* 1972: 11f.). The complex data and mathematical equations in the world model have been presented in several publications; in *Limits to Growth* the main conclusions were summarized. First, the argument went, if the present growth trends in world population, industrialization, pollution, food production, and resource depletion remain unchanged, the limits to growth on this planet will be reached within a hundred years. Second, it is possible to alter these growth trends and establish a condition of ecological and economic stability that is sustainable far into the future. Third, if the international community decides to strive fo change, the sooner they begin working to attain it the greater will be the chances of success (Meadows *et al.* 1972: 23f.).

These findings resulted in an overwhelming response and had substantial effect. In various regions of the world people acknowledged nature was finite and started to critically survey human intervention. The environment was on everyone's lips and an environmental or 'ecological' consciousness was soon evident on a global scale. However, this boom in ecological thinking was not simply grounded in the apocalyptic character of the predictions of the Club of Rome, but in the concept of ecology itself. The concept now encompassed three different levels of justification with reference to the realms of science, aesthetics, and ethics (Nennen 1991: 95ff.). It therefore offered multiple ways of identification and commitment.

The *scientific* argument within the revised and enlarged concept is based on instrumental reason and an anthropocentric idea of ecology. Man is the only subject to which the environment, or the whole of nature, is related.[2] The environment is mainly seen as an aspect of utility and has to be protected to secure the survival of mankind as

[2] This concept of ecology is opposed by the environmental theory (*Umweltlehre*) of Jakob v. Uexküll, which rejects anthropocentrism and relates a specific environment to a particular subject (Nennen 1991: 87).

well as guarantee a certain quality of life. The scientific concept of ecology—and this is important—envisions nature as a global phenomenon. It relates nature to mankind as a whole and does not segregate a particular environment for a particular people. Ecological responsibility in this context means the ability to predict, calculate, control, and manage natural processes, to anticipate and prevent damages or 'repair' previous damages. Ecology, in its system theoretical understanding, has become a discipline of crisis management and functions as legitimation (not as critique) of technology and industrial production. The domination of and mastery over nature is constitutive for ecology as natural science: it will not come to an end but will be intensified and enlarged, for example by the invention of genetic sciences and biotechnologies.

In relation to aesthetic and ethical levels of justification, only *nature*, not the environment, stands at the centre of argument and the problem at stake is the conceptual shift in the perception of nature within occidental history and philosophy. An earlier metaphysical concept of nature which assumed the indivisibility of external and human nature as well as the interconnectedness of discourses relating to *verum, bonum,* and *pulchrum,* has now been replaced by a conception in which nature is perceived as de-contextualized and as the sole object of scientific knowledge and instrumental action (Schäfer 1982; Zimmermann 1982).[3] The development from Platonic cosmology to the Copernican revolution is believed to have provided the ground for the modern scientific worldview favouring the epistemological subject and the objectification of nature. Instrumental action has gained in significance at the expense of other forms of human practice and become rational action *par excellence.* Other approaches to nature, varying from empirical science and technology, can now only claim a subjective meaning. 'Superseding the metaphysical concept of nature by the scientific one leaves behind a vacuum which is now explicitly filled by a more differentiated aesthetic concept of nature' (Zimmermann 1982: 130, my translation). In the history of ideas, the paradigmatic example of this aesthetic appropriation of

---

[3] Another approach for grasping the changing perception of nature is the confrontation of the mythic and the modern worldviews, outlined by J. Habermas (1981).

nature is Romanticism. A pantheistic identification transfigures
nature into a subject (*natura naturans*) which reveals itself to human
subjects through the medium of aesthetic experience and can be
made intersubjectively understandable through aesthetic representation (*mimesis*). The arts of painting, poetry and gardening reflect an
aesthetic approach to nature, manifest most clearly in the representation of landscape as beautiful and sublime. Mimesis serves as a
way of criticizing and replacing instrumental reason, seeking the
reconciliation of man with nature.

The aesthetic content within the concept of ecology claims to represent an alternative approach to, and an alternative form of, appropriation of nature and demands the recognition of expressive validity
claims (to use a notion of Habermas). As a critique of instrumental
reason, the aesthetic argument is closely linked with ethics, which, in
the context of ecological discourse, is far more prominent and more
widely discussed.[4] Recent philosophy has taken up the challenge of
reflecting on ecological *ethics*, and on the underlying question of how
to change man's relation to nature:

> Nature, as a human responsibility... is a new phenomenon ethical
> theory must ponder upon. (Jonas 1987: 27, my translation)

> Is the responsibility of action, even if it belongs to the realm of human
> ends, limited to the relationship between humans or must it—rather—
> also include the relationship of human beings to themselves as natural
> beings, and thus to nature as such? (Schäfer 1982: 40, my translation)

To reflect on ecological (or environmental) ethics and work out an
agenda for moral action is a task tackled not only by philosophers but
by academics in other disciplines, and by politicians and green activists as well. Accordingly, the spectrum of thought and outlines
which constitute the debate is broad based. All arguments start by
questioning the subjugation of nature and the priority given to

---

[4] 'Aesthetic experience anticipates a social condition, where the human relationship to nature is no longer primarily—or even exclusively—determined by
the interest in scientific objectivation, technical control, and economic
exploitation. A new aesthetic of nature can thus, in the last instance, only be
developed in conjunction with a new ethic of nature' (Zimmermann 1982: 147,
my translation).

instrumental reason; the arguments differ in their evaluation of the extent to which instrumental reason is permissible or inescapable, and how it should be corrected or modified.

The most radical forms of environmental ethics have been formulated in the USA. Radical environmentalism or eco-radicalism is characterized by M.N. Lewis (1992) as 'a multi-stranded philosophy' which contains *deep ecologies* (forms of 'anti-humanist anarchism' and 'primitivism'), *views from the classical left* ('humanistic eco-anarchism' and 'eco-marxism') and *ecofeminism*.[5] Lewis says all eco-radicals agree that human society in its present form is 'utterly unsustainable and must be reconstructed according to an entirely different socioeconomic logic' (Lewis 1992: 2). Deep ecology seems to be the dominant and most influential version. It seeks a new harmony with nature by denying modern technology and other elements of modern civilization. Its arguments often draw heavily on particular constructions of pre-modern societies, to which an unalienated and harmonious relation with nature, based on a pre-reflexive form of responsibility, is attributed. Deep ecology also may refer to 'Eastern' religions (Buddhism, Taoism, Hinduism) to propagate a non-destructive and conservationist manner of dealing with nature, which is said to be conveyed in such religious teachings. The romanticizing vision of 'deep ecology' sees nature as 'the other subject' and calls for communicative relations between man and nature, transcending instrumental action.[6]

Ecofeminism has its roots in the USA. It gained wider popularity in the late 1980s, especially in India. Ecofeminism in the context of the Indian debate was conceptualized in part by Vandana Shiva, together with the German scholar Maria Mies. Their project idealizes and essentializes women's relation to nature, which is seen as the embodiment of a female principle (Shiva 1988: 38). Conceptually eco-feminism also holds patriarchy responsible for subjugating nature and women and converting them into resources. The argument is that the development of modern science, with its 'reductionist or mechanical paradigm', did not emerge as a liberating force for all

---

[5] For a history of environmentalism and environmental ethics, see Guha (2000) and Guha and Martinez-Alier (1998).

[6] Sunderlal Bahuguna's 'spiritual ecology' can be interpreted as a particular form of 'deep ecology' (see Chapter 5).

human beings, but 'as a Western, male-oriented and patriarchal pro-
jection, which necessarily entailed the subjugation of both nature
and women' (Mies and Shiva 1993: 22). It is women who bear responsibility for opposing the patriarchal scientific Western project
and develop a new vision for a new society which should be 'ecologically
sound, non-exploitative, just, non-patriarchal, self-sustaining' (Mies
and Shiva 1993: 297). Mies and Shiva call their utopia the 'subsistence
perspective' or the 'survival perspective'. From this perspective, human
interaction with nature will be based on 'respect, co-operation and
reciprocity' and man's (literal and metaphoric) domination of nature
'replaced by the recognition that humans are part of nature, that
nature has her own subjectivity' (Mies and Shiva 1993: 319). Ecofeminism is directed at the 'activation' of what has been or was being
construed as 'passive'. It does not reject all science and instrumentality,
but only its patriarchal distortion. The political agenda of ecofeminism
is the creation of 'a science and knowledge that nurtures, rather than
violates, nature's sustainable systems' (Mies and Shiva 1993: 34). This
science is meant to learn from traditional knowledge preserved by
women, especially in the Third World.

Other lines of argument which look for ethics and a new relationship
with nature do not assume the revival of 'pre-modern' ways of
thinking and acting. One way forward that has been suggested is to
seek an *alternative form of reason* which should replace conventional
reason (Bookchin 1996), the other way is to find an *additional form
of reason* (Adorno 1992), which can correct instrumentality and the
subjugation of nature. A third way, pursued by Hans Jonas (1987) and
Hans Küng (1996), argues the need for a new theology (implicitly in
the case of Jonas, explicitly in the case of Küng).

Murray Bookchin, one of the pioneers of the American ecological
movement (though according to Lewis of only marginal influence)
emphasizes in his book *Philosophy of Social Ecology* (1996) those
strands of European philosophy which, he says, have been sidelined
by instrumental and analytical reason ('conventional reason').[7] Relating his meditations to Greek philosophy as well as to Hegel and

[7] Lewis categorizes M. Bookchin's approach as 'humanistic eco-anarchism'
and subsumes it under 'views from the classical left' (Lewis 1992: 31). He argues
that the explicit humanism of Bookchin's philosophy is repellent to most

Engels, he presents dialectical reason 'shorn of both its idealism and its materialism' (1996: 15) as a form of thought which can be seen as naturalistic and ecological while simultaneously accepting the distinctive place of humanity and its right to work on itself and on external nature. In 'dialectic naturalism' the reality of a thing or phenomenon embraces not only its being but also its becoming, its potentiality; and therefore the approach provides a framework for ethical judgement: the 'what-should-be' serves as an ethical criterion for judging the truth or validity of an objective 'what-is' (1996: 24).

The dialectical perspective on natural evolution involves for Bookchin the 'vision of an ever-increasing wholeness, fullness, and richness of differentiation and subjectivity' (1996: 20). Humanity's capacity to bear moral responsibility, to intervene and alter the world, is itself a product of natural evolution (Bookchin calls this 'second nature'). But humanity as it *now* exists has not fully developed its potential, it 'is *not* nature rendered self-conscious'. Therefore the future of the globe 'depends overwhelmingly on whether second nature can be transcended in a new system of social and organic conciliation' (1996: 33), which Bookchin calls 'free nature'—'a nature that would diminish the pain and suffering that exists both in first and second nature' (1996: 33).

Theodor W. Adorno, well-known leading member of the 'Frankfurt School', refers to aesthetic theory and the notion of 'mimesis' to outline his vision for reconciling human subject and objectified nature. Mimesis or mimetical art is an alternative way of cognition (*Erkenntnis*), a way of approaching nature by distancing oneself from the *hybris* of mastering nature. Mimesis is seen by Adorno as human capacity which is not subjected to but dialectically connected with instrumental reason—as not intended to replace but to correct instrumentality.[8]

American eco-radicals. Because of Bookchin's attempt to carve out an ecological content within Western philosophy, his ideas are presented here in considerable detail.

[8] See Adorno 1992. Albrecht Wellmer states: 'Art and philosophy are the two spheres of mind, in which the mind, due to the linkage of the rational with the mimetic moment, cracks the crust of reification' (1985: 12, my translation).

The philosopher Hans Jonas calls for an ethic of responsibility (*Verantwortungsethik*) suited to a technological civilization. Following the lines of Kant he words a new imperative of responsibility: 'Act in such a way that the effects of your action are compatible with the permanence of genuine human life.' He refers to the duty of ancestors ('*Pflicht der Urheber*') towards the 'being' of their descendants ('*Sosein der Nachkommen*'). The crucial statement of his ethic of obligation to the future ('*Ethik der Zukunftsverpflichtung*') is that we must here and now seek to control our power over nature which, in contemporary technological and scientific civilization, has taken on a life of its own. For Jonas this seems to be possible only with the rejection of all forms of utopia (the immodest goal par excellence), which is marked by 'Promethean presumption' and is essentially geared to progress. Protecting ourselves from the misuse of our power requires awe and fear in the religious sense. 'Only awe, inasmuch as it reveals to us something "sacred", that is something we must under no circumstances offend against (and this can be visible even without a positive religion) will also save us from violating the present for the sake of the future' (Jonas 1987: 393, my translation).

Another form of an ethic of responsibility—explicitly based on religion—has been presented by Hans Küng (1996). His ethical maxim for the third millennium is the responsibility of man to this planet ('*Verantwortung des Menschen für diesen Planeten*') (Küng 1996: 238). To carry out this responsibility, man has to become more than he is: he must become more human (Küng 1992: 240). Küng wants to harmonize Jonas's concept of an 'ethic of responsibility' with the utopian 'principle of hope' ('*Prinzip Hoffnung*') of Ernst Bloch. The new ethic he imagines has to be absolute and universal, it has to be a 'global ethics' ('*Weltethos*'). Its ultimate grounding cannot be looked for in philosophy but is to be found in world religions relating to a final and supreme reality (the absolute, God). For Küng, a global ethics does not presuppose a single world culture or world religion—it can be founded on fundamentally shared premises:

A global ethical stance, a world ethics, is nothing other than the necessary minimum of common human values, criteria and basic attitudes. Or, more precisely: World ethics is the fundamental consensus on binding values, incontestable criteria and fundamental attitudes, which can be accepted by all religions irrespective of their doctrinal differences, and also be shared by non-believers. (Küng 1996: 250, my translation)

These analytic dissections of 'ecology' reveal the currently rich and ambiguous character of the concept. Ecology encompasses aspects and attitudes of instrumentality and goal-attainment, emotionalism, expressiveness, morality, and caring (*Sorge*), but outwardly it has the image and prestige of a natural science. Ecology, in its ambiguity, is supposed to function as universal guideline for action and as yardstick for judging the interpretations and actions of others. Under the appearance of scientific objectivity, the holistic and often anti-modern understandings encompassed within ecology allow us to re-legitimize metaphysics and satisfy a desire for resisting instrumental reason, as also to authoritatively prescribe ways of interaction between humans and nature.[9] These ambiguities of ecology may explain why the concept came so easily into conflict with the dominant and popular paradigm of progress and development, creating a new challenge to that paradigm. From the early 1970s, ecology and development became two inseparably linked but contradictory key concepts continuously discussed in politics, economics, and academic circles.

4.2 Development as Concept and Praxis

Development theorists have identified 'development' as a particularly Western concept. Gilbert Rist (1997) traces its origins back to the European ancient world and to early Christian thinking. While in these periods a cyclical understanding of development prevailed, the philosophy of Enlightenment saw development as a linear, teleological process of cognitive and moral perfection in both individual and society.[10] The economic side of this process was stressed in the work of

[9] See also W. Sachs on ecology: 'The scientific term has turned into a worldview. And as worldview, it carries the promise of reuniting what has been fragmented, of healing what has been torn apart, in short of caring for the whole' (Sachs 1992: 32).

[10] For Aristotle nature—*physis*—denotes the essence of (biological and social) things which holds, as such, a source of movement, leading to a final state which corresponds with its perfect form. Thereafter, it fades and dies. According

Adam Smith (*The Wealth of Nations*, 1776). Smith presented 'the progress of opulence' as an 'order of things which *necessity* imposes' and which 'is promoted by the natural inclination of man' (Rist 1997: 40).

  Progress and development became key concepts of the evolutionism which flourished in the nineteenth century. For social evolutionists, the history of mankind was a sequence of progressive stages, which were defined in economic (Marx) or socio-cultural (Lewis Henry Morgan) terms. Although all societies were supposed to follow the same trajectory, the dynamics of development were claimed to be different. The most developed stage was said to be represented by the West to which a leading historical role was attributed. But in both Enlightenment philosophy and social evolutionism history unfolds its potentialities in an immanent and natural process of *intransitive* character. The development paradigm changed fundamentally when development came to be imagined as intentional praxis and thus as a *transitive* concept. The question when this conceptual shift took place is controversial. In the view of Cowen and Shenton (2000) it dates back to the philosophical and economical debates and practices of nineteenth-century Europe, whereas for the majority of development theorists it is a more recent event. For the latter development started with the end of World War II and is directed to the states and societies of the so-called Third World.[11] Especially

---

to ancient European ideas, growth cannot continue infinitely, for growing without limits would mean to be always and by definition incomplete and imperfect. The ancient concept of development—from birth to decay—was a cyclical one, and in the social realm it was bound to a particular local, national, or imperial history. The Christian theological history formulated by Augustinus in the fourth century still followed the cyclical idea; but as a history of salvation it was constructed as a single cycle—from creation to the end of time. It was also extended to the whole of humankind.

  [11] Cowen and Shenton argue that the transitive concept of development came up in the nineteenth century as a reaction to the social and political problems of industrialization and the politics of *laissez faire*, and was linked with the idea of *trusteeship*. Contemporary theoretical thinkers in the field of economics and philosophy came to the conclusion that the idea of progress (as objective, natural process) lost all its persuasiveness in view of the market and its un-

in the process of decolonization, development advanced into a powerful narrative and was a decisive factor in the restructuring of international relations, which was deeply linked with the emergence of the United States and the Soviet Union as new economic and political powers.

A number of development theorists (e.g. Gilbert Rist, Arturo Escobar, Gustavo Esteva, Wolfgang Sachs) regard the programmatic speech of the American President H. Truman in 1949 as the crucial event for the establishment of a new world order. Truman declared economic growth as key to global prosperity and peace, adding: 'We must embark on a bold new program for making the benefits of our scientific advances and industrial progress available for the improvement and growth of underdeveloped areas' (cited in Esteva 1992: 6). This new political programme, notwithstanding the derision it attracted from the Left, had far-reaching consequences:

- Economic development was equated with economic growth. The level of economic production, measured by Gross National Product (GNP) and GNP per capita, became the prime indicator for progress and marked the stage of development of a particular society.

---

regulated competition as well as the social disorder which characterized the capitalistic system. They asked for constructive forces (the state, the bank and bankers) who would be able to intervene with a regulative hand, working for the prosperity of all: 'No longer was development something that occurred during a period of history; it was the means whereby the present epoch might be transformed into another superior order through the actions of those who were *entrusted* with the future of society' (Cowen and Shenton 2000: 34). Primarily directed to one's own society, development as intentional praxis had become the key element of the imperial project.

It has been controversially discussed how far colonialism can be interpreted as a particular form of development. The colonial reality which makes a hierarchical divide into dominant and dominated societies perpetuates and reinforces direct economic and political dependencies, contradicting the idea of development. According to Gilbert Rist (1997), colonialism has to be understood as a transitory period, in which economic exploitation goes along with paternalistic attitudes and the mission to 'civilize' the indigenous people.

- North–South relations were no longer primarily characterized by political dependencies and considered along hierarchical categories of colonizers and colonized, or as subordination of colony to metropolis. Developed and underdeveloped states were equal *de jure*, but not *de facto*.
- International (global) economic and financial interconnections replaced political dominance as a unifying force. Economic and political interests as well as the claim to 'civilize' others merged in the concept of economic growth, which alone was said to promise wealth, prosperity, and a 'good life' for all.
- The idea of development went along with a restructuring of geopolitical space. This becomes obvious in terms like First and Third World, North–South, Centre–Periphery.
- Development received a clear transitive meaning. It could be interpreted as a 'particular universalism', as in the work of Bruno Latour, that is, *one* society is able to extend to all the others the historically constructed values in which it believes because they are inbuilt into relationships of power. In this context, development is seen as an altruistic undertaking and Western societies, above all the United States, are represented as agents of development.[12]
- The majority of non-Western cultures and societies, representing a diversity of forms and perspectives, are categorized as *underdeveloped*, thus causing them to be subsumed under a homogenizing and devaluing notion. With that these societies lose their particularity, they are denied the ability to argue options and alternative forms of human existence.

With Truman, development and underdevelopment were established all the same as key concepts in structuring the international order. Development as morally based intentional praxis gained status as 'social imaginary' and as the dominant and powerful discourse. Arturo Escobar describes development as 'a historically singular experience,

---

[12] Humanity is seen as resembling a 'family': 'Only by helping the least fortunate of its members to help themselves [can] the human family achieve the decent, satisfying life that is the right of all people' (Truman, cited in Rist 1997: 72).

the creation of a domain of thought and action' which is defined by three axes:

> the *forms of knowledge* that refer to it and through which it comes into being and is elaborated into objects, concepts, theories, and the like; the *system of power* that regulates its practice; and the *forms of subjectivity* fostered by this discourse, those through which people come to recognize themselves as developed and underdeveloped. The ensemble of forms found along these axes constitutes development as a discursive formation, giving rise to an efficient apparatus that systematically relates forms of knowledge and techniques of power. (Escobar 1995: 10, emphasis mine)

Development has thus become a discursive formation in the Foucauldian sense. Although it is possible to follow different approaches of development and debate its forms, it is impossible to call the existence of the notion of development *as such* into question: it is not possible now to think without engaging with 'development'. During the following decades, from the 1950s until the 1980s, definitions, policies, and strategies of development changed, but the basic assumption— gaining prosperity and wealth through economic growth—remained.

Economic growth through industrialization was the core idea of the first development decades (1950s and 1960s: see Rostow 1960). This was expected to lead quasi-automatically to general social improvement. In the aftermath of decolonialization, development thinking began to include concepts of political and social modernization (democracy, nation-building, entrepreneurship, an achievement orientation), and so-called 'traditional' social structures and relations were pejoratively described as 'obstacles' on the way to modernity. The second phase of development (1970–80) was marked by a deliberate revision of previous concepts and strategies. For the first time, development as an originally Western project came under critical inspection and concepts of alternative development emerged as part of the public discourse, opening up possibilities for a participatory approach. Attention was paid to indigenous ideas of development as well as to gender perspectives. According to Esteva, this second development phase was *de facto* characterized by dispersion: 'Major problems', like environment, population, hunger, women, habitat or employment, were successively brought to the forefront. Every 'problem' followed for a time an independent career, concentrating both public and institutional attention' (Esteva 1992: 14). The process of rethinking development was, on the one hand, a reaction to the demands of the countries of the South.[13] On the other hand the West realized that all its efforts to develop the 'underdeveloped' could not eliminate poverty. In 1975 the Dag Hammarskjöld Foundation published a report known by the title *'What now'?* in which the existing understanding of development was critically analysed and an alternative perspective propagated. Development, said the report, is not simply an economic process but a complex whole which has to arise endogenously within each society. *There is thus no universal formula of development* (Rist 1997: 155), and development cannot be reduced to a simple imitation of the Western trajectory. The prominent target of development should instead be seen as satisfying the essential needs of the poorest sections of the population, who should rely mainly on their own resources and capacities. Subsequently, in the second half of the 1970s, a new development strategy emerged. The ILO Conference on Employment, Income Distribution and Social Progress (1976), together with the World Bank, offered the Basic Needs Approach to achieve a minimum standard of living in all countries, and UNESCO promoted the concept of endogenous development.

Although critiques and a new rhetoric were flourishing, and although processes of revision and attempts to establish new policies

---

[13] Already in the 1960s *dependencia* theorists had criticized the integration of 'Third World' economies into the world market and identified in 'dependent accumulation' as the main reason for the 'development of underdevelopment'. Representatives of the *dependencia* school asked for a dissociation from the world market. Another trajectory of alternative development was based on the concept of self-reliance. This was, for example, propagated as a national programme in Tanzania. Earlier, Mahatma Gandhi had developed a similar vision for India. In 1974 'Third World' countries put pressure on the General Assembly of the United Nations to pass a declaration demanding a 'New International Economic World Order' (NIEO). This new order, they argued, should be based on 'equity, sovereign equality, interdependence, common interest and cooperation among all States irrespective of their economic and social systems' (cited in Rist 1997: 145).

and strategies were undertaken, the gulf between the theory and praxis of development policy widened. At the end of the 1970s 'development' was widely believed a failure and politicians and intellectuals spoke of the 'end of development'. From the middle of the 1980s, 'a new development ethos' (Esteva 1992) evolved. It focused on the concept of *sustainable development*—a concept which achieved what formerly seemed impossible: the reconciliation of two conflicting ideologies and realms of action, the 'wedding' (Sachs 1992, 1999) of environment with development. In 1983 the UN World Commission for Environment and Development (WCED) was brought into being under the Norwegian Prime Minister Gro Harlem Brundtland. The commission was advised to formulate a 'global programme for change' to secure the future of mankind. In its report, *Our Common Future*, released in 1987, the experts presented 'sustainable development' as the global key concept: 'Sustainable development is development that meets the needs of the present without compromising the ability of future generations to meet their own needs' (WCED 1987: 43).[14] The ideology of development seemed now to have legitimacy if natural resources were used in a sustainable manner, thus preserving the life basis of future generations.

The attractiveness and success of the concept of 'sustainable development' are grounded in its ambivalent character. '[T]he Brundtland Report incorporated concern for the environment into the concept of development by erecting "sustainable development" as the conceptual roof for both *violating and healing the environment*' (Sachs 1992: 29, emphasis mine). Although the new concept virtually invited politicians, planners, intellectuals, and the public to question the development ideology and hegemonic values of the West, they very largely failed in this. Development policies and strategies did not undergo any considerable change; only attempts were made to limit the ecological damage caused by them.

The concept of sustainable development seems to offer certain benefits to those living in the countries of the North and to the elites

[14] The term 'sustainability', in German originally 'Nachhaltigkeit', derives from forestry and demands that human beings maintain nature, for it is the basis of their life ('erhaltende Nutzung der natürlichen Lebensgrundlagen durch den Menschen'; Busch-Lüthy, cited in Messner 1993: 41).

of the South. First, environmental attention no longer focuses only on industrial pollution and the exploitation of finite resources but instead includes the worldwide destruction of renewable resources (forest, soil, flora and fauna), thus globalizing responsibility for the protection of nature. The present state of the environment, which obviously results from the global subjugation of man and nature in the name of technological and social progress initiated in the North but also adopted in the South, is being transformed into the global and collective responsibility of mankind. Most of the blame is now being put on indigenous cultures—on people living in a particular habitat—and their 'poverty', because 'Poverty reduces people's capacity to use resources in a sustainable manner; it intensifies pressure on the environment . . .' (WCED 1987: 49–50). From this point of view, local inhabitants are perceived as *intruders* and the preservation of nature becomes possible only by limiting and regulating local people's access to nature and natural resources.[15]

Second, development is interpreted as the 'satisfaction of needs' of the current as well as future generations. But immediately the question arises: Who defines these needs? Do different cultures have different needs? Are people allowed to increase their needs or must they limit them? And by what criteria? It seems quite obvious that those living in the industrialized countries as well as elites in the South do not intend to change their present opulent and resource-consuming lifestyle. But safeguarding any standard of life, and more so increasing consumption, presuppose controlling the development of others. The right to develop the same needs as people in the industrialized countries and striving for similar satisfaction is often denied to Third World cultures. Two connected arguments are brought forward in this context: catching up with the Western world seems impossible because it would result in unbearable environmental stress *for all* (pollution of biosphere, destruction of forests, rapid decrease of mineral resources). Further, catching up with the Western world is not on the agenda of the majority of Third World people because of fundamental differences in and the modesty of their needs. An

---

[15] See also the critique of Guha and Martinez-Alier, who argue that wealth is a greater threat to the environment than poverty (1998: 59). This critique is developed most fully in relation to India *vis-à-vis* the USA in Guha 2006.

idealized construction of so-called traditional societies—which are said to be distinguished from modern societies by their self-sufficiency, their limited needs, and their supposedly 'ecological' relation to nature—is deployed to legitimize existing economic disparities between North and South.

The promise to protect nature and environment, included in the concept of sustainable development, did not lead to any fundamental revision of the dominant development ideology. Rather, to a great extent it helped play down the problems which arise for man and nature if sustainable development is accepted:

> The existing system has taken the word 'sustainability' to its heart, and now employs it at every turn, but in a context which deprives it of its meaning. For sustainability is the most basic form of conservatism. It means not taking from the earth, from the world, from society, from each other, from life, more than we give back. But when industrial society uses the word, it means the sustaining of itself, no matter what the cost. It means sustaining privilege, sustaining poverty, sustaining abuse of the earth, sustaining inequality, sustaining starvation, sustaining violence . . . (Blackwell and Seabrock, cited in Rahnema 2000: 307)

The concept of sustainable development neither creates a world in which the rights of nature are fully acknowledged, nor helps to build a new sociality of economic justice on a global scale. Does this mean that, finally, development has been unmasked as a powerful and destructive myth? Do we live in the age of post-development, as some development theorists like A. Escobar (1995), G. Rist (1997), W. Sachs (1999), and J. Nederveen Pieterse (2001) suggest? These authors, who deal critically with development ideology in a historical perspective, argue that the period of post-development is not only marked by critique, scepticism, and disillusionment, but also by the existence of *alternative forms of development* or *alternatives to development*. Regionally (locally) and culturally, varying imaginaries of the 'good life' have started to replace, or at least challenge, the hegemonic development discourse. The erstwhile singular field of those responsible for development processes has now become pluralized and includes a multiplicity of social actors at local, micro- and macro-regional, national, and international levels. Culturally diverse and economically different ways of appropriating nature have challenged its one-dimensional perception as an exploitable resource. Different conceptual frameworks have also been created to deal with the question of development in an alternative way.

Among these scholarly approaches, 'political ecology' is one of the most well known and well established.[16] 'Political ecology' concentrates on linkages between the state of the environment and the capitalist logic of growth. Recent modifications of the concept analyse social and political institutions operating at local and trans-local levels, accentuating their interrelationship and power relations, especially with regard to environmental policy and resource management. They give attention to local actors and their diverse activities (political parties, social movements, everyday resistance) and ask questions about the relationship between civil society and its attitude towards the environment. They try to identify and discuss different and often conflicting environmental discourses existing in a particular society (see Peet and Watts 1996).

Another rather promising approach tries to give the development debate a new direction by including an ethical dimension. Development ethics acknowledges human beings as culturally different and thus having different needs, capacities, opportunities and perspectives. Development ethics has gained prominence through the work of Martha Nussbaum and Amartya Sen. Both these authors argue that development neither has a value as such nor is value-neutral. They understand development as *value-relative:* 'without some idea of ends that are themselves external to the development process and in terms of which the process may be assessed, we cannot begin to say what changes are to count as development' (Nussbaum and Sen 1989: 299). Ends and values which should guide the development process are not separate from particular ideas of the 'good life' and therefore are only to be defined through the experiences of the people concerned. Sen pleads for a concept of development which attests to individuals

[16] Political ecology was already established in the 1970s (Wolf 1972). It gained importance with the studies of Piers Blaikie and Harold Brookfield (1985, 1987). These authors discussed local forms of land use and resource utilization as well as the degradation of resources by taking into consideration social, economic, and political contexts at regional, national, and international levels.

and communities the right to define their own ends, to expand their capabilities as well as decision-making power and agency. By his 'capabilities approach' Sen connects the ethical dimension with the political demand for entitlements: Given the functional relation between the entitlements of persons over goods and their capabilities, economic development can be described as the expansion of people's entitlements and of the capabilities enjoyed by the use of these entitlements.[17] From the perspective of development ethics, the question of ends and means (what should happen and how it should happen) does not, in the first instance, address politicians and planners but the people concerned, thus being a request that people come together in a moral dialogue.

Development ethics, dealing with the future of individuals and societies, is complementary to ecological or environmental ethics, which is directed to nature. Both ethics focus on the question: *What should be?* However, as against development ethics which emphasizes local perspectives and experiences, ecological ethics is still oriented towards global solutions. Because the answer to ethical questions—in the realms of both development and ecology—cannot be found by presenting a singular model postulating universal validity, ecological ethics also needs to undergo a process of 'regionalization' or even 'localization'.

Development ethics and environmental ethics have to be reconciled and made to serve a complementary function when addressing the issue of development. In the next section I illustrate how development has been discussed in India and the ways in which ecological considerations have become part of the agenda.

4.3 Discourses on Ecology and Development in India

With independence in 1947, the agenda was set for India's political and economic future. Under Nehru India took a path to modernity

---

[17] 'Entitlement refers to the set of alternative commodity bundles that a person can command in a society using the totality of rights and opportunities that he or she faces' (Sen 1984: 497). Entitlement refers to the opportunities of exchange (*exchange entitlements*), but also to property (land) (Sen 1984: 31). For the capabilities approach, see also Sen 2000.

which neither followed Western capitalism nor simply reproduced the socialist model. The Indian modernization project was built on three pillars—democracy, secularism, and development (Kothari 1998: 25)—and held together by nationalism and a nationalist ideology. Development, in the first years after independence, was synonymous with large-scale industrialization and economic growth based on science and rational planning, the ultimate goal being to catch up with the rich and powerful nations of the world. This vision of development and modernity was linked to the ideals of ending 'all exploitation of nation by nation and class by class' (Nehru 1964: 28) and providing equal distribution, equally high living standards, and material wealth to all.

Although development was expected to bring benefits to all strata of the Indian population, it very soon exposed itself as a process of exploitation and violence against man and nature. Claude Alvarez (1992) identifies two phases of industrial development in India. In the first phase (which took shape in the colonial period) emphasis was laid on capital-intensive industrialization and urbanization in metropolitan regions. The rural areas had been encouraged to concentrate on the production of raw materials and to purchase finished industrial goods from the cities. This resulted in the decline of village-based industries (the local production, for example, of textiles, oil, and tools), and thus of local means of subsistence. People were forced to migrate to cities, increasing the country's unemployment and destitution. The second phase of development was characterized by economic 'penetration' into backward areas and the active appropriation of the rural environment for purposes of industrialization. Large factories were located closer to the resources they exploited (e.g. mining and steel production), disregarding the fact that land, forest, and water were the life bases of the local (often tribal) population. The resources and lifestyles of local residents were severely affected, if not destroyed. Conflicts over resources arose especially where large-scale projects (dam construction, open cast mining) required the displacement of large numbers of people (see e.g. Fernandes and Thukral 1989; Baviskar 1995; Dreze et al. 1997; Parasuraman 1999).

The emphatic discourse of economic growth and industrialization dominant in the 1950s lost its vigour when it became obvious that large parts of the population would not profit under the existing development strategy. With priority given to industrialization the agricultural sector had been significantly neglected. Neither land reforms nor structural adjustments and technological investments in favour of the rural population had taken place (Parekh 1995: 48). Nehru and his government started to rethink their modernization project and more attention was given to rural people, who still constituted the large majority of the population. With its integrated 'community development programme' the state now attempted to reach rural areas. It was later replaced by the system of *panchayati raj*, consisting of local bodies providing self-governance. In the 1960s the small and middle peasantry became the target group of social engineering projects such as the 'Green Revolution' and the 'White Revolution', which intended to overcome food scarcity. Peasants were no longer seen as representatives of a backward and old-fashioned mode of production, but as rational, calculating agents responding to financial incentives and capable of making proper use of state help and scientific inputs (Parekh 1995: 50).

Yet the different state strategies of rural development did not always fulfil the hopes which politicians and planners had placed on them. Community development programmes which were meant to address the rural population on a broad basis worked for the profit of the propertied classes and led to an increase in social inequality. The capitalization and mechanization of production methods which took place in the course of the 'Green Revolution' further added to structures of inequality; the rich became even more prosperous and the poor faced further impoverishment. In reaction to that the Fifth, Sixth, and Seventh Five Year Plans (1974–9, 1980–5, 1985–90) of the Indian government advised the implementation of a number of special programmes for the uplift of regionally and socially marginalized groups. The important (and still existing) Integrated Rural Development Programme (IRDP) was established 1979/80; it could also be seen as an answer to the 'basic needs approach' of the World Bank (Hazary 1994).

From the late 1980s the issue of development as well as the rhetoric of poverty alleviation and social equality were pushed more and more into the background by the new ideology of 'liberalization'. The state increasingly withdrew its economic influence in favour of a free market economy which was expected to bring technological modernization, greater efficiency of production, and decrease in the influence and power of the bureaucracies. International financial aid (World Bank, IMF) was given only on the condition of privatization and the implementation of structural adjustment programmes. The new economic strategy presented itself as openly anti-egalitarian and supportive of better-off members of the upper and middle classes. The concepts and strategies of liberalization and development have not helped create a more equal and fair society. From inside government and administration, as well as from outside (e.g. non-governmental organizations, intellectuals), critical voices have been heard loud and clear through the 1980s and 1990s. One of the reasons for the continuation of poverty and social inequality is also seen in the centralization of political and economic decision making and in the dependency of the states on the centre. Decentralization has often seemed to be the solution. Those in favour of this approach have demanded '[a] greater degree of decentralization of economic decision-making with an appropriate devolution of financial powers from the centre to the states and further to local bodies so as to further the process of development based on local resources and needs' (M.B. 1989: 1874; see also Minocha 1991: 2488). India's 73rd Constitutional Amendment (1993) was intended to create the formal conditions for political decentralization and participation by establishing a three-tier system of self-governance based on the formation of panchayats at the district, block, and village level (a continuation of Panchayati Raj). In the years following most of India's states amended their laws accordingly and started to reorganize existing structures of self-governance, transferring powers to local bodies. Control over public finance and the preparation of development and finance plans which took into consideration local conditions and needs were defined as the main tasks of panchayats.

Even a couple of years after its establishment, the new system of self-governance could not come up to expectations for three reasons: First, government officers still cling to the top-to-bottom approach. Second, there is a clear gap between duties and responsibilities of bodies of self-governance on the one hand, and their rights and powers on the other (e.g. panchayats still lack financial powers). Third, lacking education, local residents often do not have the knowledge essential for participating in structures of self-governance. Therefore, in practice, the process of decentralization has been only partly successful, and only limited successes have occurred from the promotion of local and regional development.

Discourses of liberalization and decentralization dominant in India in the 1980s and 1990s have started to incorporate or replace the hegemonic development discourse. Lately, another discourse has gained increasing importance in the critical public: the discourse of *alternative development*. This was stirred by the growing consciousness of ecological problems in the country and refers in its normative demands to the ideas and visions of Mahatma Gandhi. Before discussing the alternative development approach, I will briefly turn to the Gandhian imaginary, which has gained global importance as a political and moral guideline for many of those critical of the current world system.

India's path to modernity was never uncontested. After independence, two alternative visions indicated possible directions to the future. The architects of these visions, Gandhi and Nehru, agreed on primary objectives, namely independence and social transformation, but, as is well known, Nehru's vision of modernity entailing catching up with the rich and powerful, overthrew Gandhi's emphasis on tradition and civilizational autarky.[18] Nehru may have won the day in his time and till the 1990s, but currently, in the context of increasing liberalization and inequality, it is Gandhi's critique of consumerism that is enjoying a resurgence. Central to the Gandhian critique is a self-reliant village, 'a complete republic, independent of its neighbours for its own vital wants, and yet interdependent for many others in which dependence is a necessity' (Gandhi 1957: 70). To model such a village seems to be the 'work of a lifetime' and Gandhi called for the *reconstruction* of villages to begin at once and to be organized on a permanent basis (Gandhi 1957: 147).[19]

[18] It is argued that Gandhi thought less on the lines of an East–West opposition than focused on the differences between tradition and modernity (Sharma 1995; Chatterjee 1984).

[19] 'In the village of my dreams', Gandhi wrote, 'the villager will not be dull—he will be all awareness. He will not live like an animal in filth and darkness. Men and women will live in freedom, prepared to face the whole world' (Gandhi, 'Letter to Nehru', cited in Iyer 1986: 286).

Gandhi's village alternative to consumerist development, moreover, implies respectful dealings with nature and thus includes an ecological dimension. For many Indian activists and organizations concerned with environmental issues, the Gandhian utopia seems in fact to comprise the sanest elements that might be modified and incorporated to suit real-world needs today. When development exposed its devastating potential in the 1970s, the destruction of nature—and thus the destruction of the life bases of many tribal and farming communities in different regions of India—came sharply into focus. NGOs and social movements, in particular, brought environmental problems on the agenda and distinguished themselves as leading voices in national and international ecological debates. Pioneering work was, in this respect, undoubtedly done by Chipko as we have seen. However, the most lasting impact has very likely resulted from an initiative of the Centre for Science and Environment (CSE), Delhi. In the early 1980s the Centre published two stirring reports: *The State of India's Environment 1982* (Agarwal, Chopra and Sharma 1982) and *The State of India's Environment 1984–85* (Agarwal and Narain 1985). According to the introduction in the first compilation, the idea of preparing such an environmental report came about when the director of the CSE, Anil Agarwal, came across a short monograph titled *State of Malaysian Environment*. In less than a year the CSE produced its Indian counterpart. An important objective of the editors was to make it a 'citizens' report', a non-governmental but nevertheless authoritative publication which assessed the state of the country's environment. A wide spectrum of individuals and voluntary organizations were involved in the preparation of the report. The guideline for the report was 'to explain how environmental changes were affecting the lives of the people', and the topics which came under closer scrutiny included natural resources (land, water, forests, atmosphere), urban and rural living conditions (habitat, health, energy), the diversity of human ways of life (people), as well as flora and fauna (wildlife). Large-scale projects (dams) and environmental policies (government) came under scrutiny as well.[20] At the end of the first

[20] The topics remained the same in the second report. With the third report, concentrating on floods in India (Agarwal and Chak 1991), the editorial team changed strategy. They decided not to publish comprehensive reports but a series of reports on specific issues. This was supposed to take into account the

report the editors and the main contributors signed 'a statement of shared concern' in which they demanded a 'sustainable egalitarian development' not only for India but for the world, pointing to Gandhi's words: 'There is enough in the world for everyone's need but not enough for everyone's greed'. The CSE reports were published in English, but the first one was also translated into Hindi, Kannada, Malayalam, Marathi, Tamil, and Gujarati. The second report came out simultaneously in Hindi and English. The impact of these reports has been very considerable. Close networks of people and organizations working at the grassroots level as well as in academic and public institutions have been established. One can say without exaggeration that India's prominence in the international ecological debate is seen as a result of the widespread ecological awareness and networking which emerged in the aftermath of the CSE's seminal work.

At the level of the central government, environmental concern has slowly gained ground since the international UN Conference on the Human Environment in Stockholm in 1972. A National Committee on Environmental Planning and Coordination (NCEPC) was set up in India in 1972. In 1980, the Department of Environment was created by the Central Government and together with the NCEPC—now under the abridged name National Committee of Environmental Planning (NCEP)—and the National Eco-Development Board started to manage the country's environment. Several important laws for environmental protection have been enacted since 1972.[21] The 42nd amendment of the Indian Constitution in 1976 established

steady increase of information and allow dealing with an issue in depth. The fourth report (Agarwal and Narain 1997) focused on traditional water harvesting systems. The fifth report (Agarwal, Narain and Sen 1999) is again a comprehensive report with a statistical supplement.

[21] For example: the Wildlife (Protection) Act 1972, the Water (Prevention and Control of Pollution) Act 1974 and the Water (Prevention and Control of Pollution) Cess Act 1977, the Forest Conservation Act 1980, the Air (Prevention and Control of Pollution) Act 1981, the amendment of the Forest Conservation Act 1988. In the 'statistical database' for *The Citizens' Fifth Report* the environmental laws for the periods before 1947, 1947–72, and post-1972 are listed (Agarwal, Narain, and Sen 1999, part 2: 10.5). See also Divan and Rosencranz (2001).

the responsibility of the state as well as of the citizens of India for the protection and improvement of the natural environment.

Since the mid-1970s, as we have seen, voluntary groups have increasingly concentrated on environmental issues and the Indian government has shown some concern for the protection of the environment. Meanwhile ecology and the environment have emerged as a focal point in academic discourses (social and natural sciences) as well.[22] From the 1980s, conferences and publications in these areas of intellectual life have increased very substantially.[23]

The discourse of alternative development which evolved in the 1980s has to be placed in this context of environmentalist thought, development critique, and revival of Gandhian ideas. The alternative development approach starts from a normative-ethical perspective ('a value premise') and puts the well being of all into focus.[24] It criticizes the ethos of consumerism and economic growth as well as global political and economic structures of power and dependence. A strong argument is made against any global model of alternative development, for it is argued that such a counter model will claim universal validity and thus ignore historical and cultural diversity. Alternative development—which could also include alternatives *to*

---

[22] As an indicator I take the internationally renowned Indian journal *Economic and Political Weekly* (*EPW*), which, since its foundation, presents central topics and discussion in the social and economic sciences. Ramachandra Guha mentions an article written by B.B. Vohra dealing with problems of erosion and water logging in 1973 (Guha 1997), but this seems to have been an exception for the time. The first articles concerning environmental issues in the context of the ecological debate were published from 1978 onwards, especially after 1984. Since 1983 Indian forests, forestry, and forest management became an issue, and after 1990 discussions about sustainable development became prominent as well.

[23] A few references to stimulating publications can be given here: Bandyopadhyay, Jayal, Schoettli and Singh 1985; D'Monte 1985; Agarwal, D'Monte, Samarth 1987; Bina Agarwal 1991; Shiva and Bandyopadhyay 1991; Alvares 1992; Gadgil and Guha 1992; A. Pathak 1994; Guha 1994; Baviskar 1995; Arnold and Guha 1995. For a discussion of social-ecological research in India, see the general overview by Ramachandra Guha (1997).

[24] Sheth 1989. The journal *Alternatives* (co-edited by the Centre for the Study of Developing Societies, Delhi) provided a forum for the discussion of problems of alternative development.

development—has necessarily to be in accord with particular socio-historical conditions.

Representatives of the alternative discourse (D.L. Sheth, Rajni Kothari) agree that without a democratic framework and without a theory of action alternative concepts will meet the fate of every utopia. Neither the theory nor the process of alternative development, says Sheth, can be a-political, as democratization is integral to them: 'For the politics of alternative development to emerge, the corresponding theory should be primarily rooted in the *problematique of democratization*' (Sheth 1989: 69). New forms of democratic legitimacy (based on participation, decentralization, transparency) and alternative development seem to be mutually constitutive for each other. Concepts of alternative development are often rooted in the actions and struggles of a *particular* population. Therefore, on the one hand, local requirements (deriving from the local socio-historical and ecological context) are constitutive for these concepts; on the other, the gap between theory and praxis, between political thought and political action, between 'developers' and 'developed', is claimed to be closed. Political action is not confined to representatives of political institutions but is equally in the hands of citizens and members of civil society who act at the interface of state and society.

Concepts and strategies of alternative development or alternatives to development have become part of the wider discourse on *alternative modernities*, and, even more recently, of the discourse on *regional modernities*.[25] Recognizing the existence of multi-local forms of the modern constellation calls for recognizing the plurality of concepts and ideas of development. Instead of privileging one global history of development, leading to a universal modernity, the focus must be laid on a multitude of development *stories,* differing historically, geographically, and culturally, and giving evidence of a multitude of trajectories to a preferred future.[26]

---

[25] See Sivaramakrishnan and Agrawal 2003. For these editors 'regional' refers to the subnational as well as transnational level. The concept of 'region' is meant to challenge the hegemony of a global modernity, and to throw light on the possible existence of different patterns of the modern constellation.

[26] The notion of 'preferred futures' has been suggested by Javeed Alam (1999).

5

Discourses on Forest Rights and Forest Use in Uttarakhand

THE CHIPKO MOVEMENT INSTIGATED AN UNCEASING search for development alternatives in many parts of Uttarakhand. Local residents and social activists began to develop visions and projects with the intention of securing a better life in the hills. Although a self-determined way of controlling and managing the natural resources of the region, especially the forests, is demanded in all these visions and projects, they differ over the means and ends as well as the concept of sustainability.

The Chipko movement has also shown that the claims local residents lay to the forest challenge those of other stakeholders, namely state and central government, industry, and international agencies. Therefore discourses on forest rights and forest use which take shape at the local or trans-local (state, national, and international) level are necessarily a result of ongoing processes of interaction, negotiation, and even open conflict.

Since the late 1970s scholarly circles as well as the public recognize forests as 'contested domains' where the conflicting interests, needs, and requirements of different stakeholders meet.[1] A growing number of publications has focused on the forest issue from a historical perspective. Authors from varying disciplines have explored the history of scientific forestry and forest legislation in British India and the 'native states', as well as in postcolonial India; some works by pioneering

---

[1] In 1994 Akhileshwara Pathak published a book with the title *Contested Domains: The State, Peasants and Forests in Contemporary India*.

foresters in British India have been reprinted. Others have discussed the impact of forest laws and policies on local communities and
thrown light on the history of forest protest.[2]
It seems worthwhile to mention that even in 1931 the basic conflicts which arose between various interests groups were indicated by
the German forester Franz Heske, who worked as Forest Adviser at
the court of the Raja of Tehri Garhwal in 1928/9. Heske argued in
relation to the Western Himalayas that forests have to be seen from
three different perspectives related to particular interests and interest
groups and are therefore not easy to balance (Heske 1931):

1. Protection forests (*Schutzwald*), construed from the perspective
   of welfare (*Wohlfahrt*) and public interest: forests are seen as
   stabilizers of the North Indian ecosystem, mainly because of
   their water-regulatory function (balancing the water level
   throughout the year, intercepting rainfall, creating soil conditions that allow higher infiltrations of water, and modifying
   runoff precipitation).
2. Forest as capital asset (*Ertragswald*), construed from the perspective and interest of non-residents (e.g. outsiders, state, and
   administration): forests are seen as a commodity, a commercial
   reservoir, for example, of timber, fibre, and resin.
3. Provider forests (*Versorgungswald*), construed from the
   perspective and interest of local people: forests are seen as the
   basis of the traditional hill economy, as the source of fodder,
   fuel, fertilizer, timber etc. for the indigenous people.

In Heske's opinion the most valuable and significant perspective is
the ecological, leading him to conclude that priority should be given
to the protection of forests. At the same time he cautioned against
neglecting the other two perspectives. Heske promoted 'scientific
forestry' as the most suitable method for achieving a fair balance
between hierarchically ordered perspectives and interests. As scientific
forestry claims to take a neutral standpoint, it proposes objectivity

[2] Some of these works are: Stebbing 1982; Guha 1983a+b; Ribbentrop 1989;
Pande and Pande 1991; Rawat 1991, 1992a+b, 1993a; Gadgil and Guha 1992;
Brandis 1994; Jha 1994; Negi 1994a+b; Grove 1995; Singh 2000.

and knowledge based on a factual understanding of natural and social processes, aspects that legitimize administrative control and strategies of utilization imposed from outside.

According to Heske, ecological and commercial interests can be reconciled because strategies for increasing forest productivity are equally effective in forest conservation. First and foremost, large-scale felling must be replaced by selective felling and combined with continual afforestation. The integration of local interests, however, poses difficulties as local people use methods that are, according to Heske, detrimental to the forest. Heske did not make any attempt to analyse the concepts, practices, and strategies that constituted hill people's rationale. Guided by his own concept of rational action and his conviction of the superiority of 'scientific' forestry, he condemned their practices as destructive and accused them of disregarding their obligations to future generations.

Heske's view leads easily to the conclusion that forests have to be protected by keeping local people out. For him the state and its institutions have both knowledge and the power to regulate access to the forest by establishing state monopoly and implementing laws and rules which define user rights. From this stately and authoritarian standpoint only a restrictive management of forests can reconcile and balance the divergent needs and interests of various interest groups.

In the following I will present discourses on forest rights and forest use which took shape in the aftermath of Chipko, among social activists and local residents involved in the struggle. Their discourses are characterized by a perspective *from below*, taking into consideration the legal claims, needs, and requirements of the local population. Constitutive for these discourses are particular perspectives on development or, rather, development alternatives which determine the manner in which the forest is related to.

The formation of a discourse always happens in a particular socio-political context, and has to be seen with reference to other discourses. In Uttarakhand, local discourses refer to state discourses on forest rights and forest use, and react to strategies linked with them. As the forest policy in colonial and post-colonial India is well documented already, I will discuss state discourses and practices briefly by posing one basic question: Does the state (the government) which, even in colonial times, claims to represent the general public, acknowledge the plurality of claims to and functions of the forest, and does it sufficiently try to integrate and balance divergent needs and requirements within its respective concepts and strategies? If not, which perspective gains priority in a certain period, and why? Official discourses, which are basically related to a concept of development favouring economic growth and exploitation, take a perspective *from above*; they define interests and implement strategies by claiming to serve 'The General Welfare' of people.

5.1 Forest Legislation and Forest Policy in Colonial and Post-colonial India: Perspectives from Above

5.1.1 *Forests in British India and the 'Native States'*

The East India Company established its rule by expanding territorial control from the ports of Bombay, Madras, and Calcutta into their hinterlands. The exploitation of forests started even in the late eighteenth century because timber was needed for military and naval purposes as well as for house construction and firewood in the urban centres. The state demand for regular timber supply very soon induced plans and strategies of forest conservation in the western coastal region of India.[3] In 1806 the post of 'Conservator of Forests' was created and Captain Watson from the East India Company Police Service was appointed as first holder of this position, vested with wide-ranging powers. Within two years he established a timber monopoly throughout Malabar and part of Travancore, disregarding all previously existing rights.

Whereas early forest regulations in British India were meant to assure a regular timber supply for state needs, subsequent conservation initiatives transcended this purely economic motivation. Administrators with an environmental concern, mostly from the medical services and trained in botany and meteorology, saw close links between

---

[3] A detailed examination of early forest conservation in British India has been carried out by Richard Grove (1995, especially Chapter 8).

the condition of the environment (water, atmosphere, and forests) and public health. Especially after 1840, lobbying for forest conservation was successful, when a considerable amount of evidence on deforestation and its consequences became available in scientific circles. In 1855 Lord Dalhousie, the Governor General, outlined a permanent policy for forest conservation. His memorandum, dated 3 August 1855 and later known as the 'Charter of the Indian Forests', was basically aimed at regulating forestry in the Burmese province of Pegu. It laid down that all teak timber was state property, all benefit from it accruing to the government. Kulkarni (1983) draws attention to the fact that the establishment of exclusive rights of the state to forests involved the regulation of earlier rights and the restriction of privileges of communities and individuals harvesting or exploiting the forests. The tension, therefore, between so-called 'public' interest and the interests of users constituted one of the main problems of scientific forestry management in India from its very beginnings.

During crown rule the country's infrastructure, especially the railways, consumed large quantities of timber (for sleepers and as fuel). To ensure continuous supply as well as to stop uncontrolled felling and the deterioration of forests, a regular system of forest conservancy was required. In 1864 the post of Inspector General of Forests to the Government of India was established and the German forester Dietrich Brandis was appointed to this position.

Brandis had been trained in the tradition of German forestry, which can be described as a bureaucratic-scientific regime of natural resource management. It includes productive and protective dimensions and was concerned with controlling and restricting forest use by disciplinary measures in the form of forest laws and regulations. Three basic principles guided the approach of scientific forestry: minimum diversity, balance sheet, sustained yield.[4] Brandis established silvicultural guidelines for the working of Indian forests according to the German system. His guidelines basically lay down

---

[4] The German system of scientific forestry is discussed in Rajan 1998. The German system is also known as 'sustained yield management' (*Nachhaltswirtschaft*) The concept of sustainability, which became central in the development debate, derives from scientific forestry. The life and work of Brandis is described in Hesmer 1975, Rawat 1993b, and Saldanha 1996.

that the number of trees to be felled should never exceed their annual production by natural or artificial means. This principle became the cornerstone of Indian forest working plans (Brandis 1994: 49).

Brandis was also substantially involved in the drafting of the Indian Forest Act VII of 1865, the first step to create a state monopoly in forests and to ensure proper forest management. But it was really the Indian Forest Act VII of 1878, which classified forests into Reserved, Protected, and Village Forests, and provided the necessary laws and rules for establishing and handling an absolute state monopoly on forests.[5]

The procedures for forest settlement had been a matter of intense debates in the forest administration and the crucial question was how to balance the opposing interests of the state—as representative of a 'general public'—and local users and owners of customary rights. To 'solve' the problem it was decided within the British administration, that European legal praxis should be followed. This entailed offering compensation in the shape of money, or the grant of land in cases of restriction, or else the simple extinction of customary rights.[6]

The National Forest Policy 1894 explicitly mentions 'public benefit' as the sole object to which scientific forest management was to be directed (original text in Jha 1994; see also Kulkarni 1983). It further states that the regulation of rights and the restriction of the privileges of users, i.e. of the inhabitants of a forest's immediate

[5] *Reserved forest*: for commercial purposes of the state; only in exceptional cases were private rights allowed to be exercised. The land came under permanent settlement. *Protected forest*: Rights (for hunting, grazing, cutting timber) were not settled but could be exercised until the state decided otherwise. *Village forest*: for community use, controlled by a village (see e.g. Gosh 1993: 76f).

[6] For a critique see e.g. R. Guha 1983a: 1885; Pant n.d.[1922]: 46–7. These authors criticize the forest settlement praxis because the application of European legal ideas and procedures required, on the part of those coming under the regulations, a certain familiarity with foreign ways of thinking and acting—which were based on the idea of private property and individual rights and obligations. This meant that most of the tribal or agricultural communities whose forests were selected for reservation were incapable of understanding and acting according to European legal demands. The colonial rulers took advantage of the 'ignorance' of the 'natives', who consequently lost their rights and were deprived of and alienated from their means of livelihood.

neighbourhood, was required in almost all cases. Such people were granted access only to forests that had no commercial value.

The first half of the nineteenth century was characterized by an increase in forest exploitation—during World War I and World War II timber and bamboo were needed for military purposes (Guha 1983a)—and the emergence of local protest movements against British forest policy. Uprisings occurred in tribal areas (Sarkar 1983: 153ff.), and also in the Himalayan regions of Eastern Garhwal and Kumaon which were brought under British rule in 1815.[7] The Kumaon forests were found extremely valuable because of their fine stands of sal, devdar, cedar, oak, and chir pine, and nearly all the region's forests became reserved, contributing remarkably to the profit of the country as supplier of resin and timber.

In 1916 and 1921 protest campaigns began against British forest policy.[8] The opposition was severe and the forester Stebbing complained of all the chir forests being burnt, resulting in severe damage to the resin industry (1982, III: 659). The government was forced to react and in 1921 a committee was appointed to enquire into the grievances of people. The critical report of the Forest Grievances Committee was issued in 1926 and led towards a reclassification of forests into two classes: Class I forests, where villagers could exercise some rights and where supervision was light; and Class II forests, reserved for commercial and ecological purposes, with strict management. Parts of Class I forests came under village management in the form of *van panchayats*, which were established in 1930–1.

Forest conflicts and tensions between the state and local residents were not limited to British India but also occurred in the 'native' or 'princely states'—including Tehri Garhwal. Up to the mid-nineteenth century large parts of the state of Tehri Garhwal were densely forested, especially the catchment areas of the main rivers—the Tons, Yamuna, Bhagirathi, and Alakananda. The Raja of Tehri Garhwal

[7] For the history of forestry and forest protest in British Garhwal and Kumaon, see Pant n.d. [1922]; Guha 1983a and 1983b; Rawat n.d., 1991 and 1992a; Stebbing 1982, vol. III; and A. Pathak 1991.

[8] Resistance against colonial rule had a long history in Kumaon as the villagers opposed the systems of *utar*, *begar*, and *bardaish*, which all implied rendering unpaid services or supplying provisions to officials touring the hills (see Rawat n.d.: 26; and S. Pathak 1998).

possessed proprietary rights to the soil, but local communities or family groups actually cultivating the land enjoyed all privileges of ownership except for the right to alienate land (Guha 1991: 63). The forest, pasture, and wasteland surrounding the villages were appropriated as 'commons'.

Commercial exploitation of forests began in 1840. In parts of the forest that had been leased by Frederick Wilson, a private entrepreneur, forest produce (musk, fuel timber, animal hides) was extracted, and chir and devdar felled. After the expiry of Wilson's lease, Raja Bhawani Shah leased large forest areas to the British government. In 1885 Bhawani Shah's successor, Pratap Shah, realized the commercial value of forests and established his own forest department. In 1897, under the rule of Kriti Shah, systematic forestry was started in Tehri Garhwal State with the help of Pandit Keshava Nand from the British government. Under his control some of the best forests were demarcated and the access of village people to them restricted. In 1908 the Conservator of Tehri Garhwal State Forests, Pandit Ram Dutt Raturi, who had been trained in France,[9] established an even more efficient system by classifying the forests into three categories, similar to the classification in parts of India which were under direct British rule: first class reserve forests, second class protected forests, and third class village forests comprising all wasteland. The closure of forests by legislation included state handling of fire protection and the preservation of wild and aquatic life. It also entailed severe restrictions and prohibitions in the different categories, the erection of boundary posts (*munarband*), and the control of forest areas by forest guards. Whereas in British India complicated legal procedures had to be implemented to abolish customary rights, in Tehri Garhwal these rights were erased without legal difficulties and compensation. Traditionally, all rights in the soil ultimately vested in the king, who granted his subjects access to his land and forests. Now, traditional law was re-interpreted and what had formerly been recognized as a right was simply

[9] France had a tradition of state forestry from the middle of the seventeenth century, when J.B. Colbert, minister in the court of Louis XIV, passed an *ordonnance* which gave the king significant rights over forests. In 1820 the French national government established an independent forest administration, and in 1824 a school of forestry in Nancy. The history of French forestry is briefly discussed in Rajan 1998.

shown as a 'concession' to which no legal claims could be made (see Saklani 1987: 127).

In different periods and in different regions of Tehri Garhwal, villagers opposed the new forest policy, resorting to a traditionally legitimized means of protest, the *dhandak*.[10] Saklani mentions several dhandaks between 1878 and 1885 under the reign of Pratap Shah, when collecting and selling animal hides, horns, musk-pod, and feathers were strictly prohibited. In 1906 another uprising occurred in Chandrabadni near the capital of Tehri, directed against preparatory work for the demarcation of forests. But the most serious incident, the dhandak of Rawain, took place in 1929/30 in pargana Rawain. Villagers felt that their mode of living was threatened imminently by severe restrictions on forest use and by the burden of taxes. During their protest the raja happened to be on a trip to England and his officials displayed no interest in a possible compromise with the villagers. For the first time a dhandak was crushed by military force, resulting in a number of people losing their lives and many being seriously injured. The killing occurred on 30 May 1930, in Tilari Maidan, in the Yamuna valley, near Rajgarhi. The leaders of the uprising were imprisoned and their property confiscated by the state. (More details in Chapter 6.)

5.1.2 Forests in Post-colonial India

The national forest policy of post-1947 India served industrialization and economic growth. The industrialization project entailed a radical instrumentalization of nature, which was seen primarily as an exploitable resource. A specific national forest policy was outlined in 1952. Based on the 'fundamental concepts' of the 1894 policy, it mentioned 'six paramount needs of the country' (see the original text in Jha 1994; also in Negi 1994a):

(1) evolving a system of balanced and complementary land-use where each type of land is allotted to that form of use under which it would produce most and deteriorate least;

[10] A dhandak was directed against a deplorable state of affairs but was not aimed at attacking and altering the political system; see also Chapter 6.

(2) checking denudation in mountainous regions, preventing erosion along river banks and wastelands, preventing the invasion of sea-sands and coastal tracks;

(3) establishing treelands for the amelioration of physical and climatic conditions and promoting the general well-being of the people;

(4) ensuring increasing supplies of grazing, small wood for agricultural implements, and firewood;

(5) sustained supply of timber and other forest produce required for defence, communications, and industry;

(6) realization of the maximum annual revenue.

To fulfil these needs forests had to be classified and carefully managed. A differentiation was made between Protection Forests (to be preserved or created for physical and climatic considerations), National Forests (to meet the needs of defence, commerce, industry, etc.), Village Forests (to provide grazing, firewood, etc.), and Treelands (for physical and climatic considerations). The National Forest Policy of 1952 reflects in fact the categorization Heske had made two decades earlier. But whereas Heske had highlighted the ambiguities and tensions which necessarily arise between the perspectives, the new forest policy suggests their equivalence in the national interest. All the same, a closer look into the text reveals that 'national interests' could override the claims of local inhabitants:

> Village communities in the neighbourhood of a forest will naturally make greater use of its products for the satisfaction of their domestic and agricultural needs. Such use, however, should in no event be permitted at the cost of national interest. The accident of a village being situated close to a forest does not prejudice the right of the country as a whole to receive the benefits of a national asset. The scientific conservation of a forest inevitably involves the regulation of rights and the restriction of the privileges of user depending upon the value and importance of the forest, however irksome such restraint may be to the neighbouring areas. . . . (Jha 1994: 165)[11]

---

[11] The region which attracts special attention is the Himalayan forests, the 'greatest of national assets', to which the richness of the country is owed. Nehru himself praised the enormous wealth concentrated here, awaiting for

With the abstract category 'national interest' and 'national well being' the new forest policy creates a legitimizing concept to erase the 'privilege' of a forest population. Such rhetoric fits the early Nehruvian programme of modernization which sees 'pre-modern' villages as intellectually and culturally backward and requiring change (Pyarelal 1958: 545). Against this background, the destruction of 'traditional' lifestyles is not a loss but an opportunity for 'development'. The growth of forest industries (packaging, pulp and paper mills, matchbox, etc.) in the 1950s led to increasing pressure on existing forests (Guha 1983a, Sundar *et al.* 2001: 25). To meet the expanding demand, emphasis was laid on *production forestry* from the 1960s onwards: natural forests with 'low productivity' were converted into 'high productivity' monocultural plantations of quick-growing, high-yielding commercial tree species like teak, tropical pine, and eucalyptus. Some projects were supported by international organizations—for example the World Bank funded the Bastar Project, which attempted to replace 40,000 hectares of natural sal forest with tropical pine to provide pulpwood for paper (Sundar *et al.* 2001: 26; A. Pathak 1994: 21f.).

With such increases in the productive use of forests and the conversion of mixed forests into profitable monocultures, forest dwellers were increasingly deprived of their means of subsistence. To meet local needs for firewood, fodder, grass, and other such items, another programme was initiated: *social forestry*. This was aimed at regenerating forest resources by extending forestry into non-forest land (wasteland, community and private land) and through the involvement of the local communities in planting and managing forests. A promising strategy, this attracted local government departments and international aid agencies to pay greater attention to forestry and

---

exploitation: 'When I see a map of India and I look at the Himalayan range— I like the Himalayas myself, I like mountains and all that—I think of the vast power concentrated there which is not being used, and which could be used, and which could transform the whole of India with exceeding rapidity if it were properly utilized. *It is an amazing source of power, probably the biggest source anywhere in the world—this Himalayan range with its rivers, minerals and other resources . . .*' (in Bright n.d.).

support the programme with large funds (e.g. World Bank, FAO, USAID, SIDA). 'Social forestry' dominated forest policy after the 1970s and became a 'new paradigm of development' (Shiva, Sharat-chandra, and Bandyopadhyay 1983: 50).

The fragmentation of forestry into two different approaches—production forests 'which are the gift of nature and . . . produce valuable timber', and social forests 'which are manmade and . . . produce small timber, fuel-wood, fodder, cocoons for silk production, medicinal plants and herbs' (Jha & Sen 1991: 1)—was supposed to reconcile the two conflicting perspectives on forest as capital asset *(Ertragswald)* and as providing forest *(Versorgungswald)*. The protective role of forests, even though recognized, seems to have been of little consequence in the 1970s. This situation was to change over the next decade, when the ecological perspective began to infiltrate official discourse as well as strategy. Several crucial and interrelated events may have been responsible for the change in the state discourse relating to forests and forestry: the emerging environmental concern after the Stockholm Conference of 1972; the national and international popularity of the Chipko movement, the formation of counter-discourses; the increasing presence, self-consciousness, and influence of NGOs.

In the 1980s, the political agenda for the environment became clear. Ecological considerations became a public issue with the Forest Conservation Act 1980, the Sixth Five Year Plan (1980–5), and the new forest policy approved by parliament in 1988. Already, after the 42nd amendment of the constitution in 1976, Indian forests and for-estry were transferred from the 'State List' to the 'Concurrent List' to give the central government a more influential role, and to provide ecological concerns with a juridical and administrative basis. The Forest Conservation Act of 1980 declared that no state government could alter the status of a reserved forest or use forest land for non-forest purposes without the prior approval of the centre (see S.S. Negi 1994a: 106). In 1988, major amendments were made to the Act. With-out prior permission of the central government, states could not clear-fell portions of the forest or create rights to forest land through sale, transfer, lease, mortgage, or any other mechanism for any private person or agency, organization, or corporation not owned, controlled, or managed by the government (see A. Pathak 1994: 59–60; S.S. Negi 1994a: 125).

The Sixth Five Year Plan (1980–5) gave conservation of forests precedence over organized forestry. The plan also laid emphasis on the complete protection of selected areas, including their flora and fauna, through the establishment of sanctuaries and biosphere reserves. Strong administrative and financial support was given to 'social forestry' programmes and Rs 100 crore provided by the central government during this Sixth Plan period (1980–5).[12]

A new National Forest Policy in 1988 criticized, in its preamble, state, industry, and local communities for the degradation of forests.[13] It went on to focus on 'basic objectives', summarized in the following words: 'The principal aim of Forest Policy must be to ensure environmental stability and maintenance of ecological balance including atmospheric equilibrium which are vital for sustenance of all life forms, human, animal and plant. The derivation of direct economic benefit must be subordinated to this principal aim' (Section 2.2; cited in Jha 1994). So, now, ecology seems paramount, and a minimum of one-third of the total land area of the country is desired under forest or tree cover. This figure was set even higher for hill regions, where two-thirds of the area is projected as forest to prevent erosion and secure ecological stability. To translate these objectives into reality, basic guidelines for managing and improving the forests are now laid down. The most important are first, protection of existing forests and forest land and increase of forest and vegetal cover on hill slopes and

---

[12] 'Social forestry' came under heavy fire in academic and environmentalist discourses (e.g. Shiva, Sharatchandra, and Bandyopadhyay 1983; Agarwal and Narain 1985; Saxena 1996; Alvarez 1992; A. Pathak 1994; Saxena and Ballabh 1995). It is argued that people's participation is only partial, that it increases inequality; instead of fuel and fodder, income-generating trees are grown; it reduces the area for food crops; the planting of some species (such as eucalyptus) causes damage to the environment.

[13] Forest degradation is seen as 'attributable to relentless pressures arising from ever-increasing demand for fuelwood, fodder and timber, inadequacy of protection measures; diversion of forest lands to non-forest uses without ensuring compensatory afforestation and essential environmental safeguards; and the tendency to look upon forests as revenue earning resource' (Resolution, National Forest Policy 1988, reprinted in Jha 1994: 176 ff.; also in Negi 1994a: 104ff.).

in catchment areas of rivers and lakes; second, strengthening and extending the network of national parks and biosphere reserves for total biological diversity; and third, afforestation and promotion of fuelwood production to meet the requirements of rural people. Proper management includes, among other strategies, the regulation of rights and concessions (including grazing); the participation of tribals in the protection, regeneration, and development of forests; discouraging shifting cultivation, and regulating the establishment of forest-based industries.

Even though this new National Forest Policy strongly encourages the protection of forests and forest land, the state is given a lot of leeway: forests can be diverted for 'public benefit'. Projects and programmes such as dam construction, mining, industrial development, and the expansion of agriculture must be carefully examined by specialists 'from the standpoint of social and environmental costs and benefits', but if such experts consider the projects of sufficient benefit to the national interest, the interests of the local residents are subsidiary. The conversion of land under certain conditions is allowed to industry because of the provision of compensatory afforestation, or, in the case of mining, proper mine management plans. N.C. Saxena formulates a critique of the New Forest Policy bluntly: 'The new Forest Policy expresses concern for ecology, but . . . it appears that environment is being used as a new excuse to keep people out of forests, just as "vital industrial needs" were considered enough of a justification to deny legitimate aspirations of the poor in the past' (1996: 115).

In 1990, however, a remarkable shift in the concepts and practices of forest conservation was initiated by the Indian state. Orders and resolutions were formulated at the national level to create a 'massive people's movement' to protect and restore forests (Poffenberger and Banerjee 1996: 325). A new approach—the Joint Forest Management (JFM) programme—was launched. To motivate local populations to join the effort at forest protection, certain rights to the forest and its produce as well as other incentives were granted to them ('benefit sharing'). Since 1991, the World Bank has supported the JFM programme.[14] This shift indicates a modification in the attitudes of state

---

[14] For a critical evaluation of the JFM programme see, for example, Poffenberger and Banerjee 1996; Büttner 1996; Sundar et al. 2001).

agencies and officials towards the local population and their management of resources. Local residents are no longer seen as a 'problem'
for the forest but as responsible and knowledgeable agents who can
be involved in the search for solutions.[15]
The actual practice of JFM has attracted ample criticism (e.g.
Arora 1996; contributions in Poffenberger and McGean 1996, Sundar
et al. 2001). Yet the authors agree that JFM has opened up new spaces
to reflect on alternative and more democratic ways of forest management, taking into consideration the diversity of interests of the different stakeholders and forest users, including women, and poor and
low-caste members in the community. Even more important, JFM
has largely contributed to the fact that the rights of local residents to
their forests have been increasingly acknowledged by the state
administration, and by the media. How local communities should be
involved in the conservation of protected areas (national parks, biosphere reserves; see Kothari, Singh & Suri 1996; Saberwal and Rangarajan 2003) is also a subject of discussion.

Concepts and practices of participatory or community resource
management are not restricted to the forest but include land and
water management as well as the management of marine resources
(see e.g. the contributions in Singh & Ballabh 1996). Co-operative
projects are also not necessarily initiated and implemented only by
the state and the administration, but may follow other models (Sarin
1996: 168ff.). One type of community resource management strategy
evolves from local initiatives as a response to the hardships local people have to face because of the degradation of their resources; here
NGOs may act as strong supporters of villagers. In another model,
local welfare organizations and NGOs play the leading role; they
make the effort to mobilize villagers and try to get funding for their
projects from the state and/or international agencies. These initiatives
'from the bottom' may be embedded in much wider concepts of local
or regional development and democratization.

[15] In the 1960s and 1970s social scientists seem to have been quite dubious
about the possibility of joint management of common pool resources (CPR) by
user communities. See for example Garrett Hardin's book, *The Tragedy of Commons* (1968), Russell Hardin's concept of the 'free rider' (2003), and Mancur
Olson (1965). An elaborate critique was formulated by Ostrom (1990); see also
Agarwal & Narain 1989; and Singh, Ballabh, and Palakudiyil 1996.

5.2 Chipko Leaders and Participants:
Perspectives from Below

In the aftermath of Chipko, village and NGO-based concepts and strategies of integrated community-based resource management have evolved, contextualized by local imaginaries for regional development and participatory democracy. In the following, I concentrate on the discourses established by the two leading Gandhian activists and central figures of Chipko whom we have met earlier, namely Sunderlal Bahuguna and Chandi Prasad Bhatt. Subsequently I present the outlook of local residents of the Bhotiya villages of Lata and Raini.

Reconstruction and analysis of the discourses will give attention to several core elements:

‘ Diagnosis of the social and economic situation in the hills; the relation between tradition (the 'old' society) and modernity (the 'new', 'developed' society); the state of forests and forest rights; the significance of forests for the local community.

‘ The relationship of human beings with nature (environment).
‘ The identification of responsibility (for the degradation of forests, for the 'backwardness' of local people).

‘ Conceptualization and definition of 'development'.
‘ Imaginaries and projections of 'healing' (concepts, strategies, and agents of change, new relationship to the forest and to society).

‘ Relations between the local and the trans-local; significance of the Himalayan situation for the nation, the world.

‘ Symbolic dimensions: references to religion and mythology.

5.2.1 'Spiritual Ecology': The Vision of
Sunderlal Bahuguna

A closer examination of the vision and ideas of Sunderlal Bahuguna has to take into account the changing dynamics of his intellectual position. His thought seems to be characterized by major changes as far as the concept of development is concerned, as well as in relation to his solutions for the social and economic problems of montane

Uttarakhand. The most recent version of his position transcends an earlier narrow perspective on locality and local problems, for it takes global ecology and world politics as the largest challenge and claims to provide a remedy for healing the world. While Bahuguna understood himself earlier simply as a 'messenger' of the Chipko movement, in his later phase he has taken on the mantle of a 'prophet'. He no longer addresses only those living in the Himalayan hills; his audience in fact transcends the Indian nation.

The Early Phase: The Need for National Integration and Village Reconstruction

Our men of letters never tire of singing the praises of the Himalaya. To the pilgrims it is the land of the gods. To the mountaineers and tourists its streams, valleys, and snow peaks have a fascination they cannot resist. Enterprising traders are attracted by its untapped forests and mineral wealth and its simple hard-working labourers. But the people who live here continue their restless battle against grinding poverty. Neither the beauty of the landscape nor the spirituality of the faithful who go there on a pilgrimage has been of any help. The Himalaya today calls for workers, dedicated workers, workers with talent, energy, zeal, and ambition to serve and give off their best, workers who will identify themselves completely with the local people, who will respond not to the snowy peaks but to the starving humanity, who will endow it with hope for its future. (Cited from a speech at the conference on 'Social Work in the Himalaya', New Delhi, 21–24 December 1967, Bahuguna n.d.: 93)

Born in 1927, Sunderlal Bahuguna grew up in Sirai, a village near Tehri, the capital of the princely state of Tehri Garhwal. Although in his youth the opportunities for education were extremely limited, he succeeded in finishing intermediate college and going to Lahore for further studies.[16] Very early in his life he came into contact with Sridev Suman, a young Gandhian who was a member of the Tehri Rajya Prajamandal, a nationalist organization in Tehri Garhwal which tried to draw public attention to the grievances and oppressions of the people in Tehri State. Suman was one of the leading figures in

[16] Till 1948 there was only one intermediate college in the whole state along with 260 elementary schools and about 5 middle schools (Saklani 1987: 69).

this organization; he especially opposed the educational politics of the raja and the attempt of the ruling elite to 'keep the doors of education closed'—as Vimala Bahuguna put it—to the general population. Sunderlal Bahuguna says Suman gave his life a new direction:

> When I was 13, Shridev Suman once asked me what I would do after studying. I replied that I would seek employment in the princely court. I am a native of the poorest district of India, where people only had one dhoti to wear at that time. He asked me, 'Then who will work for these people?' I replied that I would do that as well. He then asked: 'How can one person have two Gods?' I did not have an answer and asked him to explain it to me. He said that I would have to work out the answer for myself, but I should give a serious thought as to whether I should sell myself for a few pieces of silver. So, I tell everyone that I decided not to sell myself for a few pieces of silver and decided to face the hardships of life. Thus I dedicated myself to the service of the people. (Interview with S. Bahuguna in Kishwar 1992b: 10)

Inspired by Sridev Suman, Bahuguna joined the Gandhian movement at the age of thirteen. Later he became involved in the revolt against the ruling raja and when in 1943, Sridev Suman was jailed and tortured, Bahuguna smuggled the news to the newspapers—for which he too was arrested and jailed (Kishwar 1992a: 14).[17] After completing his BA in Lahore, Bahuguna became a member of the Congress Party but gave up his political career when he married Vimala Nautiyal. In 1956 Vimala and Sunderlal Bahuguna founded Silyara ashram in the Bhilangana valley and since then both have concentrated on social and welfare work. Both are strongly committed to Gandhian ideas and strategies, which are reflected in their life and work as well as their vision:

---

[17] Sridev Suman was sentenced to two years' imprisonment. With a fast unto death he opposed the conditions in jail and violence against political prisoners. Suman died after eighty-four days, on 25 July 1944. His death added to the alienation between the raja and the people. The 'martyrdom' of Sridev Suman is still remembered; private educational institutions working in the Garhwal hills are named after him.

- *Dedication to village improvement (village reconstruction)*: In Gandhi's rural vision the village represents an ideal social organization: self-sustenance, self-reliance, and self-rule based on non-violence and truth. According to Gandhi, reconstruction work includes the uplift of Harijans and women, the foundation of village industries, sanitation and health care, basic education and adult education. Sunderlal and (especially) Vimala Bahuguna share this belief in village reconstruction and make every effort to concentrate on these tasks.

- *Idealism, practical and personal involvement*: While Gandhi was an idealist, he was never an impractical visionary, says his former secretary Pyarelal (1959); Gandhi's insights into what he claimed to be the truth were linked with practical action; he was ready to fight for truth with non-violent means and 'became the greatest moulder of men that our age has witnessed' (Pyarelal 1959: 15). Bahuguna similarly tries to convince people of his ideas with unwavering persuasiveness and like Gandhi often takes to spectacular non-violent practices such as fasts and padyatras. Like Gandhi, he dedicates his life to objectives he thinks worth fighting for.

- *The importance of a concurrence between one's life and one's message:* Gandhi once said: 'You must watch my life—how I live, eat, sit, talk, behave in general. The sum total of all those in me is my religion' (Gandhi, cited in Pyarelal 1965: I, 329). Gandhi also said that, sometimes, the way a man lives gives a much better idea of his beliefs than any verbal statement (Richards 1991: 80). Bahuguna too claims his personal life reflects his beliefs, saying: 'My life is my message.' Like Gandhi, he follows an extremely simple and disciplined lifestyle. Clothed in a white cotton kurta pajama, for several years he has lived in a small hut near the construction site of the Tehri Dam.[18] He meets people with patience and affection. As a true satyagrahi and guru, he expects from them respect and reverence for his person and his work.

- *Willingness to go to the common people and to listen to them:*

[18] In 1993 he told the researcher that he would not go back to live in Silyara ashram unless the state ceased constructing the dam.

Gandhi spent much of his time travelling through the country. He walked through villages and listened to people's grievances. Bahuguna goes a step further: he says he wants to learn from the common people. He sees a conflict between knowledge and wisdom in present times, arguing that we (the educated, Westernized) have too much knowledge but very little wisdom. 'The train of knowledge is meeting with accidents; only if wisdom becomes its driver will it run well. And wisdom is the assembled experiences of common people, which they have gained from many generations' (Interview with S. Bahuguna in Kishwar 1992b: 11).

• *The vision of the world as a moral order based on Indian values*: Gandhi's moral utopia was shaped not only by a critique of Western civilization but also based on a moral critique of fundamental aspects of civil society in general. His critique claimed universal validity (Chatterjee 1984). For Gandhi unlimited desire, produced by industrialization, is the core evil of *all* existing modern civilizations; whereas, he belives, ancient India set a limit to indulgence, deliberately deciding against machinery and in favour of what 'we can do with our hands and feet' (Gandhi, cited in Chatterjee 1984: 158). Like Gandhi, Bahuguna makes a plea for universal modesty because happiness does not come from wealth—it must be seen as a mental condition. Bahuguna makes a plea for a future world organized along the lines of a new morality, with India helping to show the way.

Similar to the ideas and practices of Gandhi, which cannot be separated from their nationalist background, the work of Vimala and Sunderlal Bahuguna (like that of other Gandhian activists) is substantially inspired by nationalist motives, for all its internationalism and spirituality.

In his early years as social activist Bahuguna concentrated on local problems. In addition to his practical work for employment generation and his support to welfare projects (mainly initiated and carried out by Vimala and other members of Silyara) he always sought to analyse the local situation and communicate problems in his locality to a larger public.

In his early phase Bahuguna depicted nature and lifestyle in the

Garhwal–Kumaon Himalayas somewhat ambiguously.[19] On the one hand he admired nature's beauty and purity; on the other he stressed its harshness. The 'inhospitability' and 'severities' of nature in his region were responsible for the fact that hill men and women have to labour hard 'even to procure the barest minimum needed to sustain life'. At the same time, this extremely burdensome life made villagers 'tough and courageous' and helped them develop outstanding skills.[20] The battle is 'so hard and relentless' that when a 'fighter' escapes to the plains he feels he is in paradise. An increasing number of educated Garhwalis (and Kumaonis) thus grab the first opportunity to 'flee to the plains for a life of ease and comfort'. Bahuguna anticipated migration as the cause of a decline in traditional lifestyles, and perceptively compared the drift of the young and the skilled to the yearly erosion of Garhwal's soil by the rains. 'The result of this exodus is that only the feeble, the aged, and the women and children are left behind to carry on as best they can.' The extreme burden of work upon hill women was seen by him as responsible for their lasting state as 'serfs', and for having 'arrested their mental and emotional growth'.

Working conditions are only one of the aspects mentioned by Bahuguna as contributing to the marginalization of the hill areas, the additional factors being lack of transport and the degradation of forests. Besides Dehra Dun, Haridwar, Kotdwar, Ramnagar, Kathgodam, and Tanakpur—the 'gateways' to Garhwal and Kumaon—no town of the region is connected to the plains by the railway. The extent of roads is comparatively low, the existing roads are small and unusable during the rains. Interior villages lack even respectable footpaths. Transport and communication problems are seen by him as the cause for the difficulties of political, social, and cultural organizations gaining ground in the hills. The lack of transport is responsible 'for people not being able to derive any significant benefit from the social-welfare measures of the administration. Schools and hospitals are poorly attended.'

[19] The following quotations are all from Bahuguna n.d. [1968].
[20] 'In the matter of intensive farming the Himalayan peasant is not to be beaten by the farmer of any country. He knows how to use the soil and the water to the maximum advantage. . . . Even the mountain slopes and the ridges have been cut up into terraced fields' (87).

Regarding forests, he says, 'the Himalayan communities have always considered it their right to make unrestricted use of the forest wealth'. He underlines that this right was intact till the middle of the nineteenth century, but then 'vested interests . . . entered the virgin Himalayan forests, and soon forest laws began to be enacted to safeguard the interest of the contractors and forest officials at the cost of the people.' Restriction of rights and oppression of the people by forest officials had two main consequences:

(1) The village economy, which centred round the forest, has been almost totally destroyed, village industries have been killed, and a situation has arisen where people must leave their families and fields in quest of gainful employment. (2) Out of resentment people began to destroy forests indiscriminately. They began to cut down trees whenever they could and became indifferent to protecting forests from fires, etc. . . .

Thus the diagnosis that Bahuguna presented in 1968 accentuates the hardships and difficulties that hill people face in their everyday life, causing migrations and a money-order economy. To prevent this drain and restore and secure the stability of the hill economy, 'It is necessary that men should be provided with the opportunity to live as men', he argues. The great necessity is 'to free man from the great burdens which keep his back perpetually bent.' The way to achieve this goal is to make better use of nature: 'Nature has endowed this area with rich resources. They only wait to be developed.'

Resource development, Bahuguna says, includes the use of rivers and streams to produce hydro-electric power in small-scale power schemes. With a sufficient supply of electricity a network of ropeways could be established to transport heavy loads, run mills, produce light. Resource development also means using the immense forest wealth of the region. 'The forests can be the only basis of a viable economy in the hills', Bahuguna argues, and recommends the establishment of cooperative societies for the handling of all forest produce, as already demonstrated by the state of Maharashtra. Intensifying agriculture and animal husbandry would be disastrous for the forests; therefore, setting up forest-based industries 'is the only way to bring prosperity to the hills', because local employment will be generated.

In these local units, the raw materials can be processed instead of in the plains. Bahuguna was convinced that the industrialization of the region would ultimately result in the protection of forests because 'people will turn their attention more and more towards utilization of the forest produce.'

Bahuguna's concept of hill development in the 1960s linked the Gandhian vision for village improvement with Nehru's call for resource utilization. He advocated a moderate form of 'modernization' and national integration through the establishment of communication networks, welfare programmes (education and health care), and local employment schemes. The basic ideas in this concept were part of the Tilari Declaration of May 1968, but they had already governed the activities and practical work done by Bahuguna in earlier years. He had, for example, put a lot of effort into the founding and support of labour cooperatives concentrating on resin extraction and running sawmills. He had himself succeeded in getting a small contractorship in the mid 1950s.[21]

Being predominantly a man of letters, he dedicated more and more time to writing, travelling, giving speeches. With the emergence of Chipko, he concentrated on the task of spreading what he believed to be the message of the movement.

'Ecology is Permanent Economy': Alternative Development through 'Tree-Consciousness'

In Uttarakhand this movement [i.e. Chipko] has created tree-consciousness. The common people have rejected the prevailing notion that tree means timber, they have now realized that trees are for their survival. (Bahuguna 1987: 254)

Whereas early on Bahuguna had supported what he later called the 'economic' face of Chipko, his views were radically transformed in the mid 1970s. From then on he advocated a complete ban on green

---

[21] Even today, villagers in the Rawain region accuse Bahuguna of having worked as a contractor. They still do not believe in his commitment to ecology, because, in their opinion, he had at one time joined hands with exploiters of the forests.

felling in the Himalayas, accentuating the ecological content of Chipko, which—as he saw it—gained momentum with the increasing involvement of women in the struggle. But what was the reason for this radical shift in his view? In an interview which I conducted with him in December 1994, Bahuguna frankly stated that in 1976 he and his followers came to the conclusion that it makes no difference whether a tree is felled by a 'foreign' contractor or by a local cooperative—in either case the tree disappears and, with it, the benefits it could provide a local community. When travelling through villages Bahuguna realized that trees growing behind the *chanis* (small huts in the fields used as stables in certain periods of the year) helped stop the erosion of the soil during landslides. He also learned about the non-commercial value of hornbeam trees (used in the textile and saddle industries), when villagers told him that during drought and fodder scarcity they have to rely on the leaves of these trees. 'This opened my eyes', Bahuguna confessed. 'With our support of small-scale industries in the hills we will give employment to a few people, but we are taking away the permanent employment of the most distressed section of the society.'

Bahuguna admits that his new insights into the need for conserving forests was the result of his continuous communication and interaction with village people: 'Whatever I have learned, I have learned from the experiences of the common people and from their struggle for survival. And whatever mistakes we have committed we committed from reading the books written by scholars and policy makers in Delhi. And whatever wisdom we gathered it was from the people' (interview, October 1993).

By emphasizing his commitment to villagers, especially to village women, Bahuguna supports his claim to represent the local population and act as their spokesman. Giving his concepts and visions a 'down to earth' note, he attempts to achieve greater persuasiveness and legitimacy. The ambiguity—identified in the context of Chipko and its representation—between attributing self-consciousness, knowledge, and agency to local people and at the same time emphasizing the need for guiding them, is quite apparent. But of course this is already inherent in the concept of the satyagrahi. As a committed satyagrahi the activist must both listen to people's voices and learn from their actions as well as give people his interpretation to seek the truth and true objectives. He must also devote himself to the attainment of these objectives: taking into account local effort, he must try to transform this into a strategy for change. Such a social activist is part of a 'creative minority' whose duty is not only to solve local problems but to heal the world.[22]

While Bahuguna may have gained insights from his interaction with the men and women of the hills, he is also deeply indebted to Richard St Barbe Baker, the 'Man of the Trees'. Barbe Baker's 'philosophy' has decisively influenced and shaped his outlook. Barbe Baker, to whom '[t]rees, conservation of nature, protection of environment, ecology' were a 'life mission' (Mehta 1989), died in 1982. Bahuguna expressed his devotion and affection in two articles published in 'A Centenary Tribute' (1989a + b). A trained forester, Barbe Baker had worked in Kenya and was prominent in the efforts to arrest the advance of the Sahara Desert in the 1960s (Mehta 1989). In Kenya he founded a conservation group, 'Men of the Trees', and later travelled the world to call for tree-planting and afforestation. In 1977, when he was 88 years old, he visited Delhi and met Sunderlal Bahuguna for the first time. Despite his failing health he decided to accompany Bahuguna to the Himalayas to learn about the Chipko movement. Bahuguna says he was deeply impressed by Baker: he calls him a 'saint' and says: 'I had come all the way from the hills to Delhi as if on a pilgrimage to have his "darshan". . . . When I touched his feet, he kept his hand on my head . . . I felt as if I was in the presence of a heavenly soul' (Bahuguna 1989b: 43).

In a speech delivered in Bombay in 1980, Barbe Baker, a follower of the Bahai religion, offers his perspective on nature: He assumes nature is endowed with subjectivity, and that all creation is imbued with life and spirit. He believes 'in the oneness of mankind and of all living things and in the interdependence of each and all' (1989: 60). The well being of the earth depends on the right balance between minerals, vegetation, animals, and mankind. He believes 'that this generation will either be the last to exist in any semblance of a civilized world or it will be the first to have a vision, a daring and a greatness to say: "I will have nothing to do with this destruction of life. I

[22] For this 'elitist' vision, see Bahuguna 1990: 24, and subsequent parts of this chapter.

1. Bhotiya woman from Lata with her Chipko certificate

2. Devrana: the old forest temple of Ludeshwar

3. Dhan Singh Rawat and his family

4. Eco-development camp, Gram Lasiyari

5. Jot Singh Rawalta

6. Nakoli: traditional Rajput house

7. Nakoli: dancing with the devta

8. Pulma Panwar returning from the forest

will play no part in this devastation of this land. I am destined to live and work for peaceful construction for I am morally responsible for the world of today and of the generations tomorrow"' (Barbe Baker 1989: 69). To take care of the earth means, for Barbe Baker, taking care of water and forests and engaging in tree planting. Women and 'simple village folk' are those who are most aware of man's responsibility towards nature. In his utopia of a harmonious world, village communities, allowed to manage their own affairs, play a crucial role: 'I picture village communities of the future living in valleys protected by sheltering trees on the high ground. They will have fruit and nut orchards and live free from disease and enjoy leisure, liberty and justice for all, living with a sense of their one-ness with the earth and with all living things' (Barbe Baker, cited in: Goldsmith 1989: 38). Barbe Baker and Sunderlal Bahuguna show a striking closeness in outlook. Both possess a strong moral attitude and a sense of mission; to a certain extent they share the same (romanticist) vision, as will become clear.

The new insight into forests for the village communities which Bahuguna and his followers enunciated in the mid 1970s found expression in public appearances, writings, and interviews after the Chipko success in 1981. In an article published in 1987 Bahuguna claimed Chipko had succeeded in creating 'tree-consciousness' in Uttarakhand. 'The common people' learned to see a tree not as source of timber but as basis for survival. Bahuguna attributes this 'tree-consciousness' primarily to women and underlines a second important achievement of Chipko, namely bringing women into public life. He characterizes hill women as 'the backbone of economic and social life' (1987: 246); Chipko women bear an even greater responsibility: they stand for 'a new socio-economic order' which is the precondition for the survival of mankind, a new order based on an alternative concept of development and a new definition of prosperity.[23] Bahuguna criticizes the 'conventional' model of development which 'encourages

[23] To underline his argument he quoted from the declaration of women delegates formulated during a women's camp held at Henvalghati: 'Any attempts to revive the commercial exploitation of forests will be opposed tooth and nail. We need natural forests for soil and water, for fuel and fodder. We stand for a new socio-economic order free from the exploitation of human beings and Nature alike' (1987: 244).

us to work towards a life style of affluence' and to exploit 'the centuries old stores . . . Nature'. Trees provide food, fodder, fuel, fertilizer, and fibre (the five F's), improve the soil, and conserve water. Instead of industry and commerce, which give employment only to a few and only for a short term, nature should be the source of a prosperity no longer defined as unlimited production and accumulation of wealth but as fulfilment of needs based on a harmonious relationship with nature.[24] Bahuguna has also created a new slogan: 'Ecology is permanent economy' (personal interview October 1993, Tehri).

With his alternative concept of development and vision of a new socio-economic order, as embodied in the Chipko struggle, Bahuguna argues a political programme with a strong ethical and moral content whose ideological foundations he traces to Indian religion and spirituality: 'The *Chipko* is a revolt against the butchery of Nature. It is an attempt to re-establish the values of *aranya* (forest) culture by making spirituality the guide of science and technology for the well being of all living beings' (1987: 247).

By the mid 1980s Bahuguna had consolidated his main vision and programmes for future society; in his later publications and speeches he worked them out and formulated them in a more precise way. His efforts show him more and more interested in transcending his earlier local frame of reference in order to heal the world. It seems striking that, in this context, the role he ascribes to local people has changed: gradually Chipko women and local villagers have lost their prominent function in his thought as agents of change and have been substituted by a 'creative minority' which is said to include literates, scientists, and activists.

'Towards a New Life': Ecological Thought and the Call for a New Moral World Order

We should work out solutions to the triple problems of war, pollution and hunger in the shape of a 'Blueprint' for the survival of our planet. This will act as guide to the groups working for change all over the world.

[24] In Chipko as represented by Bahuguna, hill women who were active in the movement invented the slogan 'Fodder, fuel, soil and water are the basis of our prosperity' (1987: 246).

The 'Blueprint' should be based upon the scientific facts of the West, but have the mystic vision of the East. (1992: 14)

The growing popularity of Chipko outside India, the internationalization of the ecological debate, and the emergence of a transnational network of environmentalists may have urged Bahuguna to pay attention to wider social and political problems. His vision and political programmes are now preceded by a critical analysis of the current global situation and claim to be applicable to all societies. One has to keep in mind that Bahuguna does not present a 'sociological' analysis and does not argue from an academic point of view. His position is that of a committed social activist with a strong moral background rooted in his own cultural tradition.

Bahuguna starts the sequence of his argument with a basic characterization of the modern world (the 'world system'): 'We live in a world of contradictions. There are democracies, but strong armies protect these. There is plenty, yet surrounded by poverty. We are prosperous, but haunted by perpetual dissatisfaction' (1992: 1). Modernity provides advantages such as individual freedom and equality, wealth and prosperity, and yet there is no peace and happiness in the world: 'This has not happened all of sudden, but it is the outcome of the progress of our materialistic civilization, a civilization which has identified development with economic growth' (1992: 1). The cause of current problems and contradictions is a materialistic definition of development, as invoked in President Truman's speech, as well as the idea that 'all the people of the earth were to move [a]long the same track and aspire to only one goal—development' (1990: 5). This concept of development presupposes a specific relationship to nature in which man is not a part but the master of nature. Nature has the status of a commodity, its free gifts are now given economic value and are placed under the control of individuals or institutions that have 'authority, wealth or arms' (1992: 1). The desire to extract from nature therefore reaches the 'extent of butchery' (1992: 1), a problem most harshly felt in 'poor countries'. Bahuguna counts three other 'gifts' of development affecting all contemporary societies: first, 'a war psychosis' all over the world because military spending has a big share in the national budget of many countries, and science and

innovative capacity are frequently directed not to life-affirming but
to life-destructive research. Second, pollution endangers life on our
planet, e.g. acid rain, greenhouse gases, the hole in the ozone layer, climatic change, air and water pollution. Catastrophes in Chernobyl
and Bhopal prove that modern technology is beyond man's control.
The third global problem is poverty and hunger. Bahuguna (1990)
refers to the WCED Report *Our Common Future*, quoting the fact that
26 per cent of the world population consume 80–86 per cent of non-
renewable resources and 34–50 per cent of all food supplies. Governments have failed to solve these problems because all political systems
follow the illusion of progress and development which is based on
consumerism and the promise of affluence (1992: 4–5).[25]

Chipko 'stands to mend these things. It is not simply to save a few
trees in [the] Himalayas' (1987: 23).[26] Chipko embodies qualities
which pave the way to a new socio-economic and moral order: respect towards human beings and nature, modesty, and self-sufficiency.
Chipko calls upon the world to redefine development.

The sources of Bahuguna's inspiration and critique lie partly in
the teachings of Gautama Buddha. Buddha, who saw all human
miseries as caused by desire, asked for desire to be overcome to enjoy
permanent peace, happiness and fulfilment. Bahuguna also quotes
the poet Kabir, who compared material wealth with the 'real' wealth
of fulfilment gained through austerity and simplicity of lifestyle. In
addition, Bahuguna also eclectically draws on statements from various
religious teachings which argue that poverty and simplicity are desirable.[27] For modern times, Bahuguna's exemplar is of course Gandhi.

---

[25] Bahuguna depicts the world system as standing on four pillars: authority,
wealth, arms, and ideology. 'Authority has given birth to statism. Wealth expresses itself in the form of capitalism. Arms have given birth to militarism and
ideology has produced a class of elite intellectuals, and thus elitism' (Bahuguna
1990).

[26] It seems to be common in certain Western critical discourses to shift the
burden of responsibility for the survival of mankind to social movements in the
'Third World' (see Linkenbach 1994).

[27] Bahuguna refers to an article by Alan Thein Durning (1991) and gives
examples from American Indian, Buddhist, Christian, Confucian, Ancient
Greek, Hindu, Islamic, Jewish, and Taoist religion and culture.

In sum, Bahuguna's alternative concept of development is marked by an emphasis on *sustainability* and *ethics* which lead to an attitude towards nature instructed by worship and respect. To achieve sustainability, care for posterity is crucial: 'Whatever benefits our generation has achieved, posterity should get at least that much, if not more' (1990: 12). Therefore the 'contract between the generations', to put it in the words of Jonas and Küng, demands not exploiting or over-exploiting non-renewable as well as renewable resources. This alternative does not dismiss science and technology, but demands they be guided by 'wisdom', which 'is neither contained in volumes of books nor in the minds of great professors, but in the lives of the common people' (1992: 9). And this wisdom lies, in part, in 'switching over from agriculture to tree farming' (1992: 10).[28] Such farming would not propagate species which are useful for commercial purposes:

> [T]he tree cover around the villages should be such as to provide food to human beings and fodder to the cattle. Priority should be given to trees yielding edible seeds, nuts, oilseeds, honey and seasonal fruits. In higher altitudes, above 1500 metres, soft walnut, sweet chestnut, hazelnut and wild apricot can be successfully cultivated. In lower altitudes mango, *amla*, *bael*, and *jamun* [indigenous names of local fruits] will thrive. An average hill family will need 300 nuts/fruits, 1500 fodder and 200 fibre trees (mulberry, *ringal*, and bamboo) to be self-sufficient. (1989c: 8)

Bahuguna claims that tree farming is not only a solution to the ecological and economic problems of the Himalayan hills, it provides an alternative for other world regions too. Tree farming can produce five to ten times more food from the same area of land as the cultivation of cereals, and the challenge for the scientist is to find suitable tree species for the different ecological regions.[29]

---

[28] Bahuguna says tribals and indigenous people still live a simple life, dependent on the immediate natural resources.

[29] Despite the claim made for its greater productivity, the idea of tree farming is obviously extremely impractical and idealistic because of the large number of trees necessary for the survival of even a single family. Growing an immense number of trees may be possible in comparatively sparsely populated areas like the Himalayas, but what about densely populated regions and cities?

Bahuguna's concept of tree farming is linked not only with vege-tarianism and rigid dietary rules, but with a political vision as well.[30] The vision, which again relies on Gandhi and his constructive pro-gramme for social change, propagates the decentralization of produc-tion as well as direct democracy. It is a plea to re-transform society into a face-to-face community within which the power of economic and political middlemen is limited or even eliminated and the im-mediate control of people strengthened.

The question remains of how this new global society can be ach-ieved. Bahuguna warns against relying on existing political parties and their leaders because they are caught in networks of power and money, they are 'captives of the system' (1992: 12). NGOs, which have emerged in India in great numbers over the last two decades, are also disqualified as agents of change because 'they receive support from governments or outside funding agencies and their style of working is more akin to those who feed them' (1992: 11). For Bahuguna, NGOs have become a part of the establishment and help to maintain the status quo.[31] To achieve real changes Bahuguna concentrates his hopes on a symbiosis of the Green Movement of the West (not the Green Parties!),[32] and sarvodaya as a non-violent movement from the East:

> The Sarvodaya inspired *chipko* movement of the East added a new dimension to the global movement for the protection of humankind by co-relating pollution with hunger and destruction of nature. There is need of a manifesto—a Blueprint for the survival of our Planet—to fulfil our aspirations to revive our dying planet from the triple threat of war, pollution and hunger. Based upon the ideas of Gandhi, the declaration should gu[a]rantee peace, clean environment and a life of fulfilment.

[30] Barbe Baker lived only on fruits; Gandhi practised vegetarianism. Food habits can be a criterion for differentiating between various strands of environ-mentalism: see Lewis 1992.

[31] Bahuguna expresses regret that former voluntary workers and organizations have been transformed into NGOs and now supplement the activities of governments. It seems obvious that the DGSM of Chandi Prasad Bhatt is seen as one of those.

[32] For Bahuguna the Green Movement includes Greenpeace, Earth First, and World Rain Forest Movement.

There should be a practical programme to convert the industrial society into a green society. For this Sarvodaya Samaj should collaborate with all such groups. They are active in ending the status-quo and in ushering in a new era. We have no time to lose. This is the practical programme to make Sarvodaya a global philosophy. (1990: 21–2)

Bahuguna considers activists engaged in these 'Western' and 'Eastern' movements as 'influence leaders', who, walking in Gandhi's wake, should command moral authority over so-called 'power leaders'. These 'influence leaders' form a 'highly creative minority' of three types: humanitarian scientists, social activists, and compassionate literary men, artists, and journalists. Scientists represent knowledge (*gyan*) and will use it to end the suffering of living beings; activists represent action (*karma*) and will bring change by non-violent means; literary men represent devotion (*bhakti*) and touch the heart of the masses (1989c: 11; 1990: 23; 1992: 11). The creative minority should listen to the people and learn from them, but it is their task to transform folk collective knowledge into strategies of action.

Bahuguna's programme for healing the world has developed into something of an elitist project, denying average men and women in their particular localities all over the world the ability to speak up and develop their own visions and projects. 'We have to become the voice of that silent minority of humankind,' Bahuguna claims, and quotes Arnold Toynbee to underline his argument: 'The growth of a civilization lies in the hands of a creative minority. This elite must have the power not only to cope successfully with the challenge to which their society is exposed, but also to carry along with them the majority of uncreative people' (Toynbee, cited in Bahuguna 1990: 24).

5.2.2 'Development without Destruction': Chandi Prasad Bhatt and the Praxis-oriented Approach

Whereas Sunderlal Bahuguna is a man of letters whose ideas and concepts can be reconstructed through his writings, Chandi Prasad Bhatt is much more a man of action whose vision and strategies unfold in his practical work. However, Bhatt has also published on Chipko and on the eco-development work he has been pursuing since the late 1970s. He has written articles which deal with ecological hazards, such as floods and earthquakes, as well as with the problems of big dam construction in the Himalayas. Bhatt is not very fluent in English and most of his publications have originally been written in Hindi. The articles I had access to were published after the mid 1980s. In these, certain passages are frequently repeated and are to be found verbatim in various of his publications. To learn about Bhatt and his work, a most valuable source of information are actually his speeches, given to common people on the occasion of eco-development camps organized by the DGSM. In 1995 I had the opportunity of participating in such a camp and recorded the meetings in which he—as well as other activists, journalists and intellectuals supporting the work of the DGSM—addressed the assembly. In contrast with Sunderlal Bahuguna, who turned from being a local activist into a global prophet, Bhatt's main concern has remained with the people on the ground and in hill localities, even though he has raised his voice in larger contexts as well and his reputation as a dedicated Gandhian worker has crossed national boundaries. Since the 1960s and 1970s, and into the present, Bhatt concentrates on local 'sustainable' development, only his strategies have changed considerably.

The Early Phase: Bringing Local Interests In

Uttarakhand which is constituted of eight districts . . . is a mountain range of glorious heights, ranging from 1000 ft to 25,000 ft; the stretches of plains or broader valleys are hardly visible in this region. A host of species of plants and trees has grown and [become] established in this region. The rich forest area and suitable climatic conditions attracted people to settle here. But with the passage of time official control was established over the forest. The trees were used to earn quick revenue. This new phenomenon worked in close design with the ever increasing needs of the communities in the region and put an end to the age-old harmony between man and nature. (Bhatt n.d.: 1)[33]

Chandi Prasad Bhatt was born in 1934 in a village located in what later became the district of Chamoli.[34] After completing his education

---

[33] This and the following quotations are cited as in the original.

[34] The following section is based on Weber (1988), as well as on personal interviews conducted with Bhatt in 1994, and with Shishupal Kunwar, Secretary of the DGSM, in 1993.

he got a 'small job' (*chhoti naukari*) as clerk in a private bus company in Joshimath. He soon realized that he was one of the few who had succeeded in getting employment in the region of his birth: most of the able men had had to migrate to the plains in search of work. He also became aware of increasing poverty in the hills and the social problems which arose because of the absence of men. When, in the middle of the 1950s, he came into contact with the Sarvodaya movement, he decided to concentrate on community building and help people gain a livelihood in the hills. Bhatt says it was a Gandhian worker named Mansingh Rawat who gave his life a new direction. Bhatt took leave from his job (which he quit in 1960) and joined the Uttarkhand Sarvodaya Mandal, in which Sunderlal Bahuguna, Radha Bhatt, and Ghanshyam Shailani were already actively involved. Together with others Bhatt toured the hills from Pithoragarh to Uttarkashi to spread the idea of *gramdan* and *bhudan*, and, from 1962 to 1967, he worked as main organizer of the Mandal.

New tasks came up in 1962. After the Indo-Chinese border war Gopeshwar became the official centre of the newly formed Chamoli District and intensive planning and construction of roads and buildings started. Contractors, who came from the plains, brought their own skilled and semi-skilled labourers; the locals got employment only as menial workers on a daily basis and for minimum wages, with no security. Bhatt and his colleagues decided to organize the workers. They founded a labour cooperative, with 30 permanent and 700 temporary members named the Malla Nagpur Cooperative Labour Society Committee. The cooperative was successful in winning several contracts from the Public Works Department to construct roads. Reasonable wages could be paid to the workers. Later, Bhatt and the other organizers of the committee began to establish village industries, focussing on metal work and carpentry. With the help of the Gandhian Khadi and Village Industries Commission they set up a workshop for wooden and iron farm implements to meet local demand. The committee, and the way it secured employment and reasonable wages for the members, seems to have been a provocation and threat to the established exploitative contractor system, and, as Thomas Weber says, 'procedural hurdles were placed in its way. . . . The organization found itself left with only two options if it was to stay in business— to reduce the wages of workers or pay bribe money to officials'

(Weber 1988: 36). The cooperative was willing to follow neither the first nor the second alternative and in 1964 its work came to an end. Bhatt and his colleagues decided to abandon construction work and, in the same year, as noted earlier, founded a new organization, the Dashauli Gram Swarajya Sangh (DGSS; later DGSM), to build village industries based on the natural resources of the forest. To get the timber which was necessary to run the processing units, the DGSM had to bid for forest lots auctioned by the Forest Department. Early on they succeeded and got several contracts. But very soon the organization had to face difficulties as established contractors tried to outmanoeuvre the newcomer. Weber says the commercial contractors bid high, 'beyond the value of the wood they were to obtain, and then made up the difference by illegal tree-felling. A Gandhian organization, naturally, could not follow suit' (Weber 1988: 36). The DGSM then turned to the collection and marketing of medicinal herbs; later it established resin and turpentine factories. But discrimination against the organization continued in several respects and became one of the causes which finally led to the first Chipko actions in 1973.

Whereas in 1964 and the following years the main target of Chandi Prasad Bhatt and the DGSM had been to provide employment for local inhabitants by using local forest resources in a sustainable way, the explicit idea of forest protection arose only at a later stage, triggered by a disastrous flood which occurred in the Alakananda valley in 1970. Bhatt wrote:

There was a devastating flood in the Alaknanda river on 20 July 1970. Its impact extended from Hanumanchatti near Badrinath and Reni . . . to 320 km downstream at Hardwar and Pathri. During this flood, in the upper catchment of Alaknanda, 55 people along with 142 head of cattle perished, 6 motor bridges and 16 pedestrian bridges were destroyed. Damage to 3 motor bridges and a 10 km stretch of motor road have rendered them useless forever. In the fury of flood 25 stranded buses, 604 houses of 101 villages, 513.30 acres of standing crop, 47 water mills, 27 cow sheds and 4 lift-irrigation machines were washed away. 100 km away at Shrinagar (Garhwal) the ground floor of the I.T.I. building got choked with a 6-feet thick layer of the silt. The Bari tal in Rishiganga, China tal in Patalganga and the part of the Gauna lake leftover from the devastation of 1894, having 1.5 km length, 700 m width and 100 m depth, was filled with silt. (Bhatt 1992: 5)

The DGSM engaged itself in flood-relief work. Along with other volunteers, Bhatt visited the remotest villages to obtain first-hand information on the cause of the flood. In our conversation, he remembered he had openly spoken against forest felling for the first time on 16 August 1970 (personal interview 1994). That was in a meeting of the DGSM with the then State Minister for Irrigation and Power, K.L. Rao, aimed at informing the minister about the flood and presenting him the conclusions of the DGSM study on the causes of the flood:

1. Heavy rainfall in the upper catchment of the Alaknanda and its tributaries viz Birahi and [M]andakini rivers and the mountains flanking the Pipalkoti and Suraithunta-Hanuman chatti on the left.

2. The catchment of the Alaknanda such as Birahi-Garuganga, Patalganga, Belakuchinala, Syalgad, Helang nala, Dhak gadhera, Ringi gad, Subhain gad and Rishi Ganga are comprised of limestone and slate. Geologically this area is prone to landslide and earthquake. The landslides of Ganai, Patalganga, Chhatana, Helang, Tangni, Redgi, Dhak, Reni, Jhinji, Patni, Gauna are some of the examples of the sensitivity of this area. Indiscriminate forest felling in the river catchment and areas prone to landslide further aggravated the situation. . . . (Bhatt 1992: 9)

Bhatt claims that between 1959 and 1969 the Forest Department cleared 16,082 acres of forest cover on the basis of their working plan. Besides that, a large number of trees had been felled during road construction. The report concluded:

[T]hough such catastrophes could not be stopped completely, man could at least avoid and minimize the magnitude of the destruction. It is worth mentioning that heavy rainfall on that fateful day also took place around Urgam to Benru-Bajni on the right flank of the Alaknanda, but except for the rise in the water level in the rivers draining through this area, no trees and boulders were physically transported by the rain water; and there were no major landslides reported. The reason being that no man-made destruction (forest cutting, road construction, dynamite blasting, etc.) was experienced by this flank of the Alaknanda. (Bhatt 1992: 10)

Realizing that the risk is higher and natural hazards more threatening in a violated environment, Bhatt argued for forest protection as a necessary means to prevent disasters affecting human beings, landscape, and flora and fauna. Already in the early 1970s, thus, his two basic targets and those of the DGSM—constantly informing their work until the present day—had been determined: to secure local employment and to protect the forest as stabilizer of the Himalayan ecosystem. In speeches, interviews, and articles Bhatt propagated these aims:

> Two things are equally important: protection of forest and protection of forest dwellers. For this noble target our samsthan has been founded. (Bhatt: personal interview 1994)

> Chipko has always insisted that all those who talk about the welfare of humankind while talking of forests, must also think of the welfare of those living near the forest. (1987b: 52)

> The use of this word 'environment' often brings out various shades of meaning. The word is used to describe rivers, forests, mountains and so on, but very often human beings are missed out. (Bhatt 1987a: 2)

> The biggest problem is that we are thinking of development without realising that the human being is the focal point of development. If we look at the way 'development people' treat forests, we find that they never think in terms of human beings at the central point. The marginalized, last person remains in a state of tremendous suffocation because his or her voice is never listened to by anybody and the number of such people in the country is very, very large and it is very important that their voices are strengthened and brought forward. (Bhatt 1987a: 4)

Bhatt favours a concept of ecology which sees human beings as part of the environment. Instead of privileging instrumental reason and legitimizing man's dominance over nature, he stresses the mutual dependence of man and nature and the responsibility of man for nature's equilibrium. Bhatt assumes this interdependence between forest and people to operate basically at two levels: through the maintenance of ecological balance, and through traditional practices. Because local inhabitants, following an agro-sylvo-pastoral lifestyle, are heavily dependent on the forest providing pasture, firewood, timber, vegetables, and medicinal herbs, 'ecological balance and traditional human relations with the forest are so intertwined that it is difficult to see them separately' (Bhatt 1987b: 47). Traditional practices, he claims, never overuse and harm the forest. The people, 'humbly limiting their needs according to whatever had been afforded to them by the kindly Nature', succeeded in maintaining a 'symbiotic' and harmonious relationship with it for a long time (Bhatt 1987c: 250).

Bhatt evidently stands in clear opposition to Heske, Hardin, Olson, and all those who blamed local communities for acting carelessly and destructively in their use of nature. Whereas Heske assumes a congruence only between the protection of forests and commercial forest use guided by scientific forestry, Bhatt postulates a congruence between ecological needs and provider forests. In his opinion it is precisely local communities who care for future generations, whereas scientific forestry and the commercialization of natural resources have to be seen as destructive elements.

However, Bhatt is eqally aware of certain other dynamics characterizing contemporary relationships between people and forest. He affirms that the harmony with nature came to an end with the state claiming control over forests and extracting forest wealth, so introducing into the region a 'commercialized approach towards Nature's gifts'. This new phenomenon 'worked in close design with the ever-increasing needs of the thriving communities in the region', inevitably changing local peoples' attitude towards the forest (Bhatt 1987c: 250). Far from railing against these new needs or preaching a restoration of old and 'harmonious' conditions, Bhatt pragmatically accepts the new demands and takes them up as a challenge in his own work. He acknowledges that the new needs cannot be fulfilled by the traditional subsistence-oriented system and require additional sources of income.[35] To prevent migration and to stabilize socio-economic

[35] Bhatt does not name these new needs. But it seems plausible that he refers to an increasing demand for education, healthcare, better clothing and food, transport and communication, etc.

conditions in the hills, Bhatt looks for alternative ways of income generation—again by using local forest resources.

The Turning Point: Chipko

In the first half of the seventh and eighth decades of this [the twentieth] century, the policy of alienating the people of the Uttarakhand region from their age-old right over the natural resources in the fragile catchment area of the Alakananda, the main tributary of the Ganga, and the unabated spate of callous exploitation of the jungles, have amounted to a threatening disbalance of the Himalayan eco-system. This hastened the people of the region to take up the road to revolution. *Chipko* (to cling to the trees in order to save them from felling) emerged as a humble, non-violent protest of the inhabitants of Garhwal against the atrocities launched by a distant 'bureaucratic set-up' at the life-giving trees. (Bhatt 1987c: 249)

In many respects, Bhatt thinks of Chipko as the turning point: it considerably altered the way in which women and men in certain parts of the hills relate to the forest, it rendered them self-conscious about their own life and future; it influenced the environmental policy of the state governments as well as the policy of the centre. And, as far as he, Bhatt, is concerned, the course and results of the Chipko movement have given his own work a particular direction and focus. 'Chipko has brought about a definite change in mentality', he says (1987c), sensing the extraordinary character of the movement. He tries to grasp the specificity and persuasive power of the *andolan* by using different rhetorical devices, deploying metaphors of war and revolution, religious symbolism, and the analytic language of the natural and social sciences. By presenting Chipko as a revolutionary (but non-violent) action, and by calling the villagers actively involved 'Chipko soldiers' (1987c: 253, 264), Bhatt conveys the immense strength of the movement which, like a revolution, was able to alter longstanding relations, practices, and attitudes. In analytic and 'objective' language he refers to scientific research on the Himalayan ecosystem; he also explains the 'pragmatic approach' (1987c: 261) of the movement, which intended to save forests to secure their potential as stabilizers of the local ecosystem and as providers of firewood, fodder, fertilizer, timber, etc. for the local subsistence-oriented economy and village industries. But the persuasiveness of Chipko, beyond all this, seems to him to derive from its religious and emotional quality. It 'germinated a devotional attitude' (1987c: 262) towards the trees, he declares, and the use of instruments such as the drum and the conch during the agitations 'significantly refers to the hill people's belief in the sanctity of the Chipko demands' (1987c: 262). Bhatt sums it up thus: 'Today, Chipko has ceased to be a movement and has become the very incarnation of bliss and benediction which affords respectability and prosperity to the woodlands and woodlanders of the region' (1987c: 264). It seems to be the immense potential of change, the purity and humanity inherent in the andolan as well as the scientific foundations of Chipko demands, which, in Bhatt's opinion, made the movement a milestone not only in the history of the region but also in the environmental history of the globe.

I have earlier argued that Chipko demands varied according to the concept and understanding of Chipko activists in different localities; the two main strands are of course represented by Chandi Prasad Bhatt and Sunderlal Bahuguna. Bahuguna was the driving force behind the memorandum for a total ban on green felling in Himalayan regions above 1000m for all commercial purposes (including village industries), which was signed by prominent public figures. It served as a basis for the moratorium of 1981 (see Weber 1988: 140, Appendix V). The six Chipko demands of Bhatt and his group differentiate between the commercial use of forests for local purposes and the exploitative contractor system which goes along with large-scale felling and the use of forest resources by outsiders: only the latter should be abandoned and all forest work should be done by cooperative societies with the involvement of the hill people, to create new job opportunities (Bhatt 1987c: 254, also n.d.: 6).

The outcome of the Chipko struggle may have been somewhat disappointing for Bhatt and his group because their demands did not find a proper echo. In the course of my interviews with both Bhatt and Bahuguna, neither of them openly criticized the work of the other; they were also not interested in explaining and commenting on their differences in either theoretical or practical matters. Bhatt's criticism was clearly directed against the environmental policy of the centre and the UP government: on the one hand, this policy seems to be a hindrance for local development; on the other, it does not consequently pursue the protection and conservation of forests. 'Although the forest department has come to acknowledge the Chipko movement, it has not been able to develop a forest conservation and development policy based on these principles', Bhatt complained (1987b: 49). Many of his critical remarks, expressed in articles or personal communications (although not very systematically), have to be interpreted in the light of this assessment. Six areas of his critique can be outlined.

First, Bhatt complains vehemently about the work of the Forest Corporation (van nigam), founded by the UP government in 1974 to control forest work and secure the employment of local labourers.

> The Corporation was established so as to fulfil the long-cherished *chipko* demand of providing respectable job opportunities to the local people of the region derived out of the forest resources and to put a final end to the contractual system. But instead of giving straight employment to the rural folk, it has been functioning by employment [of] the petty contractors. So the situation is more or less back to square 'A'. The idea behind the Corporation should have been to form a strong, effective organisation of workers who would fell trees, wherever necessary, and work simultaneously for forest conservation and enhancement. . . . Far from this, the Forest Corporation is given to 'small scale contracts' for a 'large scale logging' and has kept its hands off the responsibility of forest conservation. (Bhatt 1987c: 258)

Under the pretence of accepting the Chipko demand to abolish the contractor system, the Forest Corporation has apparently developed new means of forest exploitation—a view shared by activists and villagers living in the Chamoli region.

Second, Bhatt says environmental laws and policies do not allow the small-scale commercial use of forests by local residents. 'The main goal of the movement is not saving trees but the right use of the forest' (Bhatt, cited in Weber 1988: 73). Bhatt and the DGSM still hold the view that existing forests must be protected for ecological reasons, but they should also serve as commercial resource for local small-scale manufacturing industries. In the course of the interview I conducted with Bhatt in 1994, he mentioned, not without regret, that after 1976–7 the DGSM had to close their gram udyog. This, he added, is not necessarily a benefit for the forest because industrial production can use raw materials much more efficiently: one tree is enough to manufacture 100 yokes (*juvar*) in a small industrial venture, whereas a traditional artisan can only produce 8 yokes from a tree.

Third, with the passing of the Forest Conservation Act (1980) and its amendment (1988), the transfer of forest land for non-forestry purposes needs the approval of the central government. Bhatt accuses the centre of exceeding its competence by refusing the transfer of forest land necessary for small village-development projects such as the construction of pipelines, roads (not motorable), and schools, whereas it easily grants forest land for big projects of 'national interest', such as the construction of dams and mining. It is true, he explained to me, that trees should be saved from felling, but small projects can be realized without doing harm to the forest if natural conditions are taken into consideration. Bhatt said disappointedly that, already in 1993, he had applied to the Planning Commission, which drafts the five-year plans of the central government, to allow districts to decide on the transfer of forest land in the case of small-scale projects—but no decision had been taken (Bhatt, personal communication 1994).

Fourth, even though the traditional rights of people over firewood from dry trees have been confirmed, in practice the local forest officers (ranger, DFO) often try to prevent such use. But we do not accept any curtailment of local rights, confirmed Bhatt; 'as long as we don't have a cheap alternative [like cooking gas], our *culhas* must burn' (Bhatt, personal communication 1994).

Fifth, Bhatt criticizes the concept of 'sensitivity' which implies ending commercial tree felling only in areas above 1000m, and at a certain angle. '[T]he *chipko* interpretation of "sensitivity" does not apply any yardstick of slant and height', he stated. Landslides do not stop beyond 1000m; the whole Himalayan region is sensitive (Bhatt 1987c: 257 and personal communication).

Sixth, there is a discrepancy between the official definition of 'forest work' and the definition given by Chipko participants. 'The former regards it as [denoting] tree-felling alone, and the latter treating it as [connoting] the collection of minor forest produce and seeds for nurseries, wall-fencing for the safety of the new plantations, and digging of pits for afforestation' (Bhatt 1987c: 258).

Afforestation has been one of the central demands of the Chipko movement and, already in 1975, the DGSM had started a campaign of tree-planting, while—together with other organizations—declaring its involvement in reforestation. But the real turning point came when the ban on green felling (1977/81) and the closing of local industries forced activists to search for alternatives. To help local people secure a livelihood in the hills, the DGSM concentrated its energies on afforestation as a core part of the wider concept of eco-development.

Afforestation as a People's Movement: A Local Answer to Social Forestry

[C]hipko has been vehemently emphasizing the necessity of imparting more and more vigils to the threatened Himalayas in the form of trees who alone can stand *in loco parentis* to the mother Earth. This cannot be done unless the local people are involved in the onerous task of regreening the naked Himalayas. (Bhatt 1987c: 260)

Bhatt and the DGSM have started 'India's largest voluntary afforestation programme' (Weber 1988: 65). In different parts of Chamoli District, activists organized local afforestation camps to initiate the planting of village forests, and in the slide-prone upper catchment area of the Alakananda near the Badrinath road they took up watershed management. Here, villagers were persuaded to give up their common grazing rights and collectively reforest the area; training camps were organized, and nurseries established to provide saplings for the plantation programme; local youths were mobilized to donate their labour power as 'friends of the trees'. For this work Bhatt won the Ramon Magsaysay Award for Community Leadership in 1982 (Weber 1988: 66).

Bhatt states proudly that the DGSM, 'the parental body of *chipko*[,] has been endlessly working with the support of the local people to achieve the high goals of agro-forestry and social forestry for the last five years in 25 villages of the Garurganga area' (Bhatt 1987c: 261).

The success of the plantations, with a survival rate between 70 and 90 per cent, has been much better than that of government plantations, where only 20–50 per cent of all saplings survived. The DGSM afforestation approach joins hands with official programmes of social forestry, and to finance its projects the organization accepts money from government sources as well as from international agencies. At the same time, DGSM afforestation programmes differ fundamentally from those initiated by the government. Whereas the government 'has failed to associate and link people's support with its afforestation drives' (Bhatt 1987c: 260), the DGSM basically draws on the direct involvement of villagers. Bhatt is convinced that '[s]ocial forestry would remain a fanciful idea only unless the economic interests of the local people are tied with every tree which grows in these forests' (Bhatt 1987c: 261). Villagers should realize, he remarks in another context, 'that forests are the basic foundation of their current living standards, and that their survival will be at stake once the forests disappear' (Bhatt 1987b: 51). For Bhatt and his group real 'participation' must apply at various levels and should include all village members.

- Villagers have to be involved in planning and decision-making processes; especially, they have to decide the species of trees useful for them. Government programmes favour fast-growing conifers, eucalyptus, and poplars, but these species are not suitable for ecological conditions in the Himalayas and without much worth for the hill economy, where fuel, fodder, and fruit trees are needed.
- The work of afforestation and care of new plantations should be done by villagers. This includes preparation of the soil, digging of pits, planting of saplings, regular watering, care of young trees, wall-fencing, and protection of the plantation area.
- People should have control of their forest, including the right to use the forest and gain immediate profit from it. The government should distribute vacant forest land among the villagers and give them the right to plant and use their own jungle. Existing forests near villages should be handed over to the village community and the money for forest improvement should be given

not to government departments but to village councils and the voluntary agencies working with villagers (Bhatt n.d.: 8).

- Village men and women from all status groups should participate in forest work. Women must be made special 'partners in the protection and development of forest wealth' (Bhatt 1987b: 51). Women seem to be more sensitive towards the forest because their everyday work brings them in direct relationship with it.

Reforestation and forest conservation have become the heart of the work by Bhatt and the DGSM. Their forest work is linked with efforts to improve village life in a more general sense—it is part of the wider programme of eco-development. During my research I had the opportunity of informing myself about the DGSM' concept of eco-development through interviews, talks, visits to various villages, and participation in a training camp. Their eco-development encompasses projects promoting social and economic development in the hills; many of these aim at income generation in a sustainable way—for example cash crop production and improvements to animal husbandry. In parts of Chamoli District (e.g. in Mandal and other villages around Gopeshwar), climatic conditions allow the growth of citrus fruits, such as oranges and lemons, and people have started to convert parts of their agricultural land into orchards. With the support of DGSM, villagers were able to get loans to buy so-called Jersey cows, which give far more milk than the traditional hill breed (10–12 litres per day against 1–3 litres per day).[36] The cross-breed has to be stable-fed, and via planned planting of village forests grass and leaves are within reach. The return from selling of milk also allows the buying of additional, highly nutritious fodder. On their own initiative, village women have succeeded in organizing a Milk Production Cooperative Committee (headed by a woman president) to undertake the collection and marketing of milk. It is said that the DGSM also gave support to set up biogas plants in villages and propagated smokeless *chulas* which require less firewood. Last but not least, eco-development has a social side; it can be best grasped by the catchphrase

[36] These cows are not Jersey cows but a cross-breed between local and European varieties. All cows which give a comparatively high amount of milk are colloquially called 'Jersey'.

'empowerment': villagers, especially women, are being trained and encouraged to speak up, formulate their needs and appeal to a wider public. The number of villages cooperating with Bhatt and the DGSM seems to increase steadily, the women being the main multipliers. For example, a young woman, whose *mait* (father's house) is in a village that has made progress with the support of the samsthan, tries to convince people in the village of her *sasural* (father-in-law's house) to get in touch with Bhatt and his group. Shishupal Kunwar, secretary of the DGSM, explained that the organization does not 'advertise' its work; villages interested in getting help and guidance try to approach the samsthan on their own initiative.

Praxis as Performance: The Eco-development Camps, or How to Educate the People

Under the leadership of DGSM every year dozens of camps are organized during the monsoon and winter and people participate with great enthusiasm. In these camps environmental education activities are undertaken and people work for achieving afforestation. . . . Donation of labour (*shramadan*) is an important aspect of these camps. . . . The barren lands lying waste around the villages are greened by planting trees chosen by the village women which meet the needs of the villagers. During the five to ten days that the camp lasts there is a festive atmosphere in the village. Women from distant villages also participate and learn from each other's experiences. (Bhatt n.d.: 7)

The central role of training and 'education' included in Bhatt's development concept becomes transparent during an eco-development camp. In the following, I try to give an impression of the course and contents of such a camp based on my own observation. First, I try to describe the setting and the order of events, followed by a short comment on the tension between activists' claims to *listen* to people's voices and to *educate* them. Then I concentrate on the problems and demands of the villagers, expressed during the camp meetings. I conclude with some reflections on the performative character of the camp and on the Gandhian ideology behind.

The Setting: The eco-development camp took place from 31 May
to 3 June 1995 in Lasiyari. The village is located in the hills, not far
from Chamoli town, on the left bank of the Alakananda. The meeting
place was the building of the high school, easily reached by men and
women from the surrounding villages, mainly inhabited by Rajputs,
Harijans, and Bhotiyas.

   I visited the camp together with my young daughter, her older
friend from Nakoli, and my research assistant J.S. Chauhan. We went
by car from Gopeshwar to Chamoli and then took the main road to
Pipalkoti. After a short drive we turned right and for a few kilometres
followed a small road. When it ended we had to get out and walk up
through pine forest and fields for another four or five kilometres until we reached the camp site. On our way we passed two villages. In the
centre of each village, people had prepared a reception area to welcome Bhatt, the activists from the DGSM, and the special guests who
were expected in their company. Red carpets were spread out, chairs
and tables decorated with fresh flowers were ready. Approaching
Lasiyari one could see the high school, located outside the village on
an elevation. The footpath to the building was clean and marked with
whitewashed stones. Halfway, one had to pass a gate-like construction.
On a white cloth fixed between two decorated poles a welcome was
written in large letters: *mahila mandal Lasiyari apka svagat karti hai*
(the women's council of Lasiyari welcomes you). The meetings were
planned to take place on the veranda and in the courtyard (chauk) of
the school (rooms were reserved for those who had to stay overnight).
The chauk was covered by a multi-coloured tent-roof to protect
participants from the sun; on the floor carpets had been spread. On
one side busy helpers had installed a kitchen. In the course of preparation work for the camp two latrines and two 'bathrooms', veiled
by empty sacks, had been built. Whitewashed stones marked the way
to these facilities. From a nearby water source a pipeline led to the
latrine / bathroom complex as well as to the kitchen.

   The camp was officially opened on the evening of 31 May, with the
singing of devotional songs (*bhajans*) and a welcome address by
Shishupal Kunwar. All participants were asked to introduce themselves.
We learned that most of the participants were representatives of the
gram sabhas and mahila mandals of neighbouring villages, but some
came from more distant places in the surroundings of Joshimath.

Especially from Lasiyari and nearby localities, women joined the camp too, but—as we realized later—they kept coming and going according to their work, which often did not allow them to stay in the camp the whole day. Besides Chandi Prasad Bhatt and his son, Shishupal Kunwar, and a few other activists from the DGSM—who were all involved in leading and organizing the camp—special guests attended the event: Ramesh Pahari and Vijay Singh Asual, two journalists working with regional newspapers; Sudarshan Singh Kathet and Sundeep Rawat, two representatives of cooperating voluntary organizations, Dr Mohan Panwar, a lecturer in geography, Garhwal University; and Sri Gopalkrishna Panthri, retired principal from the intermediate college, Gopeshwar. After the introductory round the official part came to an end and people had dinner.

The programme of the second day started early morning, before 8 o'clock, with prayers and devotional songs. All participants were enthusiastically looking forward to the camp activities. In the ensuing session participants from the villages were asked to speak of troubles and problems which were under discussion within the village community. These topics were listed on a blackboard; the most important were: the village forest, school, and education, roads, 'smog' (*dhundh*), and village unity. With the listing of the problems the early morning session came to an end and people went to the courtyard to eat breakfast. Soon after, they were called by a drummer to assemble for the 'inspection tour' through the new tree plantations. Led by Bhatt and local women, the camp participants walked through the fields until they reached a formerly barren and uncultivated area where the villagers of Lasiyari had started to grow their own oak forest. Pits and saplings were examined and the activists advised villagers on how to care for the plantation further on. By 11 o'clock everybody was back in school. In between, a dispensary had been opened and those who needed medical care or medicine could ask for help until, approximately at 1 p.m., lunch was served. It was 2.45 p.m. when the next session started with the singing of bhajans. Then, alternately, one of the activists spoke to the assembly or one of the village representatives presented the particular hardships of his or her village. By 5.30 p.m. the meeting was over and tea served. Participants met again around 8 p.m. The evening session, which again started with a prayer, was primarily a social meeting. Villagers and guests were asked to speak about important events and experiences in their life, things which had impressed them or brought a personal change or that were worth remembering. Most of the stories we got to listen to related to Chipko times, to current development efforts, or to the struggle for regional autonomy going on in those days in Garhwal and Kumaon. Some stories made people laugh, some set them thinking. The session was closed by 9.30 p.m. and with a dinner the 1st of June came to an end.

Programme and course on 2 June were almost similar to those of the previous day. In the early morning session, problems listed on the blackboard were discussed. Special attention was paid to the problem of dhundh, to the foggy and smoky air caused by forest fires all over Garhwal in 1995, and to the urgent need for roads through the forest demanded by some of the village people. After breakfast a new afforestation project was started near the village of Lasiyari and women began to prepare the pits. Panthriji, the retired principal—one of the experienced guests—explained to the village folk and other participants how to dig a proper pit, how to plant saplings, and how to care for them in the following months and years. The afternoon session was again reserved for speeches and for information about problems in the different villages. As my time schedule did not allow me to stay on I had to leave the camp together with my companions on 2 June, in the late afternoon. We were told that the camp would end in the middle of the next day.

The Camp-meetings: Space to listen—space to teach? At first glance it seems that the institution of these eco-development camps provides a space to *listen* to people's voices, to learn about their particular needs so that help and support can be well directed. But this is only one side of the coin. Camps are equally, if not more, aimed at educating the village participants, at teaching them about the importance of forests and afforestation and convincing them of the absence of village jungles as their most crucial problem. In the course of the eco-development camp I learned that the camp's focus was on the planting of village forests and fruit trees. Even though the social and economic problems outlined by villagers were taken seriously and activists promised to help tackle them, attention was always redirected to the *gram van,* which was assumed to be a vital aspect of problem-solving. In this respect, it is worthwhile to take a closer look at the course of the first session.

The session was begun and chaired by Chandi Prasad Bhatt. He encouraged the villagers to ask questions and discuss problems. Then he elaborated on the importance of village forests: he demanded its own forest for every village and gave examples of people who had succeeded in reforesting previously barren land. He stressed the special task of women to plant and nurse village forests and argued that a van panchayat (forest council) was necessary to manage the forest.[37] 'To destroy a forest, that's quickly done', Bhatt said, 'but to care for a forest takes a long time'.[38] Bhatt then listed the problems the villagers had brought forward. When villagers frequently mentioned the need for schools, hospitals, roads, Shishupal Kunwar intervened: You should tell us about problems which our samsthan is able to solve, he said. Schools and road were the responsibility of government.

Later a dialogue developed between a village woman and Bhatt. The woman complained about the pradhan of two villages with a joint gram sabha and accused him of caring only for the development of his own village. There he has succeeded in opening a school, a post office, a veterinary centre, whereas in the other village there is no progress and no hope of employment, she said angrily. 'We are poor people and we depend on you and your help'—she concluded.

Bhatt: You should plant your own forest, and then you will be able to do your routine work more easily.

Woman: We tried to, but we made mistakes. We have a lot of difficulties. We need a hospital. The road is very far and if somebody falls ill we have big problems. For treatment we have to go to Joshimath, Chamoli,

[37] A van panchayat is an officially sanctioned means to secure people's participation in forest management. Panchayat forests, only found in the region of the former British Kumaon and supervised by the district magistrate, are managed by an elected van panchayat accountable to the administration and to the Forest Department. Van panchayats controlling gram van (planted and cared for by the villagers themselves) are organized according to the official structure but are probably only accountable to the villagers.

[38] This and all quotations following are translated extracts from speeches and discussions recorded during the camp meetings, or are based on interviews. Between the sessions I took the opportunity to talk with women from various villages. I asked them to elaborate on the situation of their village and the topics they had presented over the meetings.

Pipalkoti. By the time we reach the hospital, the patient may be dead—that has happened very often. And our only employment is breaking stones.

Bhatt: You should plant trees—walnut trees, areca nuts.

Woman: (supported by others): 'We have planted trees, a few orange trees, walnut trees. We don't have land for more. Also, our living conditions are bad. When a family separates, there is no place to go. We are poor, we cannot construct a house. For five years our pradhan promised a budget for our village, but nothing happened. Also the mahila mandal does not work properly.

Bhatt: What do you expect by coming to this camp?

Woman: We have a lot of grievances (*dukh*). You can see there is no development in our village. So we came to your camp.

Such dialogues, as well as later presentations, showed that if for the villagers afforestation is of crucial interest, it is nevertheless, only part of a whole bundle of demands born out of marginalization and feeling of neglect. Bhatt and the DGSM have always shown concern for the problems of villagers in a changing physical and social environment, and they are willing to give support in many respects. But this support is informed by their own imagination and concept of village life and development; it is given according to the priorities of the organization. Demands of the village men and women are evaluated and judged and are taken up only when they fit into the concept of the samsthan. To this aspect (which characterizes not only the work of the DGSM but more or less that of many other voluntary organizations) I shall later return.

The Main Issues—Village Achievements and Village Demands: The fact that village folk are able to stand up in the camp-meetings and frankly present their problems and demands is one of the considerable achievements of Chandi Prasad Bhatt and the DGSM. Villagers have not only learned to voice their concerns, they are conscious that as *citizens* they have the *right* to. Seeing that those living in neighbouring villages are often in similar difficulties stimulates and encourages them to tackle their own problems. This was evident in several statements by village representatives during the camp meetings:

'It is due to Bhatt*ji* that we have learned to speak, he has encouraged us, he has helped and educated us.'

'In the camps we meet other people and learn from them. We have learned to speak according to our opinion, to express our needs.'

'We meet people from other villages and learn about their grievances and problems. We discuss, we see that we are not the only people with problems.'

'Before we worked with the samsthan we were not vigilant, we were not aware of our problems. They have helped us to become self-conscious.'

'Today we know: if we express our demands, the samsthan will help us. If the child cries, the mother will come to feed it with milk. But if the child is quiet, nothing will happen. Only if we request a hearing, then people will listen to us.'

Many villagers spoke of their cooperation with the DGSM and what they gained. First of all 'we learned to acknowledge the value of trees', a village woman said. 'Then we thought we should have our own jungle. And now we are working in it for two years.' Those who have already succeeded in afforestation spoke of their efforts. They described how they began by fencing off the chosen plot with thornbushes, they spoke of the encouragement and financial support they got from Bhatt and the DGSM so that they could buy saplings of fodder and fruit trees and were able to construct a durable stone wall. They mentioned with pride how many *bojh* (the load a woman carries on her back) of firewood and grass they now got from their forest. Some village representatives explained that the DGSM spent money for other community purposes as well, for example to purchase equipment (i.e. blankets, carpets, kitchen utensils, large pots) needed for village functions, marriages, and pujas. These are public events when people must be fed and provided a place to sleep. To lay the foundation for development work the DGSM had also encouraged the constitution of women's councils on a voluntary base.[39] These

[39] Women's councils (*mahila mandals*) are official organizations in the context of village self-government. Often, they do not work properly, but when the councils are inspired or supported by voluntary organizations they often function well.

mahila mandals are mainly involved with preparing, planting, and nursing the village forest; some groups have started other activities as well. For example, women make sure that no alcohol is consumed, the local brew is not made; in some villages they regularly organize the cleaning of village streets and water sources; to tackle the problem of local employment some women's councils have decided to establish a *silai* (sewing) centre where women and girls can learn tailoring.

Although considerable steps forward have been taken in villages co-operating with the DGSM, a significant number of problems remain. Not all the villages participating in the camp have a gram van. Women complain that the government forest is far away, to collect firewood they have to leave their houses by 5 in the morning and then walk 5-6 km until they reach the forest. Often they have to quarrel with members of other villages who claim exclusive rights to a particular jungle. Coming back after several hours, they get no rest; they have to haul water, prepare a meal, care for the children, so there is no time left. Some villages do not have land enough for afforestation. Another problem is the damage done by wildlife. Lack of forest and decline in the numbers of prey are reasons for the permanent threat by wild animals. Panthers that once roamed the jungle now come into the vicinity of settlements, destroy fields, even attack human beings. Besides the need for village forests, the demand for roads and bridges, schools and water are most frequently expressed. Villagers do not ask for a motorable road, they simply need a road usable by children and adults over the whole year, which allows easy transportation of goods, and which links the village with Chamoli and the main valley. Villages are often located in mountainous areas traversed by small ravines and rivulets which children have to cross on their way to school. Many speakers, insisting on the need for a primary school in their own village, described the difficulties children face on their way to school. Little children are not able to manage these routes and cannot start going to school until they are 9 or 10 years old. Government employees working in distant places take their children with them for their education, a woman stated, but our children are just sitting around. Decent schooling is seen as a precondition for future development, and despite the hardship and expense, many families send their boys and sometimes even their girls to secondary schools in Chamoli and Gopeshwar.

Several villages around Lasiyari have severe water problems. The region is deforested, water sources are few, and the flow of water irregular. Especially in the dry season, women walk long distances to fetch water; sometimes they wait a long time until their vessels are full. For lack of water only a few cash crops can be grown; in some villages there are no irrigation channels to water fields and the yield is poor. Villagers ask for pipelines but are also aware that the water problem is caused by deforestation. According to a Dalit woman the water problem in Dalit settlements is even more severe. She described her situation during the camp meetings with bitter words: the lack of water for drinking, cleaning, and irrigation was only one side of the coin. The general neglect and contempt of the village Rajputs and the government towards them was the other:

> If at times in the year there is water near the village, the Rajputs say: 'This water is not meant for you, you are *dom* . . .' The government is not interested in helping us, cooperating with us. Everybody thinks *dom* can eat shit and drink urine. Nobody will help us; the government does not provide budgets, we don't have a high school, and our children cannot get a proper education. . . . If nobody will help us, the government should at least give us poison so that we can die. The government should pour poison into the water, we are thirsty, and we will drink everything. . . . We don't have employment; we have only a few fields, our children are small. We work from morning till evening, after work the children wait for a meal, but the mother says: 'Without water, how can I cook?' Bhattji, you should visit our village, see our problems, and then help us.

For every problem, villagers expect help and support from Bhatt and his organization. They are expected to help in village afforestation projects, exert influence on the government and administration, write petitions. Participants in the camp showed enormous confidence in the leaders, as well as the strong belief that they had power.

How does Chandi Prasad Bhatt, how do other activists, react to people's expectations? In his first speech on the afternoon of the first day, Bhatt took up the grievances of villagers that had been expressed in the previous session. He expressed sympathy for the demand for roads and schools; he confirmed the importance of education and complained of the dangerous trails pupils had to follow on their way to school. He concluded: 'It seems that we are not real citizens of the

country', and he promised: 'All that has been mentioned by you, it may
be forgotten by others, whereas I will try to solve your problems. But
you have to organize yourselves and you should be united. Then your
voice will be heard.'

Bhatt then elaborated on the success of the mahila mandal of Lasiyari in relation to afforestation. He urged women to emulate this success, because without forests in close proximity women suffer:

> Formerly women managed to bring the firewood and the grass from the
> forest in 1–2 hours, currently it takes them 6–8 hours per day. And what
> will happen after some time? We know about villages where women
> leave the house by 5 o'clock in the morning and do not return before 3
> p.m. Many of them have no time to eat, even not before leaving. They
> don't have strength, they fall ill. The destruction of the forest does not
> concern the government, and also not the men. It concerns the women!

> What kind of work do the women do? They collect firewood and grass,
> they fetch water, and they wash their children. If the women spend the
> whole day in the forest, children remain dirty. We have seen 2–3 year-old
> children tied on the *charpai*, they were screaming. All the time, until the
> mother returns, the child has a running nose, its face covered with flies.
> It weeps and weeps and will never become strong. Now the woman
> comes home, she lays down her bojh and stores it—the child is still
> weeping. The woman gets nervous, perhaps she will beat the child. I have
> enough problems, she may think, why do you trouble me as well? That's
> our situation.

Bhatt spoke of young women who committed suicide because of
their workload and hopeless situation. On the water issue he pointed
out that the problem existed in many countries of the 'Third World'.
Then he came back to the need for afforestation and demanded that
women plant their own jungle to solve their problems. He encouraged
women to fight van panchayat elections. He announced his willingness
to help villagers get a road and a school. He invited people to visit
Gopeshwar to work out a strategy: 'As far as village progress is concerned we [the DGSM] can make an appeal to the government, but
in the case of afforestation, the progress is your responsibility alone.
The forest you have to make on your own.'

In other speeches Bhatt elaborated on the procedure's required to create a village forest: see where empty land is available; acquire the plot; make a wall. The land for afforestation, should not be in more than 3 km from the village and it must be under village control. Dig the pits, add fertilizer, plant saplings, care for the new plantation with regular watering. And so on.

Dressed in simple khadi, Bhatt always spoke in a calm and convincing voice and seemed to inspire confidence. The contents of his speech and his choice of words were down to earth, easily understood. Other leaders and activists, being guests at the camp, praised Bhatt and the DGSM, their strong commitment to village folk. Ramesh Pahari, the journalist, encouraged the villagers to cooperate with Bhatt and the DGSM and highlighted the involvement and successes of the organization:

Our whole country knows about Bhatt, his samsthan and his afforestation projects. The practical work he is doing in the villages is very well known. And *mantriji* [Shishupal Kunwar], he is from your village, but you don't know how hard he works for the success of the samsthan. The whole team has been busy for more than twenty years, and the villages where they worked have changed completely. Villages which were in the shadow, the people forlorn and hopeless, today they have a good spirit, people are educated, have cash crops. . . . I know about these things because I work with Bhatt. Look at all the villages that showed interest in cooperating with Bhatt, their situation has improved; they are ahead of others. . . .

You are lucky, the man who can advise and help you is in your midst, and you should try to get the maximum profit from his help. You should not quarrel with each other, you should work according to the suggestions of the samsthan, you should work for environmental improvement. See, even the people in foreign countries know about Bhatt, they come to see him, to see how he works in camps [he referred to my visit].

You have a lot of problems: road, water, electricity, school, employment. . . . And you women, you have even more problems: grass, firewood, to care for the cattle, to care for the children. And how do you solve your problems? First you should come together, discuss, and analyse the problem. Then you should jointly find a solution. To accuse the government and the officials, that's not the solution. We have to think, we have to be alert: suppose we don't have grass, firewood—we can't blame the government. But we can get hold of Bhatt and Kunwar and cooperate with them. Only with this cooperation have some of you succeeded in afforestation, achieved some prosperity—due to your own work and the support of the samsthan. . . . We are *pahadi log*, people from the hills, we must find work in the villages, in our area. We must do agricultural work, we can plant cash crops,. . . . raise good cattle. Every village must have its own forest. That is important, because the government has the right to impose restrictions to the Reserved Forest. . . . We have to work for our development, and then we will be our own masters!

Chandra Singh Rana, a villager from Mandal and a member of the DGSM, has been active since Chipko times. He began and ended all his contributions to the camp with the slogan: *Kaun jage? Vanvasi jage!* (Who should be alert? The forest dweller should be alert!). In one of his speeches he distinguished three types of leaders: *asli neta* (true leaders), *fasli neta* (seasonal leaders, only for a period, like crops), and *naqli neta* (false leaders). Many of our leaders in the villages and in politics belong to the last two categories, he said, but Bhatt—he is the only true leader we have!

The Work of Chandi Prasad Bhatt and the DGSM: Concluding Remarks

The project of eco-development as designed and carried through by Bhatt and the DGSM has two aims: to empower people, specially women, and make them self-reliant. The training camps provide a space to express grievances and make sure that people's voices are heard, problems taken seriously. The camps are equally a space for self-articulation by activists who are keen to convey their ideas and vision and transform these into action. The term 'influence leaders', invented by Sunderlal Bahuguna to differentiate Gandhian workers from politicians (whom he calls 'power leaders'), well comprehends the way Bhatt and his group see themselves. 'Influence leaders' don't carry through ideas against the will of those concerned, they give attention to the needs and demands of others, they convince by argument and by their own dedication to the issues at stake. This is evident from Bhatt's deeds and his words:

Dasholi Gram Swaraj Mandal (DGSM), the mother organisation of the Chipko Andolan, has been successful in *understanding the psychology of the forest dwellers*; the organisation has been active in making villagers understand the importance of forests and vegetation and in seeking their active participation in afforestation and forest conservation. Towards this end, the mandal has been organising a series of eco-development camps in the areas seriously affected by landslides and soil erosion in the Alaknanda watershed in the Central Himalayas. The purpose of these camps is *to prepare the villagers psychologically to recognize the importance of forests as foundation for their future growth and development* without which all their economic and social values will be at stake. Once they accept this, their participation in afforestation and forest conservation follows. (Bhatt n.d.: 7, emphasis mine)

Trans-local publicity, which is also important for dissemination, seems to be one of the reasons why the camps have a *performative* character: The course of the camp follows a certain 'ritual'. Every session starts with prayers and devotional songs, producing a sense of community and indicating the moral commitment of activists. During the meetings villagers speak of their problems and activists signal understanding and suggest solutions.[40] Participants from successful villages tell of their achievements and express their gratitude to the DGSM. Every day, after the morning session, activists and participants set off to see new plantations, and the leaders and special guests offer comments on the efforts of the villagers. The camp activities are directed (even stage-managed) in such a way that leaders and activists reveal knowledge and charisma, whereas villagers tend

[40] I cannot say whether this was part of the 'ritual', but in one of the first sessions of the camp Shishupal Kunwar elaborated on the financial sources of the organization: 'There is a rumour about the money we spend for our work and people ask: where do the sarvodaya people get their money from? They have four camps a year, they provide good meals, they sponsor the afforestation.'. Then Kunwar listed the financial sources: their own small industries for turpentine production from local resin; their own nurseries growing saplings and plants for sale (and for free donation to co-operating villages); spinning mills and weaving; interest on awards that Bhatt received; national and international funding for afforestation work. Such explanations were apparently meant to inform the villagers of their fund sources largely in order to display transparency and to enlist additional financial support.

to show their 'ignorance' and dependence. In this sense, I would say, the training camps radiate the Gandhian spirit. Bhatt as well as the leading activists of the DGSM think of themselves as satyagrahis who claim to search only the truth and selflessly devote their lives to teach people, 'uplift' them. Weber stresses that even though a satyagrahi tries to convert, he must also remain open to persuasion (Weber 1988: 82). We have seen that both Gandhian Chipko leaders—Bhatt and Bahuguna—claim to have learned from the people. Nevertheless, the basic relation of activist and villager seems to be that of teacher and disciple: on the one side there is the one who knows and who teaches, on the other side are those who know less and who have to learn. The attitude of distance and respect, devotion and love, which characterizes the relationship between guru and *chela* (teacher and disciple) in traditional Indian contexts is mirrored here in the dealings of villagers with their leaders.

Another Gandhian key concept which informs activity here is *swarajya*, literally self-rule, independence. Bhatt and his colleagues, as well as many of the guests, repeatedly advise villagers not to rely on the government for help but with the support of the samsthan take the future in their own hands. Gandhi's vision of self-sufficient villages, suitably modified by realism, suffuses the work of the DGSM. Bhatt and his group do not imagine a 'survival economy' dissociated from the market and relying only on agriculture, husbandry, and tree farming—as does the more utopian Bahuguna. Although they basically aim to reduce the dependence and vulnerability of villagers through the improvement of everyday ecological conditions, they also tackle the problems of employment and income generation, of social neglect and general village development.[41] They believe villagers are no longer geographically marginalized and cut off from the larger society, that they have developed additional demands and will naturally search for more life options. Bhatt and the DGSM do not try

[41] The concept of 'vulnerability' has been developed by R. Chambers. He has defined vulnerability as 'an external side of risks, shocks and stress to which an individual or household is subject; and an internal side which is defenselessness, meaning a lack of means to cope without damaging loss' (see in Bohle 1997). The concept of vulnerability is central in the research on risk (Blaikie *et al.* 1994) and in the livelihood approach (Bohle 1997; Bohle and Adhikari 1998).

to completely alter lifestyles: they want to accommodate life to contemporary needs and end local backwardness, creating villagers who are full-fledged citizens.

5.2.3 Village Discourses in the Aftermath of Chipko: The Example of Lata and Raini

A number of villages in Chamoli District profit greatly from the welfare work of Bhatt and his organization, but there are also villages which completely refuse cooperation. Prominent examples of the latter are the villages Lata and Raini located east of Joshimath in the Niti Ghati, well known because of their Chipko struggle in 1974. In those days the inhabitants of Lata and Raini jointly fought against the felling of their jungle and were supported by, among others, Bhatt. The reason for their current mistrust of Bhatt seems to be a certain disappointment about the way he is said to have strengthened his own reputation by representing the Raini struggle, and by allegedly making use of Gaura Devi (see Chapter 4). The villagers have done some afforestation work cooperatively with Anand Singh Bisht, formerly a member of the DGSM who now runs his own voluntary organization in Gopeshwar (Jakeshwar Shikshan Samsthan).

J.S. Chauhan and I visited Lata and Raini several times between 1993 and 1996 and worked with the villagers. We realized there was a certain bitterness in their narrations about life in the aftermath of Chipko: they have succeeded in saving their own jungle from destruction but, after the establishment of the Nanda Devi National Park in 1982 (the core zone of the Nanda Devi Biosphere Reserve ranging from Raini to Malari), their conditions have worsened. People complain that, in the end, they gained nothing from Chipko and their struggle for environmental protection (see also Mitra 1993).

Lata and Raini: The Villages and Their Inhabitants: Following the Tibetan border road from Joshimath to Malari which runs parallel to the left bank of the Dhauli Ganga, a tributary of the Alakananda, the traveller passes Tapovan and then reaches Raini at the confluence of the Dhauli Ganga and the Rishi Ganga. After a few kilometres she arrives at Lata. Only dwellings used in the cold season, from November to March, are located near the roadside. To reach the main village

(2317 m) with the stone temple of Nanda Devi she has to climb up a well-kept footpath. Lata and Raini had a joint gram sabha in Chipko times; the inhabitants are Tolchha Bhotiyas who speak a mixture of Garhwali and Kumaoni.[42] According to the census data of 1981, Lata then consisted of 72 families. In 1995 I counted 84 families; 16 families belonged to Dalits (*lohar* [blacksmith] and *bajgi* [musician]), and 68 families were Rajput. My informants said Raini is inhabited by 45 Rajput families, a number which differs significantly from the 1981 census data (19 families). The village economy is based on rain-fed cultivation on terraced slopes.[43]

The main crops are wheat, amaranth, buckwheat (*phaphar*), pota-toes, and kidney beans (*rajma*). Potatoes and rajma are also produced for sale. People own a few fruit trees—walnut, apple, apricot—but some families have started small orchards for cash-crop production. Animal husbandry plays a supplementary role in the subsistence-based local economy. Most villagers in Lata keep 1–3 cows for milk as well as oxen for work; a few families own small herds of sheep and goats (not more than 5–20: only three families have bigger herds). For the long winter, grass for the animals has to be stored. A good quan-tity of grass grows on civil land, which is located on the right bank of the river. Utilization policies are decided by the village panchayat and each family gets 5–6 nali (0.3 ha) of land from which its members can cut grass; after three years the plots are redistributed.

Two bridges cross the river to the civil land. For their construction, families belonging to the village collected money and are also res-ponsible for their maintenance. Of the 68 Rajput families of Lata counted in 1995, 21 families (31 per cent) received additional income from 'outside employment' of husband or son. The men had joined military or police service (Garhwal Rifles, Border Security Force, Indo-Tibetan Border Police), others worked as peons or clerks, and

---

[42] Another group, the Marsha Bhotiya, also living in Chamoli District, still speaks a Tibetan language.

[43] I asked villagers in Lata about their land and property. According to their information, it seems comparatively low. In 1995, 58 per cent of all families owned between 5 and 30 nali (all Dalit families fall into this category); 32 per cent of all families have 30 to 60 nali, and only 10 per cent own 60 to 120 nali. These details are not based on official records.

three were qualified as geologist, medical doctor, and forester. Some of the migrants have taken their families to their place of work and have given their agricultural land for tilling to a relative residing in the village. More frequently, a married male leaves the village alone; his wife and children remain in the village and stay with the husband's family.

In the last two decades the importance of education seems to have been increasingly acknowledged by the Rajputs of Lata and, nowadays, education is highly estimated as a necessary condition for village development. Old men and women are mostly illiterate, and whereas middle-aged men often have a basic education, women of this age group remain uneducated. The situation has changed with the next generation. Men in the age group of 35 years are educated and some have even got 'higher education'. These young men have married literate girls and the couples send their children—boys and girls—to primary and secondary schools. The Dalits are less educated than Rajputs, they still keep their girls at home and send only the boys to school. But, as in many villages in the hills, many educated young men from Lata—they may even have a university degree—have no salaried employment and continue doing agricultural work in the village.

When I asked the older men about their occupation, quite a few said they had done mountaineering in earlier years. They worked as cooks, porters, and guides for the expeditions which came to climb the Nanda Devi peaks. Mountaineering was a stable source of income for the villagers, but they profited from the trekking groups in other respects as well: after the tour they could keep the trekkers' warm clothes and equipment; in cases of severe illness (when local treatment was not sufficient) they got medical help and allopathic medicines from the trekkers.[44] The mountaineers of Lata and its neighbouring villages had to stop their business when trekking was prohibited

[44] One expedition is remembered vividly by the villagers of Lata. In 1976, an American group tried to climb Nanda Devi. Among the members of the expedition were father and daughter Unsoeld. Because of his fascination for the mountain the father had given his daughter the name Devi. She died during the expedition near the peak, and people in the area believe she was an incarnation of the goddess Nanda Devi who, in the end, returned to her real home. The

with the establishment of the Nanda Devi National Park in 1980—an event which marked the beginning of severe interventions in the life of Bhotiya villagers.

Ecological Conservation at the Expense of the Local Population: The Nanda Devi National Park (NDNP) consists of an area of 624.24 sq. km and gained legal status in 1982. Following the recommendations of UNESCO's Man and Biosphere Programme the park (and a certain area surrounding it) was given the status of 'Nanda Devi Biosphere Reserve' (NDBR) in 1988. In 1992 this reserve got recognition as a World Heritage Site.[45] The NDBR occupies the whole Rishi Ganga catchment area, encircled by several high peaks (like the famous peaks of Dunagiri, Nanda Devi, Trisul). The core zone of the reserve is the NDNP, surrounded by a buffer zone of 1,612.12 sq km which includes Reserved Forests, Civil Forests, Panchayat Forests, alpine meadows and farmland. 17 villages are located in the buffer zone, 10 in Chamoli District, the others in the districts of Almora and Pithoragarh in Kumaon.

The establishment of the reserve/national park was a reaction to threats to biodiversity in the region.[46] Forests were endangered by commercial exploitation and the inability of government agencies to ensure a balance between exploitation and regeneration was obvious. Forests and pastures were threatened by overgrazing and the influx of livestock from distant villages. Non-timber Forest Produce (NTFP) was diminishing because of large-scale commercial extraction of medicinal and aromatic plants to supply the pharmaceutical and cosmetic industries. Illegal hunting was a threat to wildlife, especially

---

events are described by John Roskelley, 'Nanda Devi: The Tragic Expedition' (Harrisburg, PA., 1987). Two or three copies of the book exist in the village and are carefully kept.

[45] For details on NDBR, see Maikhuri *et al*. 1998.

[46] The flora of the reserve comprises 341 species of trees, 552 species of herbs and shrubs, 18 species of grasses; 6 plant species are endangered, 12 are rare. The fauna comprises 86 species of mammals (among them the snow leopard, blue sheep and muskdeer), 534 species of birds (among them the monal pheasant, the Himalayan snow cock, and snow partridge), 54 species of reptiles and amphibians; 7 mammals and 8 birds are considered endangered (Maikhuri *et al*. 1998: 406f.).

muskdeer (*kastûrâ*) were poached for cosmetics (Maikhuri *et al.* 1998: 410f.).

Apparently, damage to flora and fauna did not occur from the local population. Their knowledge of the regeneration cycle of plants and trees, their rules and regulations for grazing, fuelwood collection and felling of trees (for house construction and preparation of agricultural instruments) meant a sustainable use of the forests. Medicinal plants extraction was an important additional source of income for most of the families; green leaves, mushrooms and edible fruits from the forest supplemented their diet regularly but were also a security in critical periods when agricultural crops were scarce. When in 1974 the Raini forest was contracted for felling, the villages resisted because they anticipated harsh consequences to their daily life. They fought for the preservation of the forest because of its basic contribution to the local subsistence economy, to food security, and to their general ecological benefit (see Gaura Devi's demand, Chapter 4). Although the Bhotiya villagers probably found a language to express the ecological qualities of their forest in an *explicit* form only with the teachings of activists (Chandi Prasad Bhatt, Govind Singh Rawat), it seems reasonable to suppose that they had an *implicit* knowledge of the possible interrelation of forests and natural hazards for long.

According to H.S. Rawat, chairman of the van panchayat of Lata, the Panchayat Forests are located in the buffer zone of the NDBR and cover an area of 4,948 acre or 2,004 hectare.[47] Panchayat Forests are under the supervision of the district administration (sub-divisional magistrate), but the management and conservation of forests lie in the hands of the van panchayats, which are responsible for the regulation of grazing, firewood collection, timber extraction, and afforestation. Forest resources can be extracted only after permission of the Forest Department. Van panchayats were established in the Nanda

---

[47] Maikhuri *et al.* (1998) mention three van panchayats (Tolma, Lata-Raini, Paing) with a total area of 4,737.7 ha. According to official NDBR maps the villages have 9,351.4 ha at their disposal; the area of the reserve is 34,384 ha. If one takes the first (non-official) figure, only 13.75 per cent forest is under the management of the van panchayats, 86.15 per cent reserved forest. The Civil Forest located in the NDBR is said to have only very poor forest cover.

Devi area in 1964. The van panchayat of Lata consists of a chairman (*sarpanch*) and nine members; three of them are women; the members meet every three months. The van panchayat pays a watchman (*chaukidar*) who keeps an eye on the forest to prevent misuse. His salary is financed out of fines paid by those who offend regulations. Money for afforestation comes from the government, but Anand Singh Bisht's NGO also runs an afforestation project in co-operation with the villagers.

The forest area under management of the van panchayat and free for utilization by the population is very limited and people seem to have used the reserved forests for grazing, lopping, and other purposes. Therefore the transformation of the region into a national park and a biosphere reserve had extremely detrimental consequences for the local communities. No hunting, trekking, grazing, fuelwood collection, and extraction of forest produce was allowed any longer; even entry into the park was banned, except for the purpose of ecological research and patrolling staff.[48] The forests and lands in the buffer zone are allowed to be used in the context of subsistence economy, and forest produce (leaves, edible fruits, medicinal plants) can be extracted for the people's own consumption but not for commercial purposes.

'The main issues of conflict in NDNP and Biosphere Reserve are over the right of the people to use the forest resources which they had traditionally been using', write Maikhuri *et al.* (1998: 417). They mention conflicts because of livestock grazing, the ban on NTFP extraction, on mountaineering, on removal of dead logs from the van panchayat forest, damage caused by wildlife, and unemployment in the buffer zone villages. In my interviews and personal communication with the villagers of Lata and Raini I learned of precisely the same conflicts.

- *Grazing:* In the summer months the villagers of Lata and Raini, as well as those of the neighbouring villages Tolma and Paing, grazed their livestock (especially sheep and goats) at higher altitudes. The grazing grounds are located in the core zone of

[48] According to Maikhuri *et al.* (1998), local inhabitants are allowed to enter the core zone. Villagers of Lata denied this.

the park and when after 1982, access was denied to the villagers they had to search for alternatives. People had to move long distances with their cattle, for example to the region of Dunagiri. As not all families could manage to send one or more members away for several months or pay a herdsman, they had to sell their herds. Maikhuri *et al.* say people also have to pay grazing taxes when bringing their sheep and goats to the alpine meadows of other villages. The sheep and goat population has declined very steeply, which, in turn, has led to a reduction in wool production and wool-based traditional handicraft. Overgrazing of the available pastures is another negative effect of the ban of grazing in the NDNP.

- *Extraction of jadi-buti*: Extraction and sale of medicinal and aromatic plants meant a steady income for the Bhotiya people. Since the establishment of the NDBR, the collection for commercial use is banned, the source of income blocked. Villagers are only allowed to extract small quantities for their own requirement. Men and women with whom I spoke also said with the ban on extraction, local medical knowledge tends to disappear. Local ayurvedic specialists (*vaidyas*) had known of cures with local medicines, while ordinary folk had a working knowledge of these cures as well. Govind Singh Rawat complained that the equilibrium between men–animals–forest has thus been destroyed in the local ecosystem.

- *Wildlife damage:* A considerable number of livestock is killed by wild animals (leopards, jackals) roaming the park and the outer zone. Compensations seem to have been paid quickly and fairly in the beginning, but now procedures have become very long. A serious loss in agriculture and cash crop production is caused by the damage done by wild boar, monkeys, and birds. Parrots destroy the apple crop. Villagers had to face similar problems in earlier times too, but could then kill animals which caused them loss. With the Wildlife (Protection) Act (1972), the hunting and killing of animals is prohibited.

- *Removal of dead logs:* Before 1982 dead logs lying around in reserved forests could be distributed by the panchayat for local use. This is now prohibited.

- *Mountaineering*: All expeditions and trekking activities in the NDBR are banned. With this the Bhotiya lost a major source of income. Maikhuri *et al.* (1998) say that in the 1960s and 1970s the per capita income per year from tourism in Tolma, Lata, Raini, and Paing—villages located at the starting point of treks—was estimated to be about Rs 2014; the average income for all buffer zone villages was Rs 1455.

- *Unemployment:* Currently the inhabitants of Lata and Raini lack profitable sources of income. In Lata a few men have employment outside the village and usually support their families; the same is reported for Raini. People staying back in the village and its vicinity can only do labour (*mazduri*), mostly as agricultural or street labourers. Whereas for long the availability of labour was low, the situation has slightly improved with the establishment of the Jawahar Rozgar Yojana (an employment plan), financing village development projects (for example for the construction of village streets, panchayat houses, playgrounds). The construction work is done by the villagers themselves who thus earn some money. Women contribute to the family income through carpet weaving, but in relation to production time the profit is about zero (see below). According to my informants in Lata, the inhabitants of the villages most affected by the establishment of the park (Lata, Raini, Paing, Tolma) were promised by government that they would get priority in the allocation of jobs (as workers, but also at higher ranks) connected with the maintenance and control of the NDNP as a compensation for the loss of income. This turned out to be a false promise.

The economic difficulties of the Bhotiya communities in the Nanda Devi region are perceived by villagers as a real threat to their way of life; but what upsets them most is that even after the establishment of the park the illegal exploitation of timber and forest produce, as well as illegal hunting, seem to continue. Some men said angrily:

In the night we see the camp fires burning and we listen to the shots. People come from the other side, from Kumaon, that's easy. . . . They are Nepalis. Illegal activities were less when we were allowed to walk in the forest. It was a certain control—we saw if somebody harmed the forest or the animals, and we stopped him. But now entry into the park is denied to us, and all sorts of *badmashi* [bad or criminal undertakings] are going on . . .

Maikhuri *et al.* (1998) have mentioned illegal activities by hired Nepalis too:

Also the commercial exploitation of NTFP from the area has been banned since 1982 (when it was declared a National Park), yet the extraction continues because of practical difficulties in enforcing the ban. A similar situation exists in the case of poaching of wildlife. A huge number of Nepalese labourers depend upon wage earning in this area, to secure their livelihood. These people, because of their familiarity with mountain resources, are being hired by contractors for illegal commercial exploitation of resources in government forests. The advantage of engaging Nepalese labour is that the reserve officials hesitate to institute legal proceedings for punitive action against these foreign nationals. It is also practically impossible in legal terms to identify the contractors as the prime culprits. (p. 412)

When I met Govind Singh Rawat again in Joshimath in January 1999 he told me enthusiastically about a new andolan he had initiated, directed against the closure of the NDNP and demanding access to the park for the local population. The first action of this andolan took place in autumn 1998, when the inhabitants of the villages located in the buffer zone marched with singing and drumming to Lata Kharak, an alpine meadow at a height of more than 4000 m. G.S. Rawat, as well as journalists from regional newspapers, accompanied the people. Rawat took a series of photographs, which he proudly showed me. He explained that the next actions would take place in May 1999. Rawat was seriously ill in January but he was full of hope that he would recover by May. He expired a few days after our meeting, and I have no information of the progress of the protest campaigns.

Negotiating Development—The Issue of Equity: When I asked my Bhotiya respondents to compare their local way of life with that of 'people from the plains' they immediately referred to what they consider the main difference. They described their own conditions of life as 'backward' (the English word is used in the local language) and themselves as 'poor' (*garib*).[49] In this discursive context 'poor' does not necessarily relate to 'poverty' in the strict economic sense, it connotes a more general depiction of the simplicity and limited nature of their mode of life. To use the term 'poor' is also not meant to blame oneself—rather, one should read it as an accusation addressed at the non-Pahari people who hoard their economic and political power and deny opportunities to the hill population. The Bhotiyas have precise ideas about local development, the important issues being income generation, education, and health care. But the basic demand is to secure a balance between ecological requirements and the fulfilment of social and economic needs. This, they say, should be the guideline of further planning.

Income should be generated from employment in the region. Therefore, job facilities have to be created on the spot in the form of small industries, village-based handicrafts, and participation in the management of the park. The educated should be given a chance as well (in the administration, as teachers, doctors).

Women have already made efforts to contribute to the family income through carpet weaving. The mahila mandal of Raini has succeeded with government funds to establish a training centre for carpet weaving in their village where women can learn the handicraft within six months. A credit system enables those who are interested to buy a loom and wool for the carpet production. For weaving a carpet the artisan needs about 10–12 kg wool (the cost for 1 kg varies between Rs 70 and Rs 100, according to quality), and (in 1995) it could be sold for Rs 1200–1500. The production process takes 3 to 6 weeks, as weaving is only done in spare time, when the woman has finished her regular work in the house and fields. If one calculates the working hours, carpet weaving is not profitable. But 'We don't count the working hours', the women said, 'and it is not the profit which is of interest for us, it is the chance to get Rs 1500 cash on the nail when we sell a carpet'.

Education is much in demand; uneducated villagers frankly express their feeling of being dominated and manipulated by those who are

---

[49] This self-characterization seems common in the hills. Participants in the eco-development camp and villagers in Nakoli tended to describe their situation in the same way.

educated and who monopolize knowledge—outsiders as well as locals. Being educated does not simply mean reading and writing, it means becoming self-reliant, and competing with people in the plains for jobs. People demand junior and high schools, as well as inter-colleges in their vicinity. Villagers also demand schools run by qualified and responsible teachers.

The third basic condition for life-improvement, health care, is mentioned by all. The demand for local hospitals, expressed by the Bhotiyas as well as by people participating in the eco-development camp, transcends the simple wish to get treatment and medicine in case of illness. Villagers say they feel neglected: without proper health care in the locality the mortality of their children is comparatively high, epidemics like dysentery are quite frequent, long distances to medical institutions and the lack of infrastructure cause frequent deaths. Bhotiyas from Lata, Raini and the adjacent villages have to go to Tapovan or even Joshimath if somebody is seriously ill. The demands for health care as well as for schools and income generation are, together, part of the general demand for respect and the struggle for recognition.[50]

Bhotiyas in the Nanda Devi region accept and value their life and culture. They are aware of hardships, the permanent struggle to get a share of modern facilities. But the Bhotiya men and women with whom I spoke would not give up their hill life in exchange for that in the plains. In the plains there is theft and criminality, they say. Women there cannot move without fear, people have to pay for everything, even for nature's products like water and wood. They summarize the advantages of life in the hills: 'We hill people are free, our women are free, we are living in peace.'

---

[50] Axel Honneth has tried to integrate the Hegelian concept of *recognition* into a normative theory of society and to see social conflicts not only from the perspective of instrumental action but as morally motivated struggles for recognition (see Honneth 1992). Martin Fuchs makes use of this concept to analyse social movements in India, especially with reference to the Dalit movement (see Fuchs 1999).

6

The Interconnections of Forest
and Village Life in Rawain
(Western Garhwal)

6.1 The Village and the Region

THE VILLAGE OF NAKOLI (A PSEUDONYM) IS LOCATED IN
the region of Rawain, which constituted a separate administrative unit (pargana) in the former princely state of Tehri
Garhwal and which now forms the western part of Uttarkashi District
in Uttaranchal.[1] Rawain, a mountainous region with still comparatively good forests and fertile valleys, spreads between the rivers Tons
and Yamuna but also extends to the left side of the Yamuna.[2] The extensive river terraces here are the preferred sites for human settlement
and archaeology offers proof that Rawain and the whole upper
Yamuna valley, including some of its subsiding valleys, have been
populated since ancient times.[3] In Ramasirai, not far from Purola,
neolithic stone tools have been found. Recently an eagle-shaped
brick altar (*syenachiti* or *garudachiti*, 24 x 18 m) was excavated here,
dating back to the second century BC, apparently built by a Kuninda
chief for Vedic sacrifices (the Asvamedha ritual)—the Kunindas
having been the rulers of the region of Garhwal and Kumaon from

---

[1] The largest administrative unit in the princely state of Tehri Garhwal was
the riyasat, the state itself; the units below were tahsil, pargana, patti and gaon
(village). In UP the administrative units below the state are zila (district), tahsil,
patti and gaon.

[2] Rawain corresponds to the tahsils Purola and Barkot.

[3] For the prehistory and early history of Garhwal and Kumaon, see Joshi 1990
and Saklani 1987.

c. 200 BC to AD 300.[4] In the foothills of the lesser Himalayas near Kalsi (Jaunsar, the region south of Rawain), some of the best preserved rock inscriptions of Emperor Ashoka (third century BC) have been discovered.[5] According to stone inscriptions the temple site of Lakhamandal (10 km south of Naugaon, in the Yamuna valley), was constructed between the fifth and twelfth centuries AD. The temples are dedicated to Shiva and Parasurama as well as to the Pandavs, the mythic heroes of the Mahabharat. Popular narratives even date some of the constructions back to the Pandavs, who are said to have lived here around 1000 BC. In a village near Nakoli, an old stone temple resembling the smaller ones at Lakhamandal and sheltering a shivaling has been built over by a two-storeyed wooden construction. This is the contemporary village temple and serves the worship of a local deity. Shivalings made of black stone have been found in Nakoli and other villages, indicating ancient sites of Shiva worship.[6] On certain hill tops of Rawain near the banks of the Yamuna or its tributaries, the remains of old fortresses can be discovered, pointing to a later period in the history of Garhwal. According to historians, the Paurava-Varmans followed the Kunindas as dynastic rulers of the region of Uttaranchal. They exerted power only for one century and were then replaced by the Katyuris, who seemingly ruled undisputed over Garhwal, Kumaon, and parts of West Nepal from about the eighth until the twelfth century, when their supremacy was challenged by the invasion of the Mallas from Nepal (Joshi 1990: 51, 63). After that the kingdom dissolved, seemingly into several independent principalities, each confined to a smaller territory concentrated around a fortress (*garh*). Six or seven such principalities existed in Kumaon, whereas local historians mention fifty-two or sixty-four in Garhwal.[7] In comparison with Kumaon and the low mountains of the Lesser Himalaya,

[4] For the archaeological excavation of this brick altar, see Nautiyal and Khanduri 1988–9.

[5] Eleventh Rock Edict of Ashoka; the language is Pali, written in the Brahmi script (Sircar 1965).

[6] Apparently, 'folk' cults have replaced the earlier worship of Hindu gods. The folk deities are often said to be a form of Shiva.

[7] According to certain interpretations, 'Garhwal' means region of the 'garhwalas', i.e. those who reside in a garh.

194 FOREST FUTURES

the landscape of Garhwal is dominated by rugged moutain tracts and is therefore unfavourable for centralized political control. Pandit Harikrishna Raturi, the author of a history of Garhwal (*Garhwal ka Itihas,* written *c.* 1933), lists the name and locality of fifty-two garhs (1988: 154–7). These independent chiefdoms flourished until the sixteenth-century, when, in Garhwal as well as Kumaon, the petty chiefs were subjugated and unified under new dynasties. Information on this particular historical period is very poor and the history of most of the garhs has fallen into oblivion. Two of these—Mungragarh and Idiyagarh in the immediate vicinity of Nakoli—are the subject of local narratives.

Nakoli belongs to that part of Rawain which extends on the left bank of the Yamuna. From the river the landscape ascends into a mountain range which runs in an almost north–south direction and separates the Yamuna valley from the interior hills. Many villages nestle on both sides of the main ridge, belonging to two neighbouring pattis (Mungarsanti patti and Barkot patti). In Mungarsanti the different sides of the ridge are described as *alli* and *palli* (on this side/on that side) and locals speak for example of alli Mungarsanti and palli Mungarsanti. As the pattis have long existed as administrative units in the Tehri riyasat with the same boundaries, long-standing interaction networks have developed between the different villages of a patti, most clearly reflected in marriage relations. Political structures have also encouraged social interaction, and religion has played an important part as well, often transcending political boundaries. In this region three main deities (devta) are worshipped. Each has a certain realm of influence affirmed by an annual yatra when the image (*murti*) of the god is carried in a palanquin (*doli*) through the villages which belong to his area. The realms of influence of the three devtas overlap at certain points, but only in Nakoli are all three gods are worshipped, and the village is visited by all three.

In the rural regions of the upper Yamuna valley, traditionally only Brahmins, Rajputs, and Dalits were settled. In all three groups, the majority of people remain agricultural landowners. With a few exceptions (see below), they till their land themselves. Shudra castes do not abound in the region and the Vaishya castes came in as traders and businessmen only in the last few decades with the infrastructural development of the region; the places where they settled grew into small bazaars in the course of time. Villages are usually inhabited either by Rajputs or by Brahmins, but a Brahmin village and a Rajput village may be very close to each other and may even, in certain cases, have a common name. Both types of villages are inhabited by Dalit families as well. The term 'Harijan' (children of god), introduced by Gandhi, allegedly to enhance the status of the so-called 'untouchables', has for long been used as a self-descriptive term by those belonging to the lowest strata of the village; across India it has been mostly dropped in favour of the term 'Dalit'; however, 'Harijan' remains more widely used in Nakoli. Older expressions like *dom* or *mochi* (the latter relating to the profession of shoemakers) are also regarded as derogatory and no longer applied, According to narratives I collected in Nakoli and its vicinity, the forefathers of the local Brahmins and high Rajputs are supposed to have come to the region approximately ten to twelve generations ago. They met a resident population whom the villagers describe as the ancestors of today's Harijans/Dalits.

Nakoli is one of the villages inhabited by Rajputs and Dalits. It is situated on the highest part of an interior south-eastern slope at an altitude of approximately 2100–2200m. The village is surrounded by well-terraced fields, fruit orchards, and comparatively dense forest.[8] Fields cover a wide area and are located at different altitudes; they reach from a height of 2300m downwards into a fertile valley (with an altitude of *c.* 1500m) carved out by a small tributary of the Yamuna. Since 1987/8 a small motorable road connects Nakoli and the other villages situated in the interior mountain tract with the main road running through the Yamuna valley from Yamuna Pul to Hanuman Chatti, from where pilgrims have to start their walk to Yamnotri. The village has a basic school (1st to 4th class) and a junior school (5th to 8th class); an additional private basic school was

---

[8] Up to an altitude of 1800–2000m, pine and cedar forests dominate—consisting of chir (*Pinus roxburghii*), khail (*Pinus wallichiana*), devdar (*Cedrus deodara*). In higher altitudes one finds oak forests—consisting of banj (*Quercus leucotrocophora*), moru (*Quercus himalayana*), kharsu (*Quercus semecarpifolia*). The red buransh (*Rhododendron arboreum*) grows amidst pine as well as oak forests. Above 2300m, fine stands of fir and spruce are to be found, mainly the species of morinda (*Abies pindrow*) and rai (*Picea smithiana*).

opened in 1995 (it closed in 1999). The government has established an allopathic hospital. Its staff consist of one medical doctor, a pharmacist and a village nurse. A veterinary station and a PWD (Public Works Department) bungalow are also part of the village. But even though Nakoli is statistically well developed, literacy is very low and medical care is, de facto, insufficient.[9] The village got electricity only in 2004.[10]

With a geographical area of 319,391 ha, 949 inhabitants, and a total of 150 households, Nakoli is one of the biggest villages in the upper Yamuna valley.[11] The households (or families, *mauvsa*) are divisible between the Rajput clans of the Panwar (42 families), Chauhan (27 families), Nakola (16 families),[12] and Rana (1 family),[13] The Dalits/Harijans, with the common name Lal, consist of 61 families; 3 families belong to the Bajgis, a caste of local musicians with the surname Das and considered higher than the former.[14] Rajputs as well as Dalits are agriculturists but some have additional sources of income. Whereas Rajputs earn money as government employees (headmaster or teacher of a school, military service) or with small contractorships, the Dalits

[9] There are several reasons for this situation. On the one hand villagers are reluctant to send their children to school, or spend money on their health. On the other hand teachers and medical personnel do not attend their work regularly; often they are not well trained, and the medicines are old and ineffective.

[10] The village got a connection probably in the late 1980s. This connection had been destroyed by a storm before I came to the village in January 1993. It was repaired—not before 1997. In 1998 the village was again disconnected, this time from the government as supplier of electricity, because the villagers were not interested in paying for the electricity.

[11] All the following data were collected in 1993 during a village survey in the context of my field work. The data represent the situation in 1993.

[12] The 'Nakola' (I use a pseudonym) have invented their name in the course of a very recent Rajputization process.

[13] Traditionally in Nakoli there are no Ranas. The only Rana came as *ghar jawain* to the village. In a context where the residence pattern after marriage is virilocal, ghar jawain is the name for a man who moves into the village of his wife and lives with her family.

[14] It is not quite clear whether Bajgis are Dalits or not. But it is evident that they have to observe similar restrictions. In the following presentation I count them among the Dalits.

work as field labourers, as general labourers (with contractors, with the Public Works Department) or in lower (class IV) government positions (peon), but in most cases they engage in handicrafts—like weaving, sewing, carpentry, and bricklaying in addition to agriculture. Formerly, the Dalits worked as shoemakers.[15] Their duties included removing dead cattle. They have given up this profession over the past two or three decades. It is remarkable that in Nakoli and its surrounding villages no service castes—sweeper, barber, washerman— exist. The villagers do these varities of work themselves, a fact which hints at a much more flexible interpretation of pollution than in other parts of India. Everyday life in Nakoli and its vicinity offers proof that, despite clear hierarchies and the necessity of observing certain rules and regulations (non-Dalits do not eat food prepared by Dalits and do not let them enter their kitchen), Dalits can participate in all village affairs (religious as well as secular) and the social interaction between castes is frequent and often relaxed. Among the different social groups in the village, the Rajput clan of Panwars claims superiority, referring to their relation with the former ruling dynasty and their prominent role in the settlement history of the village (see below). Even though this claim of superiority may be disputed by the other Rajputs, it is reflected in property relations and marriage practices.

To give a complete picture of the inhabitants of Nakoli one must also mention the Nepalis.[16] They till the fields where cash crops are grown—as agricultural labourers or on a contract basis. As contractors they have to give a fixed sum of money to the landowner after the harvest and therefore they bear the full risk of the quality of the crop and

[15] The Dalits of Nakoli did not make shoes from leather alone. Footwear with the local name *paintran* was made of a leather sole with a piece of felt sewn with it.

[16] Nepalis are not included in the population figures of the village. Nepalis, in general young men with or without family who have come with a labour contractor or with a relative already working in India, have migrated in most cases from east Nepal and usually leave after some years. Their migration is not necessarily an answer to poverty. Often, they are part of a joint family and possess land in their home villages, but they try to earn additional income (cash) to raise the living standard of their family.

its marketing. Contractorships are given for the production of potatoes and peas, whereas apple orchards remain the responsibility of the owner. Nepalis live scattered outside the main village, near the fields they work, usually in one of the chanis of the family to which they are related.[17]

Nakoli, like other villages, is far from being a closed and self-sufficient unit. For religious and economic services the inhabitants have to rely on groups or individuals residing in other places. For religious purposes Brahmins have to be called: the family priests (*purohit*) for Rajputs and Dalits come mostly from D., a village at a distance of 7km from Nakoli; Brahmins who serve as temple priests (*pujari*) or who get possessed by the deities (*mali*) come from three different places: that is, from villages which have a special relationship with one of the local gods (for the religious structure of the region, see below). As far as economic life is concerned, most of the handicrafts (weaving, rope-making, carpentry) are done by resident Dalits, but for forging the people have to call in specialists living in another village which is exclusively inhabited by blacksmiths (*lohar*). The purohits as well as the weavers and the blacksmiths are not at everybody's disposal, but, have by tradition established special relations with particular families. A family that uses the service of a Brahmin or Dalit craftsman is classified as a *jajman* and payment for the services (in kind, or as money) is regulated by certain local (*jajmani*) standards. Exceptions are carpenters and bricklayers, who are also called *mistri* and who claim to be of slightly higher status than other Dalits, although they belong to the same category. They work for money and are not bound to a particular family. They may work in their village of residence, but can also be called from families living in other villages.

In Nakoli, Rajputs and Dalits have settled in two separate but adjacent parts of the village. The upper part is inhabited by the Panwars, Chauhans, and Nakolas, whereas the houses of the Dalits are located in the lower part. A few villagers have recently constructed new houses, shops, and 'hotels' (tea stalls with facilities for one or two

---

[17] Chanis are simple buildings usually consisting of a stable and one or two rooms. They are located at various altitudes near the fields of a particular family. Chanis are not used all round the year, they shelter cattle (and often cattle herders) in certain seasons.

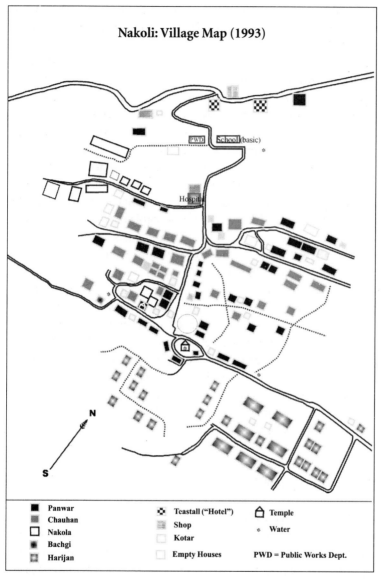

people to stay overnight) on the roadside. Rooms of their own house that open on to the road may be rented out to government employees (or to anthropologists). In the old part of the village the houses are huddled together, with only narrow paths and chauks (yards for drying fruits and grain, for threshing, etc.) in between. Traditional houses are constructed of stone, clay, and wood, the roof being covered with large flat stones (*patal*) from local quarries. The houses consist of two or three storeys, and an open veranda with carved pillars running in front of the upper rooms. Here people can sit and talk; woollen blankets are spread for visitors. In the rooms, shelves are integrated all around with the walls, which are closed with wooden doors, so that one gets the impression of a wood-panelled interior. In one of the rooms, the fireplace (chulha) is located. Here, not only are the meals prepared, but also the family members meet and talk, and sometimes they are joined by neighbours or relatives. Especially over colder days, the fireplace becomes the centre of communication. On the ground floor of the houses narrow stables may shelter the livestock in certain seasons (mainly sheep and goats). The house opens into a small yard or chauk where the threshing happens and the crops are dried. Old houses are comfortably warm in winter and comparatively cool in summer; they can give protection in case of earthquakes because the flexibility of stone and wood prevents destruction, at least in case of lighter seismic shocks.[18] But despite these advantages of the old houses, people who build new ones do not follow the traditional techniques. They prefer cement constructions, especially for the roof, while walls are often done in the old way. The main reason given is the shortage of timber, but villagers also say cement roofs are more watertight than the old roofs. Near the houses, small rectangular buildings with a veranda, carved pillars, and carved doors with metal fittings catch the view. These buildings, called *kutar*, serve as store rooms and are mostly owned and used together by a joint family. Kutars also function as places of communication where people like to meet; men may sit on the verandas, talk and smoke the huqqa, while their hands are busy rotating the spindle (the spinning of the wool of sheep or goats is done by the men); if women assemble here, they usually do some housework and watch their small children playing around. I was told that, twenty years earlier, village children gathered on the veranda of a particular kutar located in the centre of the

---

[18] Earthquakes are frequent in the Himalayas. Over the past ten years alone two big earthquakes have struck Garhwal. In 1991 many places in Uttarkashi District, and in April 1999 the towns of Chamoli and Gopeshwar in Chamoli District, were seriously affected.

village to listen to stories told by older women. Some of my informants regretted that this habit has come to an end with the increase in the number of children, with the availability of radios, and with a general change in lifestyle favouring individuality instead of a sense of community.

In what follows I give a more detailed picture of population figures, level of education, marriage relations, and property relations in Nakoli. This basic information is indispensable for understanding local hierarchies, interactions, and practices.

Population

In 1993 Nakoli had 949 inhabitants. Even though a few nuclear families did not have their actual residence in the village, they still counted as members of a joint family of Nakoli.[19] Figure 1 shows the composition of population in the form of an age pyramid.

The first significant finding by looking at the age pyramid is the balanced number of male and female children up to the age of 15. In the hills, women are valued because of their child-bearing capacity and, especially, for their labour power. In Nakoli the economic value of women finds its social expression in bride-price marriages which had been the form of marriage in former times and in some cases is still practised today. Girls are a 'source of income' and therefore are not neglected.[20] Between the age of 16 and 40 years females exceed the number of males, for various reasons. First, unmarried daughters still live with the parents because, usually, marriage is no longer performed at an early age; second, marriage practices allow polygyny. In most cases the reason for a second marriage is the barrenness of the first wife. Although polyandry was traditionally practised as well, it

[19] Migration is of marginal importance in Nakoli as well as in its neighbourhood. A few families, or members of some families, have settled in a nearby market town in the Yamuna valley, earning additional livelihood through business (small shops).

[20] In 1993 the hill districts still belonged to Uttar Pradesh. According to Drèze and Gazdar (1998: 50, Table 5) the sex ratio in the Himalayan region was the highest in UP (955); the child mortality rate (death before the age of 2 years) also showed a balance between females and males, whereas in other parts of UP significantly more girls than boys died.

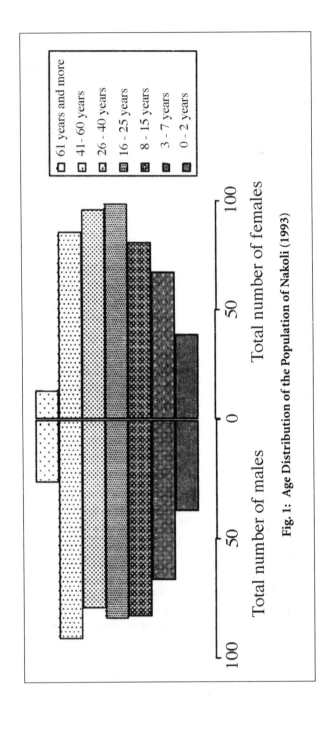

Fig. 1: Age Distribution of the Population of Nakoli (1993)

Total number of males   Total number of females

Legend:
- 61 years and more
- 41- 60 years
- 26 - 40 years
- 16 - 25 years
- 8 - 15 years
- 3 - 7 years
- 0 - 2 years

is less common nowadays.[21] The significant fall in population figures in the uppermost part of the age pyramid indicates a low life expectancy among villagers in general, caused by daily hard work, disregard of hygiene, and insufficient medical care in case of illness. Women seem to die earlier than men, their health being additionally affected by frequent pregnancies, diseases, and a greater workload.

Education

The level of formal education of adolescents and adults (all people more than 16 years old) is equally low among all communities, although the Dalits have received less (formal) education than others. An even greater difference exists between males and females and between the age groups. Generally speaking; women are much less educated than men and older people are much less educated than the young. Figure 2 shows the discrepancy between male and female literacy. Only 8.2 per cent of males and 2.3 per cent of females enjoyed a higher education (MA, BA, and Intermediate completed or ongoing).[22] 34.8 per cent of males and 7.3 per cent of females went to junior and/or high school (5th to 10th class); many of them did not enrol for the final examinations. 3.9 per cent of males and 2.3 per cent of females went to school but did not always complete basic school (1st to 4th class). 20.4 per cent of males and 9.9 per cent of females can neither read nor write properly and only manage their signature, whereas 32.6 per cent of males and 78.1 per cent of females are completely illiterate. According to the official definition of literacy given by UNESCO in 1978—namely the ability to read and write a text relating to one's everyday life—53 per cent of all males and 88 per cent of all females in Nakoli are illiterate.[23]

[21] Polyandry and polygyny as well as bride-price marriage have been declared illegal. They are still practised in a few remote areas of Garhwal (Rawain, Jaunsar). In Kumaon, under British rule from 1815, these marriage customs were prohibited much earlier and have almost disappeared.

[22] Statistical bases are formed by those who have replied to questions concerning education (males: 279, no answer 1; females 274, no answer 20).

[23] This relates to primary illiteracy (people who have never learned to read and write); the percentage is even higher if one adds those who are secondarily (functional) illiterate, i.e. people who have lost their capability to read and write.

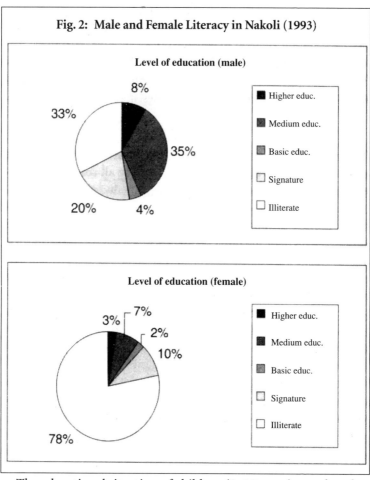

Fig. 2: Male and Female Literacy in Nakoli (1993)

Level of education (male)

8%
33%
35%
20%   4%

- Higher educ.
- Medium educ.
- Basic educ.
- Signature
- Illiterate

Level of education (female)

7%
3%
2%
10%
78%

- Higher educ.
- Medium educ.
- Basic educ.
- Signature
- Illiterate

The educational situation of children (3–15 years) reveals only a slightly better picture (Figure 3). Up to the age of 7, only 11 male and 7 female children (together 13.3 per cent) in the age group 3–7 years (total 135) had joined school. Whereas in India children usually start to go to school at an early age, this is not so in the hills. Children become schoolgoing when they are older; even then, most pupils do not participate in the lessons regularly because they are busy with household duties and other work (e.g., caring for cattle). Some of them repeat classes frequently and it is not uncommon to find 10-year-old children in the 1st class. 61 (74.3 per cent) of boys (total 82) between

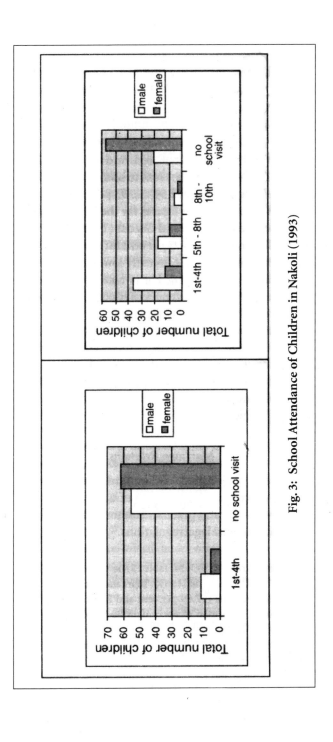

Fig. 3: School Attendance of Children in Nakoli (1993)

the ages of 8 and 15 years go to school, but only 24 (29.6 per cent) of
the girls (total 81). Very few boys and even fewer girls continue with
junior and high school after having completed their basic education.
To sum up: in total 48.6 per cent of boys and 20.6 per cent of girls between the ages of 3–15 years get a minimum formal education. To put
it the other way round: approximately 50 per cent of the boys and 80
per cent of the girls remain uneducated. And a closer look at the data
show that Dalit girls are often not sent to school (out of 58 Dalit girls
only 4 are attending school, and 54, i.e. 93 per cent, stay at home).

Compared to the education figures for the Himalayan districts of
Uttar Pradesh quoted by Drèze and Gazdar (1998: 50, Table 5), which
show an overall literacy rate of 43 per cent for females and 76 per cent
for males, literacy in Nakoli is extremely low. But to understand the
situation in Nakoli correctly one has to take into consideration the
highly significant regional differences in education and literacy in the
hill regions. In regions formerly under British rule (Kumaon, East
Garhwal, Dehra Dun), people have a higher level of education than
those living in parts of the erstwhile princely state of Tehri Garhwal
(the present districts of Tehri and Uttarkashi), where higher education
was prohibited up to 1947 for normal folk. Significant variations also
exist between urban areas or those with good infrastructure, and the
less 'developed' regions.[24]

Marriage Relations

In the so-called tribal region of Jaunsar Bawar, and in adjacent
Rawain, bride-price marriages—often of a polygynous but also of
polyandrous type—are still practised, although this practice contra-
venes post-independence legal regulations.[25] In 1993 one polyandrous

---

[24] Aggarwal and Agrawal (1995: 24, Table 19) have mentioned the districtwise
'literacy pattern' for Uttarakhand (1981). Tehri and Uttarkashi are the districts
with the lowest literacy rate (27.89 per cent and 28.92 per cent). In Chamoli,
Almora, and Nainital more than 37 per cent of the people are literate (37.46 per
cent, 37.76 per cent, 37.81 per cent), passed by Pithoragarh with 39.08 per cent.
The highest literacy is to be found in (Pauri) Garhwal (41.06 per cent) and
Dehra Dun (52.58 per cent).

[25] In British Garhwal and Kumaon the colonial administration prohibited

family was living in Nakoli (fraternal polyandry, a woman married to two brothers), whereas numerous polygynous marriage bonds could be found. Usually, a second or even third wife was taken in case of barrenness of the first one(s). Bride-price marriage (*dam vivah*) needs to be evaluated from two aspects. On the one hand it may be argued that the exchange of money degrades women to a commodity; on the other hand one can point out that paying money underlines the social value of women. Usually, bride-price marriage goes along with certain freedoms for the women, whereas the mainstream Hindu marriage (*dan vivah*) implies for greater control of the wife by the husband and his family. Primarily, bride-price marriage allows the couple to separate relatively easily in cases of incompatibility. In cases of separation the husband or his family get back the money they paid the girl's family, mostly with an extra 'interest' charge. I learned about several possible scenarios in Nakoli: A girl was married very early because the father needed money, but she continued to live in the household of her parents.[26] Her family members said if the couple decide to live together after having reached the required age, their marriage would be approved. If the couple don't got on, the girl's father is prepared to pay back the money (with 'interest'). In the course of my village survey many villagers talked about their first marriage at an early age being dissolved simply by returning the bride price. In another case the wife had started a liaison with another man who was ready to pay a large amount to her husband to secure her for himself. There are no reservations among men about marrying a woman who has been married earlier; in fact it is even considered worthwhile that a woman has 'proved' her fertility (sometimes she fetches a higher price at remarriage). Offspring from earlier marriages

---

traditional marriage practices which, under compulsion, had been given up much earlier than in the princely state of Tehri Garhwal. For polygyny and polyandry in Garhwal from an anthropological perspective, see e.g. Berreman 1987a and 1987b, G.S. Bhatt 1991.

[26] The formerly prevalent practice of child marriage (*bal vivah*), which forced child brides to live largely in the household of their in-laws from the day of marriage, has been given up in the mean time. If today a girl or a boy gets married at a young age, they continue to live in their parents' house and join each other once the girl reaches puberty.

mostly stay with the father, but may also accompany the woman into her new household.

The amount of money to be paid for a girl varies according to the age and status of the girl or the husband. In 1993 Rs 4000–10,000 was thought an adequate price, but in one case an old man without offspring paid Rs 28,000 for a young wife. The system of bride-price marriage excludes dowry; the traditional practice only prescribes that the parents of the girl give jewellery to the bride (e.g. earrings—*jhumki*; nosering—*nath*, necklace—*mangal sutra*) as well as a wooden box and some kitchen utensils of brass or copper. To be able to afford the expenses of marriage and bride-price, villagers try to accumulate money through cash-crop production, labour, or employment. The less educated are reluctant to spend money for other purposes—for proper clothing, education, hygiene, and health care. If a family cannot manage to save enough money to meet the expenses of a marriage, they borrow money from neighbours or friends (not from the bank). A few rich villagers lend money at comparatively high interest rates.

Although bride-price marriages still occur in Nakoli and the neighbouring villages, dan vivah is now preferred, especially among educated members of the Rajput clans. Dan vivah symbolizes advancement, development, modernity, whereas dam vivah is deemed the practice of remote and backward areas. Even the women, who, after marriage, know they will be subject to complete control of husband and in-laws (because the new system does not allow separation), accept the mainstream idea of Hindu marriage. Constitutive for the practice of Hindu marriage is the system of giving dowry. Dowry—which has fortunately not become utterly unbearable in the hills—is legitimated as a share of daughter(s) to the family property which, usually, is inherited only by sons.[27] Besides jewellery, which is a 'must' in every marriage, some goods are acknowledged as a necessary part

---

[27] If a couple has no male offspring they often try to marry their daughter to a man who is ready to live in the house of his in-laws as ghar jawain. The reputation of this form of marriage and residence is comparatively low because usually a ghar jawain is a person without his own property. Satirical poems and songs indicate the low prestige of a husband residing in his wife's village.

of the dowry: double-bed with mattress and bedding, sofa, stools, dressing table, metal boxes (*sanduq*) or a big wooden box (*divan box*), kitchen utensils. If a family is well off, the dowry may also include a TV, a radio, a video recorder.

Who marries whom? Who are preferred marriage partners? In Nakoli and its vicinity, so-called inter-caste marriages are very exceptional. Usually, Brahmins marry Brahmins, Rajputs marry Rajputs and Dalits form matrimonial bonds only with Dalits.[28] Intra-caste marriages allow a range of possible partners who, in the case of Rajputs, can come from different clans with different ranks. As far as North Indian Hindu marriage is concerned, the anthropological literature presupposes the practice of hypergamy—where the 'wife giver' is lower in status than the 'wife taker'. In his study on kinship and marriage in Kangra (Himachal Pradesh) Jonathan Parry (1979) has shown that hypergamy includes a well-contrived system of rights (for the wife-taker) and obligations (for the wife-giver) transcending even the life-span of a couple. In Nakoli, where bride-price marriage had prevailed a long time, no real system of hypergamy could be discovered, even though marriages show hypergamous tendencies. But to acknowledge a boy as a desirable marriage partner, high-clan status has to be combined with the financial strength of his family. In Nakoli and its vicinity Rajput families from the Chauhan, Nakola, and Rana clans prefer to give their daughters to the well-off members of the Panwar clan, but they also accept each other as wife-takers. Panwars have always tried to give their girls to Chauhans, seemingly recognized as near-equal partners. A special case is marriage bonds with the Nakolas. Whereas nowadays marriage relations between the three main Rajput clans of Nakoli are frequent, accepted, and desirable, this was not so a few decades ago. Villagers said that, formerly, nobody was interested in establishing marriage relations with the Nakolas as they were not considered Rajputs in those days (they also had a different name). Then, certain Nakolas got themselves well educated and managed to accumulate a lot of wealth, invented a new clan name, and rose in status. First their daughters were accepted as wives

---

[28] During my stay in the village I attended one inter-caste marriage. A Rajput girl from Nakoli got married to a Baniya boy from the nearby market town.

by other Rajput clans; later the Nakolas could also establish themselves as takers of girls from Chauhans, Ranas, and Panwars.

Geographically, the marriage network of the inhabitants of Nakoli covers the whole district of Uttarkashi. But whereas a few girls are taken from or given to families living in distant villages or towns, the majority of marriages have a more localized character. In 34 per cent of all cases matrimonial bonds are formed within the village. The same percentage of marriages has united partners from Nakoli and other villages of alli Mungarsanti (the direct vicinity of Nakoli), followed by 14 per cent of marriages which have established relations between families from Nakoli and palli Mungarsanti. Marriage relations also exist with villages of the bordering patti (Dashgi, Khatal, Ramasirai, Barkot), as well as with villages in the upper regions of the Tons and Yamuna (see Figure 4 and Figure 5).

The Chauhans and Nakolas tend to establish marriage bonds with the Panwars and therefore marriages within the village are more frequent. The Panwars also marry within Nakoli but, somewhat oftener, also take girls from or give girls to Rajput families residing in neighbouring villages. The majority of Dalits seek marriage partners outside the village, probably because of the close kinship bonds between families in Nakoli—they all claim their origin from one ancestor.

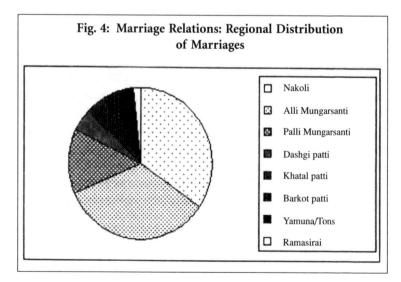

Fig. 4: Marriage Relations: Regional Distribution of Marriages

- Nakoli
- Alli Mungarsanti
- Palli Mungarsanti
- Dashgi patti
- Khatal patti
- Barkot patti
- Yamuna/Tons
- Ramasirai

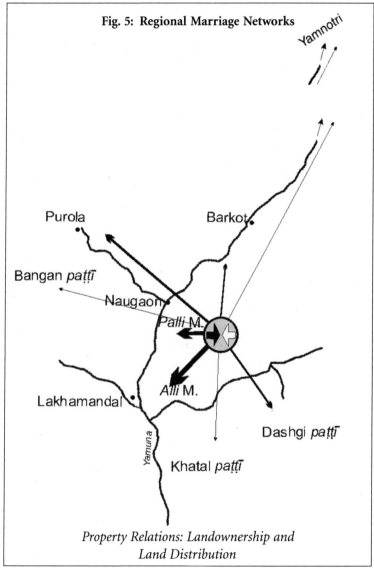

Fig. 5: Regional Marriage Networks

*Property Relations: Landownership and
Land Distribution*

With the exception of one Bajgi family which has migrated into
Nakoli, all own land and earn their livelihood basically through agriculture and animal husbandry. The production and marketing of
cash crops (apples, potatoes, peas) have gained importance in the last

ten to fifteen years.[29] It serves as an additional source of income, especially for households which do not earn money via employment,
military service, or contractorships. To grow cash crops many villagers
have acquired, and still acquire, additional land (see below).

The figures on land property and land distribution in Nakoli are
based on the records of the local *patwari* (registrar of land accounts)
who is responsible for Nakoli and five neighbouring villages.[30] Reliable
data could be collected only for 135 families, because the records
show some inaccuracies:

- Land measurements date back to 1964 and the land records have
  not been updated. So it was not always possible to relate personal names—listed in the records and indicating landowners—
  with the names of persons living/having recently lived in Nakoli
  and who claim land to be their (or their father's) property. The
  patwari explained that land may still be registered in the name
  of a forefather or another relative who is dead; or, land may be
  registered in the name of a person who is still living but—because of family separation and land division—does not own all
  the land or part of it any longer.
- Revenue land recently acquired does not show in the data
  because, usually, it is not immediately registered.

[29] The first orchards were planted *c.* 1970–5. Potatoes are said to have been
known a long time but were produced only for home consumption. Commercial
production of peas seems to have started only recently.

[30] The duty of a patwari is the administration and updating of the land register and the annual enquiry concerning the main crops (rice, wheat, barley, and
cash crops). Several land settlements happened during the reign of the Tehri
rajas: the last was completed in 1924; a revision which started in 1944 was stopped by the political disturbances in 1947 which ultimately led to the merging of
the Tehri riyasat into a new national state of India. The first settlement in
independent India was started in 1959 and completed in 1964. For the first time,
land was measured by plane table and by the use of a 55-yard chain (*jarib*). The
land register map was not done on paper but on white cotton cloth, now stored
in the office of the local patwari. The land is supposed to be resurveyed every
twenty years by a special officer (*amin*), but the actual figures date back to the
survey (*bandobast*) of 1964. For revenue administration, District Uttarkashi is
divided into 4 tahsils consisting of altogether 29 patti. A patti is a revenue circle
consisting of a group of villages (see Rizvi 1979: 104ff.).

• Figures on land property given by the families interviewed during my own village survey cannot serve as a reliable source to
correct or complete the official figures. People only gave rough
calculations, deliberately underestimating or overestimating
their property; some either did not know or did not want to dis-
close the extent of their property. One should keep in mind that
land is usually inherited by male offspring and, therefore, registered in the name of males.

In sum: in a number of cases de jure property relations differ from the
contemporary de facto situation.

Even though almost every family in Nakoli owns land, land distribution between the caste groups as well as between the different clans
and families of a caste group is unequal (see Figure 6). Whereas the
Panwar clan consists of 29 per cent of all families, its members own
40 per cent of the agricultural land. Against that the Dalits with 40 per
cent of all families own only 23 per cent of the land.

A more differentiated picture is given in Table 1: most households
of Panwars and Chauhans own between 31 and 150 nali[31] (Panwar

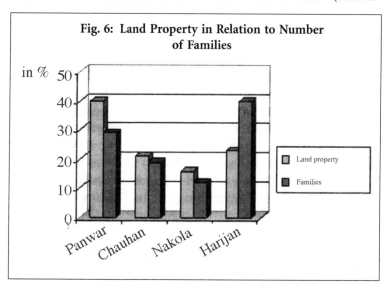

Fig. 6: Land Property in Relation to Number
of Families

in %

[31] According to the measurement system in the hills, land is counted in *mutti*
and nali (1 nali = 16 mutti). In the conversion table of the patwari in charge of

Table 7

Distribution of Land Property in Nakoli
(per cent Families)

	Land Property in Nalis										
	0–5	6–10	11–15	16–20	21–30	31–60	61–100	101–50	151–200	201–300	<300
Panwar (39)	./.	./.	2.6	2.6	5.1	20.5	23.1	15.4	7.7	15.3	7.7
Chauhan (36)	./.	3.8	./.	7.6	./.	26.9	26.9	19.2	3.8	11.5	./.
Nakola (16)	./.	6.2	./.	./.	6.2	50	6.2	6.2	6.2	6.2	12.5
Harijan (54)	./.	16.6	3.7	./.	18.5	33.3	20.3	1.8	1.8	3.7	./.

59 per cent; Chauhan 73 per cent), but 23 per cent of the Panwars own between 151 and 300 nali and 7.7 per cent even more than 300 nali. 15.3 per cent of all Chauhan households own more than 151 nali, but in no case does their property exceed 300 nali. On the other hand the core of the Dalits (72.1 per cent) have land property between 21 and 100 nali, but 20.3 per cent own even less than 15 nali and only 7.3 per cent can enjoy a land property between 101 and 300 nali. The majority of the Nakolas (62.4 per cent) have a land property between 31 and 60 nali or less, and only two families (12.5 per cent) own more than 300 nali.

When discussing land property one has to take into consideration the location and quality of the land because, in Nakoli, as in the hills in general, differences in altitude and access to water play a decisive role in cultivation. The total agricultural land surrounding Nakoli is divided into particular sections (or field areas) marked by a traditional field name. When asked about their land property, villagers usually mention the number and size of the field(s) they own in a particular section. These sections are situated at different altitudes and are for that reason favourable for different crops. The fields at lower altitudes

---

Nakoli 1 nali corresponds 0.05 acre or 0.020 ha (approximate figures). It is difficult to say how many nali of agricultural land a family needs for subsistence, because this depends on the size of the family and the number of children as well as on the quality of the land. But one can roughly estimate that a land size of 60 nali (3 acres or 1.2 ha) seems to be sufficient for a household consisting of 4–5 persons.

are irrigated and of high quality; they are mainly used for the production of paddy (*dhan*), but mustard seed (*sarson* or *rai*) and wheat (*gehun*) are additional crops. In the higher fields wheat, barley, mustard, pulses, and various sorts of millet are grown as well as apples, potatoes, and peas, which are the main cash crops. In Nakoli each family owns fields at various altitudes (even though a family does not necessarily have fields in every section) and is therefore able to plant at least basic crops for subsistence.

The villagers of Nakoli are increasingly occupied with the production of cash crops, particularly apples. For this climatic and soil conditions are conducive and the forest provides wood to for the boxes in which the fruit is transported. Villagers have also learned that prosperity and development in the neighbouring state of Himachal Pradesh is owed to a large extent to the production of apples. But although most families are interested in apple orchards, not all have sufficient land to convert their fields into plantations. When cash-crop production was started in the 1960s by a few of the villagers, new land was acquired by them. This land seems partially to have been forest land, i.e. *benap* land (unmeasured land near the fields), common (village) land, as well as revenue land (state land).[32] Later, the new owners managed to get official land titles (*pattas*) for the acquired fields. The practice of land acquisition still continues, but shortage of land causes villagers to illegally extend agricultural areas into the state forest.[33] During one of my last stays in Nakoli (1999) officials from the Forest Department made an inquiry into the practice of illegal acquisition of forest land and destroyed large numbers of newly planted trees.

In 1993, 87 per cent of the Nakola families owned orchards. The family of a village pradhan was the first to introduce apples in Nakoli when they were propagated as a cash crop by local workers of the Horticulture Department about thirty years ago. 73 per cent of the Panwar families have plantations, followed by the Chauhans with 63 per cent and the Harijans with 50 per cent. Figure 7 indicates the

---

[32] Until 1988 forest land could be given on lease. According to the personal information of a patwari, leasing contracts became permanent after 10 years.

[33] Whether villagers see it as illegal will be discussed later.

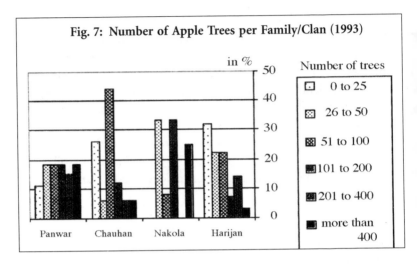

Fig. 7: Number of Apple Trees per Family/Clan (1993)

number of trees owned by families of the different clans. In the Panwar clan orchards of all sizes can be found, including very large ones with more than 400 trees. Families of the Chauhan clan as well as the Dalits generally own comparatively few apple trees, more than 70 per cent of all families have less than 100 trees, and a good deal even less than 25. The Nakolas reveal a split with 42 per cent owning less than 100 trees, while 58 per cent are proprietors of big or the biggest orchards.

For the production of other cash crops, namely potatoes and peas, villagers use agricultural land which they legally own. Because of the capacity of both crops to enhance soil quality, these are also grown on newly acquired land.[34] All cash crops are partially consumed by the villagers; some (dried) peas are stored, as well as potatoes of poor quality and some few boxes of apples. The larger and qualitatively better part of the crop is sold in the markets of Saharanpur, Vikasnagar, or Dehra Dun.

Besides basic crops, cash crops, and apple orchards, many of the village households own fruit trees, such as walnut and apricot. Walnuts are often sold locally; apricots are dried and the kernels used for

[34] Potatoes loosen the soil; peas (belonging to the family *Leguminosae*) provide the soil with nitrogen.

the extraction of oil. Some villagers also have pear trees (*nashpati*), peaches (*aaru*), and plums. There is a tendency to increase the number of fruit trees, especially walnut and apricot, because these fruits can be locally consumed and have commercial value as well.

Livestock Property

Animal husbandry is an important branch of the local subsistence economy and in Nakoli very few families are without livestock. Those who do not own animals are either 'singles' (widows, old men) or families registered in Nakoli but which have shifted their permanent residence to nearby market towns in the Yamuna valley. The following figure gives an overview of the total population as well as of the variety of livestock in Nakoli.

Water buffaloes and/or cows are reared by almost each household for its own consumption of milk and butter (1 buffalo and 1 to 2 cows on an average; some households own more, see Figure 9). In comparison with the local breed of cows, which give very little milk (1–3 kg per day), buffaloes are preferred due to their higher productivity (4–8 kg per day). A few families have started keeping more productive cross-breeds of cows ('Jersey' cows), but these

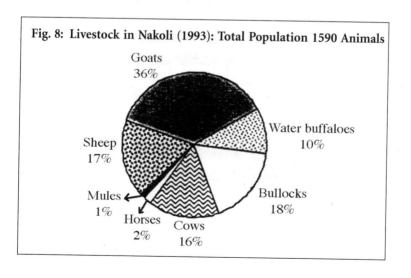

Fig. 8: Livestock in Nakoli (1993): Total Population 1590 Animals

Goats 36%

Water buffaloes 10%

Sheep 17%

Bullocks 18%

Mules 1%

Horses 2%

Cows 16%

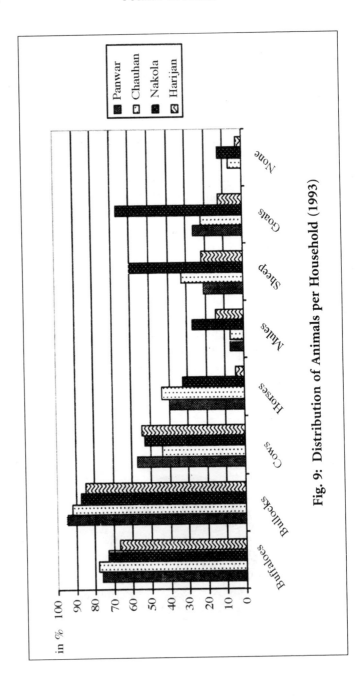

Fig. 9: Distribution of Animals per Household (1993)

animals cannot move in the difficult terrain of the hills, and need stable-feeding; their maintenance is very labour-intensive. The system of terracing in the hills where people own comparatively small fields of irregular shape, depends on animal labour for cultivation. Households keep 2 (sometimes 4) bullocks for ploughing. It is rare for a household to own only one bullock or none at all (this happens only in cases of family separation or due to an accident or sudden death of an animal). Horses and mules are used for transportation, but their total number was very low in Nakoli in 1993. This situation changed in the following years. When I revisited the village in 1998/9 I was amazed at the number of mules being used to carry firewood, dung, harvested crops, stones for house construction, etc. Obviously, a greater number of families could af-ford to buy a mule because of higher earnings. The number of goats and sheep was comparatively high in 1993 but it seemed to have been even higher in earlier decades. In former times sheep or goat wool was the only protection against winter, and shoes, thick blankets, jackets, and coats were made from it. Nowadays, wool has been partly substituted by ready-made products from the market. Keeping larger herds of sheep and goats is also very labour-intensive. The animals need grazing and pastures need to shift regularly. One male (mostly a boy or an old man) has to accompany the sheep and goats daily.

Animals are essential to the local economy. Milk and wool apart, the agricultural system is dependent on *gobar* (dung of cattle and horses) and *karish* (dung of goats and sheep) for manure. Several studies show that traditional Indian villages (especially in mountainous regions) are highly integrated 'agro-sylvo-pastoral systems', wherein different land-use components interact and an ecological balance of forest use, livestock breeding and agriculture has to be secured (see Figure 10).[35] In Nakoli, specific forest areas, clearings, alpine meadows, and wasteland are used as pasture; additionally, women cut the leaves of banj trees to feed the animals at times when they cannot graze. Women go regularly to the forest to collect dry leaves which are carried home in large baskets and stored in chanis to be used as litter. When the stables are cleaned, the animal dung is

---

[35] Agarwal and Narain 1989; Koranne 1996.

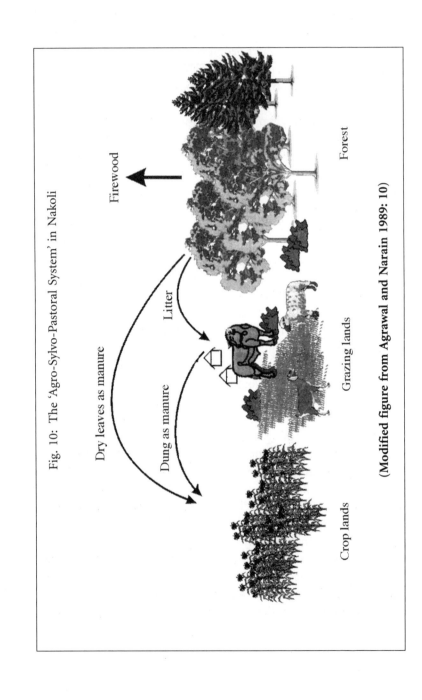

Fig. 10: The 'Agro-Sylvo-Pastoral System' in Nakoli

Firewood

Dry leaves as manure

Litter

Dung as manure

Forest

Grazing lands

Crop lands

(Modified figure from Agrawal and Narain 1989: 10)

removed and piled up outside the chani; then a new layer of litter is spread on the floor. Over time the dung heap increases but also becomes hard and dry. The manure is brought out into the fields twice (seldom thrice) a year, when harvested fields are prepared for the new crop.

70 per cent of all families in Nakoli complain that they do not have enough natural manure to fertilize fields regularly and sufficiently. In such cases, families try to get dung from related families who own enough livestock, but in general people are forced to substitute dung by simply spreading dry leaves and related matter from the forest on

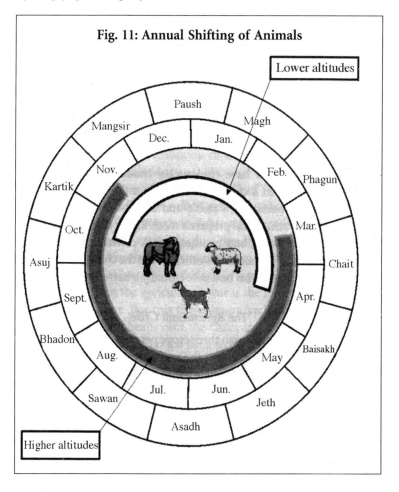

Fig. 11: Annual Shifting of Animals

to the fields. Chemical fertilizers (*khad*), although sold in the village by the local branch of the Horticulture Department at subsidized prices, is very limited in Nakoli. More than 30 per cent of all households never use khad. The rest predominantly fertilize apple orchards, potato and pea fields, and irrigated fields with chemicals. According to statements by the farmers, shortage of money is only one reason they use khad sparingly; the major fear is a possible destruction of crops if climatic conditions are not favourable. They argue that crops which are chemically fertilized are easily destroyed ('burned') if rains fail to arrive in the first period of growth and strong sun dries out the soil. During the annual cycle animals move regularly between pastures and chanis, both located at different altitudes. This 'transhumance'-like system guarantees that animals can be kept in favourable climatic conditions throughout the year, and also particular areas are not overused by grazing and lopping. This system brings animals near the fields where they can feed on the remains of the harvest (straw, stubble), and on grass growing at the borders of fields; another advantage is that fields can be manured without incurring transportation costs.

Families in Nakoli have constructed chanis in such field areas which are located at a certain distance from their village. Even the smallest chani consists of a stable and a fireplace so that a family member can live there and prepare a meal. Bigger chanis have one (or more) separate rooms and can house folk permanently with their cattle. Often, elderly men and women live in the chani, but in a polygynous family it may also be a wife (usually a barren wife) who cares for the animals.

The Agricultural Cycle

The hill climate allows up to three crops per field per year. Due to the varying elevation of fields and the sophisticated intercropping system, a broad range of crops grows at one time. People in Uttarakhand praise this system as *barahnaj* (literally: twelve seeds).

Two main harvests have to be distinguished: the *rabi* (spring harvest) and the *kharif* (autumn harvest). The following list indicates the main rabi and kharif crops in Nakoli (excluding cash crops).[36]

---

[36] The crops and their methods of cultivation are well described in vol. 1, part II, of the *Himalayan Gazetteer* by E.T Atkinson (1882; reprinted 1973).

Rabi Crops	Kharif Crops
Wheat (*gehum—Triticum vulgare*	Rice (*dhan*)—*Oryza sativa*
Barley (*jau*)—*Hordeum hexastichon*	Millets:
Mustard seed (*sarson, rai*)—*Brassica junicea*	(*mamrua*)—*Eleusine coracana*
Lentils: (*mazur*)—*Ervum lens*	(*kauni*)—*Panicum italicum/Setaria italica*)
	(*cina*)—*Panicum (virgari) miliaceum*
	(*jhangora*)—*Oplismenus frumentaceus*
	Maize (*makka, makai*)—*Zea mays*
	Amaranth (*caulai, marsa*)—*Amaranthus frumentaceus*
	French bean (*frans bin*)—*Phaseolus vulgaris*
	Black seeded kidney bean (*chimi, rajma*)—*Dolichos lablab* (different varieties)
	Rayed kidney bean (*urad*)—*Phaseolus radiatus*
	Soya bean (*bhat*)—*Glycine soja*
	Sesame (*til*)—*Sesamum indicum*

Figure 12 shows the distribution of main crops (including cash crops) according to elevation.

The agricultural year starts in the month of Phagun with the preparation of the fields for rice, millets and potatoes, the main crops of the kharif harvest.[37] Although in February the weather conditions may be bad and snow may fall, often the days are clear, the sun is strong and warms the air. Early morning, men and women set out for their chanis and fields and start their daily work. One of the first important activities in the agricultural year is the fertilization of fields with natural manure. For this the villagers hack off pieces of dried gobar from big dung heaps near the chani and pile them into large baskets which are carried on the back to the fields. Here the baskets

[37]In the Hindu calendar the Hindi names of the months are as follows: Phagun (mid-February to mid-March), Chait (mid-March to mid-April), Baisakh (mid-April to mid-May), Jeth (mid-May to mid-June), Asadh (mid-June to mid-July), Sawan (mid-July to mid-August), Bhadon (mid-August to mid-September), Ashwin, in local Pahari called Asuj (mid-September to mid-October), Kartik (mid-October to mid-November), Aghan, in local Pahari called Mangsir, (mid-November to mid-December), Pus, in local Pahari called Paush (mid-December to mid-January), Magh (mid-January to mid-February).

Fig. 12: Main Crops according to Elevation

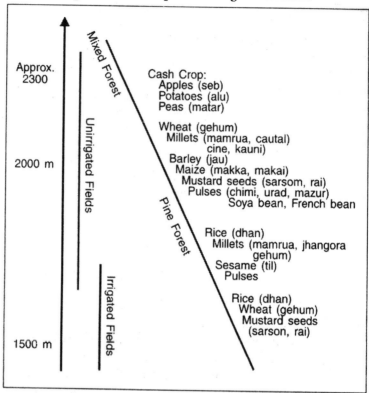

are emptied and the procedure starts again. After a while small dung heaps cover the field at equal distances. Before the gobar is spread on the soil, the stubble and roots of the last crop have to be removed and burnt at the edge of the field. When the dung is scattered the men start the ploughing.[38] At the same time, women remove stones which come to the surface. Women are also busy clearing the field borders of weeds and grass, while men repair the terraces wherever necessary. Fields are ploughed and cleared twice. The preparation of the fields continues up to the end of the month of Chait.

[38] Ploughing is a male activity; only very rarely may one see a woman behind the plough. This may happen when no male family member, relative, or labourer is available.

In the month of Chait the apple trees are in full bloom and the owners of apple orchards spray their trees with insecticide for the first time. A second spraying takes place a few weeks later, in Jeth, when fruit buds have developed. In Chait and early Baisakh people start preparing the fields for potatoes. Already in Magh the manure has been scattered and the first ploughing done. Now, the second ploughing begins and the women remove stones and weeds, hoe the whole field with their *kutla*, and crush clods. Finally, the soil is harrowed and fields furrowed for the seed. Now the farmer spreads a little khad in the fields, plants the potatoes, and closes the furrows with the ploughshare.

In Baisakh rice (on unirrigated fields) and millets are sown. Before the seed finally enters the soil, previously prepared fields are again ploughed and cleared, and this time also hoed. The seed is scattered sparingly and carefully ploughed in. On the field borders, additional crops—cucumbers, pumpkins, some pulses—are planted. In the month of Baisakh villagers also start preparing a few fields at lower altitudes as seedbeds for paddy. These fields have been manured and ploughed in Magh, but weeds have sprouted and must be cleared. The fields are ploughed a second time; subsequently, the women hoe the field and remove weeds, roots, and stones. Then, after a third and last ploughing, the seed is sown closely.

Starting with the end of Baisakh, the rabi harvest goes on during the whole of Jeth. Men and women are busy harvesting fields surrounding the village where barley, pulses, and mustard seed have ripened. The barley is cut with the sickle (*daranti*), tied in sheafs, and set up for drying. Later, the threshing is done with a stick or with the feet. The straw is stored for the animals; grain is collected in sacks after it has been separated from the chaff. For winnowing, portions of grain are put in a shovel-shaped basket (supa). This is held against the wind at an angle that enables chaff to be blown away. The grain is expertly shaken to the ground.[39] Pulses and mustard seed plants are pulled out by hand and spread out to dry. Later, pulses are dashed to

[39] The supa (Hindi: sup) is used for all crops, to separate chaff from grain as well as to clean the crops of small stones, soil, and other residue. Small portions of grain can also be cleaned by placing them on the ground and using the supa as a fan.

the ground to release their beans; mustard seed is threshed with feet. For the wheat harvest, which starts after the earlier crops have been brought in, all families get busy on the fields with cutting, tying, and drying the crop, and in the chauks of the village the threshing with bullocks goes on. All day, bullocks move in a circle, stamping on wheat under their feet, which teases out the grain. To prevent them from eating the crop they are made to wear muzzles made of plaited grass. The grain is filled into sacks, dried on large mats, and stored. It is ground to flour (*atta*) in one of the local mills (*chakki*) operated by water and owned by the village.

All the fields where the rabi crop has ripened are now empty; they have been cleaned of the remains and ploughed immediately after the harvest. Still in Jeth, a second ploughing is done and several varieties of millets, pulses, and maize are sown for the autumn harvest on fields surrounding the village, as well as further up. Since most farmers are short of manure, often only dry leaves are spread on the soil. Soon, small plants appear and a soft green covers the fields.

By the end of Baisakh the seed potatoes have developed into strong young plants and villagers start to 'hill' up the soil; they continue with this work during Jeth. Early in the morning the women leave for the potato fields, work for a few hours, and by eleven o'clock, when the sun moves to its zenith (day by day the temperature gets more and more unbearable) come back home for their meal. They set off for the fields again in the late afternoon, when the air has cooled down and the long shadows of the hills protect them from the sun. Hilling up the soil around potato plants is meant to prevent soil from being washed away in the monsoon, and this work has to be complete when the first monsoon rains start, which sometimes occurs as early as end June.

At the end of Jeth the paddy seeds have sprouted and the villagers are ready to plant the seedlings into irrigated fields (*rupai*). Sometimes whole families shift for one or two weeks to their chanis at low altitudes and they work, sleep, and eat their meals there. First, fields for the paddy are cleaned and manured, then watered and ploughed. At then seedlings are put into the irrigated soil, four to five seedlings being planted together in equidistant groups. Large groups of men, women, and children bend in the irrigated fields for long hours; often they are joking and laughing, young men and boys are playing and clobber each other with mud pies.

Although in Jeth and Asadh the weather is very hot, sudden thunderstorms and heavy rains allow the crop as well as weeds and grasses to grow very fast. Women have to go regularly to the fields for weeding work (*gudai*). This continues until Sawan, when the monsoon rains make it difficult to work in the fields. Generally, from the end of Asadh until the end of Sawan, agricultural work slows down for about four weeks. During this period the annual yatra of each of the local deities takes place and people have time to engage in the village puja and attend the fairs or melas of two of the gods (Daheshwar mela and Devrana mela of Ludeshwar). Agricultural work increases again when the first crops—early varieties of potatoes and maize—are ready for harvesting.

Potatoes are harvested in the rainy season and people set off for their fields with ploughs and bullocks when the day is bright and the rain has ceased for a while. The men carefully plough one row of potatoes after the other, then women and children search for tubers and collect them by hand. Later, the potatoes are sorted according to size and grade. The good quality potatoes are sold in the market, the rest destined for consumption and use as seeds. Soon after the harvest the empty fields are ploughed, harrowed, and manured for the planting of peas. During the month of Bhadon; the maize ripens, and by and by the cobs are cut. Many are roasted and eaten, some are also stored for the winter (villagers like popcorn). The stems and leaves are used as fodder for the cattle.

Asuj and Kartik are the two months in which the kharif harvest as well as the apple harvest goes on and people work with full strength. The apple harvest is done by all family members and/or Nepalis, who are in charge of some of the orchards. Apples are basically destined for sale and are carefully plucked, sorted according to size, colour, and grade, rolled one by one into newspapers and packed into wooden boxes. The boxes are transported to the roadside on mules or horses, from where they are loaded onto trucks or buses to be sold in Dehra Dun or the cities of the plains (Saharanpur, even Lucknow, Kanpur). Good quality apples can obtain a good price, especially when the harvest has started early and the apples are the first in the market. On an average one box with 20–25 kg can be sold for Rs 200–250, but sometimes prices can go down to much less than Rs 200, or rise to Rs 400. The sale price has to be seen in relation to the comparatively high costs of packing and transport. The boxes, which are made of local timber, are a high-cost factor on two counts—financally and ecologically. They cannot be substituted by cardboard containers, because their transportation on mules entails severe bumping and bruising.

The main kharif crop harvested is dhan. Villagers start with the unirrigated dhan, later they move down to the irrigated fields. The dhan is cut with the sickle by men and women; immediately after, it is brought to the threshing floor near the fields, where people engage in separating the grain by stamping on it barefoot. Then the grain is collected, filled into sacks, and carried home. When the days are sunny and bright, mats are laid out in the chauk and the harvest spread out for drying. After that it is stored.[40] On the empty fields in the irrigated area, mustard seed is sown immediately. It will ripen within six to eight weeks and can be cut at the end of Mangsir/beginning of Paush, before the cold period starts.

The many sorts of millet (*mamrua, cina* and *kauni*) as well as amaranth are harvested by cutting its ear while the crop is standing. The straw remains in the fields and is soon grazed by the cattle, which are allowed to move freely in the now empty agricultural area. The millets are predominantly threshed with a stick, used as a flail. The grain is cleaned and dried before it is stored in the kutar. To harvest pulses and sesame, plants are pulled out as a whole. The pulses are dashed on the ground for their beans, and then the crop is spread to dry. Sesame is threshed with a stick in the same way as the millets. Then it is dried, soaked, and again dried to remove its black skin.

During the harvest and after, villagers are busy collecting and bundling the straw of the dhan, and cutting the high grass which has grown on the borders of their fields. Straw and grass are stored on trees to feed animals in winter. Storage on trees preserves the fodder much better than by just piling it up in a heap on the floor. Even in rain and snow, tree fodder is not spoilt.

---

[40] Before consumption the husk has to be removed from the grain, and women pound the needed quantity of dhan in a large wooden or stone mortar (*ukhal*) with a pestle (*mûsal*). Only after processing is the rice called chaval.

In the months of Mangsir, Paush, and Magh there is comparatively little agricultural work; people collect firewood for the winter and grow sociable. It is the marriage season, two of the big melas take place (Magh mela in Uttarkashi, alternately Baukh or Sema mela near Nakoli, see below); also, the 'Second Diwali' is celebrated.[41] Only two crops are ready for harvesting in this period—late varieties of potato and the mustard which has ripened in the fields at lower altitudes. But in the main people are busy preparing fields for the rabi crop. They remove stems and roots and burn them at the edge of the field; they plough, collect stones, spread manure, etc. Wheat, barley, pulses, and mustard are sown until the end of Mangsir, and with that the agricultural wheel comes full circle.

Already at the end of Paush and the beginning of Magh, when the days are clear and warm, villagers engage in the first preparations for the coming season. They carry dung to the fields; sometimes even the first ploughing happens now. This, and the cutting of apple trees at the end of Magh and early Phagun, indicate the beginning of a new agricultural cycle.

6.2 Approaching the Forest Issue through Local Narratives and Practices

Bygone times and events relating to their own village, the neighbouring villages, and the patti are well remembered by the local population of Nakoli and the surrounding area, and a multiplicity of historical representations, narrated by villagers of all castes and clans, gives proof of this. The narratives concentrate on a number of central topics: on the (historical) process of land acquisition and settlement; the origin and history of clans; rulers and kings and relations between rulers and their subjects; the relation between Nakoli and neighbouring villages; the ritual sphere and the origin and realm of influence of the main local deities. Organizing the past is meaningful in relation to

[41] Diwali is celebrated all around India in Kartik. But in West Garhwal people celebrate a 'Second Diwali' as well and during the festival old and young men compete in different varieties of tug-of-war. According to some villagers, 'Second Diwali' takes place because the first cannot be observed properly due to agricultural work. Others see the origin in a historical event: once, there was a war between Garhwal and Kumaon and nobody was able to observe diwali. After the war, diwali was celebrated belatedly.

Fig. 13: Annual Agriculture Cycle

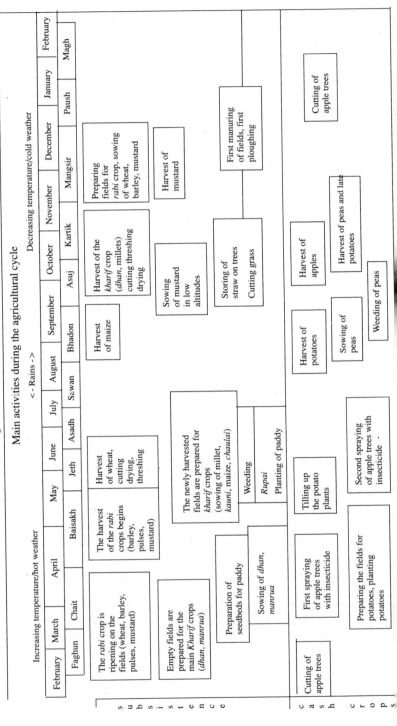

the present and operates as an important element in the process of identity formation. Memory helps to establish self-perception, for example as Rawalta (inhabitant of Rawain), as member of a village community, as member of a particular clan and therefore as holder of certain privileges and rights, or as somebody to whom such rights are denied. Narratives may either legitimate supremacy or they may serve to justify a person's or group's low status. Relationships and interactions recalled in the narratives are often reflected in contemporary practices, which, vice versa, are illuminated by them. When, in the following, I make an attempt to reconstruct local narratives and illustrate certain practices, this is not done as an end in itself but as a strategy to approach the forest issue, and to gain insights into the ways in which people relate to nature and to the forest. No discourse addresses this relationship explicitly: it seems to be 'hidden' (implied) in cultural practices as well as in narrative constructions which are part of discourses focusing on other topics, primarily on local history and religion.

What I call a narrative is not necessarily a full 'story' enacted with a plot structure and told by one person. Moreover, narratives often have to be '(re)constructed' by the anthropologist from narrative elements voiced by a person in various situations or even by different people under various circumstances. Knowledge, or rather ideas, about the past and present depend on a person's perspective; they are often limited and fragmented. Certain aspects of a story may be repeated by different speakers and so constitute a basic narrative element, whereas other elements may differ according to the status, gender, age, and education of a speaker. My field experience in Nakoli and its surroundings revealed that the unity and consistency of a story depend on its subject. When villagers relate to mytho-religious topics (the local deities, their origin and deeds) they tend to give a well-knit and detailed account, whereas stories about regional history, or about the origin and past of clans, tend to be incomplete and contested. When, in the following, I renarrate stories or compose narratives from fragments, I do not intend to give the illusion of a closed story. I try rather to give space to variations and deviations (smaller variations will be mentioned in brackets).

Narratives or narrative elements can be analysed as poetic constructions according to their form and historiographic style (White
1991). Although the stories I am going to present use certain metaphorical elements, their poetical analysis will not be in focus. Stories
can also be analysed according to their function (Rüsen 1990). From
such a perspective narratives from Nakoli and its neighbourhood
follow the pattern of traditional narrativity (*tradionales Erzählen*),
which aims to recall the origin of life situations and structures in such
a way that the actual experience of time can serve as a stimulus to
revitalize the origin as orientation for their future (Rüsen 1990: 179).
Form and function may be important subjects of analysis, but what
seems to me of special relevance is the content of a narrative. My central question therefore is not how people tell their story but what they
tell and what they want to communicate with it.

Oral narratives are not sources that allow establishing a chronology.[42] The usual way narrators in the Nakoli region locate a story in
time is to start with the introductory statement 'in the time of our
fathers and forefathers' (*dada aur pardada ke samay*) or to say it happened in olden days (*purane samay mein*). The first statement usually
alludes to a past which is not more than thirty or fifty years back; the
second may refer to a period more than 200 or even 500 years back.
Events in ancient periods are often dated with reference to the Pandavs, who are worshipped as divine heroes of the Himalayas by the
local Rajputs (*Pandavon ke samay, Bhim ke samay*).[43] What may help
the researcher date 'historical' people, events, and processes more
exactly are genealogies (*vamsalis*) and, as a turning point in the social
and political history of Uttarakhand, the Gurkha invasion. The
genealogies which some of the Brahmin and Rajput clans of the region have constructed (and which I was lucky to collect), did not go

[42] Jan Vansina says, 'the weakness in chronology is one of the greatest limitations of all oral traditions' (1985: 56). He mentions that lists and genealogies
could help to establish 'both relative sequence and eventually absolute chronology' (1985: 178).

[43] The Pandavs are the heroes of the Mahabharat, one of the two great epics
of North India, a work composed betwen the fourteenth century BC and fourth
century AD.

back more than eight to ten generations, that is, at most 200 years.[44] The Gurkha invasion, which took place between 1790 and 1798, resulted not only in political changes (the constitution of the separate realms of British Garhwal and Tehri Garhwal after the defeat of the Gurkhas by the British), but also in migration of people. Genealogies and reference to the historical event of the Gurkha invasion indicate that the colonization of the Nakoli region by Brahmin and Rajput clans may have happened around 200 years ago. After the defeat of the Gurkhas, and after having been re-established as a ruler by the British, Raja Sudarshan Shah of Tehri Garhwal explicitly called for new settlements in western Garhwal.

Reconstructing local narratives is done in order to learn about local discourses, interpretations, and outlooks, but insofar as narratives are poetic constructions of chronicled events (a 'fable', to use a term from Hayden White) they contain historical facts as well. To approach these facts a narrative has to be confronted and compared with other narratives, as also with those given by professional historians, which— in the same way as 'oral histories'—have to be acknowledged as only possible interpretations that need to be evaluated critically.

6.2.1 History, Politics, and Territory
Reconstructing the History of Nakoli and its Inhabitants

One of the upper field areas of Nakoli is known by the name *Barak*. Where today agricultural fields and common pastures are spread, in olden times a Raja lived in his fort (*garh*); this was Bariya Raja. In those days the village Nakoli did not exist, dense forest covered the landscape and only the ancestors of the Nakolas, named Mendri, as well as two other families from whom today's Dalits derive, lived around the fort. Both groups were shepherds and did some shifting cultivation but they also worked for the Raja as lower officials, servants, and herdsmen. Nothing is known of the reign of the Raja, which came to a sudden end

[44] In the hills people traditionally got married very early (child marriage); the first child may be born when the wife is only 15 or 16 years old. Therefore a generation can be counted as *c.* 20 years.

due to the punishment by Baukhnag devta. And this is the story of the Raja's offence:

Every morning, a cow of Bariya Raja went grazing to the nearby pastures, but when she returned in the evening and when the servants tried to milk her they realized that no milk [a little milk, milk from only 1 teat, from 2 teats] was left. The servants reported this to the Raja, who immediately suggested that one of his servants should follow the cow and observe what happens to the milk. The next morning a servant sneaked along behind the cow. The animal strolled to the place where, today, the village temple of Nakoli is located. In those days a *bekhal* bush grew there, and near this bush the cow [partly] emptied her udder. When the Raja learned of this he did not care to find out the reason but ordered that the cow be killed.

Continuation (version 1; Nakolas, Panwar Rajput married to a girl from the Nakola clan): A servant from the Mendri clan was encumbered with this duty. At night, after the Raja had given his order, the Mendri who was chosen to kill the cow had a dream. He dreamt that, very soon, something bad would happen to the Raja and that he himself had better leave the fort and hide in a cave. The Mendri woke up and followed the advice he got in his dream. That very night a thunderstorm came up, fire and red-glowing stones [coals] fell from heaven and destroyed the fort as well as the Raja and his whole family. The cow was saved, and so was the Mendri because of his pure heart.

Continuation (version 2; Panwar, Chauhan, and Rawat Rajputs): A servant from the Mendri clan was encumbered with this duty. The next day the Mendri set off to obey the Raja and killed the cow. But punishment did not wait long to follow. Soon, a heavy thunderstorm destroyed the fort as well as the Raja and his whole family. From that time on, the Mendri had to expiate their guilt. Until today, every year, upon the change (*sakrant*) from Chait to Baisakh, they have to prepare a small cow made of dough mixed from various millets, barley, wheat flour, and jaggery, which they must throw from a wall of the house. When in April a special puja for Baukhnag is celebrated in the forest, the Nakolas have to carry the urine of a cow.

Continuation (version 3; Nakolas): The Bariya Raja called a *mochi* (the earlier term for an 'untouchable' working with leather) to kill the cow.

But in the night, before the mochi could execute the order, a heavy thunderstorm extinguished the Raja and his family. The cow, the mochi and his family, as well as the ancestors of the Nakolas, were saved.

The end, in all versions: The place where the cow deposited her milk was considered holy. Later, a Shivling was found there, as well as the murti (image) of Baukhnag devta and a water source. But the Raja, who did not believe in the gods and did not enquire why the cow deposited her milk where she did, got the deserved punishment for his lack of faith.

The motif of the cow depositing milk at a certain spot seems to be a metaphorical way of indicating the holiness of a place. It is repeated in other narratives as well. The motif links, as a key metaphor, 'historical' memorizing with mytho-religious stories as well as with explanations of local social ranking and hierarchy. The above-mentioned stories are well known by male and female members of the different status groups of Nakoli and the neighbouring villages—although they were narrated to me only by the men. Villagers generally believe that the ancestors of the Nakolas were the first inhabitants of the place where modern Nakoli is located. They lived together with the forefathers of today's Dalits, who, as distinct from the Nakolas, are said to have migrated from outside into the region. Seemingly no (or only marginal) status differences divided the two groups (both were servants of the Raja and could be asked by him to kill the cow). When Dalits try to explain the social hierarchy between themselves and the Nakolas which exists and can be clearly observed today, they refer to the 'sibling myth', a discursive scheme well known amongst Dalits more generally in India (Vincentnathan 1993).

K. Lal, a middle-aged Dalit, says: In the times of our fathers and forefathers two brothers lived in Nakola, Gutjata and Mendri. One day, a cow died and the two brothers discussed who should remove the dead animal. Mendri, who was the older brother, refused to do the job because of his status as the first-born son, and ordered his younger brother to pull the cow away. Gutjata had no choice and threw the animal into a ravine (*khud*). In the evening the two brothers had their meal and, as usual, shared one plate. When soup was poured on the *thali* it separated the food into two parts and so indicated the (social) distance between the two brothers, which had been created by their activities. From that day on Gutjata was of lower and Mendri of higher (Rajput) status.

Much later, Rajput clans from outside enter the stage. The Chauhans—with most probably two brothers named Ladhu (Ladakh Singh) and Pithu (Pithak Singh)—are said to have come from Srinagar (the former capital of Garhwal) together with their sheep and goats. It is not clear if they reached the area of Nakoli before or after the Panwars. The latter are assumed to have migrated from Nahan (today located in Himachal Pradesh) to Manjeli (near Purola) and later to Tunalka (near Naugaon). From there two Panwar brothers, Rupa (Rupsingh) and Gulabu (Gulab Singh) finally came to the region of Nakola.[45] It is said that the (grand) father of Rupa and Gulabu had been the chief minister (*wazir*) of the Raja of Nahan, but when a conflict arose between the wazir and the Raja, the minister decided to leave his homeland.

> *S.L., an old Dalit, says*: When the Panwars came, they took all the land which formerly belonged to the Mendri and to us. Our ancestors used to be away in the jungle for many days to graze the sheep and goats. Once, when they returned, they realized that their land had been acquired by these newcomers.

Members of the Panwar clan affirmed that their ancestors had acquired as much land as possible because 'In those days the land was enough'. Even though the soil belonged *de jure* to the Raja, there were no restrictions de facto on new colonization. Whereas the Chauhans as well as the two indigenous groups appear to have primarily been herdsmen who only additionally did some shifting cultivation, the Panwars are assumed to have been the first to clear the forest and to cultivate the land systematically and permanently. According to local practices and accounts of villagers, especially from the Chauhan clan, the Panwars enjoyed a variety of privileges:

(a) The basic local political function—headman of one or more villages (*malguzar, sayana*)—was confined to the Panwar

[45] I obtained the vamsali (genealogy) of Rupa, and partly that of Gulabu. The vamsali of the Chauhans was not available (not existent).

clan. Rupa had been the first in this office, which after him was transferred in his lineage. Only after several generations, it shifted to the Gulabu line. Some say that in the beginning leadership was shared between Rupa and Gulabu.

(b) When a member from the Panwar clan died, the dead body was carried to the banks of the Yamuna for burning. The burning place was located near Mungra garh, a few hours walking distance from Nakoli, close to present-day Naugaon. In the beginning, Chauhans and the other status groups were not allowed to burn the bodies of their dead on the banks of the Yamuna. Later, the restriction was repealed, but the non-Panwars had to pay a toll to high-ranking Rajputs from a neighbouring village when passing this particular village on their way to the river. M.S. Chauhan said in 1995 that, even five years earlier, when his mother died, he was forced to pay a certain amount, but since then the toll has been abolished.

(c) In autumn, when the annual worship of the ancestors takes place (*pitra shraddha*, locally named *auns*) the Panwar clan follows a special ritual in which at least one person from each family participates. The worshippers leave the house in the early morning and with the rising sun walk to a nearby ravine (*khud*, with a small rivulet flowing in it), led by the village drummer (*bajgi*) and the oldest men of the two lineages. For their puja the old men arrange offerings for the ancestors (special food, flowers) on a bed of *kus*-grass and then put them into the flowing water. To the other clans of the village this ritual near the ravine is denied. The Chauhans, Nakolas, and Dalits celebrate auns in their houses.

The supremacy of status of the Panwars is explained (sometimes legitimized) by clan members with reference to their relationship to the ruling power: the Rajas of Tehri Garhwal are said to have been Parmars (= Panwars), claiming their descent from Kanak Pal, who came from Gujarat on a pilgrimage around AD 888 and married the daughter of a local petty chief (see Chapter 2). But status differences within the village exist not only between the Panwars and the other groups, they also occur between the migrating Rajputs (Panwar *and*

Chauhan) and the 'indigenous' Rajputs (Mendri/Nakola).[46] The lower status of the Nakolas is explained in different ways. Some hint to the fact that one of them had killed the cow of Bariya Raja, others mention that one of their elders had married (or had lived together with) a girl from the so-called 'untouchables' (*dom*), or that Mendri and Gutjata had been brothers.

Since the time when all clans were settled in Nakoli, the social ranking seemed to have developed along clear-cut lines. The lowest group were the ancestors of the Dalits, called mochi or dom. They removed dead animals, worked with leather, and consumed beef. In between the mochi and the Rajputs were the Mendri. Among the Rajput immigrants, the Chauhans were considered lower than the Panwars. This status situation has changed in the last decades. The Nakolas have succeeded in gaining a higher rank (due to education, wealth, and a new name); they are now accepted as marriage partners among the Panwars and Chauhans. The mochi have given up their degrading work as well as beef-eating and no longer demand to be taken as equal with the *chamar* who, in the pan-Indian social ranking, are one of the lower groups of 'untouchables'. The name mochi, considered derogatory, was replaced by 'Harijans'—and more recently by 'Dalits'.

Reconstructing the History of Nakoli in the Socio-political Context of the Region

Before we concentrate on socio-political relationships in the Nakoli region, it is necessary to give an idea of the territorial structure of the subregion, that is, the location and character of villages (see Figure 14).

With only a few exceptions, the villages in the vicinity of Nakoli are inhabited by Brahmins *or* Rajputs, who migrated to the area several generations ago, and by Harijans, i.e. Dalits, who have settled as artisans and/or musicians. It was not possible to get information about the origin of social groups in all the villages, but often people could

[46] The status difference between *khas* Rajput and immigrant Rajputs is (controversially) discussed in the literature on Kumaon (Sanwal 1976; Fanger 1980; Brown and Joshi 1990).

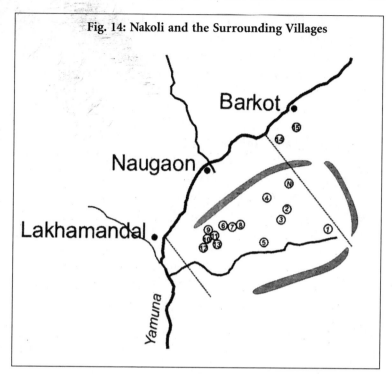

Fig. 14: Nakoli and the Surrounding Villages

give a rough idea about the place they came from and the time of migration.

Villages in palli Mungarsanti: A few decades ago a number of families from the Panwar clan as well as some Chauhans and Dalits from Nakoli founded a new village to the south-east of Nakoli (No.1). In 1981 this village consisted of 30 families and had 183 inhabitants.[47] Two other villages are located to the south-west of Nakoli (Nos 2 and 3), the first one being dominated by Rajputs from the Rana clan (32 households [h.], 172 inhabitants [inh.]), the other by Brahmin families belonging to the Nautiyal, Thaplial, and Uniyal clans (40 h., 258 inh.), who say they have come from Srinagar after the Gurkha conquest. Around 3 km to the west one finds another Brahmin village

[47] I could not carry out surveys in the neighbouring villages; therefore I rely on the census data of 1981 (Gupta [1982]; 1991). The number of inhabitants may have increased slightly in the mean time.

(No. 4, 32 h., 194 inh.). Its inhabitants, Badoni Brahmins, seem to have arrived about ten generations ago. They say that they migrated from Kangra, where they had been pujaris of the goddess Jwalamai. The Badonis are known as tantric specialists. Village No. 5, located further to the south-west of Nakoli, is exclusively inhabited by Lohars (22 h., 121 inh. [own data: 1995, 30 h.]), who said they had been requested by the local Rajputs of the region to settle down in their neighbourhood and work for them.

A number of villages are located further to the west of Nakoli. Village Nos 6, 7, and 11 are Brahmin villages. No. 6 is dominated by families from the Thaplial and Bahuguna clan (52 h., 311 inh.), No. 7 by Gangari Brahmins named Dhobal and Uniyal (41 h., 212 inh.), and No. 11 by Thaplial Brahmins (15 h., 94 inh.). The Dhobals said they left their home, Dhobalgao near the former capital Srinagar, about twelve generations ago, when the Gurkha army started to invade Garhwal. In those days large numbers of Brahmins seem to have moved further west: including the Brahmins from Village No. 3 and No. 14 (see below). Village No. 8 (44 h., 291 inh.) and Village No. 9 (27 h., 149 inh.) are dominated by Rajputs from the Rana clan, whereas in Village Nos 10 (27 h., 158 inh.), 12 (24 h., 131 inh.), and 13 (21 h., 134 inh.) Dalits form the majority; the Rajputs belong to the Bhandari, Rana, Chauhan, and Bhartwal clans. The Chauhans from Village No. 13 said they came from the region between Tehri and Chinyalisaor (Tahsil Dunda) before the time of the Gurkha invasion. The Ranas of Village No. 10 claim their origin from Jaunsar.

The next two villages I want to mention are located in Barkot patti. They are of special importance in the later discussions on religious discourses and practices, respectively, in the context of the local resistance against the forest policy of the Raja of Tehri Garhwal. Village No. 14 is separated into a Rajput and a Brahmin village. Together, it contains 127 households or 754 inhabitants (including the Dalit families living in the Rajput village). The Brahmins belong to the clans of Dhobal (from Dhobalgao) and Dimri (from the Chamoli region), the Rajputs are Rawats, Ranas, and Ramolas. The Rawats, who claim to have been the first settlers, migrated from Chandpur about ten generations ago; the Ranas claim their origin from Osla (Harki Dun valley, western Rawain); the Ramolas say they have come

from the region around Chamoli. According to the narrations, Vllage
No. 15 (78 h., 474 inh.) was founded by Rajputs from Village No. 14
and is inhabited by Rawat, Rana, and Ramola families.

Remembering regional history and politics mainly means referring
to the time of the Gurkha invasion and to the period when kings ruled
Tehri State (*raja ke zamane mein*). The narratives give evidence of
local political structures, social relations and events, but they are
often contradictory and inconsistent. The reason is that people relate
to different periods during the Tehri Raj without being able to indicate the time they talk about: they do not even consider this relevant.
Even in academic publications, written by Pahari historians dealing
with the history of Garhwal, the administrative and territorial structure
of the kingdom is not very clearly described. This structure not only
kept changing under the rules of the different rajas, the administration
had to relate to local circumstances as well. Very briefly, I give some
hints of local and temporal variations in the administration of the
Tehri Raj as described in historical accounts (Saklani 1987; Rawat
1989, 2002) because this background knowledge may help to situate
local narratives.

In 1815 the British installed Sudarshan Shah as Raja of Tehri
Garhwal. During his rule he largely relied on the old administrative
structures but tried to restrict the influence and power of the land-
owning elites and the intermediaries by abolishing their privileges.
The hitherto hereditary offices of thokdar and sayana (officials responsible for revenue collection and law and order in a certain territory or in one or more villages) were terminated and converted into
lifetime appointments; also, the Raja often refused to affirm hereditary
jagirs to old and well-known families who had enjoyed such privileges
under the rule of the former rajas of Garhwal.

Special attention was given to parganah Rawain, which remained
under British control until 1824, when it was handed over to Sudarshan Shah. Already, before the Gurkha conquest, the region was geographically and politically marginal. It was at a distance of 6-8 days'
foot-march from the capital Srinagar and the control of the central
authorities was not very strong, the feudal loyalties weak. Additionally,
Rawain was culturally distinct; its language, habitus, religious practices,
and marriage customs differed from those in the central parts of the

kingdom.[48] It is well documented that British officials often complained about the 'lawlessness' of the inhabitants of Rawain and the
disorderly state of the region (Saklani 1987; Rawat 1989, 2002). When
Rawain passed to Raja Sudarshan Shah, he started to rule the tract
with 'an iron hand' (Saklani 1987) and levied heavy taxes on the local
residents.[49] Despite this, the Raja most probably remained a distant
ruler at the local level. Here the political vacuum may have encouraged
the emergence of powerful personalities and—to a certain degree—
the establishment of autonomous structures.

In the following periods the rulers made genuine efforts to strengthen the political integration of the state and replace the administration
based on a system of patronage with a 'modern' bureaucracy. During
the reign of Pratap Shah (1871–86) the administrative territorial
units of the state were reorganized and the kingdom divided into
twenty-two pattis, each headed by a *kamdar* appointed for one year.
Later, Kirti Shah (1886–1913) subdivided the state into four divisions,
each under a deputy collector assisted by tahsildars and patwaris. He
was the first raja to start annual inspection tours of two to three
months which took him to the remoter areas of his kingdom. During
his reign Dalits got tenancy rights on their land and were allowed to
build stone houses at the outskirts of the village settlement. His
successor, Narendra Shah (1913–46), revived the old offices of diwan
and wazir. He vested them with new power and the diwan became
overall head of the executive.

---

[48] Jean-Claude Galey has elaborated on the relations between religion, politics, and social structure (kinship, clan) in the kingdom of Tehri Garhwal (1980,
1984, and 1990). Revising Louis Dumont, he locates the idea of kingship in the
heart of society. Kingship, clearly defined by its ritual and territorial dimensions,
is the constitutive principle and key concept for the understanding of social
organization. In Galey's studies structural analysis prevails against historical
analysis of processes and interactions. Additionally, concentrating on information
given by individuals from the family of the former rulers which seem to relate
basically to the core area of the kingdom, Galey's findings cannot be generalized
or mechanically applied to Rawain.

[49] When complaints were sent to the political agent, the British enquired
about the situation. Later the king was asked to renounce all oppressive measures.

When the Brahmin and Rajput clans settled in the Nakoli region at the time of the Gurkha invasion or slightly later, no clear-cut structures of power and dominance seem to have existed in the locality. The ancestors of the Panwar lineage were one of the groups which tried to profit from the political vacuum. The following passages describe what was stated by many of the Panwar Rajputs of Nakoli as well as by Rajputs and Brahmins from neighbouring villages: 'When Rupa and Gulabu reached Nasaka, they saw the vast land and decided to settle in that place.[50] They constructed a house and acquired as much land as possible.' The old house construction still exists. It is located in the very centre of the present village and the upper storey was used as the village temple. Recently, a new cement temple has been constructed, but it is only in the old one that the murti of Baukhnag is kept when the deity resides in Nakoli.

> Rupa and Gulabu were men of great influence and power, they were the thokdars of the region [they were the sayanas of their village, but were respected like a thokdar]. In the neighbourhood there were two other sayanas [thokdars], Buddi and Surmani. They were great and honourable men and were respected like Rupa and Gulabu. Rupa and Gulabu and Buddi and Surmani could punish the villagers [like a thokdar] if they did something wrong. The guilty person was made to sit in the heriberi for some hours [up to three days].

A variety of information is contained in this passage. As they were the heads of their lineages and belonged to the dominant clan, Rupa and Gulabu somewhat logically usurped the function of the village headman (sayana). They were successful and honourable and therefore vested with extraordinary juridical power, so that, de facto they became the local representatives of the ruler (i.e. thokdars). The heriberi was an instrument of torture which obviously had been used by thokars in case of minor offences. It was made of wood and, according to the description, it must have been a seatlike construction with a cross beam (like a yoke) with round apertures. The victim had to sit in it with legs crossed and arms which were put through the apertures

[50] Nasaka is the name of the field area on the top of the northern ridge. Today a small temple can be found here.

and somehow tied.[51] To control the heriberi was—in the eyes of the villagers—synonymous with power over people. But the power of Rupa and Gulabu was restricted to a certain area: it was limited by the adjoining realm of influence of two other 'big men', Buddi and Surmani, who came from two different villages (Nos 6 and 11) and who must have been Brahmins.

The area on which Rupa and Gulabu laid their territorial claim can still be imagined from the hints given by local residents. When asked about the borderlines of present Nakoli, villagers (especially from the Panwar clan) seem to have a clear picture. According to their mental map a natural borderline stretches on top of the densely forested mountain ridges which enclose Nakoli and separate alli Mungarsanti from palli Mungarsanti and parts of Barkot patti in the north, from the adjoining pattis in the Bhagirathi catchment area to the east and south-east. A socio-political (territorial) border marks the area of Nakoli in the south-west and west. The imagined borderline includes (reserved) forest areas and part of the territory of neighbouring villages. If one looks into the official records, reserved forests border the area of Nakoli in the north and east, whereas land belonging to three adjoining villages (Nos 2, 3, 4) marks the border to the south and west. But we could see that in the perception of the village Rajputs the borderlines of Nakoli run differently and they still count a much wider area as 'theirs'. Even though everyone knows about the present-day administrative divisions, village Rajputs recall and implicitly refer to their old rights on land and commons.

It is difficult to reconstruct the historical relations of Nakoli and the villages located in their former realm of influence. A Brahmin from Village No. 3 stated: 'When our ancestors migrated to this area they first settled in Maidanda.[52] The place was surrounded by jungle and bears and leopards were about. So our elders decided to shift to a place further down. In those days all the land was acquired by Nakoli; only much later the land became recorded in our name.' In the times of the Tehri Raj all land rights were vested in the king. The

---

[51] Villagers stated that the heriberi existed until a few years ago, later it was used as firewood.

[52] Name of one of the upper field areas located to the south-east of Nakoli.

cultivators were considered hereditary tenants but could not alienate their holdings by sale or mortgage. The system of land tenancy seems to have been even more complex. The literature reports three types of land tenure: *maurusidar*—possessing hereditary rights; *khaikar*—under-proprietary rights; *sirtan*—tenant-at-will (Arora 1996: 86f). In the course of my fieldwork I came across the first two categories. A few of my informants indicated that in former times members of the neighbouring villages have been khaikar. The khaikar, according to the literature, had to pay the land revenue and, in addition, give 10 per cent to the maurusidar. He also had to pay a fixed rent for his holding to the maurusidar who had no right to eject him unless he himself surrendered the holding. The interest of the khaikar was hereditary but not transferable (Arora 1996: 87). One informant described the khaikar as *karnevala* (one who works) and added: *zamin khao—tax do*, i.e. till ('eat') the land and pay the tax. But he denied that a rent had to be paid in addition to the tax.[53] Even though it is highly speculative, it seems plausible that migrants who settled in the area of Nakoli received the land with full tenancy rights (khaikar) from the dominant Rajputs of Nakoli (maurusidar).[54]

In the agricultural system of the hills, access to cultivable land is of basic importance, but it is equally essential for villagers to have access to forest and pastures. In the Nakoli region the mountain ridges are still covered with comparatively dense mixed forest (oak and pine) and, in higher altitudes, with stands of spruce and fir. In the lower altitudes pine forests dominate. For grazing, lopping, and collecting firewood and dry leaves, oak forests are of highest value. Even though the inhabitants of all the villages adjoining Nakoli have formal right to make use of their oak forest, they usually rely on the pine forest, so that the upper part is de facto mainly used by villagers from Nakoli. At first glance it seems that the inhabitants of Nakoli have access to the oak forest on account of their favourable location, but there may

[53] The literature mentions it was common to give some land to the *kul purohit*, the family priest (Arora 1996: 86).

[54] At present land may be given for tenancy on a 50:50 basis (*adhiali*). Fifty per cent of the crop belongs to the cultivator and 50 per cent has to be given to the landowner. This system is applied when the owner of the soil cannot till the land on his own. In most cases the cultivators are relatives.

be social reasons as well. I was told that inhabitants from the villages in the neighbourhood of Nakoli have to ask people from Nakoli for permission to take firewood, grass, and other forest products from the forests at the higher altitudes. One can guess that customary rights and traditional powers of control still define access to the forest and—what is very crucial in present times—also defines who can acquire new land for cash-crop production. Villagers from the adjoining settlements complain that only a few of the families in these villages managed to plant small apple orchards and that only small-scale production of potatoes and peas for sale is possible, due to lack of land. In contrast with the inhabitants of Nakoli, they also have fewer opportunities to extend their agricultural area. Even though I did not come across open conflict, tensions between the villages seemed latent.

After the period of colonization no village elders seem to have enjoyed as much power and respect in the locality as Rupa and Gulabu. With the administrative structure of the region becoming more centralized in the ensuing decades, the influence of village leaders probably declined to the same degree as the position of state officials (intermediaries acting in the locality) was strengthened. 'Political' narratives which tell of the time after Rupa and Gulabu do not any longer concentrate primarily on the villages and their sayanas, but also tell of the Thakur of Mungra garh and reflect the relation of the villagers to him.

Villagers say that Mungarsanti was already a patti in the time of the Tehri Raj, that is, the administrative unit below the pargana, consisting of a few villages. The patti was controlled by a thokdar, whereas each village (or a cluster of villages) was under the leadership of a sayana or malguzar. The position of thokdar of Mungarsanti was hereditary in the lineage (khandan) of the Rautela Thakurs who resided in Mungra garh on the banks of the Yamuna and claimed kinship with the Raja of Tehri.[55] When asked about his family and its origin, Thakur Surat Singh Rautela from Naugaon stated that four brothers had migrated from Srinagar at the same time as the Raja had to leave his

[55] Mungra garh, located on the banks of the Yamuna, is in ruins today. Over its long history the garh was destroyed by fire twice. The last fire occurred in the 1950s.

capital after his defeat by the Gurkhas. They all settled in Rawain. In a story about Mungra garh the Thakur presented another version. According to this his ancestors came to Rawain long before the Gurkha invasion. They resided in Hansura garh but left the place later for Mungra garh. Since the reign of Pratap Shah the Rautela Thakurs were installed as *jagirdars* of nine villages in the vicinity of Mungra garh (jagirdars held the right to collect and keep the total revenue).

What was the administrative role of the thokdar in the time of the Tehri Raj, and what were his rights and obligations? According to the ideas of my upper-caste informants, the thokdar was the local representative of the Raja and functioned as the connecting link between the king's court and the village headmen (sayana). The revenue collected by the village sayanas had to be handed over to the thokdar, from where it went to the state treasury. Village conflicts which could not be solved by the headmen came to the thokdar, and only if he was not able to find a solution was the problem presented to the local court in Rajgarhi or to the Raja himself. The thokdar had to keep an eye on the villagers and was expected to report local discontent, agitations, and uprisings to the *darbar* (the Raja's court).

Villagers were expected to respect the thokdar and show him reverence in various ways. When the thokdar visited a village in his administrative realm the inhabitants had to welcome him and carry him on their shoulders to the village centre, where a special place for him to sit had been prepared and a good meal with meat and alcohol served. Villagers could be asked to work on his fields free of charge. The relation between thokdar and the local population seems to have been characterized by a certain ambivalence: on the one hand villagers feared and respected the thokdar, on the other they felt oppressed and subjugated by him. Two stories give evidence of this ambivalence:

First story, by G.S. Rawat from a village in the Yamuna valley: Once the thokdar from Kumola needed labourers for the planting of paddy (dhan rupai). Besides his own people, villagers from Mungarsanti were also forced to help in the fields. The villagers of Nakoli were angry and their sayana thought of how to undermine the obligation. He proposed that they should all go to the fields of the thokdar but they should keep their shoes on and their trousers too during the work, and they should plant the rice seedlings upside down. The thokdar would then be angry and chase them away. And so it happened. Nakoli's people were cursed and chased away with the words: *Sale parvateye, tum khet ka nuksan kar rahe ho* (You dirty hill people! You are damaging the fields).

Second story, by Thakur S.S. Rautela: In former times when the Mungra Thakurs were still jagirdars and thokdars, one member of their family was an old and respected man with white hair who used to wear a white cotton cap (*topi*). One day a villager from Nakoli went to Nasaka (located on the top of the ridge) to do some work. Suddenly he saw a *langur* [long-tailed black and white monkey] but did not recognize him as a monkey. The man thought, 'Oh, this is our Thakur Sahib who will come to visit us', and hurried back to his village. When he reached back he called his fellow villagers together and said the Mungra Thakur was on his way to Nakoli and had been spotted by him in Nasaka. The people rushed to welcome the Thakur, but by the time they reached Nasaka the langur had disappeared. The inhabitants of Nakoli thought that the Thakur had become angry over something and had returned to his garh. Apprehensive, they rushed back to the village and discussed matters. They grew convinced that something must have infuriated the Thakur and decided to collect presents to conciliate him. The next day a delegation from Nakoli went to Mungra garh to present the collected goods and beg forgiveness. The Thakur was puzzled when he heard the villagers and asked: 'Why do you want to apologize and why did you collect so many things for me?' The villagers told him the whole story. Having heard the story the Thakur was even more puzzled. He shook his head and said nobody from his family had been in Nasaka. But he took all the presents and said: 'Because you have collected so many things for your thokdar and brought them to my house, I will graciously accept them.'

The political role below the thokdar was performed by the village sayana. I learned from my informants that the sayana had to be a man of good reputation and influence in the locality (*bolbala*). He was expected to know how to speak to the people as well as in front of the ruling groups. The village sayana was not elected, he was selected. Usually, the oldest son was designated to follow his father in the office, but as it was not a hereditary position the son had to be intellectually and morally qualified, else another candidate (probably from another lineage) was selected. The candidate could not be appointed to the office without the approval of the Raja. In case the Raja disliked the recommended person he was free to choose another. The sayana had a number of duties in which he was supported by a helper, the village pasvan: collecting of village revenue (*malguzari*); adjudicating minor conflicts (e.g. theft, divorce); organizing begar (transporting the luggage of officials free of cost); observing villagers and reporting any sort of agitation; controlling forest fires and organizing firefighting operations. The team of firefighters was made up of one male from each family; the work was compulsory; failure to help meant the family had to pay a fine. The sayana was entitled to keep a certain percentage of the malguzari. Often it happened that a farmer could not pay the revenue by the due date and so the sayana lent him the needed amount—a practice which could lead to financial and social dependencies and to increase in status differences. Annually, in the month of Mangsir, all village households (who could afford it) would cut a *kharu* (male sheep); of this the sayana had the right to one leg from each family. In return he was expected to invite one male member of each family and serve them a rich meal with meat.

The Raja himself remained the distant ruler who received revenue and formally installed the village sayana and the thokdar but did not intervene in the everyday affairs of the Rawaltas. Personal contact between local villagers and the Raja and his court was also comparatively rare. The raja and his subjects met during royal inspection tours, when the king visited villages in his territory. The villagers had to provide him unpaid services and collect provisions and gifts for the king and his escort. The Raja was also the final authority in legal questions and in severe cases the accused was brought in front of the king.[56]

---

[56] All legal issues which could not be solved by the sayana or the thokdar were taken to the local court in Rajgarhi or to the main court in Tehri. When no judgement could be passed, the case came in front of the Raja. But according to my informants, the Raja did not administer justice himself, the accused had to face a trial by ordeal: He was asked to stand in front of the Raja, on his head a vessel with water from the holy Ganga (*gangajal*), his right hand on his breast. The accused had to take an oath that, in case of his guilt, for example, he would accept falling ill with leprosy, or the death of his child. The ordeal was believed to punish the guilty and set free the innocent.

It seems that in the earlier days of the Tehri Raj the political and administrative constellation in that particular part of Rawain allowed some autonomy in the regulation of local affairs. Among others, the management and control of commons (forest, pastures) was still the responsibility of the villages. When scientific forestry, according to the British system, was implemented under the rule of Raja Kirti Shah and, in particular, when classification and demarcation of forests began at the instigation of Padam Dutt Raturi (the new Conservator of Forests), in 1908, it meant radical change for the local population. The new policy not only affected the local economy but denied the villagers the right of self-determination in a central aspect of their life (see below).

6.2.2 Religion and Ritual

Religious life in Nakoli and the surrounding villages is characterized by a variety of imaginations and practices relating to gods, ancestors, and supranatural beings. Religious plurality comprises the cults of regional or village gods (gaon devtas), worship of the main Hindu gods and goddesses (Shiva, Durga, Ganesha, Vishnu, Krishna, etc.), the cult of the Pandavs, the worship of family and clan gods (kul devtas), worship of minor or 'specialist' gods and spirits, pilgrimages to the four dhams Gangotri, Yamnotri, Kedarnath, and Badrinath. In the following I concentrate on those aspects of religion and religious life which provide insights into the religious significance of the forest.

Regional/Gaon Devtas: Origin, Responsibilities, and Religious Geography

In Mungarsanti patti three local deities are worshipped: Baukhnag, Ludeshwar (sometimes called Rudeshwar), and Daheshwar. All of them are said to be incarnations of Shiva. As I have mentioned before, each deity has a particular realm of influence affirmed by an annual yatra and by a mela, the highlight of the religious season. The realms of influence of the devtas partly overlap with each other, but only in Nakoli are all three worshipped and it is the only village visited by all three. Two of the devtas even reside in Nakoli alternately—Baukhnag and Daheshwar. To each of the gods at least one village temple is dedicated, as well as another which is located outside the inhabited area.

The latter temples, of Baukhnag and Ludeshwar, are each situated on a densely forested hilltop, whereas that of Daheshwar is located amidst fields not far from the village (No. 3). All deities have three main functionaries: a Brahmin pujari, responsible for the daily worship; a Brahmin mali, who gets possessed by the god and acts as his 'voice'; a wazir, usually a Rajput, who functions as the treasurer of the god and accompanies him on the annual yatras. The pujari and the mali have to follow certain restrictions for their whole life (the wazir only during the yatra): vegetarianism, teetotalism, not eating and drinking in restaurants. They, as well as their male family members, are not allowed to plough their fields on their own. All these restrictions do not affect the other Brahmins of this area.

Origin and Responsibilities

Baukhnag devta is said to be the autochthonous deity of the hills (*paharon ka devta*) and especially linked with forest and water. He is also called upon by his worshippers when things are in disarray, for example when a village and its inhabitants are threatened by illness, when the rains fail, when crops seem likely to fail. The proper residence of Baukhnag is assumed to be the approximately 3000m high Baukh-Danda, a densely forested hilltop a few hours' walk from Nakoli. My Brahmin informants stated that Baukhnag (like most gods) prefers to live permanently in the forest temple at a high altitude. This allows the deity to stay away from the noisy and dirty world of human beings and enjoy the calmness and purity of a forest environment. But because a deity needs puja every day and the Brahmins cannot abide long in forest seclusion, the god has decided to reside in village temples. The main temple of Baukhnag is located in Village No. 14. The pujari as well as the mali of the god are selected from among the Dimri Brahmins. The office of wazir has been held in the lineage of the Rawat Rajputs for a long time. The devta resides in village No. 14 for two years (because the village consists of two separate parts), then shifts annually between three other temples, one of them situated in Nakoli. Because the puja of the devta is exclusively done by Dimri Brahmins from Village No. 14, in the years when the deity stays in a distant village the pujari walks every day to that village to perform the ritual.

The origin of Baukhnag seems to be unknown and no myth speak of his descent. The god who is worshipped in villages of the pattis of Mungarsanti, Barkot, and Ramasirai is said to have reigned eternally in the hills of that particular part of Rawain. The inhabitants of Nakoli claim a special relation to the deity as they believe their village to be his birthplace or mait. The following story (consisting of already well-known motifs) was told to me by S.S. Rawat from Village No. 14:

> In Hansuragarh [on the banks of the Yamuna] lived a king named Bariya Raja. In the summer time when the water level rose with the heavy rains, the Raja shifted to Barak (above Nakoli). His cows went to the nearby pastures. One of them daily returned with an empty udder. A servant sent by the Raja to observe the cow, saw her depositing all her milk at a bekhal tree. Immediately, the Raja ordered people to dig under the tree. A murti was found and, after the people had removed it, water poured out of the place where it had been hidden in the earth. A small temple was erected near the bekhal tree and, later, the villagers of Nakoli constructed a bigger one.

The image found was the murti of Baukhnag and it is believed that the god, by appearing in Nakoli, demonstrated his close bond with the locality. G. Panwar, a middle-aged woman, explained that when the god comes to Nakoli in his palanquin (*doli*), those who carry him on their shoulders realize that the doli is very light. When the devta has to leave Nakoli the doli is heavy. This is because the god is happy to arrive but heavy with sorrow when he has to leave.[57] Brahmin informants from a neighbouring village said that only after the Rajput clans had settled in Nakoli did the worship of Baukhnag start in this part of the hills. Before, the deity was mainly linked with villages in the Yamuna valley, especially Barkot patti where three of his temples are located. The story of the discovery of the murti of Baukhnag—

---

[57] The emotions which accompany the coming and going of the male god are interpreted according to the emotions of a married girl when she visits her parents' house. I could not fathom the reason for this analogy. For the feelings of the goddess of East Garhwal during her yatra, see Sax 1991a. The term doli is used for the palanquin also, in which the bride is seated when carried to the house of her husband and in-laws.

which in its metonymic character seems to represent common pattern in the region in order to claim special closeness to God—   can be interpreted as the attempt of a dominant lineage to secure the protection of a powerful god for one's village and to stabilize its own position in the region by integrating itself with a group of worshippers.

As already mentioned, Baukhnag is related to forest and water. Even though no water can be found on Baukh Danda, the deity grants it to those who are in need and who truly believe in him. I collected many stories about how people got water with the grace of Baukhnag and present two of them. S.S. Rawat narrated as follows:

First story: Once a saint (*mahatma*) came to village B. and told the people that he wanted to go to Baukh Danda to pay homage to Baukhnag. He asked for a vessel to collect water; then he asked for somebody to accompany him and show him the way. Two young men were sent with him. Having reached Baukh Danda the mahatma asked the men to fetch water and promised them that they could go home after handing over the water. The two young men knew that there was no water available all over Baukh Danda, but they were afraid to tell the mahatma the truth. They took the vessel, but instead of searching for water they put the vessel under a tree and quietly disappeared. The mahatma waited in vain and had to face a lot of problems without water; he was thirsty, he felt pressure to relieve himself, he wanted a wash. He went in search of the two men, but when he discovered the vessel under a tree he was sure that the two had left him. In the night he had a dream in which Baukh Devta appeared to him. The god showed him where to find water and explained: 'You will meet seven canals (nalis), the first one will be of gold, but you should not scoop from that; the second one will be of silver, and again you should avoid drinking from it. The third nali will be of copper, the fourth of brass, and the fifth of iron—but do not scoop water from any of these. You should take your water only from the sixth nali, which will be made of stone. Then you will reach a seventh nali, a wooden one, and again you should not drink. Baukhnag assured the mahatma that he could stay for eight days on Baukh Danda; after that he should leave the place. The next morning the mahatma found all as had been promised to him in the dream. He stayed for eight days and then returned to the village where he told his story. Immediately, some villagers started for

Baukh Danda to find the water, but in the meantime all the nalis had disappeared.—The two men who had left the mahatma got their punishment by Baukhnag. He made them wander around in the forest the whole night long. Only in the morning did they reach the fields of Nakoli and from there returned safely to their village.

Second story: Once some shepherds brought their sheep to the lush pastures near Baukh Danda. One of the shepherds was mentally retarded. When he felt thirsty the others intended teasing him and sent him to Baukh Danda to drink—although they knew that there was no water there. But those who are innocent and trusting will always be rewarded. The shepherd went, found water, and drank. When he returned to his companions the shepherds realized his hands were wet. 'There is water', the madman said. The others rushed to the place which he showed them. Really, there was water! The shepherds were happy as it was a great advantage to have water near the pastures. They felled four trees and constructed a pond, and then hurried back to their village. The next day many villagers went to Baukh Danda to see the pond. But there was none! Even the trees felled by the herdsmen had disappeared and the forest looked as untouched as before.

Baukhnag devta is the deity called upon by his worshippers in case of drought. In summer 1995 the rains had not come in time and the crops were withering. In many parts of Garhwal and Kumaon forests burned; in the region of Nakoli the fires threatened the apple orchards. A rain puja was organized in Village No. 14. The villagers assembled and collectively shouted and prayed for rain; offerings were made to the devta. When the rains started one or two days later and extinguished the forest fires, people believed that Baukhnag had heard their prayers.

It is commonly believed that Baukhnag, who himself appears as a tiger (*sher*) in the dreams of people, controls all forms of life (plants, animals, supernatural powers) populating the forest. One Brahmin narrated that in former times people used to ask Baukhnag for permission before felling a tree. They burned some incense (*dhup*), fixed a coin (as *teeka*) and sometimes also a ribbon on the tree growing next to the one they intended to cut; by doing this people recognized the god's supreme rights to the forest. Especially the *yoginis* or *matri* (*saptmatrikas*)—female supernatural powers who live in the jungle and who mostly affect women—are said to be subordinate to him. The matri are worshipped in the form of stones; sometimes red ribbons are tied on a tree to pay homage to them. Once a year in Baisakh a puja is performed for the matri during the night at Baukh Danda. Only Rajput men are allowed to participate, and representatives of many villages join them at the small forest temple of Baukhnag.

Ludeshwar devta is a deity that 'migrated' to the region of Nakoli several generations ago. Everybody in the villages knows about the story of the coming of Ludeshwar and it is frequently narrated (with slight variations):

In olden days the people of this region used to go to Delhi to sell rice and forest produce. From the money they earned through their sales they bought sugar, salt and a few clothes—necessary goods which they could not produce in the villages. The route to Delhi led them via Chakrata; on the way they prepared their meals themselves.

In those days Ludeshwar was a Raja who went into hiding in Delhi. Suddenly he smelt the red rice from the hills and was delighted that the hill people produced and sold such good rice. When the villagers had finished their sales and purchases each of them packed his goods into his *kandi* (basket to carry on the back) and together they took off for home. Ludeshwar followed them discreetly, but later, when they had reached the foothills turned into a stone and placed himself in a kandi. After some time he shifted into another one and so on. The village men wondered. Sometimes a kandi got very heavy, then it became light again, and the next person complained about the weight on his back. They jokingly asked each other: 'Why did you place stones in my kandi?' After some time they reached Lakhamandal, from whereon the area (*ksetr*) of Baukhnag devta spread. Baukhnag realized that another power (shakti) attempted to enter his region and immediately caused a heavy rainfall. The waters of the Yamuna rose and the villagers were worried because they did not know how to cross the river. Ludeshwar realized who was responsible for the flood and intended to prove his own power as well. He made a hill collapse on both sides of the river. The stones formed a dam and the villagers could cross to the other side. But they did not think for a moment that a devta was with them.

Having reached the left bank of the Yamuna the villagers started to climb the ridge opposite Lakhamandal. They were terribly thirsty and the stone had again started to move from kandi to kandi. The men got angry and they addressed the stone: 'We are tired, we are thirsty! If there is some shakti in you, give us water. Let the water come out of that spot!' Saying so they knocked the earth with a stick. Suddenly the point of the stick disappeared in the earth and fresh water streamed up from the hole. Immediately the weight of the stone was gone. Now the villagers realized that some supernatural power had inhabited the stone. The men returned home [probably to the villages nos. 9, 10, 11] and forgot about the incident. Some days later a man went to plough his field. He started to work and suddenly a murti appeared on the surface. The eye of the statue was injured by the plough. The murti was soon brought to the village.

A short while after the murti had been found, a great stir was caused in village B. [no. 9] by an amazing incident: The villagers saw a 6-month-old child walking on the roofs of the houses. They also saw him walking in the nalis (small channels), weeping softly. The people asked the child: 'Who are you, where did you come from, what is the matter with you, what do you want?' The child, who had got his shakti from Ludeshwar, answered, and through the mouth of the child Ludeshwar explained how he came to the region. When they got to know about the new devta the villagers collected gold and silver and made a kandi, which can still be seen in the village. They also constructed a temple where the murti, found in the fields, was placed. Ludeshwar, who wanted to acquire his own territory, went to Baukhnag and asked him to grant him an area where he could exert influence. Baukhnag saw the power of Ludeshwar and decided that he should not deny him a certain number of villages. 'We will live as brothers', he said. And in the temples a murti of Baukhnag is always placed side by side with that of Ludeshwar; but Baukhnag is considered to be the elder brother.

Ludeshwar is the only one of the three main gods who has a story of origin, not only told in the villages but also sung by local bards. It is said that his realm of influence includes forty-five villages belonging to the region of Purola, to alli and palli Mungarsanti, to Dashgi patti and Khatal patti. Ludeshwar has four main village temples, two located in alli (Village Nos 9 and 6), two in palli Mungarsanti, and one temple on a saddle between two hilltops amidst a forest of cedar; this is also the place for the annual mela. The god spends, alternately, one year in each of the village temples. In Village Nos 6 and 9 the puja of the god is performed by the Brahmins from Village No. 6, in the other villages it is done by local Brahmins. In contrast with the other deities, Ludeshwar has three malis, all from Mungarsanti. The wazir of Ludeshwar always comes from the lineage of the Mungra Thakur, who held the office of thokdar under the Tehri Raja (for the legitimizing function of religion, see below). Ludeshwar is considered a very powerful devta, who is especially called upon in cases of theft and robbery. Some malis of the deity became very famous for their ability to speak the truth and ferret out the guilty.

Daheshwar devta is one of three brothers, who are all said to be an avatar of Rudra (Shiva). Whereas Daheshwar is worshipped in six villages in the Nakoli area (besides Nakoli Village Nos 1–5) the brothers exert power in other parts of the Uttarkashi District (for example in the neighbouring Dashgi patti). Brahmins say the area of Daheshwar was formerly much bigger. He had his residence in the temples which are today occupied by Ludeshwar and he was also worshipped by those who at present follow Ludeshwar. When Ludeshwar Raja came and wanted to acquire a territory of his own he tried to expel Daheshwar from his temples by showing him the leg of a dead cow. Daheshwar was afraid of the pollution and voluntarily disappeared.

Daheshwar's main temple is located in Village No. 3. Several generations ago an old stone temple with a Shivaling was discovered in this village. Its architecture shows similarities with the nearby temples of Lakhamandal. The small temple probably hints at early settlements of a population which worshipped the classical Hindu deities. The worship of regional gods seems to have started much later, when the region saw a new wave of colonization by Rajput and Brahmin clans after the invasion of the Gurkhas. The stone temple and the Shivling have been built over by a wooden construction and the Brahmins say proudly that Daheshwar is the only god in the region who has a 'natural' temple, which was probably built by the Pandavs or by the saint Shankaracharya.[58] As Daheshwar and Baukhnag are considered brothers, the murtis of the two deities are placed

[58] Shankaracharya (approximately AD 788–840) is assumed by many Paharis to have lived in the Garhwal Himalayas for a certain period. Recently the wooden temple has been pulled down and a new temple is under construction.

together in the upper storey of the wooden temple. A second temple of Daheshwar is not far from the village on the mela ground amidst the fields. It is very small and built of wood; near its entrance grows a a cedar (devdar). The puja of Daheshwar is the duty of the Nautiyal and Thapliyal Brahmins of Village No. 3, and when the god resides in Nakoli for a year they have to walk to Nakoli for the daily performance.

Stories with well-known patterns speak of how the old stone temple and the murti of Daheshwar were found. The temple is said to have been discovered long ago by the forefathers of today's villagers. The milk-depositing cow of the legends came here, to the old temple nearly covered by stones and earth, only the top its roof slightly peeping out of the ground. The murti seems to have appeared only two generations ago. A Rajput of Nakoli found the statue when he was ploughing one of his fields near Village No. 2.

People consider Daheshwar to be less powerful than Baukhnag and Ludeshwar, but they call upon him in case of illness (of human beings and cows). Daheshwar neither has a special relation to the forest nor does he have a forest temple which goes with the power to control a particular forest area (hilltop). He is mainly worshipped by those villages that formerly depended on Nakoli and which still have de facto limited access to the forest.

Religious Geography

Whereas the political geography of Nakoli region originates in the collective memory of an act of appropriation, the key to religious geography is continuous mobility: Baukhnag, Ludeshwar, and Daheshwar have to confirm their territory and realm of power by moving around and visiting the villages during the annual yatra (pilgrimage), while believers move from their villages and come to the mela of their deity once a year. The religious spheres of the gods transcend the geographical boundaries drawn by political interests. If one tries to visualize the spheres of the deities as three concentric circles overlapping in Nakoli, each circle transcends the imagined political boundaries of Nakoli and covers part of the neighbouring region: Baukhnag devta in the north-east, Ludeshwar devta in the west, and Daheshwar devta in the south. In a certain way, religion joins what politics separates.

The annual yatra leads each of the gods to the villages in which he is worshipped. The sequences of the event are almost similar, so that it is possible to describe an ideal-typic yatra. The main yatra season falls in the month of Asadh (June/July). The journey starts from the temple in which the deity has resided the previous year, and it follows an old-defined route. For the yatra the golden murti of the god,[59] which can be touched only by Brahmins, is placed in the doli, a wooden palanquin draped with red cloth and covered with an ornamented silver top. Accompanied by its main functionaries the deity moves through the forest and fields to reach its first destination. The palanquin is carried on the shoulders of male worshippers, and the younger men are eager to carry the god at least for a short while. In expectation of the god, young people from the village next in line, hurry in for his welcome. These males take the doli from the others and proudly bring the devta to their village, where they dance with the doli for a while. Then the god is placed in the centre of the village for the performance of the puja. From each family the men, women, and children come and assemble around the doli. Worshippers bring offerings like rice, wheat, ghee, coconuts, and flowers; they lay them down in front of the devta. Whenever I was present in Nakoli for the village pujas of the three deities, I noticed that in the case of Ludeshwar and Daheshwar it was performed by the mali.[60] Before the puja can start, the Brahmin mali has to fetch water from a holy source, and with this he returns to the devta and the assembled congregation. He starts the ritual by sprinkling some holy water on the doli and swivelling a flame. The most important part of the ceremony comes with the mali being possessed by the devta. First the mali trembles, then slowly the trembling increases until, in the end, his whole body seems shaken up by an inner power. He throws grains of rice into the crowd and with a loud and clipped voice starts to answer questions the villagers raise.[61] Very soon the possession comes to an end and the devta

[59] The murti of each of the three gods in the Nakoli region is not a statue, but a golden mask showing the face of the god.

[60] In principle the ceremony is the same for Baukhnag as well. But because he did not have a proper mali over the time of my field work, the ritual of possession could not be performed.

[61] Questions concern family problems, illnesses, fixing of dates for religious undertakings. In 1993, for example, the god decided the date the villagers should

leaves to visit the village temple, and, in the case of Nakoli, moves after that to a small temple in the fields worshipped specially by hunters.[62] When the devta has returned from the temple the villagers join him in dancing. The Bajgis start their drumming and one or two of the men take the palanquin on their shoulders, moving gently to and fro with the doli. Then the drumming and movements become faster and the dancers whirl around the place, the red *palki* fluttering in the wind. Men and women, young and old, rush to the dancing ground to touch the doli. Often they become possessed by spirits or minor gods and start to dance in ecstasy. After a couple of hours the ritual dancing stops. The god is either brought to the village temple to stay there overnight, or the devta moves to the next village on the same day. Before the god leaves he is carried through the village and families take the opportunity to honour him with a thali of burning incense, a coconut, and flowers. Finally, the devta circumambulates the village as a symbol of his protection. After the god has left, girls and boys immediately rush to the central village place for dancing and singing. Later they are joined by the elders, men and women equally. The performance may go on until late in the night.

A special attraction for village residents are the melas of the deities. The Baukhnag mela takes place every second year.[63] The melas for Ludeshwar and Daheshwar happen once in a year. I want to describe the Ludeshwar mela, because it was, for me, not only the most impressive but also of special interest because of the traditional relation between religion and politics

The festival takes place on the mela ground (*maidan*) near the forest temple of Ludeshwar, located on a hilltop amidst old stands of

---

start a yatra to Gangotri. It was planned that on this yatra the god should be taken in his doli.

[62] The temple is dedicated to Dulha, a young man who was an excellent hunter and who died in the forest due to the saptmatrikas.

[63] One year a mela for Baukhnag takes place on Baukh Danda, the second year people celebrate a mela for Krishna on a hilltop further away. I could not get clear information about the relation between Baukhnag and Krishna. One Brahmin placed Baukhnag and Krishna (= Trilokinag) into one line of descent, others say that Krishna asked for a place to stay after he had left Dwaraka and was on his way to the forest. He was allowed to rest at Sema Danda.

devdar. In the years of my field work the temple was still an old wooden construction with a brass-plated door.[64] Opposite the entrance stood a smaller building, a crocodile-like figure protruding from its roof. Very near the temple was a platform which was used traditionally as a place where the thokdar of Mungarsanti, the political representative of the Raja of Tehri Garhwal, who also functioned as wazir of Ludeshwar, was seated. According to Jean-Claude Galey, in the region of the former princely state of Tehri Garhwal political networks were dependent on religious identification. Galey argues that the religious foundation of political power is inherent in the constitution of royal as well as local authority (Galey 1990). When acting as wazir of the local deity and when occupying the platform in front of the temple, the thokdar claims political rights mediated through his religious authority. Old people said that in former times the thokdar was brought to the mela ground on the shoulders of village men. Today the head of the Thakur family still holds the office of wazir, but he can send another family member on his behalf to attend the mela.

The first to reach the maidan on the day of the mela are shopkeepers of the surrounding villages, street traders, and the 'hotel-wallahs' (owners of a tea or food stall). Some carry their luggage on their back, others drive heavily loaded mules or horses. Soon everybody is busy searching a good place. The 'hotel-wallahs' arrange their cooking pots and light a fire; others display their merchandise on blankets or cloth. When the first visitors arrive, a colourful scene welcomes them: numerous stands with glass bangles, necklaces, and earrings, and others with all sorts of cosmetics attract the eyes of women and adolescent girls. The children are more interested in toys, balloons, ice-cream and sweets, the men walk over to the tea stalls to chat. In the

---

[64] The old carved temple complex was torn down in 1997–8 and a new construction begun. In 2002 the new temple was nearly finished. It is much bigger than the old one; but it is also made from wood and is nicely carved. The carpenters were called from the Harki Dun Valley, as only very few artisans still know the art of carving. I was told that the pillars and sculptures of the old temple would partly be attached to the new one, and partly be auctioned. Villages interested in placing one or more pieces in their temples, can bid for them.

course of the next few hours hundreds of worshippers from the various villages reach the maidan, the younger and better-educated women and girls dressed in attractive saris or salwar kameez, the older village women still wearing the traditional ghagra (a long skirt with a braid trimming) and blouse. All these women come wearing their best jewellery. People relax on the grass or the moss-covered undergrowth; often they have a picnic, they meet relatives and friends and wait for the devta to be brought from one of his village temples. Then, suddenly, the first rolling of drums can be heard and soon the god in his doli, reaches the maidan accompanied by pandits, musicians, and young men who dance and shout. Immediately, the group is joined by men of all ages. They wield long staves and escort the doli several times around the temple, chanting all the while. After that the god disappears into the temple. When I attended the mela for the first time in 1993, visitors had to wait a long time for the main ceremony to start. At last, the mali was brought into the open. He was already possessed by the deity; he was shivering, his body motions were jerky. He was helped to a seatlike construction on the roof of the small building opposite the main temple entrance. There he flung his head up and down, babbling and incoherent. The peak of his possession arrived suddenly: with both hands he abruptly tore open his cloak and for a moment or two showed the murti of Ludeshwar fixed on his breast. After this the mali broke down and was carried off into the temple. The murti of the deity was installed in the inner shrine and the people were allowed to enter the temple to pay homage to the god, and to gain his darshan.

The Pandavs: Divine Heroes and Their Responsibilities

When Yudhishthira lost the game of dice against the Kauravas, the five Pandav brothers and their common wife Draupadi had to leave Hastinapura and go into exile. During their exile they lived for twelve years in the jungle and it is this forest with which the Pandavs are assumed to have a special affinity and where they exert special control. The Pandavs are worshipped as local heroes by the Rajput clans in Garhwal. In some of the western parts (especially the area of

Bangan between the rivers Tons and Pabar), an epic tradition of the Mahabharat is still alive. Elsewhere in the region various forms of Pandavlila, dramatic performances from the life of the Pandavs and Draupadi, are celebrated.[65] Around Nakoli people show the Pandav nritya (dance of the Pandavs), mostly in short performances which can be seen at several occasions all round the year. In these, male villagers are possessed by individual Pandavs (Arjuna and Bhima when I was around), and the women by Draupadi. Dalits are involved in the Pandav worship, too, and men from this group get possessed by a ban-devta. The identity of a ban-devta is unclear: some think of it as van-devta, a deity living in the forest, which meets and helps the Pandavs during their forest exile. The more likely explanations, which the local villagers and especially the Dalits give, refer to the meaning of ban as 'arrow', interpreted as a symbol of strength and power. In this version a Pandav and his ban-devta—which then is synonymous with his mental and physical strength—are seen as a symbiotic unity.

The most outstanding Pandav ritual is Navratra (in 1993 it took place in November), during which Pandav dances continue for nine nights. Every second year on the eighth day the Pandavs and the ban-devtas proceed through the jungle to the banks of the Yamuna on a night's journey. Here they meet with other Pandav groups from neighbouring villages. Fires are lit and they dance for several hours along the light of the flames. Then, at the first glimmer of dawn, they take a bath and dip their weapons in the holy river Yamuna. On their nocturnal journey through the forest the Pandavs pass several villages where they dance a short while and then receive and eat pure food and fruits (ghee, yogurt, apples, walnuts). The last day of the whole ritual recalls the return of the mythical Pandavs from their forest exile. The Pandavs spend half the day outside the village, at the edge of the forest, where they prepare and eat khir (rice cooked with milk); afterwards they return to the village and the great 'finale' starts. Scenes from the life of the Pandavs are performed: in 1993 the main scenes showed the hunting of a gainda (rhinoceros). The hunting is said to have taken

---

[65] In Bangan local versions of the Mahabharat are recited by local bards. One elaborated version, the Panduan, was recorded, translated, and interpreted by C.P. Zoller (1996). For the tradition of Pandavlila, see Sax 1991b.

place in the course of the Asvamedha ritual performed by the Pandavs after they had been established as the rulers of Hastinapura.[66]

One more example shows the Pandavs' relation to the forest and their special ability to control the evil powers inhabiting it. Amidst the dense oak forest a big stone is hidden in the undergrowth facing the village from the eastern hills. From this spot a direct line can be drawn to the top of the village temple. People believe that the area surrounding the stone is full of danger because it is the dwelling place of evil spirits and wild animals. The stone itself is said to have the potential to destroy the whole village or at least threaten its inhabitants seriously. Only the Pandavs and their ban-devtas have the power to control the malign energies within this stone. At regular intervals, but especially when the villagers face certain problems (illness, natural hazards), Pandavs and ban-devtas move into the forest, taking with them a big iron nail (kil; iron is said to be effective against evil spirits)). Having reached the stone they try to drive the nail into it, each Pandav and ban-devta delivering it one blow. Rusty, half-broken nails fixed to chinks on the stone as well as traces of powerful hammer blows testify to the continuous and obviously successful efforts of the Pandavs to protect the village and its inhabitants.

All the above is evidence that religious concepts and practices influence both the relations between villages, and relations between people and their forest.

(1) Religious imagination and ritual praxis transcend socio-political boundaries and create a network of relations between villages and villagers, who join in the worship of particular deities. These relations are those of solidarity between members of a religious community, but they also establish and perpetuate dependencies with Brahmins, who act as ritual specialists.

(2) The religious territory of the various gods includes villages as well as uninhabited areas consisting of forests, wasteland, pastures, and fields. The forest areas at high altitude, and in particular the surroundings of forest temples and the mela ground, are much respected

---

[66] For a discussion of the hunting of the gainda, which is a common motif in folk literature and drama (not only in Garhwal), see Zoller 1994. Villagers told me that in other years the ritual was more elaborate. For example, village members masked as animals entered the scene. But generally the performance is only accompanied by drumming: neither songs are sung nor texts recited.

by the villagers. Even though I did not come across an explicit concept of 'sacred groves', these areas are seen as the abode of gods; they are under divine control and it seems that they enjoy a certain immunity not extended to other parts of the forest.[67] The oldest and autochthonous god is said to control not only the hilltop where his temple is located but all forests in his territory. He also exerts power over the non-human inhabitants of the forest (spirits, animals). To the forest as such no sanctity or divine quality is attributed, but it is closely integrated into religious concepts as well as into religious praxis.

6.2.3 *The Forest in Everyday Life*

Everyday life in Nakoli is dominated by work—housework as well as agricultural and pastoral work—which keeps men and women busy all day. Young and middle-aged women spend many hours fetching water, cooking, washing, and cleaning. Women and men are busy in the fields, orchards, chanis, and in the forest. Women hardly enjoy any leisure time. Men work less on the average and find time to relax, but they contribute substantially to the family workload.[68]

Activities in the forest are various: people have to collect firewood and dry leaves as litter and fertilizer, they lop oak trees for fodder, in the spring the flowers of the rhododendron are collected for juice, in late summer villagers go mushroom-picking. Men or boys accompany sheep and goats, cows and buffaloes, to their pastures near the forest. In certain months the animals are taken to distant clearings in the jungle or to bugyals located at higher altitudes. Men also cut trees (cedar, fir) allocated to the household for house construction, for agricultural instruments, for boxes used in the transportation of apples. Some young men roam the jungle to hunt.

Collecting firewood is the most time-consuming and tiring work, even though the jungle around Nakoli is sufficient and close by. Women bring firewood as headloads; when men go for firewood they take a mule or a horse. They proceed to more distant parts of the

---

[67] For the concept of 'sacred groves', see e.g. Khurana 1998.

[68] When I asked a woman in Tangsa village (near Gopeshwar) if it was okay for men not to work, she disagreed. Men who work less in the house and in the fields try to earn money as labourers. *'Khali to koi nahin hai'* (no one is idle), she added.

jungle and load their animals with the heavier logs. Sporadically, villagers take a truck. In this case men, women, and older children gather at the loading area, and amidst jokes and laughter, jolt their way into the forest.

The lopping of oak trees for fodder is done by men, but also by young, agile women. The tree must be climbed, its branches cut with a sharp, sickle-like instrument (*daranti*). The lopper takes care to lop only part of the tree so that enough branches remain to allow new growth. Nevertheless the problem of overlopping exists in Nakoli because the gaps between the cuttings of branches seem to be too short to guarantee full regeneration.

Work in the forest—especially by women—has not only an economic function but incorporates a social quality as well. In his dramaturgic approach to social interaction, Erving Goffmann (1959) contrasts backstage (back region) and frontstage (front region) arenas in which social performances happen. Anthony Giddens argues, taking the analysis forward, that the spatial and social separation of these regions 'can be connected in an illuminating way to practical consciousness and the operation of normative sanctions' (Giddens 1979: 207).[69] 'Performances in front regions typically involve efforts to create and sustain the appearance of conformity to normative standards to which the actors in question may be indifferent, or even positively hostile, when meeting in the back' (Giddens 1979: 208). The distinction between front and back region seems an analytically useful way of describing people's behaviour in Nakoli, as also in other villages of Western Garhwal. An important backstage for men is the 'hotel', where they can sit and talk, drink and smoke. For women there is no such opportunity for retreat *within* the village. In the village area, women are under strong normative control; in particular young women are always watched by their mothers-in-law or by other elders. For this reason women enjoy working in the forest: it gives them an opportunity to withdraw from social control, at least for some hours.[70] I accompanied Rajput women into the forest many

[69] Gerald Berreman (1993) used the notion of backstage and frontstage to reflect on his field experience in a village near Mussoorie. He discussed especially the relation between the anthropologist and his 'object'.

[70] During my field work my room functioned as backstage for women and

times; they had necessarily to pass my room on their way to the forest and often asked me to join them. After a short climb the women stop at the edge of the forest near a small temple and wait for the others. Later they start off together—the 'official' argument for going together is safety—and talking, joking, laughing, and singing they disappear into the jungle. On the way, during and after work, they rest, smoke *bidis*, or even a cigarette, and, if available, eat some groundnuts or roasted rice. Songs, jokes, and talk are often provocative and teasing. Difficulties with husbands and in-laws are freely communicated between women friends. Girls sometimes also use forest work as an opportunity to meet and gossip with each other—they try to avoid going with older women. In short, compensating the heavy work women have to do in the jungle, the forest is for them a space of secrecy, joy, and relaxation where, for a limited time-span, are out of sight of other village people and can behave more freely.

Young and middle-aged men also enjoy the jungle for a favourite pastime: hunting. Even though hunting without a licence is strictly prohibited and has been since 1929 in the former Tehri State (Rawat 1989: 123), the practice exists and men who possess or have access to a gun are most eager to hunt. They prefer going in winter, when agricultural work has declined and the snow has caused the game to leave the more densely forested hilltops and come closer to the villages. Successful hunters were, and still are, respected persons about whom villagers talk with pride. On the one hand hunting is a good opportunity to get meat; on the other it carries on the Kshatriya tradition— by hunting men prove themselves true Rajputs. According to my informants, after the ban on hunting in 1929 Raja Narendra Shah granted to his subjects, living in villages situated at the higher altitudes, one hunting-day per year. People had to apply officially for that day before, and after a successful hunt they had to provide one leg of the kill to the local forest ranger. This day, I was told, was celebrated as a festival (*airi*). The male population of the village set out to hunt, but the animals could be killed only with the *dangra* (a battle-axe) to

---

girls, and—due to my research assistant—sometimes in the evenings the kitchen was backstage for young men. For the social dimension of forest work, see also Krengel 1989: 50f.

demonstrate individual bravery. After a successful hunt festivities took place in the village, especially if a tiger had been killed. After independence, the practice of a hunting-day was prohibited.[71]

The forest provides security and protection in times of conflict. The implementation of strict forest legislation under the reign of Raja Narendra Shah, resulting in the closing of forests and the curtailment of former legitimate rights of access to villagers, provoked serious conflicts between villagers and the ruler, especially in pargana Rawain (see below). It is recorded that, in those times, village people withdrew into the safety of the jungle when persecuted by the king's officials. During my research I observed that young men disappeared into the jungle for a couple of days after a serious quarrel. Having learned that the opposing party had approached the local police, such boys thought escaping into the jungle seemed to embody the better part of valour. They tended to creep back home after the police had left the village and, sometimes, after their families had paid a fine. And that would end the matter.

The forest is an area which separates villages from each other and from the river valleys. It may be uninhabited but is not seen as hostile. A network of small roads, broad or narrow paths, trails and tracks run through the jungle. Some of these are frequented when villagers collect firewood; others lead to pastures and are used by herdsmen. Some lead to neighbouring villages and to the more densely populated valleys; they are frequently used because personal bonds as well as

[71] Villages in lower regions did not celebrate airi, they met for a fishing festival, *maun* (fishing was also prohibited in 1929; Rawat 1989b). Whereas the airi was prohibited after independence, maun is still celebrated. In autumn 1993 I could participate in a maun, which took place not far from Nakoli, near the road to the Yamuna valley. For this festival, inhabitants of several villages meet at a particular place near a rivulet which, a few kilometres downstream, joins the Yamuna. The men bring nets to catch fish which, before being caught, are dulled by a powder prepared from the twigs of a local plant. Every year, alternately, a village is instructed to provide this anaesthetic, which is poured into the water after a signal. A yellowish dust immediately shrouds those standing nearby and, at the same moment, the men start splashing downriver to catch as many fish as possible. The catch is over when the fishermen reach the confluence. They light fires and eat the fish, accompanied with much drinking.

social and political obligations demand regular communication. Even though the forest is the living space of wild animals, gods, and evil spirits, it does not hinder translocal contact, for only certain precautions are required. To give an example: approximately 150m above the village the hills form a saddle, where a temple is located, facing a huge cedar tree. In 1993/4 this marked the northern upper borderline of inhabited and cultivated space, and from here the paths ran in different directions into the adjoining forest, some of them leading to neighbouring villages and the Yamuna valley. Here, as well as at similar crossroads, travellers pay homage to the local deities (mainly to Baukhnag who is believed to control wild animals and ghosts) for safety on the road by inserting coins or affixing ribbons on certain trees or bushes.

Even though the forest contributes in an essential way to the village economy, from one point of view villagers do see it as a hindrance—it prevents the extension of agricultural land. Expanding cash-crop production, which is valued as an alternative to outside employment, creates an unfulfilled demand for additional land.[72] People have begun clearing small strips of state forest, a practice considered illegal from the official point of view, but to the local population it represents a legitimate claim to forest rights.

6.2.4 *The Social Construction of Forest in Nakoli*

Two connected questions guided my attempt to understand the relation between people and the forest in Nakoli: how is the forest constructed in local discourses, and how is it experienced in everyday life within varying forms of social praxis? Such a contextualized and historical perspective, concentrating on the forest in a particular region and to which a particular community and social actors relate in their cultural imagination and praxis, is intended to avoid a priori constructions and essentialist assessments. The eco-feminist approach has, in particular, constructed an idealized and ahistorical image of the basic relationship between human beings and forests in India,

[72] Other possibilities of local income, for example work as a teacher, contractor, or soldier, are only accessible to educated people. A few manage to get permanent employment as labourers in the Public Works Department.

epitomized in the following two examples from Vandana Shiva's work:

> [Forests] have always been central to Indian civilization. They have been worshipped as Aranyani, the Goddess of the Forest, the primary source of life and fertility, and the forest as a community has been viewed as a model for societal and civilizational evolution (Shiva 1988: 54).

> The forest thus nurtured an ecological civilization in the most fundamental sense of harmony with nature (Shiva 1988: 55).

In this view the forest is an eternally sacred and provident space, an arena of religious contemplation associated with a harmonious life, with people's capacity to merge with the rhythms and patterns of nature. Shiva argues that the knowledge of the forest was not only the subject of the *aranyakas* or forest-books (which are part of the ancient Vedas), but also of the everyday beliefs and practices of tribal and peasant societies. Because nature is thought of in her work as a female principle,[73] women have an especially close relation to it; consequently they show a particular responsibility and nurture a conservationist attitude towards the forest. This affective relationship is challenged by the 'patriarchal project' (subjugating women and nature), expressed in modern (colonial and post-colonial) sciences and economics. As we saw earlier, the Chipko movement is Shiva's central case and Chipko women serve as her examples of this hypothetical female affinity with forests.[74] Shiva's essentialist argument is derived, it seems, from feminist theory rather than from the specificities of lived life and the relations people develop with their

---

[73] The word translated as nature is prakriti. It is 'an expression of Shakti, the feminine and creative principle of the cosmos' (Shiva 1988: 38).

[74] Several shortcomings exist in Shiva's approach: She deduces the special nature of the relationship between humans and the forest from Sanskrit texts and argues their validity for everyday life in all parts of India, for all communities, for the past, the present, the future. She also argues an ontological opposition between men and women and attributes to each sex a certain pattern of thought and action valid for all times. The relation to the forest and the relation to nature are seen as equivalent. Traditional ways of life guided by the feminine principle are predefined as being in harmony with nature, while modern ways of life, following the 'patriarchal project', are seen as destructive for nature (for a critique, see e.g. Bina Agarwal 1991).

environment at a certain place and at a certain time. Her arguments serve as a pseudo-scientific foundation and legitimation of the environmental issue, and especially women's role in it. It seems pointless to say more: my work suggests a reality very different and remote from Shiva's. Even more interesting is that, from the same Sanskrit texts to which she refers when drawing her picture of harmony between humans and forest, the *opposite* picture can also be deduced.

Indologists, who also work at a general and conceptual level, have shown that the dichotomy of *grama* (village) and *aranya* (forest) is omnipresent in Vedic literature: '*Le grama et l'aranya se partagent la totalité du monde habitable*' (Malamoud 1976: 4). In the old Vedic literature this is discussed as the duality between wilderness and civilization, nature and culture, and so has the status of a basic and quite fundamental opposition. According to this concept, the forest always remains *outside*, distanced and more or less detached from the sphere of human praxis. The relationship between forest and people, nature and culture, is not described as a state of harmony but rather as a state of tension and ambivalence.

Another interpretation given by Indologists questions the static character of the relationship between the two zones (even though the basic opposition remains undisputed) and sees it as a 'continuum' (Sontheimer 1987: 128 and 164). This interpretation starts from another conceptual pair, namely that of *vana* (forest) and *kshetra* (fields, inhabited space), which—according to Malamoud (1976) and Sprockhoff (1981, 1984)—are used in Sanskrit texts as equivalents of aranya and grama in late Vedic and post-Vedic literature. Whereas aranya and grama appear as reciprocally exclusive categories, this is not the case with vana and kshetra: they *interact* with each other and this interaction is seen as positive. Vana is the forest which supplies villagers with timber for house construction and tools; in it, herbs and wild plants are to be found; some trees acquire special ritual significance as *vanas-patti* ('Lord of the Trees': Sprockhoff 1981: 39). But vana and aranya could be perceived as complementary categories as well: the same space that was once seen as aranya, as wilderness, may become vana, utilizable forest, or land for cultivation, in course of time.

Shiva's approach, like that of several Indologists, remains at a generalized and ahistorical level. These approaches do not differentiate between (textualized) *conceptions* of human–forest relationship and concrete human *modes of dealing* with the forest. In order to understand the rationale of decisions and practices of local residents concerning the forest within a certain historical context, we need a more precise knowledge of these concrete modes of interaction, not unsound hypotheses.

From the detailed analysis I have presented thus far, the following general conclusion concerning the perception of forests can be drawn for the Nakoli region: first, the forest itself does not have any supernatural or divine quality, although it is the space for divine action and ritual praxis. Second, the forest is a vital part of the local socio-economic, political, and cultural-religious life; accordingly the forest is appropriated and seen in diverse ways. Third, the forest is part of a certain territory which is part of a recall via legend and history as the realm of local political power, and defined by divine supremacy, religious solidarity, and dependence. Finally, this territorial perspective nourishes a certain feeling of local autonomy.

Because the forest is part of a socio-politically defined territory, those who lay claim to the territory also lay claim to the forest. In this sense, rights of control and forest use, as well as responsibilities for the preservation of the forest, are vested in a local community. But the exclusive right of the community has been challenged by the state ever since the end of the nineteenth century and, consequently, forests in Garhwal have long been a contested domain. In the following, I illustrate how, in Nakoli and its neighbourhood, the assumed legitimacy of forest access is defended against the demands of the state and its representatives. The first example deals with the 'Dhandak of Rawain', the historical uprising of local hill people against the closure of forests during the Tehri Raj; the second with contemporary practices of acquisition of (forest) land in everyday life.

6.3 The Local Claim over Forest Rights

6.3.1 *The Dhandak of Rawain—Represented through a Local Narrative*

On 31 May 1930 the protest of villagers in pargana Rawain against the forest policy of Narendra Shah, the Raja of Tehri Garhwal, ended in a bloody massacre on Tilari Maidan, when military forces started to shoot at an assembly of demonstrators and petitioners. The uprising, known as the 'Dhandak of Rawain', is recorded as one of the first movements of a local population to claim their rights to forest use and forest control, and as a 'heroic' event it is still remembered in the region. It has moulded the identity of the villagers of Rawain, especially of those living in the vicinity of Tilari Maidan and those whose fathers and relatives participated in the struggle.

The Dhandak of Rawain is mentioned in publications on history and politics of the Tehri kingdom (e.g. Rawat 1989, 2002; Saklani 1987), and has a central place in Ramachandra Guha's book on peasant movements in Garhwal and Kumaon (1991). Time and again, it is discussed in regional newspapers and magazines published in Hindi. Annually on 31 May local politicians, environmentalists, and social activists meet at a place near the memorial stone of the Tilari fighters in Barkot to commemorate the event, and as we saw earlier, in 1969 the Tilari Declaration came into being there. In the following, I present the Rawain uprising and the Tilari firing from a local point of view. Jot Singh Rawalta from Kanseru, son of Dayaram, one of the leaders of the uprising, has written a short piece on the events. Jot Singh's account exists only as a single exemplar, but he generously distributes photocopies if one shows interest in it. This fragment of 'local historiography' is an example of how to construct locality as well as local identity and solidarity within the wider framework of state and nation.[75] But before dealing with the narrative of Jot Singh Rawalta it is necessary to make a few remarks on the concept and practice of the dhandak.

The dhandak, a tradition still alive in the first decades of the twentieth century, was a particular form of legitimate protest in Tehri Garhwal, open to community and locality. The dhandak affirmed relations between ruler and people (*raja* and *praja*) as constantly subject to negotiation. The concept is discussed by Saklani in his history

---

[75] For the concept of 'local historiography', see Harneit-Sievers 1998 and 2002. A 'local history' is a description of the culture and history of a certain community written by a non-professional historian for a local audience, published and sold locally. The process of reflection and representation of one's own culture and history is, for Harneit-Sievers, simultaneously a process of production of locality and local identity. (For local history writing in India, see Linkenbach 2002a.)

of Tehri Garwhal (1987), who states that the term cannot be grasped without going into historic folk memories; he quotes three different explications of the idea (1987: 75-6, orthographic mistakes in the original corrected): According to local popular perception, the dhandak was 'some sort of legitimate social device, which provided to the local populace [the] opportunity to raise their protesting voice and express discontentment against the ruling authorities.' By organizing a dhandak people demanded redressal of their grievances. Saklani cites two jurists, U.D. Dangwal, former sessions judge of the Tehri High Court, and Govind Ram Bhatt, a barrister and freedom fighter, who both explore the meaning and idea of the concept. Dangwal emphasizes that every subject of the state has the right to approach the king with his grievances, but 'when these same grievances were raised by more than one person jointly against any state official or a state department and brought to the notice of the king, this complaint or agitation was termed as "dhandak".' G.R. Bhatt characterizes dhandak as a means to deal with conflicts of interest between people and ruler; it was directed 'to regain those popular rights and customary privileges, which at times were usurped by the state'.

According to Saklani, the dhandak is different from the riot, the revolt, insurgency, and the Gandhian satyagraha because it was born out of a local tradition, could only be started to put through the demands of a group or a locality, and was not linked with a political philosophy or ideology. With reference to folk memory, an additional image is evoked (also briefly mentioned in Guha 1991):

> It [the dhandak] carried a certain connotation which proximated to an imagery of an unruly or a stubborn child, who remained doggedly insistent for the fulfilment of his simple demands. He shamed it or pretended annoyance in order to coerce small concessions and favours from the parents. Similarly, the protestations and agitations among the subjects were tolerated condescendingly as pretensions of an unruly child not to be minded as a serious offence. (Saklani 1987: 76)

Saklani, referring to Govind Ram Bhatt, adds that this image of an unruly child makes it difficult for contemporary minds 'to comprehend these humane nuances and niceties of the tradition' (Saklani 1987: 76).

The dhandak was directed against a deplorable state of affairs. Yet it was never aimed at overthrowing the political system. Protests were intended to restore the *status quo ante*. The concept presupposes a division between the ruler and his administrative body. The raja, legitimated by his status as the personification of divine power (*bolanda Badrinath*[76]), is seen as benevolent and good; problems and injustice arise only due to 'mismanagement' by state officials. This concept of dhandak is mirrored in the narrative of Jot Singh Rawalta, but, written retrospectively and after more than fifty years, later events and discourses which form part of the author's experience influence his story. The narrative follows a particular plot structure which is basically that of classical drama: a fable, situated in the past, is constitutive for a particular course of action which culminates in the climax or turning point. Then it leads to a result which is oriented towards the future. Contemporary academic works on social movements use the same dramatic pattern of presentation.

Jot Singh starts with an idealization of earlier states of affairs, then describes a process of decline of the earlier favourable conditions, these resulting in the protest by villagers. The narrative culminates in the Tilari shooting, which is then brought towards a satisfactory solution: it ends with the information that the Raja has restored the old rights and regulations, and that the person who was guilty and who caused all the problems has been punished. But a subsidiary narrative breaks the structure of the drama and, in the end, leads to a particular interpretation of the dhandak: Jot Singh tells of his own effort to convince the government to acknowledge the victims of Tilari as martyrs and freedom fighters. Why does Jot Singh want those who died in Tilari to be praised as freedom fighters—a term used in India for people who joined the national movement and opposed the British colonial regime? How can villagers who rose up to restore earlier conditions, rather than to overthrow the ruler and his oppressive system,

[76] Ramachandra Guha says the Panwar rulers of Garhwal had acquired the title of 'Bolanda Badrinath' or 'Speaking Badrinath'. The king himself is said to have been the religious head of the shrine of Badrinath located in the high Himalayas, near the source of the Alakananda. It is believed that the connection between the throne of Garhwal and the sacred shrine results from the time when Kanak Pal helped Adi Sankara expel Buddhism from the hills (Guha 1991: 64).

be deemed freedom fighters? The answer to these questions has to be searched for in later events, in Jot Singh's later experiences and political positions. His subsidiary narrative reflects increasing opposition against the ruler of Tehri Garhwal in the context of the anti-colonial movement.

From 1930 onwards, the people of the princely state of Tehri Garhwal were influenced by the national movement and Gandhian ideas. In particular, young educated men grew increasingly critical of the existing political system and its undemocratic structure. They tried to organize themselves and, in 1938, the Tehri Rajya Prajamandal was founded.[77] The organization's manifesto entailed, among other things, the demand for civil liberties, education, agrarian reforms, and development, a ban on begar, and the demand for local employment and Dalit uplift. In the following years political workers toured the villages to arouse political consciousness among the inhabitants and teach them about the aims and demands of the Prajamandal. After the Indian National Congress had passed the 'Quit India' resolution in August 1942 new agitations started in Tehri Garhwal and members of the Prajamandal demanded the king declare himself independent of the British. The political activities were suppressed by the state and many of the agitators imprisoned. One of the leading figures among the young activists was Sridev Suman, a convinced Gandhian (see Chapter Five). After his release from jail he did not cease striving for political reform and was again imprisoned in 1943. In jail he took a fast unto death to draw the attention of the public to the inhuman conditions of imprisonment.[78] Sridev Suman died after eighty-four

[77] Saklani explains: 'The Prajamandals were the individual units of "Indian States People Conference (ISPC)". This ISPC was practically the State's wing of the Indian National Congress. Through a resolution of 1928, the Indian National Congress decided that the chief aim and object of the States people's conference was the establishment of a responsible Government for the people of Indian States through representative institutions under the aegis of their ruler. Under the Gandhian leadership, the Congress party showed reluctance and hesitation in extending open support to States people movement' (Saklani 1987: 184).

[78] Saklani says the Tehri State was 'particularly infamous for barbaric conditions of its prison and atrocities committed on political prisoners' (Saklani 1987: 194).

days and his death caused a great stir in the kingdom; the confidence of the people in the ruling elite declined further. For them Sridev Suman was a martyr and even Jawaharlal Nehru paid him homage in his presidential address in the All India States People's Conference in Udaipur in 1945.[79] The death of Sridev Suman seems to have been another link in the chain of injustice and cruelty done to the people of Tehri Garhwal and together with the earlier Tilari incident it widened the gulf between raja and praja.

Jot Singh Rawalta's biography gives an explanation of why he was so involved in the public recognition of the Tilari fighters.[80] As son of Dayaram, one of the local leaders of the dhandak, he and other family members were seriously affected by the punishment given his father. Dayaram was sentenced to five years' imprisonment after the Tilari massacre, but when he was set free he spent another six years fighting for the release of his fellow prisoners, who were still in jail. Dayaram returned to his village only after eleven years. In between, the administration had confiscated parts of his land and property. Dayaram died in 1942, at this time Jot Singh was sixteen years old. He had finished only the 4th class. It was logical for this youth to support the national movement and become a critic of the political situation in Tehri Garhwal. He did not think of himself as a freedom fighter— those were people who went to jail and had to suffer, he said in the interview—but he attended and organized meetings in the region and actively supported the struggle for liberation from both colonial rule and the oppression in the princely state. Jot Singh Rawalta proudly stated that, together with other young compatriots, he once visited Nehru when Nehru was imprisoned in Dehra Dun jail.

Given the background of the political situation in Tehri Garhwal after 1930 and the biographical details available on Jot Singh, it is clear that the dhandak of Rawain was reinterpreted in the course of

---

[79] 'Of the many martyrs to our cause, I would like to mention especially the name of Shri Suman of Tehri State. Many of us will remember this brave and earnest youth, who worked for the freedom of people of the state. He was practically done to death by the treatment given to him in prison by the State authorities' (Jawaharlal Nehru, cited in Saklani 1987: 195)

[80] Information collected in a personal interview with Jot Singh Rawalta, August 1993.

later political processes, although it had primarily been a local event, traditional in form and function. The dhandak came to mark the beginning of the struggle for freedom and rights among the people of Tehri Garhwal. This reinterpretation guides Jot Singh's narrative on the Tilari Goli Kand.

Jot Singh's story is organized into 15 sequences. Instead of presenting the text as a whole and adding comments at the end, it seems more desirable to take one or more sequences (depending on their contents and dramatic structure), discuss them in the context of additional sources and information, and then turn to the next block.

Jot Singh Rawalta, President of the Heroic Tilari Martyrs Memorial Committee, Barkot, District Uttarkashi—Subject: The Tilari Goli Kand [my translation]

1. Under the rule of the Maharaja of Tehri the only life-bases and forms of love among our ancestors were cattle and the forest. From the cows and buffaloes they got milk, yogurt, and ghee, from the sheep and goats they got wool for blankets and clothing. The cattle also provided the dung to nourish the dry earth and let the crops grow. Only to bring salt our ancestors walked to Chakrata in former times, because they needed the salt for the cattle and to prepare masala [a mixture of spices].

2. Under the rule of Maharaja Kirti Shah there were no restrictions to produce marsha [amaranth] and potatoes in the forest, to graze cattle and construct chanis in the jungle; to prepare ploughs from the timber of the forest and to extract stones and plates for house construction. And for the houses trees were granted free.

3. Sri Padam Dutt, DFO [Divisional Forest Officer] went to France for forest training, and after his return from France he imposed restrictions to stop the above-mentioned practices. He ordered starting with the erection of boundary posts (munarbandi) near the nap land [measured land].

The story starts with praise of the reign of Kirti Shah, predecessor of Narendra Shah. The picture drawn shows a region with self-sufficient villages based on agriculture and animal husbandry. The people depend on the forest to fulfil their everyday needs and enjoy full freedom to use it as a 'common'. Section 3 initiates the transition by formulating the problem which sets off the ensuing dramatic events. When Padam Dutt Raturi acquired the principles of scientific forestry in France, he imposed rules and regulations which restricted access to the forest. Soon, the old favourable conditions came to an end in the Rawain hills—not the Raja's fault but that of a leading state official. When I asked elderly villagers in Nakoli and the neighbouring villages what, in their opinion, had led to the dhandak, they mentioned not only the forest legislation but also the imposition of taxes for cattle, the ban on brewing, the begar system, and the limitations on education.[81] Although the restrictions on forest use seem to have been the main reason for the uprising in Rawain, other obstructions by the ruling elite had created an atmosphere of general discontent.

4. Since Padam Dutt Raturi had started to impose restrictions, the people of this area had to face a lot of difficulties. Then the chiefs and respected elders of the region called a meeting, so that in every village the people would become alert and recognize that the Forest Department is erecting boundaries which should be torn down. When Sri Padam Dutt Raturi lodged a complaint to Wazir Sri Chakradhar Juyal concerning this matter, Sri Juyal prohibited meetings in the region. Therefore the below-mentioned elected committee was forced to hold its meetings in Lakhamandal, District Dehra Dun. The passed resolution was brought to Shimla by a messenger on foot and was presented to the British Government.

5. President: Sri Dayaram, Gram [Village] Kanseru; Vicepresident: Sri Hira Singh, Nagangao; Treasurer: Sri Kamal Singh, Dakhayatgao; Organizer: Sri Ramprasad Lala [Shopkeeper], Rajtar; Secretary: Sri Baijram, Gram Khamundi; and other important members: Sri Ludar Singh and Dalpati, Gram Barkot; Sri Jaman Singh, Gram Kanseru; Sri Fateh Singh, Gram Binai; Sri Dhum Singh, Gram Chakragao; Sri Dila, Gram Bariya. All these persons were elected members of the committee and assembled monthly for a meeting in Lakhamandal. The results of the meetings were spread to every village with drumming and blowing of *ranasimha* [a trumpet-like instrument].

[81] One of my respondents was Narayan Singh Rana from a neighbouring village, who was an active participant in the dhandak. Due to his age (in 1993 he was more than 80 years old) he could only recall the events very vaguely.

Sequence 4 describes the emergence of the protest, initiated by village functionaries and elders. The insurgents formed a committee with elected members (sequence 5) to organize the struggle. This committee met regularly near Lakhamandal, located in Dehra Dun District, which was under British administration. At the time of protest Raja Narendra Shah had left for England and a council headed by Diwan Chakradhar Juyal as president was responsible for the state's affairs. According to Jot Singh a resolution was adopted by the committee members and sent to the British Government in Shimla; why the resolution was taken to Shimla (the political agent of Tehri Garhwal had his headquarters in Nainital) is not clear. Perhaps Rawain's people hoped the resolution would be forwarded to the Raja, from whom they expected a solution to their grievances.

Ramachandra Guha and Ajay S. Rawat say that the committee members had constituted a parallel government, *azad panchayat*. Saklani, more cautiously, argues that sources which may provide more detailed information are still not available (1987: 179).[82] Guha and Rawat contradict each other in one respect. Rawat states that the parallel government was constituted according to the Nepalese system: 'Hira Singh was designated as 'Paanch Sarkar'', i.e. king, and Baij Ram was given the title of 'Teen Sarkar', i.e. Prime Minister' (1989: 164). Guha, with reference to 'an official, posted immediately afterwards to Rawain', says Hira Singh designated himself prime minister of the 'Shri 108 Sarkar'.[83] His interpretation is: 'The appellation clearly indicates the king's continuing legitimacy in the eyes of his subjects, who believed that through their actions they were helping him regain his lost powers' (1991: 75). In Jot Singh's narrative the azad panchayat is not mentioned. I cannot decide about the existence and role of this panchayat and the intention of its members. Is it a fiction of British officials and later interpreters, or, if not, was it a counter-government to the council led by Diwan Juyal, and was it even directed against the Raja's power? Did Jot Singh ignore it because his father was not involved in this parallel government? Did he even oppose it?

[82] I take the publications of Guha, Saklani, and Rawat as a contrast to the narrative of Jot Singh. All three have discussed the Rawain incident at length.

[83] King Narendra Shah was titled 'Shri 108 Maharaj' (see Guha 1991: 65).

6. To make [the work of] the members [of the committee] inefficient, Chakradar Juyal appointed Sri Ranjor Singh, Gram Koti, as Thokdar of Rawain. Sri Ranjor Singh was interested in getting the documents of the committee members and confidentially went to Chanda Dokhri [name of the meeting place], near the village of Bankoli, where at that time Fateh Singh from Binai was preparing a meal. He gave him Rs 5.00 and took all the files. When the members of the committee came, Fateh Singh told them that somebody had stolen all the papers whilst he was away to collect firewood near the riverside. The members were frightened by this.

7. At this time Maharaja Narendra Shah was abroad. All the documents and resolutions directed against the Maharaja and collected by Ranjor Singh were presented to the Maharaja, and for that Chakradar Juyal personally visited him abroad. He told him that the villagers are destroying the boundary posts and threaten the forest guards with beatings. In reaction to the complaints the Maharaja instructed Chakradar Juyal to hold a meeting in the region [of Rawain] and to find a compromise in such a way that no losses to the people should result from the enclosure. But if the people continued to tear down boundary posts, they would have to face serious consequences.

8. When Padam Dutt called a meeting at Barkot, not only were the above-mentioned committee members assembled but the ordinary people as well. They all requested Padam Dutt Raturi: 'Please, you must re-grant to [the people of] our region the former usufructs, because our whole livelihood depends on only one basis, namely cattle.' Sri Padam Dutt answered President Sri Dayaram, who had formulated the request, that all the restrictions would be completely maintained. 'If you like, throw your cows and buffaloes down the hills and butcher your sheep and goats.' As soon as Sri Padam Dutt had uttered such abuse, President Sri Dayaram quickly pulled him from his chair and with his hands and gave him a slap in front of the assembly. Immediately, Sri Padam Dutt fled and set off for Tehri. There he told Chakradar Juyal that Dayaram had pulled him from the chair and had beaten him up with a stick in front of the people. Thereafter Chakradar Juyal decided the following actions, which remained confidential.

Sequences 6 and 7 sound the bell for the coming events. Wazir Juyal,

interested in weakening the movement, appoints one of his colla-
borators as Thokdar of Rawain who, to show his gratitude, bribes one
of the rebels to get information and documents on their plans. Juyal
presents all this material to the Raja. The king, who does not want the
situation to escalate, instructs his minister to find a compromise. But
even though the ruler is ready to make concessions, his officials are
not (sequence 8). They ignore the royal order and confront the people with the message that all restrictions will be maintained. Pro-
vocatively, Padam Dutt Raturi suggests the villagers kill their cattle in
order to cope with the new regulations. The villagers take these
utterances as unambiguous disrespect for their way of life. The slap
Dayaram is said to have given to Raturi may have come from the heat
of the moment, but it shows how deeply insulted the people felt by the
words of the forest officer.

9.   On the 27th of May 1930 Sri Chakradar Juyal came from Tehri and
     brought along a military force of several hundred men. Part of them he
     hid secretly in the forests near Barkot, others in the government build-
     ing in Rajgarhi. Magistrate Sri Surendra Dutt sent a letter with false
     information to the members of the committee and to the population.
     In that letter he announced the arrival of Wazir Sri Chakradar for the
     30th of May 1930, who wanted to find a solution as far as the move-
     ment was concerned. Because of this announcement thousands of
     people from the pattis Bangan, Fateh Parvat, Ramasirai, Gadugarh,
     Jaunpur, Mungarsanti, Barkot, Gith, Bajri Thakral, Banal, Bhandasyu,
     Dashgi reached on 30th of May 1930 at Tilari Maidan. The committee
     members were asked to come to Rajgarhi at nine o'clock in the morn-
     ing. It was a deliberate false promise when they were told that the
     Maharaja had accepted their demands and that they all together
     should confront the public to give a declaration at Tilari Maidan. The
     members answered with applause and shouted 'Jai, jai'. And they lifted
     Sri Chakradar Juyal on their shoulders. But the members did not
     foresee the following fraudulent incidents.

10. On the night of 29th of May Sri Chakradar Juyal, Padam Dutt Raturi,
     DFO, Sri Surendra Dutt, Magistrate and Ranjor Singh, Thokdar, [had]
     decided in Rajgarhi to get rid of the committee members. They should
     be taken away to Tehri, but earlier, in a ravine near Nandgaon, they

should be handcuffed. The military leaders got the order to march with the Rajgarhi force to Tatau Maidan and with the Barkot jungle force to Barkot Maidan. The Chief Officer was advised to come to Tilari Maidan, there he should frighten the public by showing them the two forces and then should appeal to the people to return to their villages, because their leaders had been sent to jail by order of the Wazir Sahab.

11. The moment the leaders were handcuffed in the Nandgaon ravine, some people from Gith patti, located at the banks of Mother Yamuna, passed the spot on their way to Barkot. When they saw the committee members, with handcuffs, they immediately rushed to Barkot to give the news to the local people. Having heard the news hundreds of young people set off for the Rari Valley and, having reached there, luckily managed to snatch the guns from the hands of the soldiers and threw them [the guns] down the hill. But unfortunately the people did not know that the pistol which belonged to Padam Dutt Raturi could kill people as well. When the people were going to seize Padam Dutt, he shot two men dead and two bullets hit the legs of Magistrate Surendra Dutt. Padam Dutt himself ran away and escaped to Tehri. The young people brought Chakradar Juyal back [to Rajgarhi] and the handcuffs of the committee members were cracked open.

From a certain perspective Jot Singh's story is one of conspiracies directed against the people of Rawain. At first Ranjor Singh outwits the committee members when he bribes one of the rebels; Padam Dutt Raturi is unfaithful to the Raja when he refuses to compromise with the villagers, and then Diwan Juyal deliberately defrauds the leaders of the uprising by making them believe that the Maharaja has accepted their demands: he has already planned a military operation. Last, Chakradhar Juyal tries to ambush the leaders, to handcuff them and bring them to Tehri. This plan fails due to the vigilance of a couple of villagers who, by chance, are passing by. In the ensuing scuffle two people are shot and Surendra Dutt hit by Raturi's pistol. The capture of the leaders, the fighting and their liberation, are discussed in Saklani and Rawat as well. But all three narrations—the one by Jot Singh included—date the incident differently: the 19th of May (Saklani), the 26th of May (Rawat), the 30th of May (Jot Singh). Whereas in Jot Singh's story the military action is decided before the Rari valley incident, Rawat sees it as a reaction to the incident: only after the happenings in Rari valley, Chakradhar Juyal approaches the Governor of the United Provinces to grant permission for a punitive expedition (1989: 165).[84]

12. When the message about the capture of the committee members had reached the public in Tilari, from all sides the people started to beat the officials who had come to Tilari for negotiations. Then, from two sides the forces opened fire. 33 people died on Tilari Maidan, 2 in the Nandgaon ravine and 2 in Rari Valley[85]—totally, 37 men. One cow died in Sunaligaon. In the village Sunali 2 men were slightly injured and 17 on Tilari Maidan, but all were saved. Besides the committee members, the force took 42 men as prisoners. Including those, all in all 1250 men went to the Tehri jail. The trial against the men lasted until 1939. In 1939 the people were sentenced to imprisonment between 1 month and 10 years, and fines were imposed between 100 and 5000 Rupees. From the prisoners 13 died in jail, and as far as the Tilari incident is concerned in toto 50 men and one cow died, 19 people were injured.

Sequence 12 presents the climax of the narrative, the firing on Tilari Maidan and its consequences. Jot Singh meticulously lists the number of people killed, injured, imprisoned (the number of the last seems very high). His enumerations differ from those by Guha, Rawat, and Saklani, who rely on historical records and newspaper articles. Guha refers to the magazine *Garhwali* and states that 'Juyal's men fired several rounds and an indeterminate number of peasants were killed (estimates vary from four to two hundred)' (1991: 76). Others were drowned in the Yamuna and 164 arrested. Saklani (1987: 178) cites an article of Sunderlal Bahuguna (in *Karmabhumi*, 26 January 1956): according to him 17 people died, several were wounded, and 600 bullets were fired. Saklani adds two other sources with different figures:

[84] Saklani does not mention the British involvement. Guha (without referring to the capture and shooting) writes that Juyal got permission from the Commissioner of Kumaon and political agent of Tehri Garhwal in Nainital (1991: 75).

[85] Earlier, Jot Singh had not mentioned the two people who died in Nandgaon, but only those who died via the bullets of Padam Dutt Raturi in the Rari valley.

'one estimate' speaks of 100 people who died and an unknown number wounded; an official source (Annual Administration Report of Tehri Garhwal 1929/30) mentions 4 dead, 2 wounded, and 194 imprisoned. Rawat (1989: 166) refers to the article by Bahuguna and, additionally, cites a publication of the Information Department of UP (in Hindi, without date of publication) saying more than 200 people had died.

It seems that as many figures exist as representations of the dhandak. Only Jot Singh reports the trial and the sentences, as well as the number of people who died in jail in the years after the event.

13. Later, the persons who had joined in the movement against the Maharaja of Tehri were declared to be freedom fighters. That was when the applicant [Jot Singh] had started to teach that the Tilari Goli Kand was as hard a struggle as the event at Jallianwala Bagh, and therefore continually demanded the government to declare the brave men who had been involved in the Tilari Khand as martyrs— so that the incident be always remembered. In the year 1952, the respected Shri Chandra Bhanu Gupta, Chief Minister of Uttar Pradesh, came himself on foot to Tilari Maidan and, as a [government] representative, declared the brave warriors of Tilari to be martyrs and inaugurated a memorial.

14. Thereafter the applicant continued to work for all the persons who had joined in the Tilari incident and had been declared martyrs. The government and the district magistrate asked for prison certificates and, additionally, for certificates from two Members of Parliament and four Members of the Legislative Assembly. The applicant spent one month and five days in the office of the Tehri jail searching for the files. Thakur Jotsingh, who came from our region, worked as a clerk in the office. He did not know where to find the files, but in the same night in my dreams [the goddess] Bhagwati appeared in the room and with her finger showed me the direction and said that the files are above. According to that information, the files were discovered at the very place the next day, but, unfortunately, the rats had destroyed [parts of] the papers and after having looked through them, the lists and certificates of only 73 men—out of 1250—could be identified. After the applicant had handed out the above-mentioned certificates, in 1957 the

government declared the men to be freedom fighters. Thereafter the applicant continued with his work and demanded declaring the 30th of May as the memorial day of the Tilari martyrs, to be a holiday in the district. With a letter dated 18-4-84 the government declared it a holiday and with letters dated 6-6-57 and 31-8-57 the brave men were declared to be martyrs and freedom fighters.

Sequences 13 and 14 break the flow of the main story and tell of the later attempt of the author to get those who had suffered or who had lost their lives in the Tilari incident acknowledged as martyrs and freedom fighters. When his project is in danger of failure because the files cannot be found in the jail offices, he is saved by the goddess Bhagwati who indicates the place of the files to Jot Singh in a dream. With this rhetorical device the author legitimates his project and proves it just and pleasing to the gods. Jot Singh is convinced that the Tilari shooting was as cruel and tragic an event as the attack by General Dyer in Jallianwalabagh.[86] To compare the action of a Garhwali state official with that of a British colonial officer means showing that Juyal was as alienated from the Garhwali people as the British general from the colonial subjects. Like Jot Singh, Saklani sees a connection between the incidents at Tilari and Amritsar (1987: 179). He says there was no prior warning and the crowd was attacked without any chance of it dispersing. In both cases an ambitious official wanted to make an example of a despised population. For Saklani the influential Diwan Chakradhar Juyal is the 'embodiment of an imperialistic police officer' (1987:175).

15. When the Maharaja returned from abroad, he personally visited the region and in Barkot declared all the facilities mentioned in § 2 to be valid. These facilities are up to now valid in the districts of Tehri and Uttarkashi, thanks to the heroic martyrs of Tilari to whom we have to pay our love and respect. On one day all came together with Wazir Juyal Sahab to Narendranagar to speak with the young

[86] Jallianwala Bagh is a walled garden in the city of Amritsar where unarmed people gathered to celebrate the Sikh festival of Baisakh on 13 April 1919. They were continuously fired upon by troops on orders of Brigadier General R.E.H. Dyer. According to offical estimates, 379 persons were killed and 1200 wounded, including women and children (Mansingh 1998: 201).

Maharaja Manvirendra Shah. When he realized the extent of the atrocities, Maharaja Manvirendra Shah gouged out an eye of Chakradhar Juyal with a pen. And again it is obvious that the public is deeply indebted to the brave martyrs of Tilari. Namaskar.

Author,
Jot Singh Rawalta,
Gram Kanseru

For all the cruelties meticulously reported by Jot Singh, his narrative is a success story and an idealization of history. In his opinion the struggle and sacrifice of the Rawain villagers was not in vain. When the Maharaja returns from England he restores the old rights, which are said to be valid until today. The arrogant and uncompromising Diwan gets his punishment at the hands of the young prince and future Raja, Manvirendra Shah (who came to the throne in 1946), who demonstrates partisanship with his subjects (at the time of my research he was a BJP member of the Uttar Pradesh legislative assembly).

Jot Singh's perspective on the outcome of the struggle is widely shared by the population in Nakoli and its surroundings. It differs fundamentally from the information that professional historians like Rawat, Saklani, and Guha give about the course of events after the dhandak. According to their study of the historical sources, the diwan faced neither criticism nor punishment from the Raja. After the return of Narendra Shah, Chakradhar Juyal convinced the king of the necessity of the military action that had put an end to the Rawain uprising. As a result the ruler blamed the people for deviating from their peaceful ways and accused them of being ignorant about forest conservation (see Guha 1991: 77). None of the restrictions on forest use was repealed; the diwan was neither punished nor dismissed by the Raja. When newspapers published details of the Rawain incident, Juyal launched defamation cases—for example against the editor of *Garhwali*, who was sentenced to imprisonment (Rawat 1989: 16; Saklani 1987: 180). Two enquiry commissions were instituted in 1931, but their results remained secret (Saklani 1987: 180).

As mentioned earlier, the years after the dhandak saw the weakening of the king's position and a decline of political legitimacy in Tehri

Garhwal. To bring the statements of the villagers somehow in accord with the findings of historians, it must be assumed that the political instability in the kingdom, particularly after the 1940s, allowed the people in Rawain, de facto, to use the forests according to their customary rights, without exposure to strong control and punishment, even though, de jure, conditions remained the same and legislation underwent no changes.

6.3.2 Contemporary Efforts: Everyday Resistance

I was travelling from Naugaon to Nakoli by bus. As usual the bus was very crowded. Suddenly I realized a rumour had started in the front part of the bus. A young man with a camera around his neck was the centre of that rumour. From the snippets of conversation I learned that the young man belonged to B. [village No. 14] and that he was critical of the felling of forest trees in order to acquire land for apple orchards. He had once published an article on this issue. Now he had taken photographs of the newly planted apple trees around his village. Definitely, he intended to contact some forest officials to blacken the villagers' names. The young man was loudly abused. People shouted 'Are you Sunderlal's brother, ha?' Then he was beaten up, his camera was seized and the film destroyed. The young man managed to escape by jumping out of the bus. A lot of people in the bus watched the scene, amongst them some local government employees—but nobody intervened.

This incident, reported in 1995 by A.P., an adolescent girl from Nakoli who attended an intermediate college in the Yamuna valley, indicates the ambiguous status of illegal tree-felling for cash-crop production and the tensions which apparently exist among villagers.

Apple production was initiated in the mid-1960s by the Horticulture Department as a means of local development.[87] In the early

---

[87] In the project of apple-based horticulture, foreign aid agencies—World Bank, FAO, and EEC—played a vital role. They provided funds for apple orchards in the states of Jammu and Kashmir, Himachal Pradesh, and the hill districts of UP. According to V. Singh, apple planting was taken up as a part of the afforestation programme. The author complains that the impact of apple plantations on the ecology of the Himalayas is widely neglected (V. Singh 1993; see fn. 88 below).

years only a few Rajput families availed of the opportunity to cultivate apple orchards, but soon more and more villagers of all status groups took to apples (as well as potatoes and peas), realizing the value of cash crops. In the mid-1990s most of the families (87 per cent) owned orchards and production is still expanding. In the early period additional land was easily available: the village and soyam forest was converted into orchards, small parts of government forest were probably leased by individuals—a practice which had to be stopped with the revised Forest Conservation Act of 1988. When legal land acquisition shrank, some villagers still tried to expand their area for cultivation by clearing government forests. Others started converting parts of their agricultural land into orchards.

During the many months I lived in Nakoli I realized that educated villagers are conscious of the ecological value of forests and the damage caused by felling trees. At the same time the desire for apple orchards is overwhelming and people find themselves in a challenging situation, wondering how to reconcile the opposing interests and legitimizing the destructive practices. 'We want to protect the forests, but we also want to use them according to our needs', says Jot Singh Rawalta, author of the piece on the Tilari incident. This includes not only the use of forest for subsistence-based agriculture and husbandry, but also clearing it for cash-crop production. From the villagers' point of view, even eliminating the forest gives immediate and sorely needed benefit to local communities. So villagers excuse the violation of the environment with two arguments:

- First, they mention the need to earn money to facilitate local development, to 'stand on one's own feet'. The majority of village men and women see the cultivation of apples as well as potatoes and peas as the only way to an additional income while staying on in the village and reducing male out-migration with all its negative social consequences. Cash crop production allows maintaining the village-based socio-economic and cultural lifestyle by sharing in modern advantages such as education, healthcare, proper diet and clothing; it also allows increasing mobility and access to radio and TV. This benefits all status groups.

- Second, villagers argue that, despite the ban on green felling, illegal tree-cutting is continuously done by the Forest Department ('our forefathers planted the trees so we should use them, but today the benefit of our forest goes to people from the plains'). Additionally, the moratorium of 1981 discriminates inhabitants of villages located above 1000m against those living at lower altitudes; the latter do not suffer restrictions against tree felling and so enjoy profit from their forests.

Both arguments are strengthened by the idea that apple cultivation is good for the environment. Apple orchards are supposed to control soil erosion and surface run-off during rainfall.[88]

The justifications villagers give for felling trees and appropriating forest land conceal implicit motives which seem to account for these practices ('a hidden transcript', in the sense used by Scott 1990). Tree felling is an assertion of the customary rights of forest control and forest use dating back to the time of first settlement. These rights were challenged by the forest policy of the Raja of Tehri, and after independence by the policy of the Indian nation state. In both cases the villagers feel they were betrayed by those representing the state: In 1929/30 forest officers kept to harsh restrictions against forest use despite the order of the king to compromise with the villagers of Rawain; today bureaucrats close their eyes to illegal felling and the

---

[88] V. Singh (1993) argues that apple cultivation has a negative impact on hill ecology. Apple production is successful at an elevational range of 1600–2700m and so falls into the 'oak zone'. In order to plant apple orchards, parts of the natural oak forest are felled which, as a long-term effect, result in declining productivity within agriculture and livestock as well as in soil erosion, and disturbance to the hydrological cycle and to atmospheric composition. Additionally, apples have to be packed into wooden boxes. It is calculated that 0.17 million m³ wood was required in 1986–7 for the making of such boxes, the estimate for 2000 being 0.21 million m³. Apple cultivation demands transport facilities and therefore accelerates road construction (which is ecologically problematic in the hills). Apples need chemical fertilizers and pesticides at every stage of their growth, which adds to the pollution of the Himalayas. Many varieties of pesticide are banned in developed countries but not in India. Apple trees have extremely low water-use efficiency. They do not control soil erosion and surface run-off because their crown is much less developed in comparison with that of oak trees.

export of timber to the plains everywhere in Garhwal. Earlier, protest took the form of the dhandak. Now, cutting trees and the appropriation of forest land can be seen as 'everyday resistance'. Scott's concept of 'everyday resistance' departs from an understanding of resistance as always overt and conscious; it refers to 'those behaviours and cultural practices by subordinate groups that contest hegemonic social formations, that threaten to unravel the strategies of domination' (Haynes and Prakash 1991: 3). This resistance may take the forms of 'passive noncompliance, subtle sabotage, evasion and deception' (Scott 1990: 31); Scott in fact points to encroachments on plantations and state forest land as examples of such resistance. Such activities are not formally organized, but they are coordinated (in the same way as other social and cultural activities) by networks of understanding and practice (Scott 1990: 300-1).

But can illegality seek justification within this idea of political resistance? Scott faces this issue in relation to theft:

> When it comes to acts like theft, however, we encounter a combination of immediate individual gain and what may be resistance. How are we to judge which of the two purposes is uppermost or decisive? What is at stake is not a petty definitional matter but rather the interpretation of a whole range of actions that seem to me to lie historically at the core of everyday class relations. The English poacher in the eighteenth century may have been resisting the gentry's claim to property in wild game, but he was just as surely interested in rabbit stew. (Scott 1990: 291)

There is no easy answer. In praxis, what is illegal and seems indisputably wrong can also be justified as financially necessary and morally acceptable. Motives are entangled and, as Scott puts it '[e]ven if we were able to ask the actors in question, and even if they could reply candidly, it is not at all clear that they would be able to make a clear determination' (Scott 1990: 291). As Haynes and Prakash argue, everyday resistance highlights the 'omnipresent tension and contradictions between hegemony and autonomy in consciousness, between submission and resistance in practice' (Haynes & Prakash 1991: 13). The concept of everyday resistance, and the notion of 'hidden transcripts', refer also to the existence, obvious or buried, of divergent discourses in every socio-cultural context. They problematize and complicate issues, taking us closer to the complexity of lived problems and away from essentialist notions.

Villagers' tree-felling for apple orchards has come under fire from two sides: first, from the government. When I revisited the village in 1998 the police unexpectedly destroyed a good number of trees in the newly prepared apple orchards. Policemen arrested some of the owners who were later released after a fine. Second, there is opposition from local environmentalists. The incident reported at the beginning of this chapter indicates that the ecological discourse deriving from a particular perspective and interpretation of Chipko has gained some influence in Rawain. Nevertheless, the majority of the villagers follow another discourse, another praxis. They do not focus centrally on ecology. They place local autonomy and advancement before ecological concern.

6.4 Projecting the Future: Autonomy and Advancement

Since the mid-1960s communication networks (infrastructure, media, telephone lines) have increasingly linked the Himalayan hills with the plains and larger cities. On the one hand this process has brought an end to the relative isolation of the hill population and confronted them with alternative ('modern') ways of life. On the other hand the exploitation of natural resources, facilitated by the expanding infrastructure, has affected the traditional way of life and led to an increasing socio-economic marginalization of Pahari communities. Events like the Chipko movement and the dissemination of development discourses in its aftermath have created awareness of both ecology and the socio-economic situation of the hills among the local population.

Like the villagers in Lasiyari, Lata, and Raini, the inhabitants of the region of Nakoli want to overcome their economic and social 'backwardness', they want to be recognized as citizens with equal rights and opportunities. But unlike people in the Chipko core areas, who, in the aftermath of the movement, continued to cooperate with welfare organizations and benefited from development and empowerment strategies, the majority of villagers in the Nakoli region have not learned to speak up and formulate their needs in public. In particular, women are not able to voice their demands. The villagers know their weaknesses, which, in their opinion basically result from a lack of education; in conversations with me they have often complained of their situation. They have realized that, in comparison with the 'plains people', they lack political influence and the ability to argue their vital interests through.

Residents of Nakoli and the neighbouring villages do not co-operate with voluntary welfare organizations. I was told that in the 1960s and early 1970s a sarvoday group had founded an ashram in the region of Purola, but apparently its members stopped their work after a while. Since the beginning of the 1990s an NGO named HARC (Himalayan Action Research Center), with its main office in Dehra Dun (and co-operating with the DGSM) has opened regional field offices in Rajgarhi and Naugaon. HARC concentrates on horticulture and fruit-tree planting projects. It helps with the construction of small tanks, distributes seeds and saplings. One source of income of the NGO is the production of *badam* (apricot) oil; workers of the NGO go to villages and buy apricot seeds, which they process in their own mill. They sell the oil to the cosmetic and pharmaceutical industry. The organization met some success in the Yamuna valley as far as horticultural work was concerned. Their activists also made an effort to organize women in villages around Purola and Rajgarhi; but this venture still lacked wide reach at the time of my revisits towards the end of the 1990s.

I got the impression that villagers in my research region are not really interested in following people from outside who seek to organize and guide them. To manage their own affairs autonomously—this seems to be the motto of many residents of Nakoli and the surrounding region, and some families have started to take the future into their own hands. For the last two decades, undisturbed by ecological considerations, these villagers have systematically converted forests into apple orchards. In a very pragmatic and even materialistic way, they presume financial 'wealth' is the straight solution to their problems and cash-crop production the best way to gain it.[89] A family

---

[89] For a discussion of the ways in which people from Garhwal and Kumaon cope with modernity, see Linkenbach 2000.

with money can afford to improve the daily living conditions of its male and female members.[90] Money raises their social status, and allows for better healthcare and better education. It is education which enhances villagers' opportunities to exert their citizenship rights.

Strategies of modernization are linked with a process of selective sanskritization. In the case of Rajputs this process of sanskritization is evident for example in the change in marriage practices. More and more, Rajputs from Rawain have given up bride-price marriage, polyandry and polygyny (considered as 'backward') and turned to dowry marriages which follow the mainstream Hindu marriage of the plains. Harijans or Dalits here have made a bid for social recognition by refusing polluting occupations (leather work), and altering their eating habits (giving up beef). I have already mentioned an earlier remarkable and successful process of rajputization in Nakoli—i.e. the attempt of a low-caste group to claim descent from a high Hindu (Kshatriya) clan—which became possible with education and the accumulation of wealth. This is not to say that customs, rituals, practices, and rules of conduct here have lost their quality as a 'binding force', but to suggest that they are now more exposed to reflection and negotiation, and that old rules of social conduct are increasingly under stress. Gender and status roles, as well as family hierarchies, are losing their traditional and self-evident character; they are subject to questioning or even conflict. The process is gradual, but a new consensus and context is taking shape in relation to ecology and development.

A central part of 'tradition', even now, remain religious rituals and practices. These include daily worship (puja) of the local deities, the annual performance of yatras, the annual celebration of big religious fairs (mela), worship of the Pandavs, the 'second Diwali'. Festivals connected with the mainstream Hindu tradition relating to Shiva, Rama, and Krishna are celebrated as well. These, and marriages, celebrated with the participation of the whole village, bring together

[90] Just to give a few examples: reduction of the workload, especially among women and children, through the purchase of mules which can be used for transport (firewood, dung) and/or through the introduction of cooking gas; in diet through the purchase of more and better breeds of cattle; better housing and clothes, daily hygiene, the construction of a pipeline to the house for clean water, etc.

people and help to create or maintain a developed sense of sociality. Despite differences of property and status, despite jealousy and resentment, people feel a spirit of solidarity, or, as they call it, brotherhood.

Solidarity, religiosity, and honesty are explicitly valued as qualities of local social life. They seem almost bound to the Himalayan landscape being perceived as a sacred, divine, and morally pure space.[91]

---

[91] For the perception of nature among residents of Garhwal and Kumaon, see Linkenbach 2002a and 2005.

7

Conclusion: Lessons from Uttarakhand, or, the Locals Speak Back

IN THE 1970S AND 1980S, STRUGGLES OVER FOREST RIGHTS in the Garhwal Himalayas drew worldwide attention via the Chipko Movement. To a large extent, the literature around this movement subsumed local experiences under global discourses, and many of the messages and meanings of the Chipko movement's varied campaigns were changed, homogenized, and rewritten. The Chipko movement was deployed as support for translocal interests and strategies, in particular to strengthen ecological and eco-feministic arguments. Some representations literally invented Chipko women as constituting the vanguard of an ecologically sound mode of production which supposedly draws on traditional practices, religious symbols, and values. More generally, Chipko was brought into play to prove the anti-modern stance of a local population. This romantic view affirms 'natives' and rural folk as close to nature, satisfying limited needs, and sensibly withdrawing from modernity.

I do not argue against environmentalists, eco-feminists, and green radicals advocating their own worldviews and socio-political strategies, but I do argue against their idealizing, and essentializing representations of communities to strengthen and support their assumptions. Global representations of the Chipko struggle tend to take away narrative control from local actors and detach movements from the specificity of their locale, from their village contexts. Global representations do not adequately recognize the concepts and strategies of local actors themselves, or their needs, visions, and strategies.

The main objective of this book is to relocate forest issues and struggles over forest rights by presenting and discussing the perspectives of leading activists and local residents. I have tried to illustrate that local residents have their own interpretations of the Chipko struggle, which may differ from those of the activists; I have also tried to exemplify that the viewpoints and concepts of the activists themselves are by no means homogeneous, but heavily contested. I argue that the issues of forest control and sustainable forest use have to be seen in the context of concerns about social and economic development, regional autonomy, and the imaginaries of preferred futures among people actually resident in the region in which such issues are raised and debated.

In her recent work Meera Nanda suggestively argues that nostalgia for traditional modes of life are not to be found among the poor and marginalized but are spread by the upwardly mobile urban and agrarian middle classes. Even in a 'quintessentially peasants' and women's movement like Chipko', villagers were not agitating against development projects but for better local control and a better share of the economic pie (2004: 32). She points out that it is the village elite and the Gandhian leadership who speak a 'language of traditionalism'.[1]

I have indicated, likewise, that the two leading Chipko activists Sunderlal Bahuguna and Chandi Prasad Bhatt are devoted followers of Gandhi and, in their different ways, attempt to live and work in his spirit. However, it is misleading to ignore differences between their approaches. Bahuguna's vision of a self-reliant economy based on tree-farming embodies anti-modern, romantic elements and refers to particular interpretations of Hindu and Buddhist religion and philosophy. He sees himself as a messenger and prophet whose first duty is to teach. Bhatt, in contrast, is basically involved in practical work. Together with other members of the DGSM, he converts his programme of 'eco-development' into practice. Although Bhatt propagates the value of village life and a sound environment, he takes into consideration the fact that villagers are keen on options which modernity provides.

I have also argued that the period of post-development is marked not only by critique and scepticism but also by the existence of alternative forms of development or alternatives to development which

[1] It seems problematic to plainly state, as Nanda does, that the new alternative movements (she explicitly mentions the science movement) and Hindu nationalists are twins, both being based on the same traditionalist agenda. She distinguishes between 'left' and 'right' Gandhians (2004: 214ff.).

are based on regionally (locally) and culturally different imaginaries of the 'good life'. From this viewpoint it is, first and foremost, the individuals and communities in a particular locality that define their own ends and means of 'development' and, accordingly, try to expand their capabilities and strive for decision-making power and agency. Of course, it is also true that local ways of life often are characterized by cultural and social differences, which may result in forms of inequality and modes of oppression in relation to caste, class, and gender. Development projects which are locally created under conditions of inequality often exclude particular social groups from processes of imagination, decision-making, and improvement; agency is reserved mainly for the dominant within the locality. In these constellations the marginalized may fight for a better status, but it is also possible that they are oppressed or hegemonized into an acceptance of their deprived position and lack of access to capability-enhancing resources.[2]

Local visions and strategies for 'preferred futures' may be an outcome of protest and struggle. However, development can also be the result of a moral dialogue between members of different social groups in a locality, or even between local residents and people coming from the outside, such as politicians and planners and social activists involved in the task of 'enlightening' local residents and assisting them to improve their ways of living. Making others aware of their situation exemplifies the arguments of Amartya Sen and Martha Nussbaum, who see it as a universally valid moral claim that human capabilities should be developed even when a corresponding self-perception does not exist. From an ethical perspective the question of the ends and means of development (what should happen and how should it happen) can only be answered by taking into view the needs of at least most members of a community.

Central subjects in both the struggle and the dialogues of a local population are the questions of utilization of local resources and how to cope with modernity. It is my intentiion in this book to keep clear of generalizing approaches and a priori definitions of the way local residents relate to nature and modernity. I have argued that only an

---

[2] Hanna Papanek has described this as 'socialization for inequality' (cited in Nanda 2004: 233).

anthropological perspective based on participatory field work and discourse analytic methods allows us to get 'an intimate knowledge of the complex nature of social situations' (Werbner 1997: 56). By weaving an analytic account into the conceptual framework which people actually deploy, the anthropologist can arrive at a cogent understanding of their interpretations.

When discussing the relation of human beings to nature, two approaches seem to have become dominant: nature is either seen as a resource to be commercially used and exploited, or as a vulnerable and endangered environment which has to be protected. These perspectives do not necessarily contradict each other; they can prove to be complementary in several respects. The exploitative and the protective attitudes objectify nature and divide it into two: into parts targeted for commercial exploitation and parts marked for protection. From both perspectives local residents, relating to nature in multiple ways and using its products in their local economies, are perceived as intruders. They are accused of 'overusing' nature and therefore are held largely responsible for its degradation and destruction. Nature can only be preserved by keeping human beings out of its bounds. A third, largely idealistic, perspective is that of romanticism. From this viewpoint humans in traditional societies (tribals, Himalayan hill farmers) are seen still to be leading a life 'close' to nature and are thus regarded as its protectors. They are often mistakenly eulogized as possessors of specific 'local' knowledge and as folk who deliberately limit their needs to maintain harmony with nature.

In all these three discourses the relation between local residents and nature is essentialized and thus deprived of cultural and historical dimensions. The (anthropological) contextual approach suggests in contrast that people's relation to nature in Uttarakhand is far more varied, heterogeneous, and dynamic than postulated in any generalist account. Basically, people in the Garhwal Himalayas are not distanced from their forest—neither as 'destroyers' nor as 'preservers'. They live *in* and *with* the forest, which, as a central part of their life world, is to be appropriated via social and cultural practices in complex and diverse ways. These practices encompass aspects that are affective as well as instrumental (pragmatic, materialistic), conservational as well as destructive.

To develop visions and projects in the search for a good life within a particular locality is only the start of a larger endeavour. The crucial problem is whether such visions can be translated into action, given the existing political structures and constellations of power. It is naïve to assume that political decision-making will ever adequately consider local demands. The *sine qua non* for these demands to be heard, and to become the subject of negotiation is, in the first instance, the creation of a moral space where people can publicly raise their voices and criticize—or, as Richard Burghart calls it, the creation of the 'conditions of listening' (1996).

Burghart locates this moral space in civil society, a concept that derives from Western theory and indicates a community which stands outside the state but allows public judgement and criticism of the state. Thus, if state politics are to be influenced by local considerations, two conditions should be fulfilled. First, there is need for a 'public sphere' where people are allowed to voice their demands and which is acknowledged by the state as a moral space for legitimate criticism and suggestions. Second, it is essential that people possess reflexivity and the ability to develop a critical outlook and so are able to speak up, comment on state policies, suggest alterations.

Looking at the situation in the Himalayas, it seems that a deliberate eradication of the conditions of listening by court officials began with suppression of the Rawain dhandak, and in large measure this distance between state and citizens holds true even today, especially in relation to people remote from centres of power and authority. It was doubtlessly one of the positive outcomes of the Chipko struggle that villagers of Uttarakhand had discovered the possibility of speaking up to claim their rights, not as petitioners (as a king's subjects or subalterns) but as equally entitled citizens. The movement enabled villagers to become vigilant and alert to every form of exploitation, injustice, marginalization, and corruption.

This process of politicization had, in the case of Uttarakhand, been encouraged by non-governmental organizations focussed on environmental and development issues. Leading activists have stimulated a *discursive culture*—especially in the Chipko core areas—involving a whole network of villages and multipliers such as intellectuals, teachers, and journalists. To a certain extent one can speak of the emergence of a local 'public sphere' (*Öffentlichkeit*) in Uttarakhand and the formation of 'critical publicities' (*kritische*

Publizitäten) as their core principle (Habermas 1989). According to Habermas, the public sphere does not intend to govern, but rather control those who are in power, to negotiate rules and regulations of political and social life, and, under certain circumstances, initiate change. In this light the struggle for a separate statehood which spread in the mid 1990s and led to creation of the state of Uttaranchal in November 2000 has to be interpreted as an outcome of public criticism which became possible with civil society gaining strength in the Central Himalayan hills.

The agitation for a separate hill state started as an anti-reservation protest but was linked to the demand for autonomous statehood within the Indian nation by the regional party, the Uttarakhand Kranti Dal (UKD).[3] The new demand seemed to encompass all previous and present grievances of local residents and succeeded in mobilizing and focusing the energies of protest. The movement 'spread like a forest fire'.[4] Participation was evident among all social strata of the rural and urban population of Garhwal and Kumaon.[5] One local

[3] In summer 1994 the Chief Minister of Uttar Pradesh, Mulayam Singh Yadav, announced the reservation of 27 per cent of seats in educational institutions and services for members of Other Backward Classes (OBCs). Whereas in Uttar Pradesh at large the OBCs counted 37 per cent of the total population, in the Himalayan districts OBCs constituted less than 3 per cent. With the implementation of the new reservation quota, locals feared that members of the OBC from the plains would infiltrate the hill districts to fill the reserved seats in educational institutions and services. This would further reduce the chances of applicants from the hills. Given the background of their experience of exploitation, neglect, and domination by people from the plains, Garhwalis and Kumaonis started to agitate against the reservation policy. Students, government employees, and women were in the forefront of the 1994 struggle and engaged in sit-ins, strikes, rallies, demonstrations, and effigy-burning. For an analysis of the autonomy movement, see Mawdsley 1996, 1997; Kumar 2000; Linkenbach 2002b.

[4] For social activists Raju Lochan Shah (Nainital), Shamsher Singh Bisht (Almora) and others the movement was not created by an organization, it came only via the 'rage' (*gussa*) and informal networking of people. The intensity and spread of the movement were often compared with a forest fire (personal interviews 1998).

[5] As far as members of OBC and Scheduled Castes (SCs) are concerned, one has to differentiate. Kumar mentions that hill OBCs being small in number, were not very keen on the demand for separate statehood (Kumar 2000: 154f.).

activist said that for the first time a social movement in Uttarakhand expanded all over the region, and it seems legitimate thus to speak of it as a *jan andolan*, a 'people's movement'.

A remarkable feature of the movement was that, during its formative and most active phases, no individuals, groups, or political parties operating at regional or national level could gain (or tried to gain) leadership. Activists who had been at the centre of previous struggles—such as Chandi Prasad Bhatt—committed themselves to the autonomy movement not as leaders but as individuals whose involvement had a mobilizing effect because of widespread respect. Political parties—even those who tried to promote the demand for autonomy—were 'kept outside the arena' because people were disillusioned with their half-hearted and patronizing support (BJP), or by their factionalism (UKD) (Kumar 2000: 94ff; 107). However, in the end the movement had to rely on established politicians and parties to realize its demands, and it was the Hindu nationalist BJP which succeeded in 'appropriating' and calming the movement by announcing separate statehood after the proper parliamentary approval. This seemingly influenced behaviour at the polls: the BJP came out of the 1998 Lok Sabha elections as the strongest political force in Uttarakhand. It took the BJP until November 2000 to make good its promise.

The Uttarakhand movement succeeded in bringing social criticism out into the public. Villagers not only saw a genuine chance to raise their voices, they were also sure that mass protest would force those in power to listen to them. In that general atmosphere of hope, the residents of Uttarakhand were motivated to develop a political vision. During my field research in 1998–9 I could make out a number of broadly shared ideas which, woven together constitute the social and political imaginary of the separate state of Uttarakhand.

The notions showing up in all visions and imaginations of the future were *self-determination*, *proximity* and *transparency*. Emerging out of critiques of the prevailing functioning of politics at different

---

The reaction of SCs was twofold: Those who were more educated and articulate supported the movement, whereas the illiterate and economically deprived were often indifferent and apathetic (personal interviews; compare Kumar 2000: 154).

administrative levels, these were seen as preconditions for a grassroots democratic way of decision-making, participation, and control in politics, economics, and social life; they were core elements in the search for a 'new political culture and morality'—to quote one of the social activists. When imagining the new state, people enlarged the idealized image of a locality—a face-to-face community—into the larger unit of a separate state.

Uttarakhandis had long complained that political decisions were taken in Lucknow, the distant capital of UP, by those who were neither familiar with the special geographical and social conditions of the hill region nor interested in its development. In local government services and administrative bodies the majority of employees working in professional positions were said to be 'outsiders'. In an autonomous and self-determined state, so the local residents hoped, the capital with its main administrative bodies and jurisdiction would be nearer and within the reach of local citizens. The decision-makers and those working in administrative and key positions were expected to be from the hills proper and therefore more caring about the area's advancement. With autonomy and local control and management of natural resoures (water, forest, minerals), the flow of resources and profits into the plains would reduce and small-scale, sustainable development would be enhanced. Proximity and self-determination were thus key notions for restructuring economic and political space; they were thought to structure social space as well. Educational institutions would be opened within the vicinity of even remote villages, as would hospitals and health centres.

Proximity facilitates transparency. With the proximity of institutions and services, decision-makers and those with authority are less anonymous and can be addressed and criticized by citizens. Proximity and transparency seem to be the foundation for what Anthony Giddens calls 'dialogic democracy', a form of politics which does not focus on the state but helps create and strengthen a close relationship between autonomy and solidarity (Giddens 1997: 159).

The question of cultural identity also came into play. With economic development come a positive self-image and self-esteem, which are basic to self-assured cultural identity. In this context distinct cultural traits may serve as markers of difference without promoting ethnic

seclusion, while supporting the conviction that community distinc-
tions add to the cultural plurality of India.[6]

Five years and more after the foundation of the new state of Uttaranchal, many of those involved in the struggle for autonomy agree
that their visions and hopes are not fully realized. I am not able to
comment on their opinions at this point. To evaluate structures, policies, and decision-making processes of a new government within
newly formed structures needs time, and altogether new research.
What seems evident from the present research is the self-confidence
of a local population that has successfully intervened in political
processes through various forms of public critique (in particular via
social movements), confronting those in power with concepts and
visions of alternative ways of structuring socio-economic and political
life.

If Uttarakhand is to be really paradigmatic in the present context
of post-development, its inhabitants will reject global solutions and
propagate spatially and culturally bounded definitions and strategies
of development. At the same time, they will remain involved in trans-
local discourses, thereby transcending the dangers of parochialism.
After all, it has been because of a demonstrated capacity to envision
a better future by articulating elements of the local and traditional
with the national and global that they have achieved their present,
culturally rooted, regional modernity.

---

[6] I have argued that the regional identity of the Uttarakhandis includes a
'patriotic' dimension (Linkenbach 2002b: 96).

Bibliography

Adorno, Theodor Wiesengrund, 1992, *Negative Dialektik*, Frankfurt/Main: Suhrkamp.

Agarwal, Anil, Darryll D'Monte, and Ujwala Samarth, eds, 1987, *The Fight for Survival: People's Action for Environment*, New Delhi: Centre for Science and Environment.

Agarwal, Anil, Ravi Chopra, and Kalpana Sharma, eds, 1982, *The State of India's Environment: The First Citizens' Report*, New Delhi: Centre for Science and Environment.

Agarwal, Anil, and Sunita Narain, eds, 1985, *The State of India's Environment 1984–5: The Second Citizens' Report*, New Delhi: Centre for Science and Environment.

————, eds, 1989, *Towards Green Villages: A Strategy for Environmentally Sound and Participatory Rural Development*, New Delhi: Centre for Science and Environment.

Agarwal, Anil, and Ajit Chak, eds, 1991, *The State of India's Environment: A Citizens' Report. Floods, Flood Plains and Environmental Myths*, New Delhi: Centre for Science and Environment.

Agarwal, Anil, and Sunita Narain, eds, 1997, *Dying Wisdom: Rise, Fall and Potential of India's Traditional Water Harvesting Systems*, New Delhi: Centre for Science and Environment.

Agarwal, Anil, Sunita Narain, and Srabani Sen, eds, 1999, *The Citizens' Fifth Report (State of India's Environment 5)*, Part I: National Overview; Part II: Statistical Database, New Delhi: Centre for Science and Environment.

Agarwal, Bina, 1991, *Engendering the Environment Debate: Lessons from the Indian Subcontinent*, East Lansing, Michigan: Center for Advanced Study of International Development.

Aggarwal, J.C. and S.P. Agrawal, 1995, *Uttarakhand: Past, Present and Future*. Specifically written chapters by Shanti S. Gupta, New Delhi: Concept Publishing Company.

Alam, Javeed, 1999, *India: Living with Modernity*, Delhi: Oxford University Press.

Alvares, Claude, 1992, *Science, Development and Violence: The Revolt against Modernity*, Delhi: Oxford University Press.

Arora, Ajay, 1996, *Administrative History of Uttarakhand (Kumaon and Garhwal) during the Rule of the East India Company (1815–1857)*, Delhi: Eastern Book Linkers.

Arnold, David and Ramachandra Guha, eds, 1995, *Nature, Culture, Imperialism: Essays on the Environmental History of South Asia*, Oxford: Oxford University Press.

Atkinson, Edwin T., 1973 [1882], *The Himalayan Gazetteer*, 3 vols, New Delhi: Cosmo Publishers.

Bahuguna, Sunderlal, n.d. [1968], 'Some Problems of Garhwal and Kumaon', in Rahul Ram, ed., *Social Work in the Himalaya: Proceedings of the Seminar on Social Work in the Himalaya*, Delhi: Delhi School of Social Work, University of Delhi.

———, 1987, 'The Chipko: A People's Movement', in M.K. Raha, ed., *The Himalayan Heritage*, pp. 238–48.

———, 1989a, 'A Tribute to St Barbe', in Indira Ramesh and N.D. Jayal, eds, *Richard St. Barbe Baker: Man of the Trees. A Centenary Tribute*, New Delhi: INTACH, pp. 13–23.

———, 1989b, 'The Man Who Dedicated His Life to Forests', in Indira Ramesh and N.D. Jayal, eds, *Richard St Barbe Baker: Man of the Trees. A Centenary Tribute*, New Delhi: INTACH, pp. 43–58.

———, 1989c, *Towards Basic Changes in Land Use*, New Delhi: INTACH.

———, 1990, *'Yes' to Life: 'No' to Death*, Varanasi: Sarve Seva Sangh Prakashan.

———, 1992, *People's Programme for Change*, New Delhi: INTACH.

Bahuguna, Vimala, 1990, 'The Chipko Movement', in Ilina Sen, ed., *A Space within the Struggle: Women's Participation in People's Movements*, Delhi: Kali for Women, pp. 111–24.

Baker, St. Barbe, 1989, 'Friends of the Trees, Speech Delivered in Bombay on 20 August 1980', in Indira Ramesh and N.D. Jayal, eds, *Richard St. Barbe Baker: Man of the Trees. A Centenary Tribute*, New Delhi: INTACH, pp. 59–69.

Bandyopadhyay, Jayanta, 1999, 'Chipko Movement: Of Floated Myths and Floated Realities', in *Economic and Political Weekly*, vol. 34, no. 15, pp. 880–2.

———, N.D. Jayal, U. Schoettli, and Chhatrapati Singh, 1985, *India's Environment: Crisis and Responses*. With a foreword by Shri Rajiv Gandhi, Prime Minister of India, Dehra Dun: Natraj Publishers.

Bandyopadhyay, Jayanta and Vandana Shiva, 1987a, 'Chipko', in *Seminar* 330, pp. 33–9.

———, 1987b, 'Chipko: Rekindling India's Forest Culture', in *The Ecologist*, vol. 17, no. 1, pp. 26–34.

Banuri, Tariq, 1990, 'Development and the Politics of Knowledge: A Critical Interpretation of the Social Role of Modernization', in Frédérique Apffel-Marglin, and Stephen A. Marglin, eds, *Dominating Knowledge: Development, Culture and Resistance*, Oxford: Clarendon, pp. 29–72.

Baviskar, Amita, 1995, *In the Belly of the River: Tribal Conflicts over Development in the Narmada Valley*, Delhi: Oxford University Press.

Berndt, Hagen, 1987, *Rettet die Bäume im Himalaya: Die Cipko-Bewegung im Spiegel der indischen Presse*, Berlin: Quorum.

Berreman, Gerald D., 1987a, 'Pahari Polyandry: A Comparison', in M.K. Raha, ed., *Polyandry in India: Demographic, Economic, Social, Religious and Psychological Concomitants of Plural Marriages in Women*, Delhi: Gian Publishing House, pp. 155–78.

———, 1987b, 'Himalayan Polyandry and the Domestic Cycle', in M.K. Raha, ed., *Polyandry in India: Demographic, Economic, Social, Religious and Psychological Concomitants of Plural Marriages in Women*, Delhi: Gian Publishing House, pp. 179–97.

———, 1987c, 'Uttarakhand and Chipko: Regionalism and Environmentalism in the Central Himalayas', in M.K. Raha, ed., *The Himalayan Heritage*, New Delhi: Gian Publishing House, pp. 266–300.

———, 1993, 'Prologue: Behind Many Masks: Ethnography and Impression Management', in Gerald D. Berreman, *Hindus of the Himaayas: Ethnography and Change*, Delhi: Oxford University Press, pp. xvii–lvii.

Bhatt, Chandi Prasad, 1987a, 'Green the People: Inaugural Address', in Anil Agarwal, Daryll D'Monte, and Ujwala Samarth, eds, *The Fight for Survival: People's Action for Environment*, New Delhi: Centre for Science and Environment, pp. 1–4.

———, 1987b, 'The Chipko Andolan: Forest Conservation Based on People's Power', in Anil Agarwal, Daryll D'Monte, and Ujwala Samarth, eds, *The Fight for Survival: People's Action for Environment*, New Delhi: Centre for Science and Environment, pp. 43–55.

———, 1987c, 'The Chipko Movement: Strategies, Achievements and Impacts', in M.K. Raha, ed., *The Himalayan Heritage*, New Delhi: Gian Publishing House, pp. 249–65.

———, n.d., *A Chipko Experience: Forest Conservation by People's Participation*, Gopeshwar: DGSM.

————, 1992, *The Future of Large Projects in the Himalaya: Overcoming Incomplete Knowledge and Unsound Beliefs*, Nainital: Pahar.

Bhatt, G.S., 1991, *Women and Polyandry in Rawain Jaunpur*, Jaipur and New Delhi: Rawat Publications.

Bisht, Anand Singh, 1993, *Van jage vanvasi jage*, Almora: Uttarakhand Sewa Nidhi.

Blaikie, Piers, 1985, *The Political Economy of Soil Erosion*, London: Methuen.

————, and Harold Brookfield, 1987, *Land Degradation and Society*, London: Methuen.

Blaikie, Piers, Terry Cannon, Ian Davis, and Ben Wisner, 1994, *At Risk: Natural Hazards, People's Vulnerability, and Disasters*, London and New York: Routledge.

Bohle, Hans-Georg, 1997, 'Sozialwissenschaftliche Dimensionen der Ernährungssicherung. Ansätze Geographischer Risikoforschung, mit einem Fallbeispiel aus Nepal', in Hans-Georg Bohle *et al.* (eds) *Ernährungssicherung in Südasien: Siebte Heidelberger Südasiengespräche*, Stuttgart: Franz Steiner, pp. 39–44.

————, and Jagannath Adhikari, 1998, 'Rural Livelihoods at Risk: How Nepalese Farmers Cope with Food Insecurity', in *Mountain Research and Development*, vol. 18, no. 4, pp. 321–2.

Bookchin, Murray, 1996, *The Philosophy of Ecology: Essays on Dialectical Naturalism*, Jaipur and New Delhi: Rawat Publications.

Boughey, Arthur S., 1971, *Fundamental Ecology*, London: Intertext Books.

Brandis, Dietrich, 1994 [1897], *Forestry in India: Origins and Early Developments. Foreword by Samar Singh*. Reprint, Dehra Dun: Natraj Publishers.

Bright, S.J., ed., n.d., *Before and After Independence: A Collection of the Most Important and Soul Stirring Speeches Delivered by Jawaharlal Nehru During the Most Important and Soul Stirring Years in Indian History 1922–1957*, vols I & 2, New Delhi: Indian Printing Works.

Brown, Charles, W. and M.P. Joshi., 1990, 'Caste Dynamics and Fluidity in the Historical Anthropology of Kumaon', in M.P. Joshi, A.C. Fanger, and C.W. Brown, eds, *Himalaya Past and Present*, Almora: Shree Almora Book Depot, pp. 245–66.

Burghart, Richard, 1996, 'The Conditions of Listening: The Everyday Experience of Politics in Nepal', in Richard Burghart, *The Conditions of Listening: Essays on Religion, History and Politics in South Asia*, ed. by C.J. Fuller and Jonathan Spencer, Delhi: Oxford University Press, pp. 300–18.

Büttner, Hannah, 1996, 'Politische Ökologie der Waldnutzung in Indien: Mit einem Fallbeispiel aus Westbengalen', MA thesis, Freiburg i. Br.

Census of India 1981, *Village and Town Directory District Uttarkashi*. See Gupta, Ravindra.

Chandra, Sudhir, 1994, 'The Language of Modern Ideas: Reflections on an Ethnological Parable', in *Thesis Eleven*, 39, pp. 39–51.

Chatterjee, Partha, 1984, 'Gandhi and the Critique of Civil Society', in Ranajit Guha, ed., *Subaltern Studies III: Writings on South Asian History and Society*, Delhi: Oxford University Press, pp. 153–95.

Cowen, M. and R. Shenton, 2000, 'The Invention of Development', in Stuart Corbridge, ed., *Doctrines of Development*, London and New York: Routledge, pp. 27–45.

Das, Veena, 1995, *Critical Events: An Anthropological Perspective on Contemporary India*, Delhi: Oxford University Press.

Dewan, M.L., 1990, *People's Participation in Himalayan Eco-System Development: A Plan for Action*, New Delhi: Concept Publishing Company.

Dijk, Teun A. van, ed., 1997a, 'The Study of Discourse', in Teun A. van Dijk, ed., *Discourse as Structure and Process. Discourse Studies: A Multidisciplinary Introduction*, vol. 1, London: Sage, pp. 1–34.

———, 1997b, 'Discourse as Interaction in Society', in Teun A. van Dijk, ed., *Discourse as Social Interaction. Discourse Studies: A Multidisciplinary Introduction*, vol. 2, London: Sage, pp. 1–37.

D'Monte, Daryll, 1985, *Temples or Tombs? Industry versus Environment: Three Controversies*, New Delhi: Centre for Science and Environment.

Divan, Shyam and Armin Rosencranz, 2001, *Environmental Law and Policy in India: Cases, Materials and Statutes*, 2nd edn, Delhi: Oxford University Press.

Drèze, Jean *et al.*, 1997, *The Dam and the Nation: Displacement and Resettlement in the Narmada Valley*, Delhi: Oxford University Press.

———, and Haris Gazdar, 1998, 'Uttar Pradesh: The Burden of Inertia', in Jean Drèze and Amartya Sen eds, *Indian Development: Selected Regional Perspectives*, Delhi: Oxford University Press.

Durning, Alan Thein, 1991, 'How Much is Enough? The Consumer Society and the Future of the Earth', in *State of the World* 8, pp. 153–69

Escobar, Arturo, 1995, *Encountering Development: The Making and Unmaking of the Third World*, Princeton, N.J.: Princeton University Press.

Esteva, Gustavo, 1992, 'Development', in Wolfgang Sachs, ed., *The Development Dictionary: A Guide to Knowledge as Power*, London and New Jersey: Zed Books, pp. 6–25.

Fabian, Johannes, 1983, *Time and the Other: How Anthropology Makes its Object*, New York: Columbia University Press.

———, 1990, 'Presence and Representation. The Other and Anthropological Writing', in *Critical Inquiry*, vol. 16, no. 4, pp. 753–72.

Fairclough, Norman and Ruth Wodak, 1997, 'Critical Discourse Analysis', in Teun A. van Dijk, ed., *Discourse as Social Interaction. Discourse Studies: A Multidisciplinary Introduction*. vol. 2, London: Sage, pp. 258–84.

Fanger, Allen C., 1980, 'Diachronic and Synchronic Pespectives on Kumaoni Society and Culture', PhD dissertation, Syracuse University, microfiche.

Fernandes, Walter and Enakshi Ganguly Thukral, 1989, *Development, Displacement and Rehabilitation*, New Delhi: Indian Social Institute.

Fischer, Wolfram, 1987, 'Affirmative und Transformative Erfahrungsverarbeitung', in Jürgen Friedrichs, ed., *23. Deutscher Soziologentag 1986: Sektions- und Ad-hoc-Gruppen*, Opladen: Westdeutscher Verlag, pp. 465–71.

Frank, Manfred, 1988, 'Zum Diskursbegriff bei Foucault', in Jürgen Fohrmann and Harro Müller, eds, *Diskurstheorien und Literaturwissenschaft*, Frankfurt/Main Suhrkamp, pp. 25–44.

Fuchs, Martin, 1999, *Kampf um Differenz: Repräsentation, Subjektivität und soziale Bewegungen. Das Beispiel Indien*, Frankfurt/Main: Suhrkamp.

———, and Eberhard Berg, 1993, 'Phänomenologie der Differenz: Reflexionsstufen ethnographischer Repräsentation', in Eberhard Berg and Martin Fuchs, eds, *Kultur, soziale Praxis, Text: Die Krise der ethnographischen Repräsentation*, Frankfurt/Main: Suhrkamp, pp. 11–108.

Gadgil, Madhav and Ramachandra Guha, 1992, *This Fissured Land: An Ecological History of India*, Delhi: Oxford University Press.

Gadgil, Madhav and Kailash C. Malhotra, 1995, 'Ecology is for the People', in *South Asian Anthropologist*. vol. 6, no. 1, Special Issue, pp. 1–14.

Galey, Jean-Claude, 1980, 'Le créancier, le roi, la mort: Essai sur les relations de dépendance dans le Tehri Garhwal (Himalaya indien)', in *Purusartha*, vol. 4, pp. 93–163.

———, 1984, 'Souveraineté et justice dans le Haut-Gange: La fonction royale au-delà des écoles juridiques et du droit coutumier', in Jean-Claude Galey, ed., *Différences, valeurs, hiérarchie: Textes offerts à Louis Dumont*, Paris: Éditions de l'École des Hautes Études en Science Sociales, pp. 371–419.

———, 1990, 'Reconsidering Kingship in India: An Ethnological

Perspective', in Jean-Claude Galey, ed., *Kingship and Kings*, Churchill: Harwood Academic Publishers, pp. 123–87.

Gandhi, Mohandas Karamchand, 1957, *Socialism of My Conception*, Bombay: Bharatiya Vidya Bhavan.

Giddens, Anthony, 1979, *Central Problems in Social Theory: Action, Structure and Contradiction in Social Analysis*, London and Basingstoke: Macmillan Press.

——, 1997, *Jenseits von Links und Rechts: Die Zukunft radikaler Demokratie*, Frankfurt/ M.: Suhrkamp.

Giri, V.V., n.d. [1968], 'Inaugural Address', in Rahul Ram, ed., *Social Work in the Himalaya: Proceedings of the Seminar on Social Work in the Himalaya*, Delhi: Delhi School of Social Work, University of Delhi., pp. 14–17.

Goffman, Erving, 1959, *The Presentation of Self in Everyday Life*, New York: Doubleday.

Goldsmith, Edward, 1989, 'The Vision of St. Barbe Baker', in Indira Ramesh and N.D. Jayal, eds, *Richard St. Barbe Baker: Man of the Trees. A Centenary Tribute*, New Delhi: INTACH, pp. 31–9.

Gosh, A.K., 1993, 'Forest Policy in India', in Ajay S. Rawat, ed., *Indian Forestry: A Perspective*, New Delhi: Indus Publishing Company, pp. 69–84.

Grove, Richard H., 1995, *Green Imperialism: Colonial Expansion, Tropical Island Edens and the Origin of Environmentalism 1600–1860*, Cambridge: Cambridge University Press.

——, Vinita Damodaran, and Satpal Sangwan (eds), 1998, *Nature and the Orient: The Environmental History of South and Southeast Asia*, Delhi: Oxford University Press.

Guha, Ramachandra, 1983a+b, 'Forestry in British and Post-British India: A Historical Analysis', in *Economic and Political Weekly*, vol. 18, no. 44, pp. 1882–96, and vol. 18, nos 45 and 46, pp. 1940–7.

——, 1991, *The Unquiet Woods: Ecological Change and Peasant Resistance in the Himalaya*, Delhi: Oxford University Press.

——, 1993, 'The Malign Encounter: The Chipko Movement and Competing Visions of Nature', in Tariq Banuri and Frédérique Apffel-Marglin, eds, *Who Will Save the Forests? Knowledge, Power and Environmental Destruction* (A Publication of The United Nations University, World Institute for Development Economics Research—UNU/ WIDER), London and New Jersey: Zed Books, pp. 80–113.

——, ed., 1994, *Social Ecology*, Delhi: Oxford University Press.

——, 1996, 'Two Phases of American Environmentalism: A Critical

History', in Frédérique Apffel-Marglin and Stephen A. Marglin, eds, *Decolonizing Knowledge: From Development to Dialogue*, Oxford: Clarendon, pp. 110–41.

———, 1997, 'Social-Ecological Research in India: A "Status" Report', in *Economic and Political Weekly*, vol. 32. no. 7, pp. 345–52.

———, 2000, *Environmentalism: A Global History*, Delhi: Oxford University Press.

———, 2004, *The Last Liberal and Other Essays*, Delhi: Permanent Black.

———, 2006, *How Much Should a Person Consume: Thinking Through the Environment*, Delhi: Permanent Black.

———, and A. Martinez-Alier, 1998, *Varieties of Environmentalism: Essays North and South*, Delhi: Oxford University Press.

Gupta, P.N., 1957, *Working Plan for the Yamuna Forest Division, Tehri Circle, Uttar Pradesh, 1954–55 to 1968–69*, Lucknow: Superintendent, Printing and Stationery, Uttar Pradesh.

Gupta, Ravindra, [1982], *Village and Town Directory District Uttarkashi* (Census of India 1981, Series 22 Uttar Pradesh, District Census Handbook Part XIII-A), Allahabad: UP Printing Press.

Habermas, Jürgen, 1981, *Theorie des kommunikativen Handelns*, vol. 1: Handlungsrationalität und Gesellschaftliche Rationalisierung. Vol. 2: Zur Kritik der funktionalistischen Vernunft. Frankfurt/Main: Suhrkamp.

———, 1989, *The Structural Transformation of the Public Sphere: An Inquiry into a Category of Bourgeois Society*, Cambridge: Polity Press.

Hardin, Gerrett, 1968, 'The Tragedy of Commons', in *Science*, vol. 162, pp. 1243–8.

Hardin, Russell, 'The Free Rider Problem', *The Stanford Encyclopedia of Philosophy* (Summer 2003 Edition), in Edward N. Zalta, ed., URL = <http://plato.stanford.edu/archives/sum2003/entries/free-rider/>.

Harneit-Sievers, Axel, 1998, 'New Local Historiography in Africa and South Asia: A Workshop Report', *Anthropos*, vol. 93, 1998, pp. 579–85.

———, ed., 2002, *A Place in the World: New Local Historiographies from Africa and South Asia*, Leiden: Brill.

Harrison, Robert Pogue, 1992, *Forests: The Shadow of Civilization*, Chicago and London: University of Chicago Press.

Haynes, Douglas and Gyan Prakash, 1991, 'Introduction: The Entanglement of Power and Resistance', in Douglas Haynes and Gyan Prakash, eds, *Contesting Power: Resistance and Everyday Social Relations in South Asia*, Delhi: Oxford University Press, pp. 1–22.

Hazary, Narayan, 1994, 'Perspectives on Rural Development: Administration in India', in Murali K. Manohar, K. Seetha Rama Rao, and B. Janardhan Rao, eds, *Political Economy of Rural Development*, Delhi: Kanishka Publishers, pp. 34–53.

Heske, Franz, 1931, 'Probleme der Walderhaltung im Himalaya', in *Tharandter Forstliches Jahrbuch*, vol. 82, pp. 545–94.

Hesmer, Herbert, 1975, *Leben und Werk von Dietrich Brandis 1824–1907: Begründer der Tropischen Forstwirtschaft. Förderer der Forstlichen Entwicklung in den USA. Botaniker und Ökologe*, Opladen: Westdeutscher Verlag (Abhandlungen der Rheinisch-Westfälischen Akademie der Wissenschaften; 58).

Honneth, Axel, 1992, *Der Kampf um Anerkennung: Zur moralischen Grammatik sozialer Konflikte*, Frankfurt/Main: Suhrkamp.

Iyer, Raghavan, ed., 1986, *The Moral and Political Writings of Mahatma Gandhi*, Oxford: Clarendon Press.

Jain, Shobita, 1984, 'Women and People's Ecological Movement: A Case Study of Women's Role in the Chipko Movement in Uttar Pradesh', in *Economic and Political Weekly*, vol. 19, no. 41, pp. 1788–94.

Jha, L.K., 1994, *India's Forest Policies: Analysis and Appraisal*, New Delhi: Ashish Publishing House.

——, and P.P. Sen, 1991, *Social Forestry*, Bombay: Himalayan Publishing House.

Jonas, Hans, 1987, *Das Prinzip Verantwortung: Versuch einer Ethik für die technologische Zivilisation*, Frankfurt/Main: Insel Verlag.

Joshi, M.P., 1990, *Uttaranchal (Kumaon-Garhwal) Himalaya: An Essay in Historical Anthropology*, Almora: Shree Almora Book Depot.

Kannabiran, Vasantha and K. Lalitha, 1989, 'That Magic Time: Women in the Telengana People's Struggle', in Kumkum Sangari and Sudesh Vaid, eds, *Recasting Women: Essays in Colonial History*, New Delhi: Kali for Women, pp. 180–203.

Khurana, Indira, 1998, 'Best Kept Sacred', in *Down To Earth*, vol. 6, no. 23, pp. 34–9.

Kishwar, Madhu, 1992a, 'A Woman with Rocklike Determination: Interview with Vimla Bahuguna', in *Manushi*, vol. 70.

——, 1992b, 'Sunderlal Bahuguna's Crusade: Interview with Sunderlal Bahuguna', in *Manushi*, vol. 70, pp. 3–11.

Koepping, Klaus-Peter, 1987, 'Authentizität als Selbstfindung durch den Anderen: Ethnologie zwischen Engagement und Reflexion, zwischen Leben und Wissenschaft', in Hans Peter Duerr, ed., *Betrug in der Ethnologie*, Frankfurt/Main: Suhrkamp, pp. 7–37.

————, 1994, 'Ethics in Ethnographic Practice: Contextual Pluralism and Solidarity of Research Partners', in *Anthropological Journal on European Cultures*, vol. 3, no. 2. (Anthropology and Ethics, co-ed. Klaus-Peter Koepping), pp. 21–38.

Koranne, K.D., 1996, 'Technologies for Improving Productivity of Hill Agriculture System in North-Western Himalayan Region', in Giri Raj Shah, ed., *Uttarakhand: A Blue Print for Development*, pp. 121–38.

Kothari, Ashish, Neena Singh, and Saloni Suri, eds, 1996, *People and Protected Areas: Towards Participatory Conservation in India*, New Delhi: Sage Publications.

Kothari, Rajni, 1998, 'The Democratic Experiment', in Partha Chatterjee, ed., *Wages of Freedom: Fifty Years of the Indian Nation State*, New Delhi: Oxford University Press, pp. 23–36.

Krengel, Monika, 1989, *Sozialstrukturen im Kumaon: Bergbauern im Himalaya*, Stuttgart: Steiner Verlag Wiesbaden GmbH.

Küng, Hans, 1996, 'Das eine Ethos in der einen Welt: Ethische Begründung einer nachhaltigen Entwicklung', in Hans G. Kastenholz *et al.*, eds, *Nachhaltige Entwicklung: Zukunftschancen für Mensch und Umwelt*, Berlin: Springer, pp. 236–53.

Kulkarni, Sharad, 1983, 'Towards a Social Forest Policy', in *Economic and Political Weekly*, vol. 18, no. 6, pp. 191–6.

Kumar, Pradeep, 2000, *The Uttarakhand Movement: Construction of a Regional Identity*, New Delhi: Kanishka Publishers.

Lewis, Martin W., 1992, *Green Delusions: An Environmentalist Critique of Radical Environmentalism*, Durham and London: Duke University Press.

Linkenbach, Antje, 1994, 'Ecological Movements and the Critique of Development: Agents and Interpreters', in *Thesis Eleven*, vol. 39, pp. 63–85.

————, 2000, 'Anthropology of Modernity: Projects and Contexts', in *Thesis Eleven*, no. 61, pp. 41–63.

————, 2001, 'The Construction of Personhood: Two Life Stories from Garhwal', in *European Bulletin of Himalayan Research*, nos. 20–1, pp. 23–45.

————, 2002a, A Consecrated Land: Local Constructions of History in the Garhwal and Kumaon Himalayas, North India', in Axel Harneit-Sievers, ed., *A Place in the World: New Local Historiographies from Africa and South Asia*, Leiden: Brill, pp. 309–30.

Linkenbach, Antje, 2002b, 'Shaking the State by Making a (new) State: Social Movements and the Quest for Autonomy', in *Sociologus*, vol. 52, no. 1. 2002, pp. 77–106.

———, 2005, 'Nature and Politics: The Case of Uttarakhand (North India)', in Gunnel Cederlöf and K. Sivaramakrishnan (eds), *Ecological Nationalisms: Nature Livelihoods and Identities in South Asia*, Delhi: Permanent Black.

M.B., 1989, 'Liberalisation Road to Economic Ruination', in *Economic and Political Weekly*, vol. 24, no. 36, pp. 1873–4.

Maikhuri, R.K., *et al.*, 1998, 'Traditional Community Conservation in the Indian Himalayas: Nanda Devi Biosphere Reserve', in Ashish Kothari *et al.*, eds, *Communities and Conservation: Natural Resource Management in South and Central Asia*, Delhi: Sage, pp. 403–23.

Malamoud, Charles, 1976, 'Village et forêt dans l'idéologie de l'Inde brahmanique', in *Archives Européennes de Sociologie*, vol. 17, no. 1, pp. 3–20.

Mansingh, Surjit, 1998, *Historical Dictionary of India*, New Delhi: Vision Books.

Mawdsley, Emma, 1996, 'Uttarakhand Agitation and Other Backward Classes', in *Economic and Political Weekly*, vol. 31, no. 4, pp. 205–10.

———, 1997, 'Nonsecessionist Regionalism in India: The Uttarakhand Separate State Movement', in *Environment and Planning*, vol. 29, pp. 2217–35.

McGregor, R.S., ed., 1993, *The Oxford Hindi-English Dictionary*, Oxford and Delhi: Oxford University Press.

Meadows, Donella H., *et al.*, 1972, *The Limits to Growth: A Report for the Club of Rome's Project on the Predicament of Mankind*, New York: Universe Book.

Mehta, G.S., 1996, *Uttarakhand: Prospects of Development*, New Delhi: Indus Publishing.

Mehta, Kisan, 1989, 'Barbe Baker, Crusader and World Citizen', in Indira Ramesh and N.D. Jayal, eds, *Richard St. Barbe Baker: Man of the Trees. A Centenary Tribute*, New Delhi: INTACH.

Messner, Frank, 1993, 'Das Konzept der nachhaltigen Entwicklung im Dilemma internationaler Regimebildung', in *Peripherie*, vol. 13, nos 51–2, pp. 38–57.

Mies, Maria and Vandana Shiva, 1993, *Ecofeminism*, New Delhi: Kali for Women.

Minocha, A.C., 1991, 'Indian Development Strategy', in *Economic and Political Weekly*, vol. 26. no. (43), p. 2488.

Mitra, Amit, 1993, 'Chipko, An Unfinished Mission', in *Down to Earth*, April 30, pp. 25–36.

Monier-Williams, Sir Monier, 1994, *Sanskrit-English Dictionary. Etymologically and Philologically Arranged with Special Reference to Cognate Indo-European Languages*. New edn, greatly enlarged and improved with the collab. of E. Leumann, C. Cappeller and other scholars, New Delhi: Munshiram Manoharlal.

Nanda, Meera, 2004, *Prophets Facing Backward: Postmodernism, Science, and Hindu Nationalism*, Delhi: Permanent Black.

Nautiyal, K.P. and B.M. Khanduri, 1988–9, 'Excavations of a Vedic Brick Altar at Purola, District Uttarkashi, Central Himalaya', in *Puratattva*, vol. 19, pp. 68–70.

Nautiyal, R.R., R.S. Negi, and H.R. Nautiyal, 1996. 'Forestry for Community Development in the Hills of Uttar Pradesh', in D.C. Pande, ed., *Dimensions of Agriculture in the Himalaya*, Almora: Shri Almora Book Depot, pp. 283–8.

Negi, S.S., 1994a, *Indian Forestry Through the Ages*, New Delhi: Indus Publishing.

———, 1994b, *India's Forests, Forestry and Wildlife*, New Delhi: Indus Publishing.

Nehru, Jawaharlal, 1964, *Nehru on Socialism: Selected Speeches and Writings*, New Delhi: Perspective Publications.

Nennen, Heinz-Ulrich, 1991, *Ökologie im Diskurs: Zu Grundfragen der Anthropologie und Ökologie und zur Ethik der Wissenschaften*. Mit einem Geleitwort von Dieter Birnbacher, Opladen: Westdeutscher Verlag.

Nussbaum, Martha C. and Amartya Sen, 1989, 'Internal Criticism and Indian Nationalist Traditions', in *Relativism, Interpretation and Confrontation*, ed. Michael Krausz, Notre Dame (Indiana): University of Notre Dame Press.

Olson, Mancur, 1965, *Logic of Collective Action: Public Goods and the Theory of Groups*, Cambridge, Mass.: Harvard University Press.

Ostrom, Elinor, 1990, *Governing the Commons: The Evolution of Institutions for Collective Action*, New York: Cambridge University Press.

Palni, Uma Tewari, 1996, 'Cattle Feeds of Central Himalaya: Problems and Prospects', in D.C. Pande, ed., *Dimensions of Agriculture in the Himalaya*, Almora: Shri Almora Book Depot, pp. 345–60.

Pande, I.D. and Deepa Pande, 1991, 'Forestry in India through the Ages', in Ajay S. Rawat, ed., *History of Forestry in India*, New Delhi: Indus Publishing, pp. 151–62.

Pant, B.R., and M.C. Pant, eds, 1995, *Glimpses of Central Himalaya: A Socio-Economic and Ecological Perspective*, vols 1 and 2, New Delhi: Radha Publications.

Pant, Govind Ballabh, n.d. [1922], *The Forest Problem in Kumaon: Forest Problems and National Uprisings in the Himalayan Region*. With a Commentary by Ajay S. Rawat, Nainital, UP: Gyanodaya Prakashan.

Parasuraman, S., 1999, 'The Development Dilemma: Displacement in India', The Hague: Institute of Social Studies.

Parekh, Bhikhu, 1995, 'Jawaharlal Nehru and the Crisis of Modernisation', in Upendra Baxi and Bhikhu Parekh, eds, *Crisis and Change in Contemporary India*, New Delhi: Sage, pp. 21–56.

Parry, Jonathan, 1979, *Caste and Kinship in Kangra*, London: Routledge & Kegan Paul.

Pathak, Akhileshwara, 1994, *Contested Domains: The State, Peasants and Forests in Contemporary India*, New Delhi: Sage, in association with The Book Review Literary Trust.

Pathak, Shekhar, 1998, 'State, Society and Natural Resources in the Himalaya: Dynamics of Change in Colonial and Post-Colonial Uttara-khand', in Irmtraud Stellrecht, ed., *Karakorum–Hindukush–Himalaya: Dynamics of Change*, Part II, Rüdiger Köppe (Culture Area Karakorum Scientific Studies: 4), pp. 167–86.

Peet, Richard and Michael Watts, 1996, 'Liberation Ecology: Development, Sustainability, and Environment in an Age of Market Triumphalism', in *Liberation Ecologies: Environment, Development, Social Movements*, ed. Richard Peet and Michael Watts, London and NewYork: Routledge, pp. 1–45.

Pieterse, Jan Nederveen, 2001, *Development Theory: Deconstructions/ Reconstructions*, London: Sage Publications.

Poffenberger, Mark and Ajit Banerjee, 1996, 'Conclusion', in *Village Voices, Forest Choices: Joint Forest Management in India*, Delhi: Oxford University Press, pp. 324–32.

Poffenberger, Mark, and Betsy McGean, eds, 1996, *Village Voices, Forest Choices: Joint Forest Management in India*, Delhi: Oxford University Press.

Pyarelal, 1958, *Mahatma Gandhi: The Last Phase*, vol. II, Ahmedabad: Navajivan Publishing House.

———, 1959, *A Nation Builder at Work, Gandhi Memorial Lectures 1951*, Ahmedabad: Navajivan Publishing House.

———, 1965, *Mahatma Gandhi: The Last Phase*, vol. I, book 1, Ahmedabad: Navajivan Publishing House.

Rahnema, M., 2000, 'Towards Post-Development: Searching for Signposts, a New Language and New Paradigms', in *Development: Critical Concepts in the Social Sciences*, ed. Stuart Corbridge, London and New York: Routledge, pp. 304–30.

Rajan, Ravi, 1998, 'Imperial Environmentalism or Environmental Imperialism? European Forestry, Colonial Foresters and the Agendas of Forest Management in British India 1800–1900', in Richard H. Grove, Vinita Damodaran and Satpal Sangwan, eds, *Nature and the Orient: The Environmental History of South and Southeast Asia*, Delhi: Oxford University Press, pp. 324–71.

Raturi, Pandit Harikrishna, 1988 [1933], *Garhwal ka Itihas*, Tehri: Bhagirathi Prakashan.

Rawat, Ajay Singh, n.d., 'Commentary', in Govind Ballabh Pant, *Forest Problems in Kumaon: Forest Problems and National Uprisings in the Himalayan Region*, Nainital: Gyanodayan Prakashan, pp. 13–27.

———, 1989a, 'Commentary', in *Berthold Ribbentrop: Forestry in British India*, New Delhi: Indus Publishing Co., pp. 9–24.

———, 1989b, *History of Garhwal 1358–1947: An Erstwhile Kingdom in the Himalayas*, New Delhi: Indus Publishing Co.

———, ed., 1991, *History of Forestry in India*, New Delhi: Indus Publishing Co.

———, 1992a, *History and Growth of Panchayati Forests in the Kumaon Himalaya*, New Delhi: Centre for Contemporary Studies, Nehru Memorial Museum and Library, Occasional Papers on Perspectives in Indian Development, 31.

———, 1992b, *History of Forest Management in Tehri Garhwal State*, New Delhi: Nehru Memorial Museum and Library, Occasional Papers on Perspectives in Indian Development, 32.

———, 1993a, ed., *Indian Forestry: A Perspective*, New Delhi: Indus Publishing Co.

———, 1993b, 'Brandis: The Father of Organized Forestry in India', in Ajay S. Rawat, *Indian Forestry: A Perspective*, New Delhi: Indus Publishing Co., pp. 85–101.

———, 2000, *Forest Management in Kumaon Himalaya: Struggle of the Marginalized People*, New Delhi: Indus Publishing Co.

———, 2002, *Garhwal Himalaya: A Study in Historical Perspective*, New Delhi: Indus Publishing Co.

Rawat, D.S. and K. Kumar, 1996, 'Problems and Development of Agriculture in the Hills of Uttar Pradesh', in D.C. Pande, ed., *Dimensions of Agriculture in the Himalaya*, Almora: Shri Almora Book Depot, pp. 35–45.

Ribbentrop, Berthold, 1989 [1900], *Forestry in British India.* With a Commentary by Ajay S. Rawat, New Delhi: Indus Publishing Co.

Richards, Glyn, 1991, *The Philosophy of Gandhi*, Calcutta: Rupa & Co.

Rist, Gilbert, 1997, *The History of Development: From Western Origins to Global Faith*, London and New York: Zed Books.

Rizvi, Saiyed Ali Akhtar, ed., 1979, *Uttar Pradesh District Gazetteers: Uttarkashi*, Allahabad: Govt of Uttar Pradesh.

Rostow, Walt, 1960, *The Stages of Economic Growth*, Cambridge: Cambridge University Press.

Rüsen, Jörn, 1990, *Zeit und Sinn: Strategien historischen Denkens*, Frankfurt/ Main: Fischer.

Saberwal, Vasant K. and Mahesh Rangarajan, eds, 2003, *Battles over Nature: Science and Politics of Conservation*, Delhi: Permanent Black.

Sachs, Wolfgang, 1992, 'Environment', in Wolfgang Sachs, ed., *The Development Dictionary: A Guide to Knowledge as Power*, London and New Jersey: Zed Books, pp. 26–37.

————, 1999, *Planet Dialectics: Explorations in Environment and Development*, London and New York: Zed Books.

Saklani, Atul, 1987, *The History of a Himalayan Princely State: Change, Conflicts and Awakening. An Interpretative History of Princely State of Tehri Garhwal, U.P.; A.D. 1815 to 1949 A.D.*, Delhi: Durga Publications.

Saldanha, Indra Munshi, 1996, 'Colonialism and Professionalism: A German Forester in India', in *Environment and History*, vol. 2, pp 195–219.

Sanwal, R.D., 1976, *Social Stratification in Rural Kumaon*, with a foreword by M.N. Srinivas, Delhi: Oxford University Press.

Sarin, Madhu, 1996, 'From Conflict to Collaboration: Institutional Issues in Community Management', in Mark Poffenberger and Betsy McGean, eds, *Village Voices, Forest Choices: Joint Forest Management in India*, Delhi: Oxford University Press, pp. 165–209.

Sarkar, Sumit, 1983, *Modern India 1885–1947*, Madras: Macmillan India.

————, 1993, 'Forest Satyagraha in the Non-Cooperation and Civil Disobedience Movement', in A. Rawat, *Indian Forestry: A Perspective*, New Delhi: Indus Publishing.

Sax, William, 1991a, *Mountain Goddess: Gender and Politics in a Himalayan Pilgrimage*, New York and Oxford: Oxford University Press.

————, 1991b, 'Ritual and Performance in the Pandavalila of Garhwal', in

Arvind Sharma, ed., *Essays on the Mahabharata*, Leiden: Brill, pp. 274–95.

Saxena, N.C., 1996, 'Political Issues in Forestry', in M.S. Rathore, ed., *Environment and Development*, Jaipur and New Delhi: Institute of Development Studies, Rawat Publications.

———, and Vishwa Ballabh, 1995, 'Farm Forestry and the Context of Farming Systems in South Asia', in N.C. Saxena and Vishwa Ballabh, eds, *Farm Forestry in South Asia*, New Delhi: Sage, pp. 23–50.

Schäfer, Lothar, 1982, 'Wandlungen des Naturbegriffs', in Jörg Zimmermann, ed., *Das Naturbild des Menschen*, München: Wilhelm Fink Verlag, pp. 11–44.

Schmidt-Vogt, Dietrich, 1994, 'Deforestation in the Nepal Himalaya: Causes, Scope, Consequences', in *European Bulletin of Himalayan Research*, vol. 7, pp. 18–24.

Scott, James, 1990 [1985], *Weapons of the Weak: Everyday Forms of Peasant Resistance*, Delhi: Oxford University Press.

Sen, Amartya, 1984, *Resources, Values and Development*, Cambridge, Mass. and London: Harvard University Press.

———, 2000, 'Capability and Well-Being', in *Development: Critical Concepts in the Social Sciences*, Stuart Corbridge, ed., London and New York: Routledge.

Sen, Ilina, ed., 1990, *A Space within the Struggle: Women's Participation in People's Movements*, Delhi: Kali for Women.

Sharma, Kumud, n.d., 'Role and Participation of Women in the "Chipko' Movement in the Uttarakhand Region in Uttar Pradesh', in Kumud Sharma and Meera Velayudhan, *Women in Struggle: Two Case Studies of Peasants and Workers*, New Delhi: Centre for Women's Development Studies.

Sharma, Suresh, 1995, '*Hind Swaraj* as a Statement of Tradition in the Modern World', in Vasudha Dalmia and Heinrich von Stietencron, eds, *Representing Hinduism: The Construction of Religious Traditions and National Identity*. New Delhi: Sage, pp. 283–93.

Sharma, T.R., 1996, 'Sustainable Agricultural Development in Western Himalayan Region: Present Scenario and Future Strategies', in D.C. Pande, ed., *Dimensions of Agriculture in the Himalaya*, Almora: Shri Almora Book Depot, pp. 139–47.

Sheth, Dilip L., 1989, 'Catalyzing Alternative Development: Values, the Knowledge System, Power', in Poona Wignaraja and Akmal Hussain, eds, *The Challenge in South Asia: Development, Democracy and Regional*

Cooperation, Tokyo: The United Nations University and New Delhi: Sage, pp. 61–74.

Shiva, Vandana, 1988, *Staying Alive: Women, Ecology and Survival in India*, Delhi: Kali for Women.

———, in association with J. Bandopadhyay *et al.*, 1991, *Ecology and the Politics of Survival: Conflicts over Natural Resources in India*, New Delhi: Sage.

———, H.C Sharatchandra, and J. Bandyopadhyay, 1983, 'The Challenge of Social Forestry', in Walter Fernandes, Sharad Kulkarni, eds, 1983, *Towards a New Forest Policy: People's Rights and Environmental Needs*, New Delhi: Indian Social Institute, pp. 48–72.

Singh, Chhatrapati, 2000, *India's Forest Policy and Forest Laws*, Dehra Dun: Natraj.

Singh, Katar and Vishwa Ballabh, eds, *Cooperative Management of Natural Resources*, New Delhi: Sage Publications.

Singh, Katar, Vishwa Ballabh, and Thomas Palakudiyil, 1996, 'Introduction and Overview', in Katar Singh and Vishwa Ballabh, eds, *Cooperative Management of Natural Resources*, New Delhi: Sage Publications, pp. 13–38.

Singh, Surendra, 1995, *Urbanization in Garhwal Himalaya: A Geographical Interpretation*, New Delhi: M.D. Publications.

Singh, Vir, 1993, 'Himalayan Ecology Threatened by Indiscriminate Apple Cultivation', in S. Rawat and S. Ajay, eds, *Indian Forestry: A Perspective*, New Delhi: Indus Publishing Co., pp.351–81.

Sircar, Dines Chandra, 1965, *Indian Epigraphy*, Delhi: Motilal Banarsidass.

Sivaramakrishnan, K. and Arun Agrawal, eds, 2003, *Regional Modernities: The Cultural Politics of Development in India*, Delhi: Oxford University Press.

Sontheimer, Günther-Dietz, 1987, 'The *Vana* and the *Ksetra*: The Tribal Background of Some Famous Cults', in G.C. Tripathi and H. Kulke, eds, *Eschmann Memorial Lectures Vol. I, 1978–86*, Bhubaneshwar: Eschmann Memorial Fund, pp. 117–64.

Sprockhoff, Joachim Friedrich, 1981 and 1984, 'Aranyaka und *vanaprastha* in der vedischen Literatur: Neue Erwägungen zu einer alten Legende und ihren Problemen', in *Wiener Zeitschrift für die Kunde Südasiens und Archiv für indische Philosophie*, vol. 25, pp. 19–90 and n.28, pp. 5–43.

Stebbing, E.P., 1982 [reprint], *The Forests of India*, vols I–III, New Delhi: A.J. Reprints Agency.

Sundar, Nandini, Roger Jeffery, and Neil Thin, with Ajith Chandran *et al.*, 2001, *Branching Out: Joint Forest Management in India*, Delhi: Oxford University Press.

Taragi, R.C.S. and K. Kumar, 1995, 'Migration Pattern in the Central Himalaya', in B.R. Pant and M.C. Pant, eds, *Glimpses of Central Himalaya: A Socio-Economic and Ecological Perspective*, vols 1 and 2, New Delhi: Radha Publications, pp. 168–82.

Valdiya, K.S., 1996, 'Distinct Socio-cultural Identity, Profiles of Resources and Planning for Development of Uttarakhand', in K.S. Valdiya, ed., *Uttarakhand Today*, Almora: Shree Almora Book Depot, pp. 7–44.

Vansina, Jan, 1995, *Oral Tradition as History*, London: Currey.

Vincentnathan, Lynn, 1993, 'Untouchable Concepts of Person and Society', in *Contributions to Indian Sociology*, new series, vol. 27, no. 1, pp. 53–82.

Weber, Thomas, 1988, *Hugging the Trees: The Story of the Chipko Movement*, Delhi: Viking.

Wellmer, Albrecht, 1995, *Zur Dialektik von Moderne und Postmoderne: Vernunftkritik nach Adorno*, Frankfurt/Main: Suhrkamp.

Werbner, Pnina, 1997, '"The Lion of Lahore": Anthropology, Cultural Performance and Imran Khan', in Steven Nugent and Chris Shore, eds, *Anthropology and Cultural Studies*, London: Pluto, pp. 34–67.

White, Hayden, 1973, *Metahistory: The Historical Imagination in Nineteenth-century Europe*, Baltimore and London: Johns Hopkins University Press.

Wolf, Eric, 1972, 'Ownership and Political Ecology', in *Anthropological Quarterly*, vol. 45, pp. 201–5.

World Commission on Environment and Development, ed., 1987, *Our Common Future*, Oxford: Oxford University Press.

Zimmermann, Jörg, 1982, 'Zur Geschichte des ästhetischen Naturbegriffs', in Jörg Zimmermann, ed., *Das Naturbild des Menschen*, München: Fink Verlag, pp. 118–54.

Zoller, Claus Peter, 1994, , 'Saying Good-bye the Himalayan Way', in Dilip Chitre, *et al.*, eds, *Tender Ironies: A Tribute to Lothar Lutze*, New Delhi: Manohar Publishers.

———, 1996, '*Die Panduan: Ein mündliches Mahabharata-Epos aus dem Garhwal-Himalaya*', habilitation thesis, University of Heidelberg.

Index

326 INDEX